SUSQUEHANNA UNIVERSITY STUDIES

Jewish Settlement and Community in the Modern Western World

Susquehanna University Studies is an annual interdisciplinary scholarly journal published as part of the Susquehanna University Press. Each issue is devoted to a theme or themes of academic interest. The editors invite manuscript submissions prepared in accordance with the *Chicago Manual of Style*, 13th edition.

Contributors should send manuscripts with a self-addressed, stamped envelope to Editor, *Susquehanna University Studies*, Susquehanna University, Selinsgrove, Pennsylvania 17870.

MEMBER

(CELJ)

Council of Editors
of Learned Journals

SUSQUEHANNA UNIVERSITY STUDIES

Jewish Settlement and Community in the Modern Western World

Edited by
RONALD DOTTERER,
DEBORAH DASH MOORE,
and STEVEN M. COHEN

SELINSGROVE: SUSQUEHANNA UNIVERSITY PRESS
LONDON AND TORONTO: ASSOCIATED UNIVERSITY PRESSES

Associated University Presses
440 Forsgate Drive
Cranbury, NJ 08512

Associated University Presses
25 Sicilian Avenue
London WC1A, 2QH, England

Associated University Presses
P.O. Box 39, Clarkson Pstl. Stn.
Mississauga, Ontario,
L5J 3X9 Canada

The paper used in this publication meets the requirements
of the American National Standard for Permanence of Paper
for Printed Library Materials Z39.48-1984.

The Library of Congress has catalogued this serial
publication as follows:
Susquehanna University
   Susquehanna University studies.   v. 1–   1936–
Selinsgrove, Pa., Susquehanna University Press
[etc.]
      v. diagrs.   23–31 cm.
   Annual
   Indexes.
      Vols. 1–5, 1936–56, in v. 5; Vols. 1–8, 1936–70, in v. 8.
      ISSN 0361-8250 = Susquehanna University studies

   I. Susquehanna University. Studies.   II. Title.

LH1. S78S8   082   38-14370
                                                                          MARC-S
Library of Congress   [8708-87]rev2

ISBN 0-945636-13-X

Printed in the United States of America

Contents

Preface

This collection of essays traces and analyzes changing patterns of Jewish mobility and settlement as well as their consequences for Jewish affiliation and community building. It focuses on how Jews in different eras and societies have used local environments to establish a sense of community, preserve their religious and ethnic identity, and interact with the larger society around them.

Traditional Jewish community depended on and fostered a degree of residential concentration and segregation. Subsequent entry of large numbers of Jews into major metropolitan areas, coupled with opportunities for social mobility, posed new challenges—similar to those faced by many other ethnic groups—to a group committed simultaneously to integration and group survival.

This volume's perspective is both historical and sociological— and, to be candid, frankly revisionist. Its first section contains four essays exploring settlement patterns in the premodern world and their relation to traditional modes of Jewish community. These essays analyze how political changes reshaped the small, semi-autonomous village communities. With new opportunities—political, economic, social—emerging in the nineteenth century, modernizing Jews migrated to Europe's growing urban areas, creating new kinds of communities that straddled tradition and modernity while reflecting limited integration into partially open Western society. Although Jews in western and central Europe established the new settlement patterns in the nineteenth century, east European Jews continued the process well into the twentieth century. These historical essays also examine the selective process of migration and its impact not only on new urban settlements but on the lives of those who remained in the villages. Contrary to popular perceptions, the Jews who migrated to urban areas usually were among the more successful. Their ambition often propelled their physical mobility as their relocation subsequently spurred their social mobility.

The second set of four essays offers different interpretations of the consequences of Jewish settlement in urban areas. The two historical essays discuss the political and ideological challenges that flowed from the migration of east European Jews westward and the efforts made to incorporate these Jews into a redefined community. The two sociological studies introduce ecological models in comparative and case study perspectives. Both suggest the need to modify the typology of the gradual dispersion of the ghetto as the predominant pattern of Jewish settlement in the modern world.

The third section contains two personal narratives of the two modern Jewish communities that have entered the popular imagination as preeminent examples of Jewish urban life: immigrant New York City at the turn of the century and contemporary Jerusalem. These narratives relate the individual's perceptions of daily life, both recorded and remembered, and reveal how communal values influence the individual Jew's urban existence.

The subject of Jewish settlement and community is a necessary prerequisite for an understanding of Jewish political, economic, social, and cultural activity. As the locale of Jewish life changed, so did the possibilities of Jewish endeavor. Jews who migrated and established the new settlement patterns implicitly understood the consequences of their behavior, although they could hardly be expected to have foreseen the results. Now a generation of scholars, schooled in the historical and social sciences, is exploring the new world these Jews created. As the essays demonstrate, it is a world both modern and traditional, innovative and conservative, linked simultaneously to past and future.

Steven M. Cohen

Deborah Dash Moore

SUSQUEHANNA UNIVERSITY STUDIES

Jewish Settlement and Community in the Modern Western World

Part I
The Transition from Rural to Urban Community

1

Village Jews and Jewish Modernity: The Case of Alsace in the Nineteenth Century

Paula E. Hyman

Like most European Jews on the eve of emancipation, those of Alsace were village Jews, and they remained so until the very end of the nineteenth century. Indeed, until their emancipation in 1791, Jews were not permitted to reside in the largest cities of Alsace, including both Strasbourg and Colmar, and were scattered among 183 localities. Alsatian Jews also were the first in Europe to experience both the benefits and challenges of emancipation; together with their cousins in neighboring Lorraine, they constituted more than three-quarters of French Jewry at the time of the Revolution.[1]

Village and small-town Jews have been virtually overlooked as historians have rushed to study the articulate urban elites who served as models for the rapid social mobility and acculturation that characterized the Jewish experience in western and central Europe. We know a great deal about the patterns of acculturation, socioeconomic development, and ideological pronouncements of the urban leaders who shaped Jewish institutions, formulated political policy, and defined the nature of modern Jewish consciousness in the nineteenth and twentieth centuries.[2] We know far less about the ways in which the masses of Jews, living in tight-knit communities in villages and small towns, responded to the new conditions and opportunities that citizenship and capitalist expansion offered them. Yet these village Jews, living in Alsace, or Baden, or Württemberg, were more typical of the Jewish social and cultural condition in western and central Europe in the age of emancipation than were the Jews of Paris, Berlin, or

Hamburg. Moreover, village and small-town Jews were the source of population growth in the major urban Jewish communities of Europe and tended to maintain traditional Jewish values and patterns of behavior while many of the children of the early urban elites were dissociating themselves from Jewish observance and communal activity. If we are to understand the factors that enabled European Jews in the nineteenth century to integrate into modern societies while retaining (and refashioning) Jewish identity and building a complex institutional infrastructure, then we must examine the Jewish masses whose origins lie in villages and small towns as well as their more cosmopolitan coreligionists. Looking at the socioeconomic and cultural behavior of ordinary Jews permits us to assess the impact of the ideological visions associated with emancipation upon the reality of Jewish individuals and communities.

The Jews of Alsace are a particularly fruitful population to study the social consequences of emancipation for a nonurbanized traditional Jewish community. At the end of the eighteenth century and for several generations thereafter, they were religiously observant, spoke their own variant of Yiddish, and were touched only gradually by secular culture. A rural but nonpeasant population, they served in a limited range of roles as middlemen in the rural economy. They were peddlers and dealers in old clothes, commercial brokers and petty merchants, cattle and horse dealers, traders in grain and money lenders—all occupations that offered occasion for friction with the local peasantry. Indeed, the commercial court records of the Department of the Lower Rhine in the 1820s through the 1860s reveal that Jews figured in one-quarter to one-third of the cases, although they were less than three percent of the department's population.[3] Periods of political unrest, as during the Revolution of 1848, witnessed riots against a number of local Jewish communities.[4] Their occupational profile thus defined Jews as an economic caste as well as a religio-ethnic community.

The social, economic, and cultural patterns of Alsatian Jews emerge from a variety of sources, often overlooked by modern Jewish historians. In addition to the well-mined communal records, government reports, memoirs, and novels, such documents as manuscript censuses, marriage records, and notarial lists provide useful information on Jews. The marriage records are particularly valuable for studying migration patterns and intergenerational mobility, because they list the bride and groom's place of birth and present domicile as well as the domiciles of their parents and the occupations of all males concerned.

For my study I have gathered material on the total Jewish population of four different Alsatian communities from 1820 through 1870: Strasbourg, the largest city and Jewish community of the region, with 2,229 Jews in 1861; Bischheim, a nearby town of more than 3,000 inhabitants at midcentury with a Jewish population of 750; Niederroedern, a village of 1,245 inhabitants located northwest of Strasbourg, one-quarter of whose population was Jewish; and the hamlet of Itterswiller, also in the Lower Rhine, more than 40 percent of whose 483 residents were Jews.[5]

The emancipationist ideology challenged traditional Jewish culture by introducing a new hierarchy of values and new perceptions of the Gentile world. But pre-emancipation attitudes and behavior survived among village and small-town Jews into the second half of the nineteenth century, embedded in continuing socioeconomic roles in the countryside and in the powerful bonds of Jewish communal life.

Despite efforts to channel village Jews into productive occupations—that is, agriculture and artisan trades—the socioeconomic composition of Jewish villages barely altered in the years between the Napoleonic period and the German annexation of Alsace in 1870. In these three Alsatian villages, 40 percent of the heads of households supported themselves during the Napoleonic period in the typical Jewish street trades of peddling, dealing in old clothes, and petty brokerage. Another 28 percent were engaged in the cattle, horse, and grain trade, and 9 percent were butchers, leather and textile merchants, and scrap metal dealers. Only 2 percent were artisans.[6] In 1846 5 percent of the employed residents of the villages had learned a trade, but 87 percent were engaged in commerce. Peddlers, second-hand dealers, and petty agents still accounted for approximately 40 percent of all Jewish occupations.[7] Twenty years later a similar pattern emerged: peddlers and hawkers predominated (36 percent); the cattle, horse, and grain trade retained their significance; and artisanry and industry attracted a meager six percent of village Jews.[8] Only in the city of Strasbourg did a new occupational pattern develop— one of settled commerce, commercial employment, and artisanry.

This economic stability was accompanied in the countryside by a steadfast adherence to the traditional features of Alsatian Jewish life—the use of Yiddish, a high degree of religious observance, and a penchant for what we might call the practices of folk religion. This resistance to cultural innovation, which I have elsewhere labeled cultural conservatism,[9] gave rise to conflicts between the village Jewish populace and the notables of the consistories who administered the local Jewish communities from their urban seats of power.

Although the Jewish villages of Alsace remained stable in population, economic structure, and cultural patterns until well into the second half of the nineteenth century, that stasis masked considerable movement among Alsatian Jews throughout the century. Actually, the stability and conservatism of village society is linked to the patterns of migration of Alsatian Jews.

To the Jews of Alsace, who had been restricted in their rights of residence both during the *ancien régime* and the reign of Napoleon I, the most significant benefit of emancipation was the geographic mobility it offered. They could move wherever their pursuit of prosperity might lead them. And they did move, both within the province and to other parts of France and abroad. The 1872 census revealed that at least 34 percent of Paris's Jews had been born in the provinces of Alsace and Lorraine.[10] As a result of high fertility and the immigration of Jews from neighboring German states, however, the Jewish population of Alsace increased until midcentury. By 1863, the effect of outmigration from the provinces became apparent as the Jewish population of the Department of the Lower Rhine declined 8 percent in one decade.[11] The Jews also became more concentrated, with half of them living in communes of more than two thousand inhabitants and more than 13 percent in the urban center of Strasbourg alone.[12]

In the half century after the removal of Napoleon's ban on Jewish mobility within France, Alsatian Jews participated in three streams of migration. The smallest contingent left to seek their fortunes abroad. Among the children of Alsatian Jews who left estates in the 1850s and 1860s, five percent had settled in foreign countries, with the United States the most favored, although not the sole, destination.[13] Thus Alsatian Jews participated in the establishment of California's Jewish community during the gold rush and formed a noticeable segment of the emerging Jewish settlements of South America. Aron Dreyfus, for example, born in Wissembourg in 1791, made his fortune as a businessman in Rio de Janeiro before returning to France to settle in Metz, where he purchased a house for 12,500 francs in 1855.[14] Those who emigrated from France were recruited from all social classes. Aron Dreyfus was the son of a prosperous merchant and sometime butcher. Among the Jewish emigrants abroad, however, the rural poor predominated, as one 1837 governmental list of emigrants from the Lower Rhine revealed explicitly. The twenty-six Jewish household heads, comprising fifty individuals, were mostly peddlers, brokers, and artisans and averaged only 273 francs per person in money taken with them, as compared with 571 francs per person for all the emigrants from the department in that decade. Sixteen of the twenty-six were emigrating alone.[15] It even became Jewish communal policy to solve the social problems of begging and vagrancy by encouraging the poor to emigrate. Thus in 1853 the Strasbourg consistory established a short-lived committee to provide financial assistance to emigrants.[16]

The vast majority of Alsatian Jewish migrants, however, remained within Alsace itself. The marriage records and notarial documents suggest that between 1820 and 1870 one-third to one-half of the Jews of Alsace relocated at least once, with two-thirds of the migrants remaining within the province.[17] As often occurs, migration was a phenomenon of youth, usually taking place before marriage or for the purpose of marriage. In fact, women were more likely to migrate regionally than were men, because they tended to settle in their husband's place of residence. Therefore, 35 percent of the male heirs at midcentury had left their parents' hometown, and 53 percent of their sisters had done so.[18]

Because Alsatian Jews were overwhelmingly village dwellers, it is not surprising that more than two-thirds of the migrants came from villages and towns of less than five thousand persons. However, migrants were disproportionately recruited from towns and cities of five thousand to fifty thousand residents in which urban skills were more likely to be sharpened and communal ties were more relaxed than in the villages (table 1). Those who came from Jewish communities with the highest concentration of Jews (more than 25 percent of the total population) were distinctly underrepresented among the migrants. In those communities, one might posit, the bonds of communal feeling and constraint were so strong that migration was discouraged (table 2).

Table 1

Geographical Origin of Grooms by Size of Place of Birth, 1820–1862 (%)

Less than 2,000	34	37
2,000–5,000	31	45
5,000–50,000	11	5
More than 50,000	4	6
Foreign born	21	6
	(N = 112)	(N = 454)

Table 2

Jewish Population Density of Groom's Place of Birth, 1820–1862

	Groom Migrated(%)	Total Sample(%)
Less than 3% population	10	9
3–10%	33	18
10–25%	43	50
More than 25%	15	23
	(N = 112)	(N = 454)

Most striking is that the migrants differed in socioeconomic status from their stationary brethren (table 3). Both migrating grooms and migrating parents were more than twice as likely as nonmigrants to come from the highest economic strata; conversely, they were far less likely to be located at the bottom of the Jewish socioeconomic scale, plying their wares in the traditional Jewish street trades. In the case of grooms, migrants were almost twice as likely to engage in crafts and to enter commercial employment as nonmigrants. Part of this disparity can be attributed to the economic differential between large town and village. Even those migrants who settled in towns no larger than those they left, however, also were more likely than their stay-at-home brethren to assume new economic positions. Moreover, parents

Table 3A

Socioeconomic Status of Migrants vs. Nonmigrants, 1820–1862 (%)

Groom's Occupation	Groom Migrated	Groom Stationary
Bankers, professionals, wholesalers	18	6
Merchants, semi-professionals	36	41
Commercial agents, employees	18	21
Artisans	17	11
Peddlers, street trades	9	19
Unskilled laborers	2	2
Rentiers, students, unemployed	1	1
	(N = 148)	(N = 454)

Table 3B

Socioeconomic Status of Migrating vs. Stationary Fathers (%)

Father's Occupation	Father Migrated	Father Stationary
Bankers, professionals, wholesalers	12	6
Merchants	38	43
Commercial agents, employees	21	21
Artisans	8	7
Peddlers	10	17
Unskilled laborers	4	2
Rentiers, unemployed	8	5
	(N = 112)	(N = 428)

Table 4

Socioeconomic Status of Grooms' Fathers and Migration

Father's Occupation	Groom Migrated(%)	Groom Stationary(%)
Bankers, professionals, wholesalers	14	6
Merchants	54	42
Commercial agents, employees	12	24
Artisans	8	6
Peddlers, street trades	9	18
Unskilled laborers	2	2
Rentiers, students, unemployed	2	1
	(N = 145)	(N = 452)

of the migrant grooms also were drawn disproportionately from the highest status rankings and in surprisingly low numbers from the ranks of peddlers and street hawkers (table 4). Furthermore, although Alsatian Jews as a whole had a high rate of literacy, as determined from the signatures of marriage documents, migrants tended to be more literate, especially in Latin script, than stationary Jews (table 5). They also married later, at a median age of 32.4 years, compared with 28.8 years for stationary grooms.

These differences between the mobile and stationary Jews suggest that a combination of success in the village economy and high aspirations stimulated migration. Put another way, upward social mobility preceded migration for the majority of those on the move. Although there were poor migrants, migrants often were recruited from among the elite in the countryside and those attuned to new economic possibilities. The lists of members of the College of Notables from both the Lower and Upper Rhine reveal the extraordinary geographic mobility of this wealthy elite. In 1828, only seven of the twenty-five notables of the Lower Rhine and eleven of the twenty-two notables of the Upper Rhine were living in their place of birth.[19] Significantly, those who followed the most traditional Jewish economic patterns—that is, peddlers and their children—were underrepresented among the migrants. It would seem that in choosing a traditional Jewish mode of employment peddlers were less likely to break with the customary and confront the changes necessitated by migration.

This phenomenon of elite migration from the villages is confirmed by a letter from the Administrative Committee of the Jewish community of Bischheim in response to a request for a donation from the Society for the Encouragement of Work (a philanthropy devoted to artisan training for the children of poor Jews). The letter stated that the community could not provide the suggested contribution because its "most heavily taxable [mem-

Table 5

Literacy and Migration

	Groom Migrated(%)	Father Migrated(%)	Nonmigrants(%)
Groom illiterate	0.9	1.9	2.2
Father illiterate	1.8	2.7	4.2
Bride, groom, and all parents sign in Latin script	40.2	37.4	23.9

bers] have just left our community to fix their domiciles in Strasbourg."[20]

Although our conclusions are derived primarily from data on mobility within Alsace, Doris Bensimon-Donath's analysis[21] of the Parisian Jewish population of 1872 reveals that Alsatian-born Jews living in Paris were remarkably similar in socioeconomic profile to those migrants who remained in the eastern provinces (table 6). Both groups had broken with traditional patterns of Jewish economic activity to enter the new sectors of artisanry and commercial employment. The larger number of proprietors and rentiers among the Parisians can be attributed to the differences in age structure between the two populations. Our sample, consisting of grooms with a median age of 32 years, would necessarily contain fewer older heads of household living on investments and pensions. Alsatian Jewish migrants to Paris, however, were more likely to engage in artisanal trades than their coreligionists who remained in Alsace, partly because of the opportunity structure of the Parisian economy.

In their socioeconomic profile Alsatian Jewish migrants, both those who remained in the region and those who relocated in Paris and other French cities, differed substantially from non-

Table 6

Socioeconomic Profile of Jewish Migrants: Alsace and Paris

Occupation	Regional Migrants 1820–1862 (Grooms)(%)	Alsatian Migrants to Paris, 1872 Census (%)
Proprietors and rentiers	3	8
Liberal and superior professions	6	7
Independent commerce	48	35
Employees	15	19
Artisans, skilled labor	17	20
Street trades, unskilled	11	11
	(N = 148)	(N = 1825)

Jewish migrants in France. Although the general overpopulation of Alsatian villages spurred the migration of Jews, unlike the masses of Gentile migrants, they were not peasants who had been forced from the land. Many were recruited, as we have seen, from towns of substantial size. Moreover, even those who lived in rural communes had some experience with the workings of a commercial economy. When they reached their final destination, Jewish migrants entered the commercial sectors of the urban economy while their Gentile fellow migrants swelled the ranks of the urban working classes. Finally, Jews tended to migrate in family groups; women were equally represented with men among the migrants, even in long-distance internal migration. Siblings also often migrated together. Thus in Strasbourg, at least twenty percent of the Jews had close relatives within the neighborhood. These factors enabled Jewish migrants to flourish in their new locations.[22]

The consequences of elite migration were considerable for Alsatian Jewry. It spurred social change and acculturation in the cities, removed potential agents of change from the countryside, and consequently retarded economic, religious, and cultural innovation there. Patterns of cultural conservatism found in the countryside thus were related to the structure of migration.

Voluntarily uprooted from their small traditional communities, the Jews who moved from village to town or city were freed from the constraints of social disapproval that prevailed in village society. The city permitted a social anonymity to its new inhabitants. Often more adventuresome than those who did not move, migrants also may have been predisposed to experiment in matters of social, cultural, and religious behavior as well as geographical mobility. In the second half of the century, the Alsatian Jewish storytellers Daniel Stauben and Léon Cahun both point to the deleterious impact on traditional ways of life of migration to the large city. Cahun's hero Anselme, the village schoolteacher, gives up regular synagogue attendance when he settles with his family in Paris, although he continues to celebrate Jewish festivals and the anniversary of his parents' death. In Cahun's words, "Now . . . . the bonhomme Anselme feels that he has left the narrow circle of the Jewish community to enter in the great French family."[23] Stauben expresses his longing to immerse himself once more "in this simple life, the last vestige of a civilization which is disappearing. In Paris ancestors, alas, are too quickly reduced to memories."[24] Such rapid adaptation to the different conditions of a new locale suggests that the oft-noted traditional piety of Jews in Alsace can best be characterized as "milieufrömmigkeit," a type of

cultural behavior not based on ideological conviction but inti-
mately linked with the entire social fabric that sustains a culture.[25]

Both Stauben and Cahun describe a migration to Paris and are
writing in a nostalgic vein, but the effect of moving to such cities
as Strasbourg and Mulhouse, although less pronounced, was
similar. Indeed, a non-Jewish and not particularly sympathetic
observer of Jewish practices in Alsace in the 1860s and 1870s,
Edouard Coypel, noted that in the cities Jews were more sensitive
to Gentile opinion and introduced changes in their funerals, for
example, "so as not to present too great a contrast to Gentile
customs."[26] Similarly, in his study of Judeo-Alsatian humor Rabbi
S. Debré, writing of his childhood in the 1860s, commented that
the Jews in the villages remained observant while those in the
cities had not.[27] Although the urban/village distinction cannot be
explained entirely by the phenomenon of migration, the newness
of the urban settlements contributed to the undermining of traditional custom. The phenomenon is more striking in new urban
communities composed of immigrants from abroad, such as
London in the Georgian period and American cities in the years of
mass immigration,[28] but the nonideological assimilation that
seems to accompany migration also was visible in the urban Jewish centers of Alsace.

The siphoning off of those with the greatest interest in new
ideas and aspirations enabled Jewish village society to conserve
traditional religious and cultural patterns until after 1870. Unlike
the situation in Germany, where young university-trained rabbis
took their first pulpits in villages and small towns and often
introduced reforms in ritual along with new models of appropriate behavior,[29] French rabbis, particularly in Alsace, were conservative. Until 1870 most had been trained in traditional *yeshivot*,
and the few who were graduates of the new Ecole Rabbinique in
Metz lacked the broad secular education which characterized the
nineteenth-century German rabbinate.[30] Only compulsory elementary schooling, most often in consistorial and state-super-
vised Jewish public schools, introduced the values of
emancipation to village Jews. That schooling, however, did not
become widespread in the countryside until the 1840s, when
clandestine *heders* finally succumbed to a combination of consistorial and governmental pressure.[31] Yet, as long as the village
economy offered Jews their traditional middlemen roles and the
village social structure remained intact, Jews in villages and small
towns usually persisted in their traditional religious observance,
practice of folk customs, and occupational profile. As Vicki Caron

has shown, only after the loss of Alsace to Germany did the erosion of the Jewish economic role in the countryside combined with anxiety about German rule lead to the massive outmigration and urbanization that transformed Alsatian (and French) Jewry in the years before World War I.[32]

Because rural Jews in Alsace acculturated so gradually in the wake of emancipation, they left a particular imprint upon the development of French Jewry. As the major source of opposition to the reformist tendency of the bourgeois leadership of the consistories—the governmentally recognized communal institutional network of French Jewry—they acted as a brake on religious reform. Petition campaigns and a threat of schism emanating from Alsace, the heartland of France's Jewish population, persuaded the consistorial elite to adopt a moderate approach. The traditionalism of Alsatian village Jews also was reflected in the French rabbinate, because Alsace and Lorraine were virtually the exclusive recruiting grounds for the rabbinate until the arrival of east European immigrants at the turn of the century. Finally, Alsatian Jews rooted in the village and small town retained a traditional definition of international Jewish solidarity, later expressed in support for Zionism that surpassed that of their Parisian cousins.

The Alsatian countryside, therefore, was not simply the biological reservoir of French Jewry; it also provided a communal social setting that cushioned the potentially disruptive impact of their new legal status on the self-concept of a newly emancipated Jewish population. The experience of Jews in Alsatian villages and towns suggests the limits of ideology in promoting change and gives evidence of the prolonged persistence, under certain circumstances, of traditional cultural and economic patterns in the face of emancipation.

Notes

1. On Alsatian Jewry see Elie Scheid, *Histoire des juifs d'Alsace* (Paris: 1887); Freddy Raphael and Robert Weyl, *Juifs en Alsace: culture, société, histoire* (Toulouse: Privat, 1977) and *Regards nouveaux sur les juifs d'Alsace* (Strasbourg: Istra, 1980); Georges Weill, "Les Juifs d'Alsace: Cent ans d'historiographie," *Revue des Etudes Juives* (hereafter, *REJ*) 149, no. 1–3 (January–September 1980): 81–108, and "Recherches sur la démographie des Juifs d'Alsace du xvie au xviiie siècle," *REJ* 130 (1971): 51–89; David Cohen, *La promotion des Juifs en France à l'époque du second empire (1852–1870)*, 2 vols. (Aix-en-Provence: Université de Provence, 1980); and Arthur Hertzberg, *The French Enlightenment and the Jews* (New York: Columbia University, 1968), pp. 164–70. For a sociological analysis of village Jews, see Werner Cahnman, "Village and Small-Town Jews in Germany: A Typological Study," *Leo Baeck Institute Yearbook* (hereafter *LBIYB*) 19 (1974): 107–

30. On the distortions caused by the emphasis on urban elites, see Jacob Toury, "Deutsche Juden im Vormärz," *Bulletin des Leo Baeck Instituts* 8, no. 29 (1965): 65–82, and Steven M. Lowenstein, "The Pace of Modernisation of German Jewry in the Nineteenth Century," *LBIYB* 21 (1976): 41–56. On the socioeconomic evolution of rural Jews in Germany, see Monika Richarz, "Emancipation and Continuity: German Jews in the Rural Economy," in *Revolution and Evolution: 1848 in German-Jewish History* ed. Werner Mosse, Arnold Paucker, and Reinhard Rürup (Tübingen: Mohr, 1981), pp. 95–115.

2. See, for example, Jacob Katz, *Out of the Ghetto* (Cambridge: Harvard University, 1973), or Michael Marrus, *The Politics of Assimilation* (Oxford: Oxford University Press, 1971).

3. U 2300, U 2310, U 2320, U 2330, U 2340, Archives départementales du Bas-Rhin (hereafter, ADBR).

4. See Jacob Toury, *Mehumah u-mevukhah b'mahpekhat 1848* (Tel Aviv: Moreshet, 1968), pp. 24–31, and Zosa Sjakowski, "Anti-Jewish Riots in Alsace during the Revolutions of 1789, 1830, and 1848" (Hebrew), *Zion* 20 (1955): 82–102.

5. The census data are drawn from manuscript censuses, ADBR 7 M 719, 726, 733, 740 (Strasbourg: 1846); 7 M 720, 727, 734, 741 (Strasbourg: 1856); 7 M 722, 729, 736, 743 (Strasbourg: 1866); 7 M 459 (Itterswiller: 1836–66); 7 M 266 (Bischheim: 1836–46) and 7 M 267 (Bischheim: 1856–66); and 7 M 562 (Niederroedern: 1836–66). The marriage records used include ADBR 4E 330, Niederroedern (1793–1830 and 1831–1862); 4 E 226, Itterswiller (1793–1830 and 1831–1862); and Bischheim (1813–1832, 1833–1842, 1843–1852, and 1853–1862); 5M1 1663, Strasbourg (1823–1824, 1825–1826, 1827–1828, 1844–1845, 1846–1847, 1860, 1861, and 1862; Archives départementales du Haut-Rhin (hereafter, ADHR) 5E 105, Colmar (1822–1828 and 1845–1848) and 5M1 66R.50 (1860–1862). All marriages involving Jews in Bischheim, Niederroedern, and Itterswiller from 1820 through 1862, a total of 368, were coded. For Strasbourg all marriages involving Jews during 1823–1828, 1844–1847, and 1860–1862 and for Colmar during 1822–1828, 1845–1848, and 1860–1862 were selected, a total of 176 marriages for Strasbourg and 64 for Colmar. These marriages represented grooms domiciled in 63 locales in Alsace and 21 elsewhere.

6. Lists of Jews applying for patents to engage in business, 1808–1813, Patentes des Juifs d'Alsace, HM 2 782a and 782b, Central Archive for the History of the Jewish People (hereafter, CAHJP), Jerusalem.

7. Manuscript censuses, 1846, Bischheim, Niederroedern, and Itterswiller, ADBR 7 M 459, 7 M 266 and 267, and 7 M 562.

8. Manuscript censuses, 1866, ADBR, 7 M 459, 7 M 267, and 7 M 562.

9. See my "Emancipation and Cultural Conservatism: Alsatian Jewry in the Nineteenth Century" (Hebrew), *Umah v'Toldoteha*, 2 (1984): 39–48.

10. See Doris Bensimon-Donath, *Sociodémographie des juifs de France et d'Algérie, 1867–1907* (Paris: Publications orientalistes de France, 1976), p. 94.

11. My calculations, based on governmental census data found in the Archives Nationales, Paris, A.N.F[19] 11.024 and consistorial censuses located in the LBI Archives (New York), AR-C 1088 2863, folios 34–39, 80–101. See also Phyllis Cohen Albert, *The Modernization of French Jewry: Consistory and Community in the Nineteenth Century* (Hanover, N.H.: New England University Press, 1977), p. 18.

12. Ibid.

13. My calculations, notarial records of the court of Mutzig, ADBR.

14. See Judith Laiken Elkin, *Jews of the Latin American Republics* (Chapel Hill: University of North Carolina, 1980), pp. 34, 37, 39, 44–46, 50, and Robert

Levinson, *The Jews in the California Gold Rush* (New York: KTAV, 1978), pp. 6, 146. On Aron Dreyfus and the contract of sale for the Metz house, see the Dreyfus family papers, P90 g, CAHJP.

15. "Emigration en Amerique d'habitants du Bas-Rhin—états numériques et nominatives, 1828–37," ADBR, 3M 703. Because I selected only those emigrants whose names were distinctively Jewish, it is likely that the total of Jewish emigrants exceeded 50. I wish to thank Vicki Caron for bringing this source to my attention. For a stimulating discussion of the evolution of emigration from Alsace, see Caron's *Between France and Germany: Jews and National Identity in Alsace-Lorraine 1871–1918* (Stanford University Press, 1989).

16. Consistoire israélite, Registre des proces-verbaux, 1853–1858, Jewish community archive, Strasbourg.

17. My calculations, based on marriage and notarial records cited above.

18. Notarial records, court of Mutzig, 1855–1864, ADBR.

19. Etat nominatif des notables de la circonscription consistoriale de Strasbourg, 1828, ZF 659 and Etat nominatif des notables de la circonscription consistoriale de Colmar, 1828, ZF 745, CAHJP.

20. Letter of the Administrative Committee of Bischheim, 20 February 1848, HM 5520, CAHJP.

21. Bensimon-Donath, *Sociodémographie des juifs,* p. 150.

22. For a discussion of general migration in France, see Leslie Page Moch, *Paths to the City: Regional Migration in Nineteenth Century France* (Beverly Hills, Calif.: Sage, 1983).

23. Léon Cahun, *La vie juive* (Paris: 1886), p. 108.

24. Daniel Stauben, *Scenes de la vie juive en Alsace* (Paris: 1860), p. 96.

25. For a similar analysis of East European Jewish immigrants to the United States, see Charles Liebman, "Religion, Class and Culture in American Jewish History," *Jewish Journal of Sociology* 9, no. 2 (December 1967): 227–41.

26. Edouard Coypel, *Le Judaïsme: Esquisse des moeurs juives* (Mulhouse: 1876), p. 158.

27. S. Debré, *L'humour judéo-alsacien* (Paris: Durlacher, 1933), p. 291.

28. See, for example, Todd Endelman's fine discussion of behavioral assimilation among the urban Jewish lower classes in *The Jews of Georgian England: Tradition and Change in a Liberal Society* (Philadelphia: Jewish Publication Society, 1979). Although Endelman does not stress the immigrant origins of the Anglo-Jewish community in that period, his evidence supports our argument. On the erosion of the traditional culture of Jewish immigrants from eastern Europe in New York City, see Moses Rischin, *The Promised City: New York's Jews* (Cambridge: Harvard University, 1962).

29. See Steven M. Lowenstein, "The 1840s and the Creation of the German-Jewish Religious Reform Movement," *Revolution and Evolution,* pp. 257–58, 265–66, 271. Residential restrictions also kept the Jewish elite in German villages longer than was the case in France.

30. Tableau du personnel des ministres du culte israélite, 1864, LBI Archives, AR-C 1088 2863, folios 80–101. On the French rabbinate, see Albert, *The Modernization of French Jewry,* pp. 240–302. On the German rabbinate, see Ismar Schorsch, "Emancipation and the Crisis of Religious Authority—The Emergence of the Modern Rabbinate," *Revolution and Evolution,* pp. 205–47.

31. As late as 1842, the Strasbourg Consistory deplored the condition of Jewish primary education in the district. Strasbourg Consistory, minutes, 15 June 1842, HM 5503, CAHJP. Although many villages had no authorized Jewish

elementary schools, until midcentury parents often refused to send their children to the local public schools, which were viewd as Christian. See Zosa Szajkowski, *Jewish Education in France, 1789–1939* (New York: Columbia University Press, 1980), p. 10. For an assessment of the impact of the new Jewish primary schools, see Jay Berkovitz, "Jewish Educational Leadership in Nineteenth Century France—The Role of Teachers," *Proceedings of the Ninth World Congress of Jewish Studies*, division B, vol. 3, *The History of the Jewish People (The Modern Times)* (Jerusalem: 1986), pp. 47–54.

32. Caron, *Between France and Germany,* passim.

2

From *Judenrein* to Jewish Community: Origins and Growth of Jewish Settlement in Cologne, 1798–1814

Shulamit S. Magnus

Between 1792 and 1794, troops of the French Revolution swept through the left bank of the Rhine, bringing the entire territory from Karlsruhe to Cleves under the banner of the tricolor. For the nearly two million inhabitants of the region, the coming of the French spelled drastic change. An ancient political order was brought down and foreign rule imposed on what had been the most politically fragmented territory of the Holy Roman Empire. Economic crisis followed the influx of a debased paper currency, the levying of a crushing burden of taxes, and the disruption of commerce and farming. Soldiers were quartered forcibly in the homes of resentful citizens whose sensibilities were further enraged by the confiscation and secularization of hundreds of churches, monasteries, and convents. Liberty trees were ceremoniously erected in ancient town centers and a new religion of equality and fraternity proclaimed.

For the twenty-three thousand Jews of the region, the coming of the French also meant disruption, although not all of it unwelcome.[1] To the French, ghettos were as much a symbol of tyranny as feudal taxes and princely palaces, and wherever they were encountered—in Mainz and Bonn, for instance—their walls were razed and the Jews freed to live where they wished.

Freedom of settlement for Jews under the new regime did not only apply within cities, however, but also to the entire French-held territory, which was annexed by France in 1798 and divided into four *départements* made fully subject to French law in 1802. Jews, whose freedom of movement and residence had been restricted severely by the Jewry ordinances of the small states that had previously governed the Left Rhine, now for the first time were able to move where opportunities beckoned. In particular contrast to the pre-French era, rural and town Jews were free to move to cities. One example of urban migration is examined here: the settlement during the French years of Jews in Cologne, the most populous and commercially most important city on the left bank of the Rhine.

In Cologne there was no Jewish ghetto for the French to destroy because the city, a *Freie Reichsstadt*, or autonomous city within the Holy Roman Empire, had excluded Jews from its precincts for nearly four hundred years. Jews had not only been barred from residence but even from entering the city on business. On the rare occasions that they were permitted to pass through it en route to business elsewhere, they paid for the privilege and were forced to submit to a conspicuous and humiliating escort by a city guard from gate of entry to gate of exit.

In 1794, then, to use an unpleasant but expressive term, Cologne was *Judenrein*. By 1814, when the city fell from the French to the Prussians, my reconstruction of the records shows more than two hundred Jews in the city with a total approximate population of fifty thousand.[2] It was a sizable Jewish population in a region in which the typical Jewish community numbered less than fifty and the important and long-established community of Bonn, former residence city of the Electors, numbered 300 in 1808.[3] Unlike the Jews of Lübeck, another city that had excluded Jews until the coming of the French and from which Jews were expelled after Napoleon's defeat, the Jews of Cologne became the nucleus of a permanent and fast-growing settlement. Unlike Lübeck, Cologne did not regain its municipal autonomy. Although Prussia did not extend the 1812 Edict of Emancipation to its newly acquired Rhine territories, neither did it allow a return to the status quo ante, and Jews became a permanent reality in the city's life. Cologne's Jewish population had reached thirty-two hundred by the time of German unification in 1871 and was the fifth largest in the country after Berlin, Frankfurt am Main, Breslau, and Hamburg.[4]

The progressive urbanization of German Jewry in the nineteenth century is one of the larger chapters in German Jewish social history and, as Jacob Toury, Monika Richarz, and Steven Lowenstein have stressed, it was particularly a phenomenon of the latter half of the century.[5] If historians rightly study the causes and effects of accelerated Jewish urbanization in the second half of the century, it is equally important to understand the character of

Jewish urbanization in the earlier period when the phenomenon was less common. What brought rural and small-town Jews to German cities in this period? Having broken one prevailing norm, were such Jews more likely to pioneer in other areas as well—in commercial techniques or religious behavior? What factors equipped these Jews to make the urban move and how did their integration proceed?

These questions were more acute in Cologne, because every adult Jew in the city in the French period really was not only an immigrant but also a pioneer. Given the historical circumstances, Jews could have had no prior personal nor professional ties luring them to Cologne or facilitating their integration. The physical look of the city, apart from its riverfront facade, must have been utterly unfamiliar to them. There were no major antisemitic outbreaks in Cologne's surrounding environs in the French period that could have driven Jews there simply in search of safety. We are left only with the possibility of economic motivations for the migration, but then we must ask whether it was desperation driving a predominantly poverty stricken and reluctant group to Cologne, or whether it was desire for betterment by an already comfortable or economically secure group whose move was a conscious choice infused with expectation and hope.

The answer has no small bearing on the kind and degree of economic, social, and political integration that the Jewish group achieved in the city. Other factors influencing the group's integration would have been its degree of prior urbanization—how much its members were familiar with the dimensions and economic rhythm of city life—and finally, the group's familiarity with the language and economic patterns of the region as a whole. Recalling the manifold difficulties of east European Jewish immigrants in central and western Europe in the nineteenth century, the advantages that regional indigenousness would have bestowed on a Jewish group migrating to the city cannot be over-emphasized. If the first Jews who came to Cologne were largely of north Rhenish origin, far less psychic as well as physical dislocation was entailed in their move than in that of Jews making a long-distance urban migration. Such a group would have had a powerful advantage toward successful integration.

Finally, can anything be concluded about the ties to Jewish traditionalism of a group that, at the dawn of the age of emancipation, when Jews were overwhelmingly still tradition bound, was willing to move to a city without a Jewish community? What was the impact on Jewish group cohesiveness and community build-

ing of the lack of a ghetto and of an established Jewish neighborhood?

According to several histories written of the Jewish community
of Cologne, these questions seem to be answered. The first Jews
of Cologne are presented as predominantly lower middle class,
with a sprinkling of wealthier Jews who led the community and
represented it to the authorities.[6] An organized Jewish community, we are told, was established easily in 1801; a constitution
was drawn up, officers appointed, and the rabbi of neighboring
Bonn was appropriated to serve Cologne as well.

My reading of the sources preserved in municipal and regional
archives yields a different interpretation of the socioeconomic
character of the Jewish group and a more complicated picture of
religious outlook and behavior in the early community. I believe
that the Jewish group, on the whole, was wealthier and significantly more culturally forward-looking than previous treatments
have suggested. Although modern German Jewish history has
taught us that the ability of Jews to integrate into a society is
determined ultimately by the receptivity of that society, absorption of such a group would be much smoother than that of a
poverty-stricken, unacculturated group of Jews. My research indicates that the city's Jews achieved a remarkable degree of economic integration during French control, even after the
introduction of anti-Jewish legislation, the "infamous decree" of
1808. The nature of the Jewish immigration was a direct, if not the
sole, cause of this happy outcome and is worthy of fresh attention.

Like the proverbial journey of a thousand miles beginning with
a single step, modern Jewish settlement in Cologne began with
the move of a single family. "On the second day of the new month
Iyyar 5558 [17 April 1798], we, the undersigned, moved to Cologne," Joseph, son of Isaac Stern, and his wife Sara later recorded
in the *Memorbuch* of the Jewish community of Cologne. After
pointedly recalling the exclusionist and degrading policies of the
old city authorities to Jews, the Sterns continued, "We applied to
the French municipality for permission to reside here . . . obtained justice a few days ago and so moved here directly."[7] Thus a
permanent Jewish presence was established in the city for the first
time since 1424.

Stern and his family came to Cologne at virtually the first
moment it was sensible for any Jew to do so, which was not in
1794, when the city first fell to the French, but in 1798, after the
French had abolished the old City Council and set up a new

municipal regime. The Sterns came with an infant and for a time were the only Jews in the city, a situation with its own distinct anxieties. One night Stern heard a call from the streets for barrels of water to quench a fire, but mistakenly understood it to be a call to expel the Jews and had the momentary horror of fearing that he and his family were about to experience a personalized pogrom.[8]

Despite the uncertainties and fears that life in such circumstances necessarily entailed, Stern, a wealthy grain merchant from the nearby commercial town of Mülheim, was soon joined in Cologne by Salomon Oppenheim, Jr., of Bonn, scion of an illustrious family of court Jews and himself banker to the last archbishop-elector of Cologne. Oppenheim also was married with a young family. Although the records show that Oppenheim's wife and child did not, like Stern's, accompany him to Cologne (a second child was born to the Oppenheims in Bonn in 1800), the entire family was established in Cologne by 1802, where eight more children were born to the family between 1802 and 1813.[9]

Soon another Jew came from Bonn, Samuel Benjamin Cohen, son of the *Landrabbiner* of the former electorate of Cologne and still the most important religious figure in the territory. The younger Cohen, however, was a wealthy metal merchant. Cohen married in 1798, the same year he moved to Cologne. Like the prolific Oppenheims, the Cohens had seven children in rapid succession.

Other less exceptional Jews soon began to arrive in Cologne, including transients and undesirables, but it is striking that the first Jewish men to open up the city to Jewish settlement in 1798 were wealthy and young (all in their twenties), and whose domestic lives indicated an intention for permanence.[10] Unlike the destitute or single migrants, they had much to lose in making the move and therefore much had to be drawing them.

Indeed, their move must be taken as a vote of confidence in the economic promise of Cologne under French rule. The city had always been a major transshipment port for goods travelling the Rhine, but its economy had stagnated badly in the eighteenth century under the stifling guild-dominated municipal government, the same regime that had excluded Jews from the city. After important new stimuli were injected into the economy through absorption by France and the old City Council and guilds were abolished, Jews had every reason to expect both enhanced opportunity in Cologne's open economy and, crucially, full access to that opportunity.

Yet it was not just Jews in general, but wealthy Jews in particular, who were drawn to Cologne. Analysis of the migrating group shows that by 1809, Stern, Oppenheim, and Cohen were joined by seven other wealthy Jews, whose standing I have deduced from explicit mention of wealth by French authorities or reliable secondary sources—occupational titles, city addresses, and amounts paid to the fledgling Jewish community.[11] Together they constitute a significant element in the Jewish group, and it is not their economic standing alone but a complex of behaviors that interests us.

Six of the seven were in their twenties or thirties at the time of their migrations; thus, in a vigorous stage of life. Three were either married with several children or recently married and beginning families. Five of the seven were brokers ("commissionaire"); the others included a merchant-annuitant and a pawndealer, respectively. Clearly, it was "pull" rather than "push," expectation rather than desperation, that brought these Jews and their families to Cologne. If one considers the disproportionate number of brokers among them, Cologne's position as Rhine River entrepôt attracted them. The wealthy Jews tended overwhelmingly to remain in Cologne once established there: all but one of the ten wealthy Jewish households of the French period appear on the first records compiled by the Prussians. For these people, Cologne had been a deliberate choice whose wisdom, they obviously felt, had been well confirmed.

We know the addresses of nine of these families. Eight were in the two best sections of town, those fronting on the river where the cathedral and city hall were located. Not surprisingly, all but one of the wealthy male heads of household had either been born in cities or had lived in cities before migrating to Cologne. For six of the ten, moreover, migration had either been from Bonn or Mülheim, which were both within twenty kilometers of Cologne. Although the others had migrated from faraway locations—Amsterdam, Mainz, Fürth, and Würzburg—as a group, they were familiar with the ambiance of city life, and had no serious linguistic disadvantage in Cologne, even if they were unfamiliar with the city's peculiar dialect.

The sons of at least three of these families, including the grandchildren of the entirely traditional rabbi who served Bonn and Cologne, attended Christian schools and were tutored by Christians at home.[12] These families clearly had every intention of making it in Cologne's non-Jewish society, if only economically, and important elements in their backgrounds facilitated this drive.

To avoid an erroneous impression, it must be noted that of the

five wealthy male householders in Cologne in 1801, when a synagogue community was formally established, four made generous
contributions to its founding, assessing themselves or voluntarily
bidding about half the total sums raised in membership and
building fund dues.[13] As was universal Jewish practice, the
richest served on the synagogue board, except Oppenheim, who
was the wealthiest. But Oppenheim more than made up for this
exemption by representing the Roer *département*, in which Cologne was located, at Napoleon's Assembly of Notables in Paris (a
task he undertook reluctantly because of the losses his business
would suffer during his absence).[14]

The synagogue founded by these men was entirely traditional,
as its constitution testifies. This is to be expected at this point in
German Jewish history; rumblings of religious reform in the first
years of the century were usually confined to the long urbanized
and highly acculturated but unemancipated Jews in Berlin and
Hamburg.[15] The community in Cologne was like dozens of others
of its size that did not have complete communal institutions,
relying instead on those of nearby communities. This alone
would have predisposed its institutions to traditional forms, because there were no heterodox communities or leaders in the
Rhineland at that early date.

Despite traditional behavior, a substantial percentage of Cologne Jews had progressive outlooks: in 1805, when there were
perhaps forty-eight Jewish households in the city, ten Cologne
Jews subscribed to Mendelssohn's translation of the Psalms.[16]
Unfortunately, it is unknown which ten subscribed, but we can
hazard a guess. If Mendelssohn's biblical translations were meant
to draw acculturating Jews back to their own sacred literature and
to serve as primers in studying pure German, even without knowing the identities of the subscribers, one can conclude that a
significant proportion of Cologne's Jews were interested in meeting the outside world on high ground.

The economic upper stratum, which I am assuming also was
culturally forward looking, was a significant element within the
larger Jewish population. In 1808, according to my count, there
were 174 Jews in the city, of which fifty-five, or 32 percent of the
Jewish population (including Jewish servants and nonimmediate
family) lived in wealthy households.[17] This was a different community than that which has been depicted in the literature. A
good percentage of it was anything but hapless immigrants.
Whatever anxiety and discomfort may have been entailed in their
move to a city with an established anti-Jewish reputation and

which initially lacked all Jewish services, such as a synagogue, school, or *mikvah* (ritual bath), much in their socioeconomic profile equipped them admirably for life there. In short, it was a "perfect match."

Cologne's "other Jews" fit the description that generally has been ascribed to the entire group, judging by the relatively low amounts pledged to the synagogue and by the predominance of addresses in unspectacular sections of town.[18] In 1806 the main occupations of the twenty-five nonwealthy Jewish male householders in the city were peddling, trading, and butchering; two were teachers. Yet even if one can agree with Kober that the scale of the livelihoods was petty, especially when compared with that of the upper stratum, one must not assume indigence or mere scraping-by. The founding constitution of the community does not mention poor relief, a traditional concern and one that Jewish communities saw to if only to head off non-Jewish hostility. An 1806 police survey of Jewish households reveals that out of twelve employing servants, eight belonged to this lower class of Jews.[19] Here I agree completely with the findings of social historians Edward Shorter, Louise Tilly, and Joan Scott that the term *servants* means assistants or apprentices rather than domestic employees.[20] But that is precisely the point. One-third of the Jews we have classed as having petty occupations, including two peddlers, engaged assistants in their businesses, probably paying them room and board rather than salaries.

A Jewish butcher from this class augmented his income by renting out rooms to the family of a French tax collector, to whom he also occasionally extended loans. This knowledge is available because the French family, behind in its rent and loan payments, accused the Jew of ritually murdering a young Christian boy in the cellar of the house.[21] The Jew was acquitted eventually. What is important for our purposes are the insights that a butcher, in occupational taxonomy often assumed to be poor, had the means to buy or rent a house large enough for subletting, and that moneylending was a further source of income. This Jew was not the only one who moonlighted.

Another thing is striking about the occupations of the nonrich Jews of Cologne. Of twenty-five such Jewish males in 1806, six were butchers. Obviously, all could not have been serving the needs of the Jewish population. Dealing in animals and meat, however, was traditionally one of the most guild-restricted sectors of Cologne's economy, so much so that before French annexation, meat shortages were regular occurrences.[22] Whatever the purely legal status of the guilds under French rule, guild members and their economic interests did not disappear. Some evidence indicates that Jewish butchers encountered resistance from the city's traditional meat dealers, who were able to enlist French support against Jewish encroachment.[23] And yet, the Jewish butchers persisted nonetheless. I conclude that Cologne's meat provisioning needs were to these Jewish butchers what the city's brokerage opportunities were to wealthy Jewish brokers—a specific lure. This also suggests that this was a highly conscious urban migration even for the less economically established migrants, who, like their wealthier confrères, found a niche in Cologne's economy.

Were these Jews also disposed to successful integration in the big city because of previous urbanization and north Rhenish origin? Did their migration also tend to be permanent?

Information about birthplaces and intermediate places of migration (sites other than birthplaces from which the move to Cologne was made) confirms the picture of Cologne Jewry as largely local in origin—*local* defined here as a site within 100 kilometers of Cologne. Jews who were born in faraway regions of Germany, such as Bavaria and Lübeck, or in non-German territories (Holland and Lithuania) tended to have made an intermediate move to a Rhenish site and to have spent at least a decade there before moving to Cologne.[24] As a result, they came to Cologne acclimatized to the economic rhythms and language of the region.

These immigrants generally were not used to a big city. Of forty-six male householders for whom the information is available, only five were born in cities of Cologne's size or larger. Most (twenty-six) were born in towns with populations of less than five thousand. Even Jews with recorded intermediate places of migration did not show histories of having moved from small birthplaces to larger-sized sites before moving to Cologne.[25]

This also reinforces the impression that the move to Cologne was deliberate. Although we have no testimony from average Jews of Cologne explaining why they moved, perhaps the words of Glückel of Hameln about the reasons she and her husband left tiny Hameln and the bosom of family for the great city of Hamburg, which had a history of expelling Jews, is typical. "Hameln," she wrote in her famous *Memoirs*, "was not a trade center and my husband did not wish to confine himself to money lending among the country folk."[26] Whatever Jews, an overwhelmingly mercantile group, did for a living could be done on a larger scale in the big city, where new opportunities also beckoned.

My count shows thirty Jewish transients in Cologne who either drop from the records during the French period or fail to appear in Prussian records. There were also Jewish "undesirables," including a Jewish thief who was guillotined in the city in 1802 and a single Jewish woman who lived with her two illegitimate children in 1808. There is a lengthy correspondence in the city archives concerning a Jew accused of dissimulations, including failure to mention that he had a starving family elsewhere while he lived, according to the accusation, with "a Jewish prostitute" in Cologne.[27] There also may have been other unrecorded Jews who had no established occupations or addresses in the city.

But the overall impression left in the sources is of a *bürgerlich* group of Jews, the majority of whom remained in the city, including the less wealthy. Lacking the tradition of a preexisting Jewish neighborhood, they dispersed in all four sections of the city, their addresses determined by their incomes. They were not avid synagogue attendees, because much of the founding constitution of the community was devoted to means of attaining a *minyan* (prayer quorum of ten adult men), especially on Mondays and Thursdays, when Jewish law enjoins public Torah reading. Geographic dispersion made attendance more difficult to secure.

There was little ambivalence about emancipation, however, specifically its economic promise. This group embraced the new era with open arms. In 1808, when they became subject to the discriminatory legislation of Napoleon like all the Jews of France, it was not because they fit the Jewish profile of an economically and culturally retrograde group that preferred the ties of traditional economic and religious behavior to the possibilities of integration in the larger society. Ultimately, the Jews of Cologne, like those of the rest of France or Germany, could not earn emancipation. The granting of emancipation, as Reinhard Rürup has insistently demonstrated, was ultimately a function of liberal society and not of the individual or collective efforts of Jews.[28]

That view, however, is the product of historical hindsight. To the Jews of Cologne in the French period, it could only have seemed that all the conditions had been met.

Notes

1. This essay is based on the second chapter of my dissertation, "Cologne: Jewish Emancipation in a German City, 1798–1871" (Columbia University, 1988). For background see Adolf Kober, "Aus der Geschichte der Juden im Rheinland," *Rheinischer Verein für Denkmalpflege und Heimatschutz* (1931), 11–98. Statistic cited, p. 98.

2. On Cologne, see Eberhard Gothein, *Verfassungs- und Wirtschaftsgeschichte der Stadt Cöln vom Untergange der Reichsfreiheit bis zur Errichtung des Deutschen Reiches* (Cologne: 1916), and Pierre Ayçoberry, *Cologne entre Napoléon et Bismarck* (Paris: Aubier-Montaigne, 1981). Rather than relying on official population statistics, I constructed a count of the Jewish population by counting any Jew mentioned in any record as living in Cologne, then subtracting those who drop from the records. This resulted in a higher count than that in the secondary literature on Cologne Jewry. My sources and methodology are described in detail in note three, chapter two, of my dissertation.

3. Typical Jewish community size derived from statistics cited in Kober, "Aus der Geschichte," 90ff; statistic on Bonn cited on p. 94.

4. Monika Richarz, *Jüdisches Leben in Deutschland* (New York: Leo Baeck Institute, 1976), 1:31.

5. Jacob Toury, *Soziale und politische Geschichte der Juden in Deutschland, 1847–1871* (Düsseldorf: Dreste, 1977), pp. 27ff; Monika Richarz, "Jewish Social Mobility in Germany During the Time of Emancipation (1790–1871)," *Leo Baeck Institute Yearbook (LBIBY)* 20 (1975): 69–77; Steven M. Lowenstein, "The Pace of Modernisation of German Jewry in the Nineteenth Century," *LBIYB* 21 (1976): 41–56.

6. There have been several histories of the Jews of Cologne from Roman times through those of their authors: Ernest Weyden, *Geschichte der Juden in Köln am Rhein von der Römerzeiten bis auf die Gegenwart* (Cologne: 1867); Carl Brisch, *Geschichte der Juden in Cöln und Umgebung aus ältester Zeit bis auf die Gegenwart*, 2 vols. in one (Mülheim am Rhein: 1879); Adolf Kober, *Cologne* (Philadelphia: Jewish Publication Society, 1940). More recently, Alwin Müller has written a methodologically sophisticated social history of the Jews in Cologne in the first half of the nineteenth century, *Die Geschichte der Juden in Köln von der Wiederzulassung 1798 bis um 1850* (Cologne: Dme-Verlag, 1984). Our works overlap somewhat but differ significantly in basic approach. Müller (p. 15) hints at but does not pursue a dissenting view of the socioeconomic character of the first Jewish immigrants to Cologne. Gothein, *Verfassungs-*, p. 313, states flatly that the earliest Jewish settlers were "poor beggars, peddlers and petty pawn brokers."

7. A copy of the "Memorbuch" is preserved in the Archives of the Jewish Theological Seminary of America, History Mic. 8600.

8. Incident related in Weyden, *Geschichte der Juden*, pp. 275–76, who records it as a piece of oral history gleaned from one of Stern's daughters.

9. Deduced from "Nachweisung der in hiesiger Stadt wohnhaften Juden" of 29 June 1820, in Historisches Archiv der Stadt Köln (hereafter HASK), Oberbürgermeisteramt, 400-II-13-C-10.

10. Although women are mentioned occasionally, information about the Jews of Cologne is overwhelmingly about men. Subsequently, the words *Jew, immigrant,* and so on refer to men.

11. HASK, Französische Verwaltung, 2470, 4888; Weyden, *Geschichte der Juden*, pp. 274–78; Brisch, *Juden in Cöln*, 2: 146–51; Kober, *Cologne*, p. 319; Hauptstaatsarchiv Düsseldorf, Zweigarchiv Kalkum (henceforth HSTA-D-K), reg. 3691.

12. Weyden, *Geschichte der Juden*, pp. 286–87.

13. Based on analysis of the founding constitution of the synagogue, whose original German text is preserved in the Archives of the Leo Baeck Institute, New York, Adolf Kober Collection, box 7 (translated in Kober, *Cologne*, 317ff), and on the record of an auction of synagogue seats, HSTA-D-K, Reg. 3691.

14. Almost all the writing on the Jews in Cologne or the Oppenheim family mentions that Salomon Oppenheim represented Roer *département* Jewry at Na-

poleon's 1806 Assembly of Notables. Oppenheim was not eager to serve, however, and he petitioned for exemption. His petition is preserved in Hauptstaatsarchiv Düsseldorf, Französische Abteilung, II Div. 1 Bureau, 1799, p. 1.

15. See David Philipson, *The Reform Movement in Judaism* (New York: Macmillan, 1931), 21ff; Steven M. Lowenstein, "The 1840s and the Creation of the German-Jewish Religious Reform Movement," in *Revolution and Evolution, 1848 in German-Jewish History,* ed. Werner E. Mosse, et al. (Tübingen: Mohr, 1981), pp. 255–97.

16. Kober, *Cologne*, p. 184.

17. Based on analysis of sources cited in note 11.

18. Analysis of Jewish residence patterns is based on several citywide surveys of the Jewish population conducted in 1806 and 1808, HASK, Französische Verwaltung, 2470 and 4884. These surveys also provided details on household composition and occupation of adults.

19. HASK, Französosische Verwaltung, 2470.

20. Edward Shorter, *The Making of the Modern Family* (New York: Basic Books, 1975), pp. 32–37; Louise Tilly and Joan Scott, *Women, Work and Family* (New York: Holt, Rinehart, Winston, 1978), pp. 13ff, 83, 95, 108–9, 116ff, 153–54, 181–82.

21. Weyden, *Geschichte der Juden,* pp. 282ff; Brisch, *Juden in Cöln,* 2:150ff.

22. Hans Pohl, "Wirtschaftsgeschichte Kölns im 18. und beginnenden 19. Jahrhundert," in *Zwei Jahrtausende Kölner Wirtschaft,* ed. Hermann Kellebenz with Klara van Eyll, vol. 2 (Cologne: 1975), p. 54.

23. See HASK, Französische Verwaltung, 2468, document 2, letter of the police commissioner dated 10 Brumaire, An 8.

24. Analysis of migration patterns based on information in the "Nachweisung" of 19 April 1817, and the "Namentliches Verzeichnis" of 25 September 1817, HASK, Oberbürgermeisteramt, II, 4-C, Bd. 1.

25. This is in keeping with the fact that all the intermediate migration places were in northern Rhineland, where most towns had fewer than 2,500 inhabitants.

26. Marvin Lowenthal, trans., *The Memoirs of Glückel of Hameln* (New York: Harper, 1977), pp. 32–33.

27. Information on all these cases derived from HASK, Französische Verwaltung, 2466 and 2468; Kober, *Cologne,* p. 185, and *Das Namensregister der Kölner Juden von 1808* (Berlin: 1926), p. 14.

28. Of Rürup's many works, see this thesis succinctly stated in "Jewish Emancipation and Bourgeois Society," *LBIYB* 14 (1969): 67–91; "Emancipation and Crisis," *LBIYB* 20 (1975): 13–25; and "German Liberalism and the Emancipation of the Jews," *LBIYB* 20 (1975): 59–68.

3

Social Mobility and Ethnic Assimilation in the Jewish Neighborhoods of Vienna, 1867–1914

Marsha L. Rozenblit

The Jews who migrated to Vienna in the second half of the nineteenth century arrived in the Habsburg capital from a variety of backgrounds and with a wide range of expectations of urban life. In Vienna Jews from Bohemia, Moravia, Hungary, and Galicia shed many of the social and economic peculiarities that had branded them as Jews and rushed to take advantage of the new economic, educational, and social opportunities that only such a great metropolitan center could provide. Their eagerness to assimilate into Austro-Hungarian society, however, did not herald the end of Jewish group distinctiveness. Jewish immigrants to Vienna, and their Vienna-born offspring, chose new urban occupations, but ones that continued to mark them as Jews. Moreover, despite rapid acculturation and secularization, they tended to inhabit a Jewish social universe: befriending and marrying each other, joining Jewish social and political organizations, and, above all, living in Jewish neighborhoods. Like Jews in New York, Paris, or Budapest, Jews in Vienna lived with other Jews, and not with Gentiles with whom they shared social class or geographical provenance. Jews in Vienna, like those in the other cities of Central Europe, assimilated into European culture in the company of other Jews, and this guaranteed continued Jewish distinctiveness and group identity.[1]

The Jewish community of Vienna in the late nineteenth century consisted almost entirely of immigrants and their children. Before 1848, only a few wealthy Jews, along with their families and servants, received imperial patents of toleration allowing them to reside in the capital.[2] With the lifting of traditional restrictions on Jewish residence after the Revolution of 1848, Jews from the Austrian provinces and Hungary streamed into Vienna, creating an extremely large Jewish community by World War I. In 1848, between two thousand and four thousand Jews lived in Vienna; by 1910, more than one hundred seventy-five thousand Jews resided in the Habsburg capital.[3] The first Jewish immigrants to Vienna came from Bohemia and Moravia, provinces to the north and northwest of Vienna in what is today Czechoslovakia. These Jews were quickly overwhelmed by a massive influx of Jews from Hungary, particularly from western Hungary and western Slovakia, due east of Vienna. Finally, at the turn of the century a large number of Jews migrated to the Austrian capital from the Polish- and Ruthene-speaking province of Galicia. These three overlapping waves of migration created a community that was 20 percent native born, 20 percent Bohemian and Moravian, almost 40 percent Hungarian, and 20 percent Galician (see table 1). In effect, two Jewish communities existed in Vienna, one composed of German-speaking Jews from the Czech lands and Hungary, and the other consisting mostly of Yiddish-speaking, traditionalist Jews from Galicia.[4]

Jewish immigrants to Vienna arrived with a wide variety of

Table 1
Land of Origin of Jewish Fathers, 1869–1910 (%)

	Overall* N = 1060	1869 N = 324	1880 N = 146	1890† N = 179	1900 N = 241	1910 N = 170
Vienna	17.6	21.3	11.6	16.8	16.2	18.2
Other Lower Austria	1.2	0.6	–	3.4	0.4	2.9
Bohemia	8.2	8.6	11.0	8.4	7.1	6.5
Moravia	12.5	13.0	15.1	14.0	12.9	7.6
Silesia	0.8	0.3	0.7	1.1	1.7	–
Galicia	18.0	10.5	13.7	15.6	20.7	34.7
Bukovina	1.0	–	1.4	1.1	0.8	2.9
Other Austria	0.4	0.3	–	1.1	–	0.6
Hungary	35.8	42.3	44.5	35.8	33.6	19.4
Other foreign	4.3	3.1	2.1	2.8	6.6	7.1

*Overall statistics are based on land of birth for 1869, 1880, 1900, and 1910, and on land of legal residence rights for 1890, the year in which land of birth was not indicated in the birth records. Austrian law accorded everyone legal residence rights in the communities from which they came.
†Statistics on land of legal residence rights.

skills, expectations, and prior experience with urban life. Unlike migrating Jews in Germany or France, most Jews who came to Vienna had not been born in villages and small towns. On the contrary, most came from larger towns and cities, and a substantial number had been born in the other metropolises of the Monarchy, in Budapest, Prague, Lemberg, and Cracow. Most Jews in Vienna came from those urban areas whose populations ranged from ten thousand to one hundred thousand, places like Brody and Rzeszow in Galicia, Pressburg/Poszony and Stuhlweissenberg/Szekeszféhervar in Hungary, and Prossnitz and Gaya in Moravia. On the average, among the non-Viennese-born Jews marrying in Vienna between 1870 and 1910, 4 percent had been born in villages of fewer than 500 residents, and 16 percent came from small towns of 500 to 1,000 residents, more than 35 percent came from towns with 2,000 to 9,999 inhabitants, and slightly less than half were born in cities with more than 10,000 residents, including 11 to 12 percent who came from large cities with more than 100,000 residents.[5]

The extent to which Jews lived in cities before their immigration, however, in no way indicates their degree of assimilation. On the contrary, the most assimilated Jews in Vienna, the Bohemians and Moravians, came from smaller-sized towns than did the least assimilated, the Galicians, who were the most urban of all Jewish immigrants to the capital. Only about 6 percent of all Galician Jews in Vienna had been born in towns with fewer than two thousand inhabitants, but about 39 percent of the Bohemians and 21 percent of all Hungarian and Moravian Jewish immigrants came from such small towns. The evidence suggests that large cities with substantial Jewish communities provided a sounder basis for continued Jewish affiliation and identity than did the small towns and villages with their tiny Jewish communities.

Whether from Bohemia, Moravia, Hungary, or Galicia, Jews in late nineteenth-century Vienna quickly abandoned traditional Jewish occupations in petty trade to take advantage of urban opportunities. Unlike Jewish immigrants elsewhere, however, they did not become garment center manufacturers and professionals. On the contrary, they embraced new careers as clerks, salesmen, and managers, as white-collar "business employees" in industrial and commercial enterprises. This changing occupational preference was most typical among the young. In samples of Jewish bridegrooms from 1870, 1880, 1890, 1900, and 1910 (table 2), the proportion of young Jews pursuing careers as merchants declined from 55.6 percent to 33.3 percent between 1870

Table 2
Occupations of Jewish Grooms, 1870–1910 (%)

	1870 N = 72	1880 N = 107	1890 N = 155	1900 N = 206	1910 N = 261
Civil Servants	2.8	–	1.9	2.9	3.8
Professionals	11.1	7.5	11.6	13.1	11.1
Industrialists	5.6	1.9	3.9	3.4	3.4
Merchants	55.6	57.0	45.8	33.0	33.3
Business employees	2.8	15.0	22.6	29.6	35.2
Artisans	19.4	15.9	10.3	13.1	8.0
Workers	2.8	2.8	3.9	4.9	5.0

and 1910. At the same time, the popularity of careers as business employees rose from 2.8 percent of those Jewish men who married in 1870 to 35.2 percent of those who married just before World War I. This transformation is even more significant than these figures indicate given the massive influx of Galician Jews, most of them traditional petty traders, who diluted the percentage of grooms practicing new occupations. During this period the number of Jewish artisans declined; those who chose careers as civil servants—a field largely closed by de facto discrimination—grew modestly; and the percentage of Jews who practiced a profession (medicine, law, journalism) did not change.[6]

The move into salaried employment did not typify only the young or the poor, nor was it related to the life cycle alone. Fewer of Vienna's prosperous Jews worked as clerks, salesmen, and managers than was true in the Jewish population at large. Nevertheless, an increasingly larger number of those Jews rich enough to pay taxes to the organized Jewish community (*Israelitische Kultusgemeinde* or IKG) also chose careers as business employees (table 3). From 1855 to 1867 and between 1868 and 1879, only 2.8 percent and 7.1 percent, respectively, of new entrants to the IKG taxrolls worked as business employees, but by the last decade before World War I, 28.3 percent held such positions. Moreover, few IKG members (11 percent) who began such careers left those jobs to become independent entrepreneurs. The free professions attracted more of the sons of the middle and upper classes than they did among the Jews as a whole, but even among the prosperous, the new "Jewish occupations" provided an important vehicle for occupational advancement.

It should come as no surprise, of course, that this pattern of occupational transformation was most typical of second-generation Viennese Jews; that is, the sons of immigrants who were born in the city and were more prepared linguistically and culturally for careers as business employees. Between 1880 and 1910 (the 1870 numbers are too small to be statistically significant) the percentage of merchants among native-born Viennese Jews declined from 62.5 percent to 28.4 percent. At the same time, the percentage of grooms who were clerks, salesmen, or managers rose from 12.5 percent to 43.2 percent, a higher rate than the 1910 average of 35.2 percent.

The mobility pattern of Viennese Jews certainly differed markedly from the legendary social mobility of New York Jews in which skilled laborers became manufacturers and entrepreneurs and their sons became professionals. Despite this difference, the occupational transformations described here represent significant upward social mobility for Viennese Jewry. The transformation from petty trader to clerk meant a guaranteed income and a secure position, a true rise in both social status and wealth for the sons of "merchants," many of whom were probably peddlers barely making a living. According to conventional social mobility scales, of course, clerks enjoy much less status than merchants. In Vienna, where merchant meant anything from international businessman to destitute peddler and most merchants were petty traders, the supposed downward mobility from merchant to clerk in fact represented profound advancement.[7]

Viennese Jews demonstrated their successful acculturation by entering these new professions. To obtain and retain these jobs, Viennese Jews had to speak, read, and write German fluently, and dress and behave like other Viennese burghers. Moreover, in clear violation of Jewish religious precepts, they also had to work on the Sabbath. Despite this acculturation and secularization, Jewish economic transformations continued to mark them as a group apart. Jews entered occupations different from those of the

Table 3
Occupations (%) of New IKG Taxpayers, Entering Tax Rolls
in the Following Years:

	1855–1867 N=177	1868–1879 N=350	1880s N=319	1890s N=433	1900–1914 N=501
Civil servants	0.6	2.9	1.6	2.5	5.6
Professionals	11.3	10.6	9.1	12.5	13.8
Industrialists	8.5	4.6	10.3	6.5	2.8
Merchants	65.0	61.7	47.6	42.5	38.5
Business employees	2.8	7.1	15.4	21.9	28.3
Artisans	11.9	13.1	16.0	14.1	11.0
Workers	–	–	–	–	–

Viennese working population, occupations that continued to mark them as Jews and that provided them with opportunities to meet and befriend other Jews. Jews simply traded in one "Jewish occupation" for another. Economic modernization did not lead to economic assimilation.

Jews in late Habsburg Vienna remained occupationally distinct from the rest of the Viennese workforce. In a city in which half of the workforce labored in factories and another larger percentage worked as employees of the imperial or municipal government, the Jews concentrated in trade or held clerical and managerial positions in business enterprises. In general more than half of all Jews were self-employed, about one-quarter held salaried positions, and fewer than a tenth worked for wages. In the total Viennese workforce, by contrast, only 25 percent were self-employed, 14 percent held salaried positions, and more than 60 percent were workers.[8] Even within such economic sectors as industry or trade and transport, Jews and Gentiles clustered differently. In industry Jews worked as jewelers, tailors, carpenters, painters, or paperhangers, while non-Jews worked in a wide range of industries and dominated the garment industry. Similarly in trade and transport, Gentiles worked in transport, and Jews traded in goods and money.

The most noticeable differences between Jews and Gentiles, however, were in the economic sector that the Austrian authorities labeled "public service and free professons." In the early twentieth century, 64 percent of all Viennese in this sector worked in civil service and the military but only 12 percent of the Jews did so. On the other hand, Jews were two to three times as likely as all Viennese to pursue careers as doctors and lawyers and, more importantly, they chose careers in private office work more than twice as often as other Viennese. In 1910 only 12.5 percent of all Catholics in Vienna worked as clerks, salesmen, or managers in private enterprise, but 30.8 percent of all Jews did so.[9]

Jews also generally remained distinct from Viennese in their ability to use a relatively closed economic system to achieve upward social mobility. Most Viennese experienced no social mobility in the decades before World War I, and those that did rise did not do it through clerical work. Although Vienna experienced considerable capitalist expansion at this time with a growing array of banks, insurance companies, and other business enterprises, the percentage of the Viennese workforce that chose to work for such companies remained the same in this period. Between 1890 and 1910 the percentage of salaried employees (*Angestelle*) in the

Viennese workforce for both civil service and private business remained constant at about 13 percent (including the Jews); however the percentage of Jews in this category rose from 25.8 percent to 41.7 percent.[10]

Viennese Jews easily used occupational distinctiveness to their ethnic advantage. Jewish business employees organized to associate primarily with other Jews and assert their solidarity. Associations of Jewish business employees multiplied. In addition to protecting the rights of Jewish clerks and forming a social nexus for Jewish officeworkers, many of these organizations endeavored to instill Jewish national consciousness in their members.[11]

Occupational peculiarities did not provide the only or most important vehicle for Jewish distinctiveness in fin de siècle Vienna. Jews created separate Jewish neighborhoods in the Austrian capital, and these neighborhoods indicated their desire to live with other Jews, to inhabit a Jewish social milieu, and to create social distance from Gentiles, even when they shared the same social class and geographical provenance as those Gentiles. These neighborhoods thus served to remind the Jews and non-Jews alike of continued Jewish identity. In Vienna, as in such other centers of modern Jewish settlement as New York, London, Paris, and Budapest, Jews congregated in certain neighborhoods that enabled them more easily to avoid what sociologists call structural assimilation—that is, forming many friendships and other intimate relationships with non-Jews. In the neighborhoods Jews met and befriended each other, attended school together, and enhanced the perception among Jews and non-Jews alike that Jews formed a distinct group on the urban scene.[12]

In Vienna Jews concentrated in three adjoining districts (see table 4 and map). The primary focus of Jewish life, the district in which more than one-third of the Jews lived and with a population more than one-third Jewish, was the Leopoldstadt, Vienna's second district and site of the seventeenth-century Jewish ghetto. Jews also lived in the Inner City (district I) and the Alsergrund (district IX), the district in which the university was located. In the years immediately preceding World War I, Jews also began to move into Mariahilf-Neubau (districts VI and VII), and into the fancy, villa sections of Währing and Döbling (districts XVIII and XIX) on the outskirts of the city. In 1900, 55.2 percent of the Jews lived in districts I, II, and IX, but only 17.8 percent of all Viennese lived there. In 1880, 75 percent of all Viennese Jews had resided in these three districts.

Viennese Jews selected their residences based on their ethnicity

Table 4
Percentage of All Viennese Jews Living in Each District

		1880 N = 73,222	1890 N = 118,495	1900 N = 146,926	1910 N = 175,318
I	Inner City	17.1	10.9	7.7	6.2
II	Leopoldstadt	48.3	41.7	35.8	32.4
III	Landstrasse	7.5	6.2	5.6	5.7
IV	Wieden	2.7	2.0	1.7	2.2
V	Margarethen	2.6	2.3	2.0	2.1
VI	Mariahilf	4.3	3.9	4.0	4.7
VII	Neubau	4.2	3.9	4.3	4.6
VIII	Josefstadt	2.3	1.7	2.0	2.7
IX	Alsergrund	9.5	10.1	11.7	12.3
X	Favoriten*	1.5	1.8	2.1	1.9
XI	Simmering		0.4	0.4	0.3
XII	Meidling		1.2	1.1	1.1
XIII	Hietzing		0.6	0.7	1.9
XIV	Rudolfsheim (Sechshaus)		1.9	2.1	2.1
XV	Fünfhaus		1.9	1.6	1.4
XVI	Ottakring		2.9	2.8	2.6
XVII	Hernals		2.8	2.5	2.0
XVIII	Währing		2.9	2.3	2.3
XIX	Döbling		1.1	1.3	2.2
XX	Brigittenau†			7.6	8.1
XXI	Floridsdorf‡				1.0
Military				0.5	0.5

*Vienna only included districts I to X until December 1890 when many suburbs were incorporated into the city as districts XI to XIX.
†Brigittenau (XX) was part of district II until 1900.
‡Floridsdorf was incorporated into the city in 1904.
Sources: Stephan Seldaczek, *Die k.-k. Reichshaupt- und Residenzstadt Wien: Ergebnisse der Volkszählung vom 31. December 1880* (Vienna: Verlag des Wiener Magistrates, 1887), II, pp. 24, 126–27; idem, *Die definitiven Ergebnisse der Volkszählung vom 31. December 1890 in der k.-k. Reichschaupt- und Residenzstadt Wien* (Vienna: Alfred Hölder, 1891), II, pp. 50–53, 63–65; *Statistisches Jahrbuch der Stadt Wien* (1901), pp. 50–51; (1911), endpaper.

and not primarily on economic concerns. In a city in which the working classes lived in the outer districts, the middle classes in the inner districts, and the wealthy in the Inner City (district I) or Wieden (district IV), rich, middle-class, and poor Jews lived together in the Jewish neighborhoods, although not necessarily on the same streets of those districts. Jews did not disperse into the rich, middle-class, and poor sections of the city, but chose to live with other Jews regardless of income. The fact that the Viennese

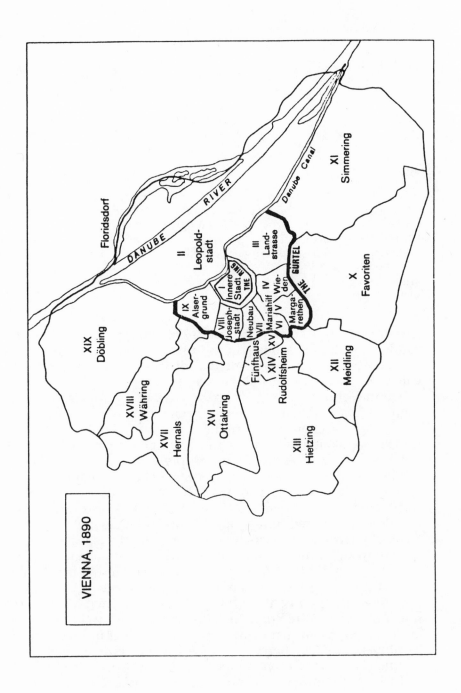

VIENNA, 1890

DANUBE RIVER

Floridsdorf

Danube Canal

XI
Simmering

II
Leopold-
stadt

III
Land-
strasse

THE RING

I
Innere
Stadt

IX
Alser-
grund

VIII
Joseph-
stadt

VII
Neubau

IV
Wie-
den

VI
Mariahilf

V
Marga-
rethen

THE GÜRTEL

X
Favoriten

XIX
Döbling

XVIII
Währing

XVII
Hernals

XVI
Ottakring

Fünfhaus

XIV

XV
Rudolfsheim

XIII
Hietzing

XII
Meidling

Table 5A
Residential Distribution* of Jewish Grooms and Brides, Composite, 1870–1910,
and IKG Taxpayers, Composite, 1855–1910 (%)

	Grooms N = 881	Brides N = 884		IKG Taxpayers N = 1883
I	8.6	9.3		23.0
II	33.6	36.3		25.1
III–V, X	9.5	10.4		12.4
VI–VIII	10.2	11.1	VI–VII	11.0
IX	9.8	9.8	VIII–IX	14.3
XI–XIX	11.7	10.5		11.6
XX†	3.3	4.0		1.6
Other	13.3‡	8.6‡		0.8

*Districts are grouped here and in the next table to make analysis easier. Because few Jews lived in III–V, X, and XI–XIX, they are grouped together.

†District XX appears lower than the census statistics for 1900 and 1910 because the sample is a composite of 1870–1910, and Brigittenau was only separated from the Leopoldstadt in 1900.

‡Those living in the provinces and "imported" to Vienna by their respective spouses.

Jewish poor were not working class, but rather poor traders and peddlers, certainly facilitated this trend.[13]

A comparison of the residential distribution of average Jews with rich and poor Jews (tables 5a and 5b) reveals the similarity of residential choice among Viennese Jews of all classes. Table 5a compares the residences of Jewish brides and grooms, who represent a cross section of all Viennese Jews, with that third of the Jewish population who were rich enough to pay taxes to the *Israelitische Kultusgemeinde*. Table 5b presents the residential distribution of destitute Jews who received charity from the organized Jewish community. Poor Jews shunned residence in Vienna's working-class outer districts (X to XVII) to live near other Jews. Rich Jews continued to rent apartments in the Leopoldstadt, the focus of Jewish life in Vienna, when one might suspect that their income would induce them to find better accommodations.

Differences did exist. Poor Jews rarely lived in the fashionable Inner City, and a higher than average percentage of prosperous Jews did rent apartments in this prestigious district. Many destitute Jews lived in the Brigittenau (district XX), a run-down section of the Leopoldstadt made into a separate district in 1900, and no wealthy Jews lived there. Poor Jews also were more likely than middle-class Jews to rent apartments in the working-class outer districts. More important than these differences, however, is that rich, middle-class, and poor Jews lived together in the Leopoldstadt and in the Alsergrund (district IX). The Leopoldstadt served as home for more than half of the Jews receiving charity, about one-third of all Jews, and even one-quarter of the richer Jews. Moreover, the Leopoldstadt, not merely an "area of first settlement," remained attractive to Jews as they rose in social status and wealth. About 25 percent of all IKG taxpayers lived in district II, but as many as 15 percent of those who paid annual taxes of 30 to 99 Kronen and 11 percent of those in the very highest tax brackets lived in Vienna's so-called Jewish ghetto.

Rich and poor did not necessarily live on the same streets within the Jewish districts; wealthy Jews inhabited a different part of the Leopoldstadt than their poorer coreligionists. A comparison of the addresses of all Jewish taxpayers from the Leopoldstadt in 1896 with those who paid more than 200 Kronen in that year indicates that the richest lived to the east of the Taborstrasse, a major commercial artery of the district; average taxpayers lived to the west of that street. Undoubtedly, the middle-class Jews lived on the better streets of central Leopoldstadt, while poor Jews resided on the back streets and alleys, and in the section's back courtyard apartments.

Table 5B
Residential Distribution of Jews Receiving Charity from the IKG (%)

	1894–1903 Centralstellung für das Armenwesen N = 518	1893–1899 "Charity" N = 337	1896–1914 "Armenamt" N = 325
I	1.4	2.4	0.6
II	57.7	57.0	41.8
III–V, X	6.9	9.8	10.8
VI–VII	3.3	2.7	4.3
VIII–IX	10.2	8.0	12.3
XI–XV	3.9	8.0	8.0
XVI–XVII	8.5	8.0	5.5
XVIII–XIX	4.4	4.2	4.6
XX	3.7*	†	11.4
XXI	–	–	0.6

*Brigittenau (XX) was only a separate district after 1900, so the figure is low.

†Brigittenau was not yet a separate district, so its residents are included in district II.

Source: Central Archives for the History of the Jewish People, AW 1890, 1899, 1897.

Viennese Jews also avoided living near non-Jews who had migrated from the same part of the Dual Monarchy as they. The
Czechs formed the largest immigrant group in Vienna. Jews from
Bohemia and Moravia avoided the Czech neighborhoods of
Vienna to live beside Hungarian and Galician Jews. The Czech
neighborhoods in Favoriten (district X) and to a lesser extent in
Ottakring (district XVI) consisted mostly of working-class Bohemians and Moravians who labored in factories on the outskirts of
the city. Middle-class Czechs clustered in Landstrasse (district
III).[15] Bohemian and Moravian Jews rarely lived in these districts,
but like all Viennese Jews lived in the Leopoldstadt, Alsergrund,
Inner City, Mariahilf, and Neubau. Because they were not working class, it is not surprising that Bohemian and Moravian merchants, factory owners, professionals, and clerks avoided the
Czech neighborhoods on the outskirts of the city. But Czech Jews
avoided middle-class Czech neighborhoods as well because they
felt no ethnic or cultural bonds with Bohemian and Moravian
Gentiles.[16] Jews from that region lived with other Jews with
whom they shared cultural and ethnic loyalties.

With the important exception of Galician Jews, no differences in
residential distribution based on land of origin can be detected
within the Viennese Jewish community. Geographical origins
were insignificant as long as one's neighbors also were Jews.
Galician Jews did concentrate more heavily in the Leopoldstadt
(district II) and the Brigittenau (district XX) than any other group
of Viennese Jews. On average 57 percent of all Galician Jewish
grooms between 1870 and 1910 lived in these two districts, compared with two-fifths of the grooms from Hungary and Moravia
and 30 percent of the grooms from Bohemia. Even rich Galician
Jews were more likely to reside in the Jewish "ghetto" of Vienna
than other rich Jews. Of all Galicians who paid taxes to the
Israelitische Kultusgemeinde, 40 percent lived in the Leopoldstadt,
compared with 25 percent of all those who paid their taxes overall. This heightened preference for the largest Jewish neighborhood in Vienna may have derived from the more recent
immigrant status of most Galician Jews in the capital. They also
may have chosen to live together because they perceived that the
Hungarian, Moravian, and Bohemian Jews in the city disliked
Polish Jews. Galician Jews also tended to marry each other, to
create their own synagogues and social institutions, and to propa-
gate a sense of the worthiness of Polish-Jewish culture in German
Vienna.[17] Nevertheless, despite the cohesion of Galician Jews in
the city, Viennese Jews did form one united community, and their

residential distribution indicates that unity. After all, the Leopoldstadt did serve as the home for Jews from all over the Dual Monarchy.

The area of the city that came to typify the new breed of urban Jew was the Alsergund, Vienna's ninth district. The Jews in this district congregated in a small area located adjacent to the Ring and Inner City, and across the Danube Canal from the Leopoldstadt. Rich and poor, recent immigrants, and native-born Jews all lived in this middle-class area. Most of the Jewish men in this district, however, worked as business employees or professionals. Here, on Berggasse 19 lived Sigmund Freud; around the corner on Pelikangasse 16 lived Zionist leader Theodor Herzl and his family; and playwright Arthur Schnitzler lived at Frankgasse 1.[18] More Jewish men who lived in the Alsergrund worked as clerks, salesman, and managers than in the Jewish community as a whole. About 25 percent of all Jewish men worked as clerks or managers, but 39 percent of the Jewish residents of the ninth district held positions in the business offices of the city. In 1910, when 35 percent of all grooms worked as clerks, salesmen, or managers, such business employees made up half of the grooms from the Alsergrund. Young Jewish business employees also moved into Mariahilf and Neubau (districts VI and VII) in this period.

One of the important results of this neighborhood concentration was that Jews attended school—a major force for acculturation and assimilation—with other Jews. Thus they studied the classics, German literature, and history with other Jews, and acculturation became a Jewish group experience. School did not provide young Jews with guaranteed structural assimilation, because they did not have many opportunities to meet and befriend non-Jews. School may have inducted Jews into German culture and Western civilization and prompted them to value that culture over Jewish tradition; it did not, however, generate or accelerate the dissolution of Jewish group identity.

Jewish students in the *Gymnasium*, the elite institution of secondary education emphasizing the Greek and Latin classics which provided the only entree to the university and high-status careers, invariably attended schools in which the overwhelming majority of the student body was Jewish. Although Jews formed 8 to 9 percent of the city's population, they provided 35 percent of all *Gymnasium* students. Most Jewish secondary school students (70 percent) attended the schools in the first, second, or ninth districts. On the average between 1875 and 1910, Jews formed more than 40 percent of the student population in the two *Gymnasien* in the Inner City, between two-fifths and two-thirds in the *Gymnasium* in the Alsergrund (district IX), and about 75 percent in the two schools in the Leopoldstadt (district II).[19] Thus Jews attended *Gymnasium* with other Jews in an environment in which most of the friends they would make were similarly acculturating Jews.

Most Jews in Vienna did not attend the prestigious humanistic *Gymnasien* of the city, because secondary education in nineteenth-century Europe was the preserve of the elite and nowhere served as a primary vehicle of upward social mobility.[20] Nevertheless, Viennese Jews did manage to use a relatively closed educational system to accelerate their social mobility. Jewish students in secondary schools may have come from middle-class homes, but that middle class was more broadly based than that among Gentile students. Thus Jewish merchants and business employees sent their sons to elite schools, often with the help of tuition exemptions. Gentile students, on the other hand, all came from the Viennese upper class, with fathers who pursued careers as army officers, upper-level bureaucrats, and professionals. Education therefore allowed the offspring of a broadly based Jewish middle class to enter the more prestigious world of the professional middle class as lawyers, doctors, writers, and managers.[21] The neighborhood base of that education, however, prevented that upward mobility from leading to total assimilation.

Modernizing Jews in Vienna also created a whole range of Jewish religious, charitable, social, and political organizations that fostered Jewish separateness and articulated new forms of Jewish identity on the urban scene. In particular, the last decades of the nineteenth century witnessed an upsurge of assertive secular Jewish nationalism, especially Zionism, which sought a Jewish state in Palestine, and diaspora Jewish nationalism, which worked for the recognition of the Jews as one of the nations of Austria-Hungary. Both of these movements were inviting to the Jews following the new Jewish occupations and living in the new Jewish neighborhoods, especially Alsergrund (district IX) and Mariahilf and Neubau (districts VI and VII). With 240 members, the Mariahilf-Neubau chapter of *Zion*, the organization of political Zionists, was the largest in the city. Moreover, a large percentage of Shekel payers, those who paid dues to the World Zionist Organization, lived in Alsergrund, Mariahilf, and Neubau.[22] Even more important, in the biennial elections to replace one-third of the Board of the *Israelitische Kultusgemeinde*, the Zionist candidate lists in the early twentieth century sometimes won a majority or two-thirds of the vote, and at least two-fifths of the vote in Mariahilf, Neubau, and Alsergrund. In 1906, the year of their greatest pre-World War I victory, the Zionists won 42 percent of the overall vote, but an absolute majority of 65 percent in Mariahilf and Neubau and 45 percent in the Alsergrund and Leopoldstadt.[23] Zionist support may have been more widespread in the Leopoldstadt than the voting figures indicate, but the many poor Jews who lived in the second district could not afford to pay Jewish community taxes and vote in IKG elections. Rich Jews in the Inner City apparently found the Zionist solution to the Jewish problem unpalatable, but Zionism did appeal to an important segment of Viennese Jewry, and Zionists quickly learned how to organize those Jews on the neighborhood level. Although the Zionists only came to dominate Jewish communal politics in 1932, they succeeded in inculcating their ideology in the last years of the Habsburg monarchy.

Between their emancipation in 1867 and World War I, Viennese Jewry rapidly acculturated into Austro-German culture, but it did so in a decidedly Jewish way and it adopted new behavior patterns that assured Jewish distinctiveness. Moreover, Jews maintained group identity by living in Jewish neighborhoods and associating primarily with other Jews. An antisemitic environment assuredly helped them to hold fast to Jewish identity, but their own desire to create a vibrant Jewish life also contributed significantly to continued Jewish identity in Vienna.

Notes

1. This essay presents themes discussed extensively in my book, *The Jews of Vienna, 1867–1914: Assimilation and Identity* (Albany: State University of New York Press, 1983).

2. Israel Jeiteles, *Die Kultusgemeinde der Israeliten in Wien mit Benützung des statistischen Volkszählungsoperatus vom Jahre 1869* (Vienna: L. Rosner, 1873), pp. 40–42; Akos Löw, *Die soziale Zusammensetzung der Wiener Juden nach den Trauungs- und Gebürtsmatrikeln, 1784–1848.* Unpublished Ph.D. dissertation (Vienna, 1952), pp. 161–62. For a general discussion in English of Viennese Jewry in this *Toleranzperiode*, see Max Grunewald, *Vienna* (Philadelphia: Jewish Publication Society, 1936), pp. 113–69.

3. Jeiteles, *Die Kultusgemeinde*, pp. 40–42; Löw, *Die soziale Zusammensetzung*, pp. 161–63; K.k. Statistische Central-Commission, *Österreichische Statistik*, N.F. 2:1, 33*.

4. All material here on the geographical origins, occupational transformation, and residence patterns of Viennese Jewry is based on a computer-assisted analysis of three sample populations—947 Jewish brides and grooms; 1,387 Jewish mothers and fathers; and 2,809 people who paid taxes to the organized

Jewish community. The sample of brides and grooms derives from every fourth Jewish marriage in Vienna in 1870, 1880, 1890, 1900, and 1910; and the sample of mothers and fathers reflects every fourth Jewish birth in 1869, 1880, 1890, 1900, and 1910. Because the Jewish community acted as the official registrar of all Jewish births and marriages, these records are still housed in the offices of the present *Israelitische Kultusgemeinde* (the organized Jewish community) in Vienna, Wien XIX, Bauernfeldgasse 4. The tax sample consists of every third Jewish taxpayer to the Jewish community between 1855 and 1914 whose name falls between *Ko* and *Q*, the only files that are still extant. These files are located at the Central Archives for the History of the Jewish People (hereafter CAHJP), files AW 805/1–25, in Jerusalem. See Rozenblit, *The Jews of Vienna*, pp. 13–45.

5. Rozenblit, *The Jews of Vienna*, pp. 37–41. In general I have used the German names for all Austro-Hungarian towns and cities. In deference to the dualist compromise, however, I have used both the German and the Hungarian names of Hungarian cities.

6. Ibid., pp. 47–70.

7. For the conventional social mobility scale, see Stephen Thernstrom, *The Other Bostonians: Poverty and Progress in the American Metropolis, 1880–1970* (Cambridge: Harvard University Press, 1973), pp. 289–302. Even the social mobility scale devised by Michael B. Katz, *The People of Hamilton, Canada West: People and Class in a Mid-Nineteenth-Century City* (Cambridge: Harvard University Press, 1975), p. 142, appendix 2, does not adequately measure Jewish social mobility in Vienna.

8. *Österreichische Statistik*, 66:2, 49; *Statistisches Jahrbuch der Stadt Wien* (1901), pp. 67–68.

9. For Viennese occupational distributions, see *Österreichische Statistik* 33:1, viii, xxiv–xxv, lxvi–vii; 66:1, xvi; 66:2, 2–64; N.F., 3:1, 13*, 118–33, 145; 3:2, 38–45, 132; *Statistisches Jahrbuch der Stadt Wien* (1901), pp. 67–68, 73–94.

10. Even in America, Jewish social mobility surpassed that of other ethnic groups. See, for example, Thernstrom, *The Other Bostonians*, p. 152, and especially Thomas Kessner, *The Golden Door: Italian and Jewish Immigrant Mobility in New York City 1880–1915* (New York: Oxford University, 1977). Unfortunately, no one has undertaken a study of social mobility in the Viennese workforce. On Viennese capitalist expansion in this period, see Gunther Chaloupek, "Der unvollendete Boom: Die Entwicklung der Wiener Wirtschaft in der Ära des Liberalismus," in *Wien in der liberalen Ära*, Forschungen und Beiträge zur Wiener Stadt-Geschichte, vol. 1 (Vienna: Verein für Geschichte der Stadt Wien, 1978), pp. 31–43.

11. See, for example, appeals of the *Jüdischer Handlungsgehilfen-Verband* in *Jüdische Zeitung*, 26 September 1913, p. 6, and 8 October 1913. For a list of organizations of Jewish clerks, see Rozenblit, *The Jews of Vienna*, appendix 2.

12. On the role of ethnic neighborhoods in retarding assimilation, see Stanley Lieberson, *Ethnic Patterns in American Cities* (New York: The Free Press of Glencoe, 1963), pp. 6, 10, 189; and Deborah Dash Moore, *At Home in America: Second Generation New York Jews* (New York: Columbia University Press, 1981), pp. 4–5, 61–62.

13. For a fuller discussion, see Rozenblit, *The Jews of Vienna*, pp. 71–98. On the differentiation of the city into different areas for the working class and other classes, see Hans Bobek and Elisabeth Lichtenberger, *Wien: Bauliche Gestalt und Entwicklung seit der Mitte des 19. Jahrhunderts* (Graz: Verlag Hermann Boehlaus Nachf., 1966), pp. 86, 91–92, 116–17; Eugen von Philippovich von Philippsberg,

Wiener Wohnungsverhältnisse (Berlin: Carl Heymann, 1894), pp. 16–26; Franz Baltzarek, Alfred Hoffmann, and Hannes Stekl, *Wirtschaft und Gesellschaft der Wiener Stadterweiterung*, vol. 5 in *Die Wiener Ringstrasse: Bild einer Epoche*, ed. Renate Wagner-Rieger (Wiesbaden: Franz Steiner, 1975), pp. 293–99, 305–6, 332–36.

14. Addresses of a sample of every fifth taxpayer in 1896 from *Verzeichnis der im Wiener Gemeindegebiete wohnhaften Wähler für die Neuwahl des Cultus-Vorstandes im Jahre 1896* (CAHJP, AW 48/1) and a sample of every fifth taxpayer who paid more than 200 Kronen in 1900 from *Verzeichnis der im Wiener Gemeindegebiete wohnhaften höherbesteuerten Wähler für die Neuwahl des Cultusvorstandes und der Vertrauensmänner im Jahre 1900* (CAHJP, AW 50/10).

15. Monika Glettler, *Die Wiener Tschechen um 1900: Strukturanalyse einer nationalen Minderheit in der Grossstadt* (Munich and Vienna: R. Oldenbourg Verlag, 1972), pp. 44, 54, 56–57. See also *Statistisches Jahrbuch der Stadt Wien* (1901), pp. 54, 60.

16. On the German orientation of Bohemian and Moravian Jews, see Hans Kohn, "Before 1918 in the Historic Lands," in *The Jews of Czechoslovakia*, vol. 1 (Philadelphia: Jewish Publication Society, 1968), pp. 17–18; Ruth Kestenberg-Gladstein, "The Jews between Czechs and Germans in the Historic Lands, 1848–1918," in ibid., pp. 32–34, 43–45; and Gary B. Cohen, "Jews in German Society: Prague, 1860–1914," *Central European History* 10 (1977): 28–54.

17. The antipathy of Western Jews to Eastern Jews typified Jewish communities in Western Europe. See, for example, Jack Wertheimer, *Unwelcome Strangers: East European Jews in Imperial Germany* (New York and Oxford: Oxford University Press, 1987), pp. 143–61; Steven E. Aschheim, *Brothers and Strangers: The East European Jew in German and German-Jewish Consciousness, 1800–1923* (Madison: University of Wisconsin Press, 1982). For a few Viennese examples of these perceptions, see *Österreichische Wochenschrift*, 17 April 1908, pp. 292–93; *Neue National-Zeitung*, 29 May 1908, pp. 3–4; 10 June 1910, pp. 1–2; and George Clare, *Last Waltz in Vienna: The Rise and Destruction of a Family, 1842–1942* (New York: Holt, Rinehart and Winston, 1982), pp. 31, 67.

18. Israelitische Kultusgemeinde Wien, *Verzeichnis der im Wiener Gemeindegebiete wohnhaften Wahler für die Neuwahl des Cultus-Vorstandes im Jahre 1896* CAHJP, AW 48/1.

19. *Österreichisches statistisches Jahrbuch* (1875), 5, pp. 32–43; *Österreichische Statistik*, 3:2, 32–33; 40–41; 35:4, 30–31, 38–39; 70:3, 32–33; N.F. 8:2, 40–43. For more detail on Jewish *Gymnasium* attendance in Vienna, see Rozenblit, *The Jews of Vienna*, pp. 99–125.

20. See, for example, David Crew, *Town in the Ruhr: A Social History of Bochum, 1860–1914* (New York: Columbia University Press, 1979), pp. 93–94.

21. This discussion is based on an analysis of fathers' occuaptions of students in three Viennese *Gymnasien* in 1890/91 and 1910/11: the *Franz-Joseph-Gymnasium* in the Inner City, the *Erzherzog-Rainer-Gymnasium* in the Leopoldstadt, and the *Maximilian-Gymnasium* in the Alsergrund. For a fuller description, see Rozenblit, *The Jews of Vienna*, pp. 108–14.

22. "Statistik des österreichischen Verbandes 'Zion,' 1901," Central Zionist Archives, Z1/6; Schekelzahlerlisten, 1898–1904, CZA, Z1/440-43.

23. "Wahlprotokolle 1902," CAHJP, AW 51/9; "Wahlprotokolle 1906," CAHJP, AW 53/10; "Wahlprotokolle 1908," CAHJP, AW 54/12; "Wahlprotokolle 1910," CAHJP, AW 55/8.

4

Communal and Social Change in the Polish Shtetl: 1900–1939

Samuel D. Kassow

People often forget that Gebirtig's famous "Es Brent" did not appear during World War II but one year before, in 1938. By that time, one-quarter of Polish Jews lived in one of the five largest cities and two-fifths lived in settlements of more than 10,000 Jews. The city, not the shtetl, was the center of new political parties, trade unions, newspapers, youth organizations, credit associations, and dramatic and literary networks revolutionizing Polish Jewish life. Yet the shtetl's hold was still strong; its crisis and decline had become a central theme of modern Yiddish literature. Asch's sentimentalism, Veissenberg's brilliant treatment of the shtetl in revolution, Rashkin's cutting dissection of the demoralization of the postwar shtetl, Peretz's depressing travel sketches—despite their wide range, all attested to the importance of the shtetl theme in the Jewish imagination.[1] Gebirtig, the great folk poet, lived in Krakow but used the shtetl, not the city, as the symbol of endangered Polish Jewry, pleading

> *oyb dos shtetl iz aykh tayer*
> *nemt di keylim, lesht dos fayer*
> *lesht mit ayer eygn blut*
> *bavayzt az ir dos kent.*

[If you care about the shtetl, get some gear and douse the fire, even with your own blood, show at least you can.]

More than nostalgia explained the pervasiveness of the shtetl theme in Yiddish letters or the effort to clarify the significance of the shtetl as a form of Jewish settlement or community. In the gap between the myth of dignified poverty sanctified by communal holiness and the grim realities of social conflict and economic desperation, couldn't there be a reciprocal and dynamic relationship affecting shtetl culture?

Even after the rise of modern centralized organizations providing secular bases of association, the local community retained a fundamental place in Polish Jewish life. Historically, a Jew could identify more easily with a specific town than with a province or country—especially after he or she emigrated and wondered about *"vos tut zekh in der haym"* (what's doing back in the home shtetl). Provincial and national organizations affected an individual life less than local structures.[2]

In its ideal type, the shtetl was a settlement in which the Jewish relationship to the outside world minimized any dangers of cultural assimilation. The ideal shtetl was a Jewish market town trading with a rural gentile hinterland. Economic relationships with gentiles were complementary rather than competitive. Because the gentiles were mainly peasants with a smattering of landlords and officials, the non-Jewish environment posed no cultural threat, although the physical threat was real. The shtetl also acquired a specific rhythm of time and place, with market day and the Sabbath as the two main events of the week. The market day itself was divided into the morning hours, when peasants sold their products, and the afternoon, when they went into the Jewish shops to buy goods. On nonmarket days the shtetl was eerily quiet.[3] Transporation and communications dictated a static economic structure: the shtetl mainly served peasants coming to town with horsedrawn wagons and returning home the same day.[4] Unless there was a major river system or railroad, entrepreneurial opportunities were rare and credit was a persistent problem, so much so that a major function of communal organization often was extending credit to buy goods for the market day.

The shtetl had enough Jews to support a basic network of community institutions—the *Bes Medresh* (synagogue), *khevra kadisha* (burial society), a rabbi. But it was small enough so that everyone was known, ranked, socially pressured, and most often fixed in the community's mind by an apt nickname. Jewish custom legitimized strong social cross-currents. Seating arrangements in the synagogue, *aliyes* (synagogue honors), place of burial in the cemetery, financial criteria for voting in *kehilla* (community) elections—all of these factors were reminders of a clear caste system: *sheyne yidn* (elite Jews), *balebatim* (proprietors), *baal-melokhes* (artisans), *balegoles* (teamsters). Even within the lower ranks of artisans, there were clear status gradations depending on the tailoring or shoemaking being performed.[5] Watchmaking ranked even higher.

But certain safety valves countered the humiliations of the caste system. Simple *baal-melokhes* could have prestigious *aliyes* by the expedient of starting their own *minyan* (prayer quorum), which also doubled as a fraternal association.[6] If a rich man showed little social responsibility or gave too little to charity, his heirs were likely to face an enormous bill from the *khevra kadisha*. Especially in Congress Poland and Galicia, Hasidism was a powerful social force establishing subcommunities with close contact between rich and poor, although often at the expense of women and family life.[7] If social differences and prejudices were real, they lacked clear legal and moral underpinnings; a flexible Jewish culture nourished new social attitudes. One example of prejudice, however, was the traditional shtetl bias toward trade [*miskher*] and against physical labor. After World War I, the collapse of Jewish commerce was counterbalanced by a far-reaching transformation of attitudes engendered by the youth movements[8] and new artisan organizations such as the Handverker Farayn, a shift that attached a new note of dignity to physical labor [*melokhe iz melukhe*].

Tension between social hierarchy and cultural safety valves provides one way to understand the shtetl's complicated social evolution between the end of the nineteenth century and World War II. There was no straight linear evolution from tradition to modernity. Although the *shtetlekh* on the eve of World War II had caftaned Agudaniks and militant young Bundists or Halutzim in blue shirts tramping off to football matches on Saturday afternoon, most shtetl Jews fell between these extremes. A basic modernizing influence was the shtetl's growing economic and cultural dependence on outside organizations: the *landsmanshaft*, the Joint Distribution Committee (JDC), the central headquarters of the political party or youth group, the touring Yiddish theater troupe, or the daily newspaper coming from Warsaw or Vilna. Economic desperation and these new outside currents imparted a certain logic to the shtetl's social organizations. Young people could not afford books and newspapers but developed libraries within the framework of youth organizations. Youth organizations altered the position of young women and relationships between young men and women. A growing need for credit gave the Joint Distribution Committee an opportunity to begin a democratic credit organization, the *Gemilas Khesed Kasse*. But traditional patterns and organizations remained strong even as political currents and modernizing trends reached the shtetl through new organizations and older ones. Social and religious issues were intertwined. Conflicts arose, for example, over electing new rabbis: humble artisans could soak the rich by gaining control of the *khevra kadisha*. Traditional *minyanim* and *khevras* often assumed a particular political complexion. Religion's hold remained strong, if only in the form of doing things for appearance's sake [*haltn shtat*]—until the very end.

1. The Shtetl and General Trends in Polish-Jewish Settlement

The patterns of Jewish settlement in interwar Poland continued, with certain modifications, trends underway since the midnineteenth century: urbanization, a steady decline in the Jewish percentage of urban population (especially in midsized cities), a decline in the number of settlements with Jewish majority, and a shift in the center of Jewish settlement in Poland from the north and east toward central geographic areas. This latter development was not as significant in the interwar period as it had been between 1850 and 1914. Overall, Jewish settlements in small towns (less than twenty thousand inhabitants) were marked by demographic stagnation, emigration to larger cities, and—especially in the 1930s—economic decline.

An ever-smaller proportion of Polish Jewry lived in the *shtetlekh*. Between 1855 and 1931 the percentage of Polish Jews (within the 1931 borders of the Polish Republic) living in communities of more than ten thousand Jews grew from 11.2 to 41.9 percent.[9]

1855–1860	156,789	11.2
1897–1900	715,210	24.3
1921	1,124,533	39.5
1931	1,304,569	41.9

The percentage of Polish Jews living in cities of more than one hundred thousand increased from 16 percent in 1897, 22.4 percent in 1921, and 27.4 percent in 1931. According to the 1931 census, of Poland's 3,113,933 Jews, 46.5 percent lived in cities of more than twenty thousand inhabitants, 29.8 percent lived in cities of two thousand to twenty thousand inhabitants, and 23.5 percent lived in village settlements of less than two thousand inhabitants. Excluding the Jewish village population,

Lestchinsky's calculations show a pronounced shift from small town toward larger city.[10]

	1921	1931	Non-Jews (urban only) 1921	1931
More than 100,000	29.9	36.3	33.2	40.5
50,000–100,000	7.6	7.0	9.5	7.0
20,000–50,000	17.5	17.6	14.4	16.3
2,000–20,000	45	39.1	42.9	36.2

The only settlement category that declined in absolute numbers between 1921 and 1931 was towns of two thousand to five thousand inhabitants.[11]

The absolute increase in Polish Jewish population between 1921 and 1931 failed to halt a continued decline in the Jewish percentage of total population. Only backward Tarnopol province and Krakow showed an increase in the Jewish percentage; Lodz, still attracting a sizable Jewish inmigration, almost held its own. Areas of greatest decline included the city of Vilna and the provinces Polesie, Bialystock, Wolyn, Stanislawow, and Poznan. Certain midsized cities such as Lublin, Luck, and Rowno suffered large declines in Jewish population.[12]

This decline in the Jewish percentage of urban settlement had already emerged in certain areas before World War I. Of 182 towns in Congress Poland, 143 increased in Jewish percentage, thirty-two decreased, and seven experienced no change between 1827 and 1857. Of 110 towns between 1857 and 1897, forty-nine had an increase in percentage, sixty a decrease, and one had no change. Of 111 towns between 1897 and 1921, only twenty-one increased in percentage and ninety decreased.[13]

Although the Jewish percentage was much higher in towns in the northern and eastern areas of the 1931 Polish Republic (part of Bialystock province, Wilno, Nowogrodek, Wolyn, and Polesie provinces), the rate of decline between 1897 and 1921 was exceptionally rapid.[14] This area saw large migration to the United States, and according to the Polish demographer Wasiutynski, to Warsaw and Lodz.[15] The decline stabilized after 1921 in towns in Wilno province but continued in the rest of this area.

In Galicia, Jewish population grew more rapidly than general population between 1869 and 1900. Between 1890 and 1910, general population grew 20.6 percent, while Jewish population increased by only 13 percent. General population decreased 7 percent while Jewish population decreased 15.1 percent between 1910 and 1921. At the same time, major Galician cities such as Lwow and Krakow had a continued Jewish influx.[16]

Within the area of former Congress Poland, there was a clear shift in the center of Jewish settlement from the north and east toward the west and south. If one divides Congress Poland into two categories, A (Lublin, Siedlce, Lomza, Plock, and Suwalki provinces) and B (Warsaw, Piotrkow, Radom, Kielce, and Kalisz provinces), the following pattern emerges[17]:

	Percentage of Jewish Population in Congress Poland		
	1843	1870	1879
A	61.8	46.8	36.2
B	39.2	53.2	63.8

A major facet in this shift was the rapid growth of Warsaw and Lodz as population centers. In Warsaw, the number of Jews increased from 44,149 to 219,128, and to 352,659 in 1856, 1897, and 1931, respectively. Their numbers increased in Lodz from 397 to 98,386, and to 202,497 in 1827, 1897, and 1931, respectively. Age structure also varied markedly between the large cities and the smaller towns.[18] In addition, clear regional differences existed in small town Jewish population as well as in the Jewish occupational structure.[19]

2. Institutional Changes

The shtetl as ideal type had heuristic value, but no two *shtetlekh* were alike. Each shtetl had its own particular economic characteristics and occupational patterns, although a secondary occupation as supplemental income was common feature, especially for Jews dependent on trade.[20] Regional differences appeared in institutional, educational, and political patterns. For example, *shtetlekh* in the eastern, non-Galician provinces had a much larger percentage of Jewish children attending private schools than government-sponsored public schools.[21] Voting patterns showed marked differences depending on size of settlement and region. Small towns in the central provinces, for example, were a stronghold of the Agudas Yisroel (with many exceptions), while small towns in the eastern provinces favored the various Zionist parties.[22]

One shtetl might have a Tarbut school for its children; a neighboring one might support a Yiddishist school.[23] Adjoining *shtetlekh* would support a totally different constellation of youth organizations. For example, Sokolow was a Poalei Zion stronghold, and Lukow's major organization was the Hashomer Hatzair—differences arising not from economic or social factors but from purely personal reasons and acquaintanceship.

One major difference between the structure of communal life in the bigger cities and in the *shtetlekh* was in the role and functions of the *kehilla* (organized Jewish community). Under partition, the various parts of Poland had different Jewish community-council legislation.[24] The common denominator of the pre-1914 *kehilla* was its restricted suffrage and purely religious competence. Although reform of the *kehilla* was a major concern of Zionists and Bundists before World War I, little happened until the German occupation and subsequent Polish independence.[25] By 1928 new *kehilla* legislation allowed all men older than 25 years to vote for the *kehillas*. Their function was still primarily religious, but they were allowed to spend money on social needs.[26] In short, the *kehilla* became a catalyst for developing local Jewish politics embracing all strata of the population—a markedly different situation than that of the prewar period. Election campaigns sometimes became violent, especially when the Aguda turned to the local authorities to void Bundist and left-wing Zionist victories.[27]

The politicization of local Jewish affairs also was affected by new organizations developed by *amcho*—the poorer Jews—after World War I. In the prewar shtetl, the *pnei* (the well-to-do) controlled local politics. In Congress Poland, the *kehilla* was often called the *dozer shtibl*[28] and excited little interest among the Jewish population. Most Jews could not qualify to vote in the *kehilla* elections and generally did not care.

After the war, in addition to political parties, new craft organizations mobilized previously dormant shtetl groups. One of the most important was the Handverker Farayn, or "Artisans Union." In some *shtetlekh,* depending on personal and local factors, the Handverker Farayn worked with the Aguda; in others, with the Bund or the Zionists. What mattered was the effort of the *farayn* to give Jewish artisans new self-respect and to inspire them to play more assertive roles in the affairs of the shtetl.[29] The Handverker Farayn appealed to long years of pent-up resentment against the *balebatim*. But in many *shtetlekh* artisans were intimidated, too unsure of themselves to contest local politics with the *balebatim*.[30] One of the ways the Handverker Farayn tried to build up spirit was through song:

Handverker fun ale fakhn / glaykht di rukns oys / derloybt nisht mer fun aykh tzu lakhn / geyt shtolz, mutig un farois / zingt un loybt glaykh mit laytn / di arbet nor iz unzer makht / fargest di alte, alte tzaytn-der handverker hot tzurik ervaknt! amol iz geven a groyser khet / tzu zayn a blekher, shloser, shmid, / yeder yakhsn hot zikh tzuredt: baal-melokhe-nidriger yid / inm klal fun lebn keyn onteil genumen / fun ale gevezn farakht-gey funvanen du bist gekumen / vi a nidriger brie hot yeder getrakht

[Artisans of all trades / stand up, straighten your backs / don't let them laugh at you / go proudly forward . . . forget the old times / the artisan has awakened. / It used to be a big sin to be a tinsmith or a locksmith. / The rich Jews thought that artisans were low / we took no part in communal life / all taunted us / go back where you came from, they said / they thought we were a lower form of life][31]

The transformed shtetl also integrated previously autonomous societies into communal institutional structures. Although not universal, the *kehilla* tended to assert its control over the *khevra kadisha* and *shekhite*.[32] Previously the *khevra kadisha*, at least in many *shtetlekh*, was a closed group inspiring both respect and fear. Conflicts broke out often over competing would-be *khevres*. The *khevra kadisha* buried the poor for nothing but could charge intimidating sums if it thought the family could pay. Often it had other sources of income, in Zhetl, for instance, a bathhouse.[33] One notable feature of the *khevra kadisha* everywhere was its legendary banquets. Kotik recounts how in Kamenetz in the midnineteenth century, the president of the *khevra kadisha* repeatedly forced himself to vomit so he could stay longer at the banquet.[34] At least one rabbi tried to curb this kind of extravagance.[35]

In the interwar period, the *khevra kadisha* remained a focus of conflict. One source of tension was the funerals of leftists, especially former members of youth organizations. In Kazimierz, a shoving match at a funeral over the issue of wearing yarmulkes resulted in the president of the *khevra* being pushed into an open grave.[36] Violence broke out in Demblin after the *khevra* buried a member of the Poalei Tzion near the cemetery fence. His friends reburied him and guarded his grave.[37]

After World War I, the *khevra* often shared burial fees with the *kehilla*. Communal political alignments were reflected in *khevra* policy. In Minsk Mazowieck, where the Handverker Farayn managed to bring the *khevra* under its influence, rich families often had to bargain for days before their relatives could be buried.[38]

One difference between large-city *kehilles* and those in the smaller towns was how they spent their money. Although revenue sources were largely the same—the meat tax, the poll tax [*etat*], and burial revenues—*kehilles* in large cities spent a larger proportion of their budgets on education and social welfare. In smaller towns, the major concern continued to be the rabbi's salary and upkeep of traditional religious institutions[39]—a major issue of small-town politics, as various parties called for more disbursements to help particular schools or credit unions. As was common in the shtetl, lack of funds severely limited available choices.

One reason for differences in *kehilla* budgets was that larger cities already required extensive institutionalization of social services, while the shtetl still relied on traditional patterns of philanthropy. Passover relief [*meos khitim*] and dowries for poor brides were organized by local rabbis or individuals.[40] Health organizations such as the *Linas Hatzedek* raised money at Purim. The *shtetlekh* tried to keep their social safety net in place: the synagogue oven that warmed the poor, the *hekdesh*, *nadoves* (alms) for wandering beggars.

In the interwar period, the *landsmanshaftn* and individual remittances from the United States played a critical role in keeping the *shtetlekh* alive. Ironically, the worse off a shtetl had been before World War I, the more help it was likely to get from emigrants, because the highest proportion of migration occurred from the poorest *shtetlekh*.[41] The following figures on 1937 Passover relief show a clear relationship between the size of settlement and the ability of the local community to bear the burden.[42]

Passover Relief 1937

Size of Community	% From Local Jews	Landsmanshaftn and Other Foreign Sources
Less than 2,000	22.6	77.4
2,000–5,000	44.2	55.8
5,000–10,000	77.7	22.3
More than 10,000	81.6	19.4

There was a clear relationship between *landsmanshaft* and per capita aid per family: the more a community relied on the *landsmanshaft*, the more money each family was able to receive; the greater the role of local resources, such as the *kehilla*, the less money was available per capita.

3. Economics

The shtetl's basis for existence—its economic role as a market and craft center for the surrounding countryside—suffered heavy blows during World War I. But the real crisis developed in the late 1920s.

Unlike the urban Jew, the small-town Jew could not be an anonymous economic actor. His economic position was personal and conspicuous, dependent largely on specific relationships with individual Gentiles. Equally important, the Gentile in the village or small town could not hide that he was buying from a Jew. Thus the *shtetlekh* were much more vulnerable to economic warfare: boycotts, pogroms, peasant cooperatives, and government-assisted programs to settle nonlocal gentile shopkeepers and craftsmen in formerly Jewish areas.

The economic crisis of the shtetl was general, but its specific intensity corresponded to the wide regional variations marking Jewish occupational structure.[43] Even before World War I, the Jewish share of commerce in Congress Poland and Galicia had been declining, while crafts and industry employed a larger percentage of the Jewish population. In the interwar period, Jewish commerce and crafts was highest in the economically backward eastern provinces, especially in the white Russian areas. If the positive side of the ledger here was the relative weakness of gentile economic competition, the negative side was the much lower purchasing power of the gentile population.[44] In the Polish central provinces and in Galicia, the economic situation of the Jewish small town was collapsing because of political as much as economic factors.

Jews fought hard to survive economically. As Joseph Marcus points out, Jewish shopkeepers often outbid Polish competitors for peasant business by lowering prices. In turn, with local authorities determined to maintain order, boycotts were less successful. The growing threat of Christian competition (1931–37) can be illustrated in the following table.[45]

Jewish and Non-Jewish Shops 1932–37

Region	Jewish Shops			Non-Jewish Shops		
	1932	1973	% Increase or Decline	1932	1937	% Increase or Decline
A	4634	4675	+0.9	944	1944	+105.9
B	2272	2305	+1.5	225	469	+108.4
C	2010	1888	−6.1	118	245	+107.6
D	663	563	−15.1	58	310	+434.5

A: 46 towns, central; B: 24 towns, northeast; C: 11 towns, southeast region; D: 11 towns, Bialystock.

The smaller the town, the greater the non-Jewish competition. The decline in the number of Jewish shops would have been more severe had it not been for an influx of Jews from more exposed villages into the *shtetlekh*.[46] Specific towns were particularly vulnerable to pogroms. In Minsk Mazowiecki, for example, the Jewish share of commerce declined from 81 percent to 63 percent after the June 1936 pogrom.[47]

The crisis in Jewish craftwork, whose overall quality had not been high before World War I, paralleled the crisis in trade. In the apprenticeship system, apprentices spent as much time doing housework for the master's wife as they did learning a trade.[48] But at least Jewish youth and Jewish artisans could eke out miserable existences without facing the formidable legal barriers erected by the new Polish republic. Stricter licensing requirements, examinations requiring knowledge of the Polish langauge, and high fees for the yearly artisan's license forced most Jewish craftsmen into illegal status.[49] Thus Jewish craftsmen, especially in small towns, were at the mercy of local police and gentile competitors, who could set up shop using cheap government credits. Equally serious, the new legal requirements made it difficult for Jewish craftsmen to employ Jewish apprentices, shutting off much economic opportunity to Polish Jewish youth just when the outlook for alternate occupations in trade was bleaker than ever.

A few figures might illustrate the truth about shtetl poverty. The JDC archives contain situation reports on various towns. A spot survey taken in Ostrog (Volhynia) in the 1930s showed that 59 percent of the Jewish families received social assistance, mostly Passover relief. In four of the poorer city streets, of 386 children under age sixteen, 82 were younger than seven, 262 were seven to fourteen (school age), and 42 were fourteen to sixteen. Of the 262 children of school age, only 109 were in school. Of the 159 not in school on the day the investigators came, 117 were staying home because they had no shoes. Most children (267) ate only twice a day, and 242 got no milk. An examining physician found only 67 healthy children. Of the 42 children fourteen to sixteen years old, only three had a contract to learn a trade.[50]

A report from Wegrow noted that weekday synagogue attendance was down because of the increased number of beggars crowding around the synagogue door. Jews with little to give were ashamed to come to the synagogue empty-handed, so they stayed home.[51]

Besides help from the *landsmanshaftn*, the *shtetlekh*'s major weapon for fighting back was the credit union—especially the JDC-sponsored Gemiles Khesed Kasse. Development of these *kasses* played a crucial role in the interwar period in shtetl life, not only as an economic lifeboat but also as a social institution fighting the politial parties and ideologues' influences.

Credit had always been important in the traditional shtetl, both interest free [*gemiles khesed*] and more conventional loans. But traditional credit organizations depended largely on private individuals. Interest rates on conventional loans were high, and the old Gemiles Khesed Kasses required the posting of articles as security.[52]

In 1926 the JDC laid the groundwork for establishing a network of *Gemilas Khesed Kasses;* by 1937 it included 870 towns and cities (of 1,013 settlements) of more than 300 Jews.[53] The *kasses* were to give small, interest-free loans (averaging 95 zloty) to Jewish artisans or traders who needed a loan to buy wares for the market day, a new horse, or an artisan's license. To force the Jewish community to work together without the party strife plaguing Jewish local politics, the JDC stipulated that "all social and economic groups in the town be united in the *kasse* work . . . and that there exist no *kasses* for special groups or unions. . . ."[54] The JDC gave a town seed money after ascertaining that a suitable committee, able to command respect and trust, could manage the *kasse*. The town was expected to supplement the JDC's capital with its own contributions and eventually pay back the JDC. The strategy was successful. The *kasse* won the trust and respect of the Jewish public, and by 1936 the JDC's share of the total *kasse* capital declined to 47 percent (from 58 percent in 1919); the *Kasses*' total 1936 capital amounted to ten million zloty. The smaller the town, the higher the proportion of Jewish population dependent on the *kasse*.[55] A survey in the late 1930s showed that Jewish small traders received half their total credits from the *kasses*. One-half of all borrowers were small traders, and one-third were artisans.[56]

In many *shtetlekh* more than 90 percent of the working population joined the *kasses*, whose membership elected the supervising committee each year. The committee met once a week, usually Sunday, to hear loan requests. Each loan applicant went to the *kasse* and petitioned for a loan to be repaid in three to twelve months. Records of the *kasses* provide a valuable glimpse into the problems of shtetl life. This case, taken from the *kasse* report of Wengrow, was typical.[57]

A woman enters with tears in her eyes. "Jews," she says, "you know that my husband is a scribe and makes 8 zlotys a week. Of course you know that one can't live on that wage. My children don't have any bread. . . . I would like to open a soda water stand . . . some soda water, some apples, and I'll be able to make do [*ikh vel zekh an aytze gebn*]. But a license costs 28 zlotys. . . . Please Jews, lend me 25 zlotys. I'll pay back one zloty a week."[58]

The JDC investigated extensively any charges of corruption or personal bias. Unlike the credit cooperatives for more affluent merchants, the Gemiles Khesed Kasses were almost free of any charges of favoritism or corruption.[59]

In addition to the new *kehilles* and the political parties, the *kasses* mobilized groups previously uninvolved in the shtetl's communal affairs. Unlike the first two organizations, however, the *kasses* imposed a spirit of communal cooperation rather than competition.[60]

4. Youth Movements

Of all new currents changing the *shtetlekh*, perhaps the most significant was youth culture. Although ideological movements swept East European Jewry before World War I, they did not become mass movements until after the war, and their vital core was the youth organizations. The latter were certainly not rebelling against the leadership of adult parties, but Jewish parliamentary politics in interwar Poland could not bring about a marked improvement in the condition of Polish Jewry. The political movements were more successful, however, in creating a framework for new social networks and organizations. In the context of the Jewish youth movement, it would be reasonable to say that literature played as large a role as ideology. Discussions of literary as well as ideological questions and intense interest in amateur theater gave the youth movement in the small towns its own peculiar cast as a counterculture, a home away from home.

A major reason for the youth movement was growing economic hopelessness. Traditional shtetl options for young people had included taking a dowry and starting a store; going to a master, either in the shtetl or the big city, and learning a trade; studying in the *bes medresh* in the hopes of impressing a rich father-in-law; entering the parents' business; or emigrating. All these options narrowed after World War I. Jewish commerce was in shambles, and only a tiny proportion of Polish Jewish youth could enter trade schools. In Glebokie, a relatively wealthy shtetl in Vilna province, only 39 percent of boys and 17 percent of girls between 16 and 20 years old had any work.[61] Another offshoot of the economic situation was late marriage. In Horodno, 33 of 44 young people in the 25 to 29 age group were still single.[62] Thus most of the Jewish shtetl youth were unmarried and unemployed. One positive factor in the early 1930s was the low numbers of youth coming of age because of the demographic impact of World War I. But the number of Jewish children turning 13 increased from twenty-four thousand in 1930 to forty-five thousand in 1938, putting added pressure on limited employment opportunities. Most parents could no longer offer their children the hope of a better future. A growing proportion of shtetl youth turned to the youth movement.

Youth organizations offered evenings of intense discussion about values, literature, and the chances for a better, more hopeful, and dignified life.[63] There was always the slim possibility that years of back-breaking work in *Hachshara* might produce an emigration certificate to Palestine. Working-class youths found the Bundist youth movement supportive, encouraging respect for the dignity of their labor and giving them heightened self-esteem by fostering cultural and dramatic talents in the language they knew best—Yiddish. Despite their ideology, the structure of these youth organizations was largely the same. A rented room, the *lokal*, was the center or organizational activities. The *lokal* usually had a library where books, too expensive for most to buy were available and served as the basis for debates [*kestl oventn*] and discussions. The organizations sponsored amateur plays, trips to neighboring *shtetlekh*, and long hikes. All but religious youth organizations scheduled trips on Saturday, thus straining relations between young people and religious parents.

As Moshe Kligsberg points out, values encouraged by the

youth movement were a powerful antidote to traditional shtetl attitudes denigrating manual work and respecting commerce. If caste divisions did not disappear in the youth movement, at least they provided a new structure in which young people of different classes could meet on equal terms. However, few youths from *balebatishe* families entered the Bundist youth movement, which remained predominantly working class. (The Communists were a different story.) There was more social integration in the Zionist youth organizations, although they also saw a certain division of class lines, with the Hashomer Hatzair attracting predominantly middle-class youth, and the leftist Poalei Zion attracting young people from poorer backgrounds.[64]

The youth movements played a major role in changing relations between young men and young women. Hikes, discussion groups, and *kestl oventn* allowed young people to meet away from parental supervision. Parents tried to stop their daughters from joining youth organizations, but few succeeded. A hapless father in a Lithuanian shtetl, told that his daughter was going on picnics in the woods on Saturday afternoon and even carrying baskets of food, replied *"Male vos zey trogn in vald iz nor a halbe tzore. Di gantze tzore vet zayn ven zey veln onhoybn trogn fun vald* (I'm more worried about what she'll be carrying from the forest than what she carries into it [*trogn* means both to carry and to be pregnant])."[65]

5. A Shtetl Near Warsaw: Minsk Mazowiecki

Minsk Mazowiecki, a village belonging to a succession of Polish princely families, did not attract any recorded Jewish settlement until the beginning of the nineteenth century.[66] After 1800 the town, 39 kilometers east of Warsaw, went through various stages of development as a Jewish community.

Jewish Minsk did not start as a market town. The community began with the arrival of Jewish contractors and craftsmen working on the high road between Warsaw and Brest-Litovsk. The village, destroyed in the Napoleonic Wars, was only beginning to recover, thanks to the establishment of a small cloth factory and distillery. Among the Jewish arrivals was Ezra Bernstein (Ezra Podriadchik), a contractor from Suwalki who brought along several Jewish stonecutters and pavers. One, Shmuel Shteinklapper, lived until the beginning of the twentieth century.[67]

The earliest institutions, the old *bes medresh*, the old cemetery, and the *mikveh* were all located on the west side of the Serebrna River, then the edge of the city. The city center, including the market and the main church, were on the river's east side, later the center of Jewish settlement.[68] Although direct documentation is lacking (the pinkas of the *Khevre Kadisha* was burned during the War), it is possible that the earliest Jews may have encountered residence restrictions.

After 1820 the town continued its slow growth. In 1827 there were 66 houses and 646 inhabitants, including 260 Jews. At that time the Jews were affiliated with the *kehilla* of Kaluszyn, with a Jewish population of 1,455. By 1857 Minsk already had a Jewish majority: 620 in a population of 1,203. Its location on the main road between Warsaw and Brest stimulated the town's development, but the growth rate still lagged behind that of Kaluszyn. At midnineteenth century the town got its own rabbi, Reb Yisroel Yankl. In 1864 the town records show that the Jewish *kehilla* was paying rent of fourteen silver rubles, and that Jews owned 44 of the 136 houses.

Between 1860 and 1897, Jewish settlement in the town entered a new era. Completion of the Warsaw-Terespol railroad, linking Minsk with the capitol, helped to double the town's population between 1861 and 1877. Jewish settlement moved to the river's east side and concentrated on the Shenitser and the Rebbe's (Narzeczna) Gas, the two streets flanking the old market. By 1897 there were 3,445 Jews in a total population of 6,196, and the Jewish percentage rose from 51.5 percent in 1857 to 55.6 percent in 1897. Minsk's Jewish population increased fivefold between 1857 and 1897, largely a result of immigration from surrounding towns and villages. After the Polish uprising of 1863, the Russians moved a military garrison into the town. The garrison, numbering about 2,500, became a major source of income for the local Jews.

According to the 1897 census, 29.2 percent of Minsk's Jews were employed in trade, 35 percent in crafts and industry, and 18.4 percent in household service and daywork (including 62 percent of the 221 Jewish women who were employed). Rents and capital supported 8.1 percent, 3.5 percent were coachmen, 3.2 percent were *melamdim*, and the rest were scattered among a variety of occupations, including tavernkeeping. Jews accounted for 94 percent of all those employed in trade and 67 percent of all employed in crafts and industry. The biggest craft category was clothing, employing 155 Jews. Although the proportion of Minsk Jews employed in crafts and industry was similar to that of the rest of Congress Poland, a much smaller proportion was employed in trade.[69] Perhaps one factor was the yeshiva (discussed below), which added a large number to the "education" and "rents and capital" categories.

Despite the relatively low proportion of Jews in trade, Minsk in 1897, according to all memoirs, was a Jewish market town. There was little overlap of economic function between Jew and Gentile. Both traders and artisans worked for peasants of the surrounding countryside.[70] Good communications with Warsaw made Minsk a transfer point where manufactured goods from Warsaw were sold to the peasantry.

The network of old Jewish families contributed to the communal development of Jewish Minsk. Ezra Podriadchik's two daughters married Nokhumke Kalina and Sane Yankl Edelshtein. Nokhumke, who came to Minsk from Lomza, was a dyed-in-the-wool *misnaged* with enough influence in the town to install Yekhiel Mikhel Rabinovitz as Minsk's rabbi in 1874. He sold iron goods, opened a vinegar factory, and built the new *bes medresh* in the southwest corner of the market. His wife, Khane Leah, died in 1937 at the age of 107.

Sane Yankl started out as a Kotzker hasid, but later lapsed [*er iz kalie gevorn*] and began to wear modern dress. In 1906, when his wife, one of Ezra's daughters, died, the *khevra kadisha* demanded a huge sum of money for the community's needs. Sane Yankl refused, and his wife's body lay unburied for two days. Incensed, he took the whole *khevra kadisha* to the gentile court, violating one of the most important unwritten rules of communal tradition.[71] The court sentenced nine Jews to six months' imprisonment, but they were soon pardoned in a general amnesty.

Another major factor in Minsk's development was the Novominsker hassidic court. In 1873 Yankele Perlov, grandson of the Koidenover Rebbe, settled in Minsk as founder of the Novominsker dynasty. Remaining in Minsk until 1914 when Yankele's son, Alter-Shimon, moved to Warsaw, the Novominsker court brought streams of visitors and students into the town. Yankele founded a large yeshiva. One of his wealthy disciples, Shloime Folman, built the most imposing building in Minsk, the "Rebbe's *Bes Medresh*" on what was henceforth to be called "Rebbe's Gas" on the market's west side. A three-story brick building containing a large synagogue and dormitories for the yeshiva students, it was built to last as the proud center of a new hasidic dynasty and yeshiva in Poland. World War I uprooted the court, however, and the yeshiva also disappeared. After the War the "Rebbe's *Bes Medresh*" became the center of a local Talmud Torah, a far cry from Folman's dreams.[72]

According to the memoirs of Minsk Mazowiecki-born Hebrew writer Yeshurun Keshet, most Jews in Minsk at the turn of the century were *hasidim*, although few followed the Novominsker.[73] Major hasidic currents were the Gerer, Alexanderer, Radzyner, Parysover, Kaluszyner, and Skiernevitzer. Each *shtibl* (conventicle) became its own social network as well as a miniature political party, ready to act as a unit in the town's conflicts. Relations between the *shtiblekh* were not always cordial. The Gerer ridiculed the Alexanderer, and the blue *tzitzis* (fringes) of the Radzyner made the other *hasidim* see red. The Parysover were known for their special brew of coffee at morning prayers; the Kaluszyner and the Skiernevitzer were simple but honest. Rich mingled with poor, dancing, drinking, or traveling together.

At the turn of the century relations between the *hasidim* and the town rabbi, Yekhiel Mikhl Rabinowitz, were good. His book [*sefer*], a commentary on *halakha* called *Galei Yam*, (Waves of the Sea) earned him wide respect. One custom in the town was to invite the rabbi to be the *sandek* at all circumcisions. He answered questions on difficult points of law (routine questions of *kashrut* fell within the province of the *moreh-horaah*) and settled legal disputes between Jews. Even more important was his role as the leader of the community. In the Jewish town the rabbi did not enjoy automatic respect. In many communities he had to beg the *kehilla* for a decent wage.[74] It was not unusual for a rabbi to supplement his often meager income by sitting in a market stall. But a rabbi earned respect and authority not so much by erudition as by force of personality. A good rabbi kept communal disputes from erupting into serious conflict and acted as a leader without seeming to become a politician. Rabbi Rabinowitz succeeded on all these counts. Perhaps his most difficult moment came shortly after the First Zionist Congress when a Zionist speaker asked to be allowed to speak in the new *Bes Medresh*. The rabbi, a secret Zionist sympathizer, quelled some vocal opposition and gave the speaker his forum.[75]

By 1900 Minsk was ready for a new stage of development, although few Jews could have foreseen it at the time. The city's first major industrial enterprise, a factory that built bridge sections, opened in the town's southern part, east of the new railroad station. Rudzki's factory, which never employed Jews, soon attracted more than a thousand workers. From that time a new process began: a steady increase in the Polish percentage of Minsk's population. Growth of the town's Jewish population slowed because of growing Jewish emigration to Warsaw and the

United States. Between 1897 and 1908, Minsk's Jewish population declined slightly, from 3,445 to 3,344.

Minsk's main axis of growth and development then shifted from the Jewish streets east of the river to the river's west side.[76] The Kolie Gas, stretching from the Varshever Gas to the railroad station, attracted many Jews, but most of the new streets, which expanded south and west, were Polish. As before, trade remained in Jewish hands.

Community life before World War I encountered two serious crises. The first was Zionism, which penetrated the yeshiva and the hasidic *shtiblekh*. Although Zionism caused serious rifts within families, before World War I it remained a movement of individuals who talked about Herzl, read Hebrew newspapers, and bought the shekel; only during the World War I did it become a mass movement. The Skviernevitzer *hasidim* were so swayed by a Zionist speech that the whole *shtibl* decided to buy the shekel, until they were abruptly called to order by a telegram from their rebbe.

The second pre-World War I crisis occurred after the death of Rabbi Rabinowitz.[77] Two serious candidates as successor emerged. Most of the *hasidim* favored Aryeh Aizntzveig, the Mekhever Rav. The younger Jews, *maskilim*, Zionists, and the Skiernevitzer *hasidim* wanted Rabbi Joseph Kaplan, a young rabbi from Brest Litovsk. On an evening in 1913 the whole town gathered in the fireman's hall to vote for the new rabbi. The Mekhever won by a narrow margin, and then trouble began. Rabbi Kaplan's supporters decided to install him as their rabbi anyway. The town now had two rabbis. To make matters worse, each rabbi's supporters divided on which ritual slaughterer could be trusted. Thus the town split into two camps, and members of the same family often stopped eating together.

When World War I broke out, the Mekhever Rabbi fled to Warsaw. Rabbi Kaplan stayed, and his supporters persuaded the German commandant to recognize him as the town rabbi. When the war ended, the Mekhever returned, but by this time Rabbi Kaplan had the upper hand, aided largely by a great upsurge in non-hasidic and Zionist Jewish elements as a result of the war. The Mekhever filed suit in a Warsaw rabbinical court and eventually settled for a large sum of money. Rabbi Kaplan remained Minsk's rabbi until his death in 1929, succeeding in winning over most of the town. Once a neighboring Jewish community, Kolbiel, burned down. The following Saturday Rabbi Kaplan halted the reading of the Torah until each Jew went home and brought back

Genesis 18:1–22:24) and was a major event in the town. Members of the society also went from house to house during Purim, dressed in outlandish costumes, and raised money in return for songs and skits.

The pogrom of June 1936 accelerated the slow economic decline of Jewish Minsk.[93] Expansion of the city limits in the interwar period had greatly increased the Polish population, so that in 1935 there were 4,792 Jews and 8,193 Poles. In 1925, the same figures were 4,860 and 6,511, respectively. The Jewish share of commerce had declined from 94 percent in 1908 to 81 percent in 1935.[94] There also was much stronger Gentile competition in tailoring and other crafts. After emigration to the United States was closed, the main outlets in the interwar period were France and Latin America. Various informants also state that many young people left Minsk to seek work in Warsaw.

A month before the pogrom's outbreak, Polish antisemites had murdered a young Jew, Israel Tzilikh, while he was walking home from the railroad station. At Tzilikh's funeral Polish socialist workers joined the procession in a show of solidarity with the Jews, enraging the local political leadership. In the interwar period, Minsk's Poles had consistently given a plurality of their votes to the antisemitic National Democratic Party.

On Monday, 1 June 1936, a mentally-ill Jewish ex-soldier walked up to his former officer sitting in the town garden and shot him. Immediately, mobs began running through the Jewish streets, smashing windows and burning stores. The sudden eruption of violence threw the Jewish population into panic.[95] Most Minsk Jews ran to the railroad station and fled to Warsaw; others stayed in town and hid in cellars. The mob set several Jewish homes on fire, including some in "mixed" neighborhoods. Coincidentally, a Bundist relief expedition from Warsaw arrived just as the sparks from a burning Jewish home set fire to a neighboring Polish house. Bernard Goldstein (Khaver Bernard), a prominent Bundist leader, leaped onto the roof and helped put out the fire. The Bundist *Folkstzaytung* reported that Goldstein then lectured the onlooking Poles that they were ultimately linked to the Jews by a common fate.[96]

The pogrom led to a serious morale crisis in Jewish Minsk. Articles in the Warsaw Jewish press, as well as Lestchinsky's dispatches in the *Forverts*, accused the Minsk Jews of cowardice, and the community leadership, most of whom joined the flight to Warsaw, of abdication of responsibility. The rabbi was singled out for special criticism.[97] Several articles drew unflattering comparisons between the Minsk Jews and the Jews of Przytyk, who stood their ground and fought the pogromists. The local Zionist leader and head of the Tarbut school, Leib Garbovnik, fueled the controversy by giving an interview in *Dos Naye Vort* accusing his townsmen of excessive panic. A handwritten description composed by a young boy, found in the YIVO archives, makes clear the pogrom's economic damage and the moral questions that threw Minsk Jewry into a deep depression.[98] There was a rapid decline of the Jews' economic position, notwithstanding an immediate donation of $15,000 sent by the JDC and large contributions from the United States and France.[99] A detailed survey of the pogrom's economic effects showed that local Polish authorities took advantage of the opportunity to encourage Poles to set up competing businesses. In the year after the pogrom, 26 Jewish shops closed and 44 new Polish shops opened. The Jewish share of commerce slid from 81 percent to 63 percent. Meanwhile, the boycott ruined many Jewish artisans.[100] After the pogrom about two hundred Jews left Minsk for France;[101] many others fled to Warsaw. But for most there was nowhere to go.

6. A Tiny Shtetl in Lithuania

Because each shtetl had its own characteristics, a quick survey of a small town on the Polish Lithuanian border, far from railways or other quick communication with the big city, might be a useful supplement to the above account of Minsk Mazowiecki. Perhaps Minsk was at one end of the continuum—slowly losing its Jewish character, affected by growing links to the nearby capital. If so, then the shtetl Wysokie might be on the other end. The statistician Hirsh Abramowicz visited Wysokie, his home town, in 1925 and published his impressions in the almanac of the Vilna regional EKOPO. It is an invaluable source.[102]

Wysokie was on the Lithuanian side of the border, 35 kilometers from the nearest railroad station and 60 kilometers from Wilno. In the midnineteenth century, the town belonged to a prince. Reb Leizer was "boss" of the town's Jews in the nineteenth century. Until Vitte introduced the liquor monopoly, the best business in the town was selling liquor to the Gentiles.

Leizer was able to dictate most behavior to other Jews. In the synagogue he could force everyone to stay longer and chant any *piyutim* that he wished, even the longest ones. But in 1900 the younger generation rebelled against his authority and elected a rabbi. This split the shtetl into two sides—for the rabbi and against him. The first side won a narrow victory and the rabbi came, but he never got much respect: most Jews called him *rebl* (little rabbi). Because he received no salary, he was forced to open a store, a move that angered Jewish shopkeepers. When Abramowicz visited the shtetl in 1925, the rabbi was still sitting in the marketplace.

Of the town's 559 people, 272 were Jews (65 families). Because most Jews had at least one secondary occupation, it was difficult to compile an accurate economic profile of the town. Abramowicz concluded that 17 families earned a living from trade, 17 from crafts, and the rest included bathhouse attendants, *luftmenshn*, village peddlers, and others. Jewish commerce was in rapid decline since 1920: in that year 30 Jewish families lived from trade. Another ominous sign was the small number of Jewish children learning a trade: of 48 young people between 10 and 20 years old, only five boys and five girls were studying a craft. Most handicrafts were of poor quality. Bitter competition kept average turnover in a market stall to the equivalent of five dollars per week. Before the war, sons-in-law would take their dowry and open a store, but this now became impracticable.

A partial counterweight to poverty was the town's rural location. Of the sixty-five Jewish families, thirty-two owned cows and five had a goat. Before the war, cow ownership was much higher, but after the Lithuanian landlord raised the rent he charged for pasture rights, the animals no longer paid for themselves. Twenty-two families had their own gardens cultivated by peasant women. In exchange the Jews would include large buckets of manure in their payment. Of the thirty-five rural Jews [*yishuvnikes*] who lived in the surrounding countryside before the war, only five remained. In the old days, the *yishuvnikes* had been a vital part of shtetl culture; a whole genre of "yishuvnik jokes" developed. But the general economic crisis and agrarian reform begun by the Lithuanian government drove the *yishuvnikes* out. They stopped coming in their wagons and holiday best to spend the major festivals as guests of the town Jews.

One ideal of shtetl Jews was to live in their own houses and 57 percent did, although all but three had to pay yearly fees to the peasants for ground rent. Almost all the houses were built of wood and consisted of two rooms. In a few *balebatishe* houses, floors were washed once a week, but that was the exception rather than the rule. Standards of hygiene and nutrition were low. During the week the main diet was herring and potatoes. Most children were scrawny and undernourished. About 60 percent of the women used the *mikveh,* but it was dirty and in disrepair. The public bathhouse was in no better condition, and no one had indoor plumbing.

Abramowicz made a distinction, brought out in many *yizkor bikher* as well, between real religious spirit and a sense of tradition [*haltn shtat*].[103] The town was characterized by the latter. Everyone went to Saturday services, but only 35 percent of the men prayed every day in the synagogue. Anyone who did not go to services encountered severe social pressure. Every Saturday there was a *tuml* (commotion), as Jews held up the reading of the Torah to air personal grievances. There were five or six regular tummlers.

One interesting feature of the shtetl's life was the commotion on Tisha B'Av. As Jews recited the *kinot,* youngsters threw burrs at them, which would stick to the clothing of the victims.[104] If a Jew kept quiet, the youngsters would leave him alone. But if a Jew began screaming at them, he would be bombarded by a barrage of burrs. Fights usually resulted between the victims and parents rushing in to save their children from beatings. Often the police had to intervene and close the synagogue.

A Zionist youth club was the only political organization in town when Abramowicz was there. After the war Zionism had affected everybody, but adults were now beginning to lose interest. The younger generation, however, was still enthusiastic, and opened a library with four hundred books. Only 15 percent of the members were adults. No one had private subscriptions to newspapers and periodicals; the library was the only place to read them.

Economic difficulties were changing shtetl customs. Before the war weddings lasted four or five days, during which a lot of good-natured hazing of the groom took place. The whole town attended the wedding and danced, heard the couplets of the *badkhn* directed at each Jew, and gave wedding gifts [*droshe geshank*]. If the bride were poor, the whole town contributed to *hokhnoses kale.* After the war, weddings got smaller, and only close relatives attended. Young men still demanded large dowries, averaging about four hundred dollars. This "son-in-law problem" reflected a basic issue of postwar Jewish life—the pauperization of the former *balebatim.* Families could no longer afford to give traditional dowries, but for a young man a dowry was often the last chance to begin the climb to economic independence and security.

Of the sixty-five families in the shtetl, 85 percent were getting help from the United States—the critical margin enabling the shtetl to exist, especially when a family needed money for dowry or clothes. The town was fortunate that many Jews had gone to America before the war.

As in other *shtetlekh*, the *khevre kadisha* intimidated many local Jews. Here, too, a family would often have to wait two or three days before burial. In Wysokie the *khevre* was a closed society, electing its own members.

In 1919, when the town was under Polish rule, the EKOPO opened a modern school to teach the children Yiddish literature and spoken Hebrew, and the teachers took the students on many nature walks. The adults became suspicious and hostile—*zey batlen tzayt oif puste mayses* (they're wasting time)—and were unwilling to support the school. As in many other *shtetlekh*, the school closed. The only Jewish school in 1925 was the *heder*, where the *melamed*, who doubled as *shames*, was thought to be incompetent. But parents refused to draw obvious conclusions: "After all, we have to teach our children to be a Jew." In addition to their distrust of modern education, the general consensus was that all families, however poor, had to give their children the rudiments of a Jewish education. Eight girls attended the local Lithuanian *gymnasium*, but no boys. This also was typical of small town life (and often big cities): Jews were more willing to allow girls than boys to get a secular education.

Relations with the local Christians had been good, but trouble was on the horizon. The small local Lithuanian intelligentsia, as well as the priest, were antisemitic. Furthermore, a cooperative store had just opened that threatened to damage Jewish trade.

One feature of the shtetl's life was the prevalence of nicknames fixing the public image of each Jew and representing, in Abramowicz's words, the "power of the shtetl." A stammerer was called Itze Bolbe (Itze the babbler). The father whose child was born three months after the wedding was called *der berieh* (the whiz). One unlucky young man who held out for a large dowry and settled for less was called *Di Metzieh* (the bargain). Nicknames stuck for life. Few Jews, whom everyone respected, escaped them. Newcomers were scrutinized carefully until the town thought up a name.

This was a shtetl in clear decline. Although some Jews enjoyed more respect than others, there were no more leaders or authority figures. Economic situations, as in other *shtetlekh*, affected every aspect of town life: wedding customs, education, housing conditions. Young people seemed to have no future. Underneath the decay, however, the shtetl still retained a basic sense of community. If a Jew were seriously ill, everyone contributed to send him to a city hospital. Abramowicz, certainly no apologist for his home shtetl, noted that the shtetl Jews gave a higher proportion of their money to charity than did Jews in the big city.

Unlike Minsk, this shtetl had no large factory, large Gentile middle class, strong competing Gentile culture (Jews were not that attracted to Lithuanians), or direct links to a major city. In all *shtetlekh* there was a delicate relationship between economic poverty and the community's ability to maintain a network of organizations—religious, social, and political. The higher the critical mass, the more possible it was for a Jewish town to maintain a variety of institutions. The four thousand Jews of Minsk barely supported a Tarbut school and a Talmud Torah.

There was enough support for a *Linas Ha-Tzedek*, a *Gemilas Khesed Kassa*, and several political, social, and religious organizations. In the smallest shtetl the most stable organizations continued to provide the bare minimum of Jewish communal life—a synagogue, a *mikveh*, and a *khevre kadisha*. New secular institutions were represented by the library, maintained lovingly by its youth.

The larger the shtetl, the greater the possibility that enough Jews would survive to write a *Yizkor Bukh* (Memorial Book) extolling the town that went up in ashes and smoke. The *Yizkor Bikher* are eulogy rather than history, and it would be wrong to expect anything different. Today they are the only reminders of that sense of community that lasted through all the conflicts, tensions, and defeats of shtetl life.

Notes

1. I. M. Vaysnberg, *A Shtetl* (Chicago: 1959); Y. L. Peretz, *Bilder un Skitzn* (New York: 1920); L. Rashkin, *Di Mentshn fun Godlbozhits* (Warsaw: 1936); Sholem Asch, *A Shtetl*. Rashkin, whose name was Shaul Fridman, gives an important portrayal of the impact of World War I on the shtetl's social structure. The war afforded numerous opportunities for quick profits through smuggling. As a result, although many former *balebatim* were ruined, former *amcho* used their new money to climb to the top of the shtetl social structure and take over its institutions. An aspect of this issue is discussed in Petertz Granatshtein, *Mein Khorev Gevorene Shtetl Sokolow* (Buenos Aires: 1946), p. 133. The best work on the image of the shtetl in Yiddish literature, an interpretative essay rather than a monograph, is Dan Miron's *Der Imazh fun Shtetl* (Tel Aviv: 1981).

2. For a fine essay discussing this point, see A. Menes, "Di Kemerlelch fun Tzibur Lebn Bei Yidn," *Yivo Bleter* (1931): 193–99.

3. An excellent description of the shtetl's silence on nonmarket days is found in a report on conditions in Węgrów that I discovered in the Lestchinsky Archive, the Hebrew University, Jerusalem, file number 258.

4. For a discussion of this point see Khaim Sosnov, "Kalkala v'khevra b'Kolno beyn shtei milkhamot ha'olam" in *Sefer Kolno* (Tel Aviv: Privately published, 1971). As a student, Sosnov collected data on economic conditions in the *shtetlekh* for the YIVO.

5. For castes among Jewish artisans, see Note Koifman, "Dos Yidishe Ekonomishe Lebn in Sokolov," *Sefer Sokolov* (Tel Aviv: Privately published, 1962), pp. 156–70. I also know this from numerous interviews.

6. A discussion of the reasons why artisans tended to start their own *minyanim* is found in Yakov Malavanchik's article, "In Katzevishn Bes Medresh," *Sefer Shedletz* (Buenos Aires: Privately published, 1956), pp. 581–84. Also see Mendele's "Dos Kleyne Mentshele," *Ale verk fun Mendele Mokcher-Sforim* (Warsaw: Farlag Mendele, n.d.), II:1–148.

7. Yekhezkel Kotik, *Mayne Zikhroynes* (Warsaw: 1913), pp. 399–415. This is an excellent discussion of the social impact of hasidism.

8. The best treatment of the youth movements is in Moshe Kligsberg's "Di Yidishe Yugnt Bevegung in Polyn Tzvishn beyde Velt Milkhomes," in *Studies on Polish Jewry*, ed. Joshua Fishman (New York: 1974), pp. 137–228. Also Rachel Ertel, *Le Shtetl: la bourgade juive* (Paris: 1982), p. 243.

9. I am following Lestchinsky's work here. See "The Jews in the Cities of the Republic of Poland," *YIVO Annual of Jewish Social Science* 1 (1946): 156–77.

10. Ibid.

11. Szyja Bronsztejn, *Ludność Żydowska w Polsce w Okresie Międzywojennym* (Warsaw: 1963), p. 129.

12.

Polish Jewish Population 1921, 1931

	1931		1921		
	% of Jewish Population	Jewish % in	% of Jewish Population	Jewish % in	Concentration Coefficient
Poland 100	100	9.8	100	10.5	−6.7%
City of Warsaw	11.3	30.1	10.7	33.1	−9.1
Warsaw province	7	8.7	7	9.6	−9.4
Lodz province	5.6	8.7	6.0	9.5	−8.4
Lodz city	6.3	33.5	5.5	34.5	−2.9
Kielce province	10.2	10.8	10.5	11.8	−8.5
Lublin province	10.1	12.8	10.1	13.7	−6.6
Bialystok province	6.3	12	6.8	14.9	−19.4
Wilno province	1.8	5.6	1.6	5.2	0
Wilno city	1.8	28.2	1.6	36.1	−21.9
Nowogrodek province	2.7	7.8	2.6	9.2	−5.9
Polesie province	3.6	10.1	3.8	14.3	−29.4
Wolyn province	6.7	10	6.3	11.4	−12.3
Poznan province	.2	.3	.3	.4	−25
Poznan city	.1	.8	.1	1.1	−27.3
Pomorze province	.1	.3	.1	.3	0
Silesia	.6	1.5	.6	1.5	0
Krakow province	3.8	5.6	3.8	6.0	−6.7
Krakow city	1.8	25.8	1.6	24.8	+4
Lwow province	7.8	8.6	8.3	9.4	−8.5
Lwow city	3.2	31.9	2.7	35	−8.9
Stanislawow province	4.5	9.4	4.9	11.2	−16.1
Tarnopol province	4.3	8.4	4.5	8.0	+5

This table is taken from Bronsztejn, *Ludność Żydowska*, 114. The 1921 figures for Wilno city and part of Wilno province date from 1919. The "Concentration Coefficient" refers to the percentage increase or decrease of the Jewish percentage of the total population of a given locality.

13. Bohdan Wasiutyński, *Ludność Żydowska w Polsce* (Warsaw: 1930), pp. 38–41.

14. H. Alexandrov, "Di Yidn in di Shtetl un Shtetlekh fun Vaysrusland," *Tzeitshrift Minsk* 14 (1926–31): 338–39. Alexandrov compares population figures for 1897 and 1921 and Jewish settlements in the Belorussian SSR and the White Russian provinces of Poland. For Poland the settlements are those areas included in the 1921 census (i.e., excluding a certain part of Vilno province). The Soviet figures are from 1923. Alexandrov found that in 125 settlements on the Soviet side of the border, the overall population increased 11.5 percent and the non-Jewish population by 46 percent; the Jewish population declined by 13.7 percent. Of 167 settlements in Poland, the overall population declined by 15.6 percent and the non-Jewish population by 1.4 percent; the Jewish population decreased by 24.7 percent. The unsettled conditions of 1921 probably helped overstate the decline. But high emigration before World War I played a key role, as did a large exodus to the Russian interior during the war.

15. Wasiutyński, *Ludność Żydowska w Polsce*, p. 214. One statistic Wasiutyński uses is the ratio of the 50+ age group to the 30 to 49 age group. In Warsaw, for every 100 Jews aged 30 to 49 there were 51.3 older than 50. In Lodz and Kielce, the corresponding figures were 57.6 and 63.7. In the eastern provinces, the ratios were higher: 100.1 (Nowogrodek), 99.4 (Wilno province under Polish control in 1921), 89.6 (Bialystock), and 88.2 (Tarnopol). Wasiutyński argues that a high ratio indicated considerable Jewish inmigration. Although Wasiutyński does not explain some obvious objections to the validity of this method, the clear differences in ratio between the central provinces and the northeastern provinces at least suggest that a higher proportion of the able-bodied Jewish population was leaving the eastern areas.

16. Ibid., pp. 102–31.

17. The A and B divisions, as well as the 1843 and 1870 figures, are taken from Jacob Shatzky, "Di Yidn in Poyln fun 1772 biz 1914" in *Di Yidn in Polyn* (New York: 1946), p. 628. I added the 1897 figures.

18. Bronsztejn, *Ludność Żydowska*, p. 138.

Age Distribution of Jewish Population
Jewish Population in %

Area	0–14	15–49	50–64	65+
a	29.6	53.8	11.3	5.3
b	28.7	54.9	11.3	5.1
c	26	58.5	11.1	4.4
d	29.5	54.7	10.9	4.9
e	31.1	51.7	11.4	5.8
f	32.9	501	11.1	5.9

a = city and village Jewish population; b = all cities; c = five largest cities; d = all cities with population more than 20,000 excluding five largest; e = all cities with population less than 20,000; f = villages (all settlements with population less than 2,000).

19. Bronsztejn, *Ludność Żydowska*, p. 206.

20. This becomes very clear in the various JDC reports. One example is Probuźna in Galicia. Of the 1,104 Jews in the town, 40.2 percent depended on trade and 26.8 percent were in crafts and manufacturing (percentage of employed). But for 185 families in trade, sixty-two had a second occupation. Of 121 families dependent on crafts, seventeen had second occupations (JDC Archives, Poland, Reconstruction, Localities, Probuźna). It is interesting that of thirty-eight market stall owners, all but eight had another occupation.

21. "Uczniowie Żydzi w Szkolach Powszechnych," *Biuletyn Ekonomiczno-Statystyczny*, September 1937. In the central provinces, 81.9 percent of Jewish children attended state schools and 18.1 percent attended the various Jewish private schools (Tarbut, Cysho, Yavneh, and so on). In four eastern provinces (Wilno, Nowogrodek, Polesie, and Wolyn), 58 percent attended state schools and 42 percent attended private schools. In Galicia 95 percent were in state schools; in Wilno province, 56.3 percent of the children attended Jewish private schools.

22. Leon Ringelblum, "Di Valn tzu di shtotratn in Poyln in 1934," *Dos Virtshaftlikhe Lebn*, nos. 8–9 (1934). As discussed below, the political party was only one of

many factors in shtetl politics.

23. This becomes clear in examining a detailed survey of all the *shtetlekh* in Vilna province in 1929. In 49 *shtetlekh*, 2,250 children were in Tarbut schools (23.2 percent), 2,103 in Polish government schools (22.7 percent), 1,081 in Cysho schools (11.7 percent), 11.7 percent in Polish *gymnasien*, and the rest in *heders* and Talmud Torahs. A shtetl rarely could afford to support more than one private school at a time, so the type of school established depended on personal factors (which particular individual cared enough to interest others in his project). In Szarkowszczyzna (my mother's shtetl), seventy Jewish children attended a Cysho school while another thirty-five studied in the local Talmud Torah. In nearby Dolhinow (my father's town), the main Jewish school was Tarbut. Between 1929 and 1937 there was a steady trend toward sending children to the Polish government schools. This was primarily caused by economic circumstances. See Moshe Shalit, ed., *Oyf di Khurves fun Milkhomes un Mehumnes: Pinkes fun gegentkomitet fun YEKOPO* (Wilno: 1930), p. 688.

24. On the details of *kehilla* legislation, see "Ustawodawstwo Polski Odrodzonej o gminach żydowskich," in *Żydzi w Polsce Odrodzonej* 2 (1935): 242–49.

25. For a valuable account of the importance of this issue in pre-1914 Jewish politics in the Russian Empire, see Genrikh Sliozberg, *Dela Minuvshikh Dnei*, vol. 3 (Paris: 1934), pp. 263ff.

26. "Ustawodawstwo," pp. 242–49.

27. This happened often. Article 20 of the election statute disqualified those who openly proclaimed their religious nonobservance. In Sokolow-Podlaski, after the Agudah joined forces with the Handverker in voiding a Poalei-Zion victory, the Poalei Zion supporters hurled rocks through the windows of the Agudah leader and invaded the kehilla building, overturning desks and chairs. Granatshtein, *Mein Khorev*, p. 66.

28. *Sefer Shedletz.*

29. For the memoirs of a leader of the Handverker Farayn in Poland, see Elimelekh Rak, *Zikhroines fun a Yidishn Handverker Tuer* (Buenos Aires: 1958).

30. A good description of this is found in Yakov Rog, "Tzvey Khevres," *Sefer Ratne* (Buenos Aires: Privately published, 1952) pp. 141–47.

31. Rak, *Zikhroines fun a Yidishn*, p. 151.

32. *Sefer Shedletz;* Pinkes Zhetl (Tel Aviv: 1957), pp. 99–109, 177–79.

33. For one example of conflict over competing *khevre kadisha*, see Yakov Rag, "Tzvei Khevres," *Sefer Ratne*, pp. 141–47; also Joseph Zelkowitsch, "A Picture of Jewish Communal Life in Poland in the Second Half of the Nineteenth Century," *YIVO Annual of Social Science* 1 (1946): 253–66.

34. Kotik, *Mayne Zikhroynes*, p. 72. Kotik gives an unmatched description of shtetl life in the midnineteenth century. Some of the customs described by Kotik persisted in the smaller *shtetlekh* until World War II. For example, the whole shtetl accompanied the deceased to the cemetery or went to a wedding. In another custom, young boys threw burrs at adults in Tisha B'Av. When a young man was about to marry and leave the town to live with his in-laws, the *shamesh* would take him around to pay calls on all the important *balebatim*.

35. Pinkas Zehtl, p. 106.

36. *Sefer Yizkor Kehilas Kuzmir*, ed. David Shtokfish (Tel Aviv: Privately published 1970), p. 195.

37. *Sefer Demblin*, ed. David Shtokfish (Tel Aviv: Privately published, 1969), p. 127.

38. Personal interviews with Esther Rokhman, Moshe Borenshtein, and Ephraim Shedletzki, July and August, 1982.

39. JDC Archives, Poland, General, 326a, Sotziale Arbet in Poyln; Y. Bornshtein, "Di Struktur fun di Budzhetn fun di Yidishe Kehiles in Poyln," *Dos Virtshaftlikhe Lebn*, nos. 1, 2 (1934): pp. 16–18.

40. JDC Archives, Poland General, 326a, Sotziale Arbet in Poyln. The report on Probuzhna, cited above, mentions that all charity was organized by the rabbi. In *Sefer Kolno*, Sosnow tells us that his father objected to the institutionalization of the town's aid to the poor because it was not "Jewish."

41. This is discussed in the JDC report on Sokolka. JDC Archives, Poland, Reconstruction, Localities, Sokolka.

42. Hersh Shner, "Ankete vegn Pesakh Shtitze in di Yorn 1935–37," *Yidishe Ekonomik* 1 (1937): 65.

43. The Jewish percentage of those engaged in trade was 6 percent in the western provinces, 56 percent in the central provinces, 68 percent in the Galician provinces, and 73 percent in the eastern provinces. They constituted more than 70 percent of the artisans in Bialystok, Wolyn, Polesie, and Nowogrodek provinces, and more than 50 percent in Wilno, Kielce, and Lublin provinces, as well as the city of Warsaw. See Bornsztejn, *Ludność Żydowska*, pp. 221–24.

44. The per capita commercial turnover was 829 zl. in the western provinces, 598 zl. in the central provinces, 338 zl. in the Galician Provinces, and 235 zl. in the eastern provinces. Bornsztejn, *Ludność Żydowska*, p. 224.

45. Menakhem Linder, "Der Khurbn funem Yidishn Handel inem Bialystoker Raion," *Yidishe Ekonomik* 2 (1937): 33. See also Joseph Marcus, *Social and Political History of the Jews in Poland 1919–39* (Berlin/New York/Amsterdam: Mouton, 1983).

46. This is discussed in the JDC report on Wysokie Mazowiecki, JDC Archives, Poland, Reconstruction, Localities, Wysokie-Mazowiecki; also Granatshtein, *Mein Khorev*, pp. 119–22.

47. Jacob Lestchinsky, "Der Yidisher Handl inem kleinem shtetl fun Poyln," *Yidishe Ekonomik* 1 (1937): 17.

48. See *Sefer Sokolow-Podlaski*, p. 164.

49. For an excellent discussion of the crisis of Jewish crafts and apprenticeship, see Y. Giterman, "Di Gefarn far der yidisher melokhe un di mitlen zei oystzumaydn," *Dos Virtshaftlikhe Lebn*, nos. 1–2 (1934).

50. JDC Archives, Poland, Reconstruction, Localities, Ostrog.

51. In the mid-1930s, a family in a central Polish shtetl needed about 35 zlotys a week to live at a minimal level of decency. A very good independent craftsman could earn about 40 zlotys a week, a young worker 15 zlotys a week, an older worker between 25 and 30 zlotys. A daily family budget was 3 zlotys for food, 50 groszy for rent, 75 groszy for heating, 1 zloty for clothing, 50 groszy for sundries (*Folkshilf* (1933): 6–7, 30.) A Hebrew teacher in a Tarbut school in eastern Poland earned about 100 zlotys a month.

In the small *shtetlekh*, wages were lower than in the big cities, but so were expenses. Many shtetl Jews had their own gardens, especially in the eastern areas.

For a good discussion of the wages and living costs of Jewish workers in Warsaw, see *Biuletyn Ekonomiczno-Statystyczny*, September 1937.

52. JDC Archives, Poland, General, 326a, Sotziale Arbet in Poyln. In *Yunge Yorn*, Sholem Asch gives an interesting description of Leibl, who enjoys walking around the town intimidating all those to whom he lent money. For a good

description of the Jewish credit bank before World War I, see *Sefer Shedletz*, 425–48. One constant problem in Jewish credit organizations was the incessant tug of war between artisans and traders.

53. JDC Archives, Poland, Reconstruction, Gemilas Khesed Kasses, n. 398.

54. Ibid.

55. JDC Archives, Poland, General, 326a, Sotziale Arbet in Poyln.

56. JDC Archives, Poland, Reconstruction, Gemilas Khesed Kassas, n. 398.

57. Lestchinsky Archive, n. 258.

58. Ibid.

59. JDC Archives, Poland, Reconstruction, Gemilas Khesed Kassas, n. 398.

60. This is a very good report of the Kasses in the Lestchinsky Archive, n. 258. Especially valuable are the reports on Wegrow, Eisiskes, and Swienciany.

61. N. Sh. Yididovitch, "Di Yidishe Befelkerung fun Glebok In Tzifern," *YIVO Bleter* (1931), pp. 414–20. Much of this "work" actually consisted of helping parents in their stores.

62. A. Tzinaman and L. Shlamovitch, "Di Yidishe Befelkerung in Horodne," *Dos Virtshaftlikhe Lebn*, nos. 8–9 (1935): pp. 92–105. In Glebokie 53.6 percent of the Jewish population depended on crafts and 26.2 percent on trade. This is one indication of wide occupational disparities between small towns.

63. See Kligsberg, "Di Yidishe Yugnt," pp. 137–228. Much of my information about youth movements in the interwar period came from extensive conversations with Jacob Kassow and Lawrence Kraut. Almost every *yizkor bukh* includes the youth movements as a major theme. Granatshtein is an especially valuable memoir source on the youth movements. In one chapter of his book he recalls going to neighboring Sterdyn with his other friends from the Poalei Tzion to attend the wedding of some friends. The leader of the Sterdyn Poalei Zion (P.Z.) youth group wanted to use the wedding to recruit new members. The brother of the bride, a Bundist, objected to the political speeches and suggested that everyone just relax and have a good time. When the Sokolow guests supported his suggestion, the Sterdyn Poalei Zion got up *en masse* and left the wedding. This is one example of how seriously the youth movements took ideology. But it was very common for a young person to leave one organization and go to another. Lazar Kraut told me that in Glebokie, Ha-Shomer Ha-Tzair was the most popular organization "because it was the best place to meet girls."

64. The question of social stratification of shtetl youth and its relationship to the youth movements is complex. In the interwar period it is possible to classify social groups in the shtetl in the following order: (1) rich merchants; (2) rich artisans who employed others; (3) middling merchants and artisans bringing home about 40 zlotys a week; (4) poorer merchants and artisans at 20–35 zlotys/week; (5) artisans working for someone else, workers in industrial enterprises at 20 to 35 zlotys a week; and (6) porters, teamsters. Of course, doctors and teachers ranked very high on the social scale, but in the small towns, their number was very small. Kligsberg points out two main factors in the determining status: (1) the degree of thought that went into the job [Laygn Kop] and (2) independence.

The youth movement tended to counterbalance social distinctions but did not eliminate them entirely. A working-class youth could show a sincere interest in Hebrew and Palestine and find a warm welcome in a Zionist youth movement that consisted of young people from wealthier families (Granatshtein, "A Tregeryung vos redt Hebraish," 154; *Pinkas Britscheve*, 337). But in most *shtetlekh* young workers felt more comfortable in leftist organizations: the Bund (Tzukunft), the Communists, or the Left Poalei-Zion.

A good commentary on class and youth movements is also found in *Sefer Lukov,* ed. B. Heller (Tel Aviv: Privately published, 1968), p. 143.

65. This is a pun on the double meaning of the Yiddish word "tzu trogn": to carry and to be pregnant. See Shalit, *Oyf di Khurves,* p. 362.

66. It is probable that individual Jews may have lived there and have been linked to the *kehilla* of Kaluszyn. See Tadeusz Lalik, "Mińsk-Mazowiecki w Polsce Przedrozbiorowej," in *Dzieje Mińska-Mazowieckiego* (Warsaw: 1976).

67. A. Ben-Moshe, "Khroniker Dertsayln," in *Sefer Minsk-Mazowiechi,* (Jerusalem: Privately published, 1976), p. 26. Henceforth, this source will be called *Sefer M.M.*

68. Marian Benko, "Rozwój Przestrzenny Mińska Mazowieckiego," in *Dzieje M.M.,* pp. 257–71.

69. The results of the 1897 census are contained in *Pervaia Vseobschchaia Perepis' Naselenii Rossiskoi Imperii,* vol. 51 (Saint Petersburg: 1904).

70. Moshe Teiblum, "Ha-ir k'fi sh-ani hekartiha," *Sefer M.M.,* pp. 39–43.

71. Leibl Farbman, "Khronik fun a Mishpoke," *Sefer M.M.,* p. 35.

72. Ephraim Shedletzki, "Vi in kholem farfloygn," *Sefer M.M.,* pp. 266–68.

73. Yeshurun Keshet, *Bein Ha-Armon ve Ha-Lilakh,* (Tel Aviv: 1967), pp. 9–10.

74. Peretz, "Der Tishovitzer Rov," in *Bilder un Shkitzn,* pp. 23–26; also Shalit, *Oyf di Khurves,* p. 364. For a suggestive story of a small-town rabbi, see Chaim Grade's "Di Rebbetzin," in *Di Kloyz un di Gas* (New York: Schulsinger Brothers, 1974), pp. 237–364.

75. Yaakov Eliav, "Reshita shel Ha-tenuah Ha-Tzionit be-Irenu," in *Sefer M.M.,* p. 47.

76. Benko, "Rozwój Przestrzenny," pp. 257–71; also Mordecai Vaysbrot, "Mayn Foter's Hoys oif der Ban-Gas," in *Sefer M.M.,* p. 299.

77. Personal interview with Moshe Zisserman, 16 August 1981. Also see his "Dos Kehile Lebn un di Rabonim Makhloikes," *Sefer M.M.,* pp. 93–99.

78. Yehoshua Budvitzki, "Bein Noar Dati," in *Sefer M.M.,* p. 93.

79. Yosef-Ber Popavski, "In di Yorn fun der ershter velt-milk-home," in *Sefer M.M.,* pp. 198–217.

80. Moshe Zisserman, personal interview.

81. On the Handverker Farayn, I relied on a personal interview with Efraim Shedleztki, 19 August 1982. On the funerals: personal interviews with Esther Rokhman and Moshe Borenshtein, August 1982.

82. Personal interviews with Moshe Zisserman and Ephraim Shedletzki; Pinkas Korman, "Unzer Hoyf oyfn Rebbns Gas," in *Sefer M.M.,* pp. 363–64.

83. Korman, "Unzer Hoyf oyfn Rebbns Gas," pp. 363–64.

84. Ephraim Shedletzki, personal interview.

85. On the Jewish Left, I relief heavily on several personal interviews with Moshe Borenshtein, a former Communist leader in the town; also Borenshtein's memoirs in *Sefer M.M.,* Leibl Grinberg, "Unzere Heldn," in *Sefer M.M.,* pp. 555–65; Jan Kosinski, "Z historii ruchu robotniczego w Mińsku Mazowieckim," in *Dzieje M.M.,* pp. 383–91.

86. On the Bund, see Popavski, "In di Yorn," pp. 198–217; also personal interview with Moshe Borenshtein.

87. One interesting example was Leizer Berger. He came from a religious family, studied in Warsaw University, and joined the orthodox student group "Moriah." But the University changed him, and he turned into a leading Communist. When he came home, however, he donned hasidic garb and went with his father to the Gerer Shtibl. After the war he took an Italian name and became a leading professor of law in Warsaw. Also, personal interview with Ephraim

Shedletzki; Budvitzki, "Bein Noar Dati," p. 93.

88. Borenshtein interview; also, the memoirs of Sz. J Rozenberg in the YIVO youth autobiography collection, no. 143793/3755.

89. On the financial difficulties of the Tarbut school in Minsk, there is a good report in the Lestchinsky Archive, no. 288.

90. Shedletzki, "Vi in Kholem farfloygn," in *Sefer M.M.*, p. 249.

91. *Folkshilf*, no. 84 (1937).

92. Personal interview with Moshe Zisserman; also, Shedletzki, "Vi in Kholem farfloygn," pp. 236–40.

93. Personal interviews; reports in Lestchinsky Archives, no. 288.

94. Lestchinsky, "Der Yidisher Handel," pp. 1, 17. The 1908 figure comes from Wtodimierz Wakar, *Rozwoj Terytoryalna Narodowosi Polskiej* (Warsaw: 1917).

95. A most interesting report on the pogrom is an entry by M. Rosenberg for the YIVO autobiography competition. This is contained in the YIVO Archives, no. 143644/3753. Other sources on the pogrom are personal interviews (Ephraim Shedletzky, Miriam Carmi, Moshe Zisserman) and the contemporary Yiddish press.

96. *Folkstzaytung*, 6 June 1936.

97. *Moment*, 7 June 1936.

98. See footnote 95; also, Lestschinsky's account of his visit to Minsk in Lestschinsky Archives, no. 288.

99. JDC Archives, Poland, Reconstruction.

100. Lestschinsky Archives, no. 288; personal interviews with Moshe Zisserman, Ephraim Shedletzki.

101. Leybl Grinberg, "Minsk Mazowiecki in Frankraykh," in *Sefer M.M.*, p. 613.

102. This report is in *Shalit*, Oyf di Khurves, 362ff. The discussion below follows Abramowicz's dispatch.

103. The concept of "haltn shtat" seems more entrenched in the non-hasidic, Lithuanian *shtetlekh* than in the hasidic towns of central Poland. The connection is an interesting cultural question and deserves further study.

104. My mother remembers this custom in Szarkowszczyzna in the 1930s.

Part II
Interpretations of Jewish Settlement in Urban Areas

5

Englishmen, Jews, and Immigrants in London, 1865–1914: Modernization, Social Control, and the Paths to Englishness

David M. Feldman

1

In what sense and to what extent was it possible for Jews and Jewish immigrants to become English in the late Victorian and Edwardian years? In this essay I examine the problem of anglicization in its most obviously ideological aspect: how immigrants adjusted and were enjoined to adjust politically and culturally to English conditions. There was a profusion of articles, pamphlets, and speeches prescribing different alignments of Jewish and English, immigrant and native identities in this period. These diverse projections of the Jewish future in England, their expression, and partial realization in conflicting institutions are the center of my discussion.

During the last two decades the history of the Jewish minority in England, and particularly the history of Jewish immigration from eastern Europe, has received an increasing amount of attention from historians. One stimulus to this minor renaissance has been the increased number and diversity of immigrants and ethnic minorities in postwar Britain. As these groups have been perceived in relation to problems of social policy and political practice, it is not surprising that some have turned to the study of historical precedents.[1]

Therefore the history of Jewish immigrants has sometimes been

---

This essay is reprinted with permission, from *Patriotism and the Making of British National Identity*, vol. 2, ed. R. Samuel (London: Routledge, 1988).

presented as a model that other, more recent, newcomers might follow profitably. This view draws upon the celebratory and modernizationist perspectives dominating mainstream Anglo-Jewish historiography. The celebration is twofold. British society is applauded for being tolerant and accommodating of its Jewish minority. At the same time, the established Jewish community is congratulated for aiding East European immigrants in adjusting to the exigencies of life in Britain.[2] Lloyd Gartner's *The Jewish Immigrant in England* most clearly presents the immigrants' history as one of their entry to the modern world. In this interpretation their origins in the small towns and villages of Lithuania, Poland, and the Ukraine were bounded by a "traditional way of life," and their "enlightenment" in England was "simply . . . an inevitable consequence of migration to a western country." The immigrants' own efforts, in contrast, are seen to have been aimed largely at preserving the habits of life in eastern Europe.[3]

In this interpretation relations of power are not considered to have been central to the processes of cultural transformation; rather, the experience of Jewish immigrants is rendered as a history of socialization and adaptation. As elsewhere in social history, in the historiography of Jewish immigration models of "socialization" have been challenged by historians who see instead the action of "social control."[4] This reinterpretation has been allied to a Marxian analysis that emphasizes class interest and class conflict as central organizing principles of the Jewish past in England. Accordingly, the immigrants' anglicization is seen as an expression of a successful program of bourgeois social control: one in which the Anglo-Jewish elite played a central role. Writing about Manchester, for example, Bill Williams has argued that the immigrants' anglicization "served most of all the class ambitions of the Jewish bourgeoisie."[5]

After their emergence in other areas of inquiry, such concepts as modernization and social control have been brought to bear upon the history of Jews in England. This essay emphasizes these concepts' shortcomings by explaining the process of anglicization among Jewish immigrants. The attempt to provide an alternative perspective may have wider applications for our understanding of cultural change. In another respect, too, this is a history whose interest extends beyond the study of the Jewish minority. Jews and immigrants were two groups against which the nature and limits of national identity were tested and contested between 1865 and 1914; thus they can illumine its history from a pertinent and unfamiliar perspective.

2

Colonies of Jewish immigrants from Russia, Poland, Galicia, and Rumania gathered in several English cities between 1870 and 1914, primarily in the East End of London. Between 1871 and 1911 the Russian and Russian-Polish population in London, a modest indicator of the Jewish immigrant presence, increased from five thousand to sixty-three thousand. Throughout this period about 80 percent of these immigrants were concentrated in an expanding Jewish East End. The Jewish population of the district was much larger than the number of immigrants alone. This occurred partly because of an earlier Jewish settlement, but it also reflected the rapid rate of natural increase among the immigrants. In 1903 it was estimated that between 45 and 50 percent of the population of St. George's in the East and Whitechapel was Jewish.[6] To many English observers the immigrants' English-born children dramatized the need for an effective program of anglicization.

Jewish immigrants to London entered a city containing an established Jewish population there, numbering more than forty thousand and comprising two-thirds of all Jews in England in 1880. The leaders of Anglo-Jewry sought to exercise the predominant influence over the immigrants' anglicization. As others have noted, this elite was anxious to present a favorable image of Jews to Gentile society.[7] Consequently, the nature of their interaction with the state and society was central to their responses to Jewish immigration.

The institutions of London Jewry were reformed in the mid-nineteenth century in ways that highlight the pattern of the communal elite's social and political integration within the majority society. In 1859 the distribution of poor relief was reorganized, along lines adopted later by the Charity Organisation Society, by the newly established Jewish Board of Guardians (JBG). Equally significant was the consolidation of the Jewish Board of Deputies' (JBD) role as mediator between the state and organized Jewry. In this respect the Marriage Registration Act of 1836 was a landmark. The Act recognized the JBD as the competent power to record marriages and to ensure they were performed correctly "according to the usages of the Jews."[8] These institutions and others were dominated by a "cousinhood" of leading families.[9] At the summit, prominence in Jewish affairs was accompanied by recognition in the majority society: in business, philanthropy, and, increasingly, politics. Thus Jewish immigrants entered a city in which there was an established structure of communal authority and a leadership that sought to mediate Jewish integration with the state and to shape Jewish images within public discourse.

English Jews did not welcome immigration from eastern Europe. Some of the greatest efforts of Anglo-Jewish institutions were spent in preventing migrants from settling in Britain. This policy reflected the general fears of the capital's propertied classes for the effects of immigration on the labor and housing markets of the East End.[10] Yet there also were particular problems confronting English Jews because of the influx. These stemmed from the uncertain integration of English Jewry within the polity and the nation.

The Parliamentary Oaths Act of 1866 allowed Jews to sit in Parliament on equal terms with other Englishmen. The acquisition of virtual political equality by Jews, however, failed to kill the Jewish question; their place within the nation remained problematic and subject to debate. As with other groups, the admission of Jews to the political nation was conditional upon their conforming to ideals of citizenship and respectability. It depended on their abandonment of signs of Jewish particularism that might offend these ideals—primarily signs of national separateness.[11] Religious toleration thus developed alongside demands for other conformities.

Jewish emancipation was an expression of the political nation that was in one obvious sense more inclusive. In this, Jewish emancipation contributed to the forces undermining its own stability. The demands for conformity with the nation now reached beyond the former inability of professing Jews to take a Christian oath, on which ground they had been excluded from parliament and other offices, and touched more widely on their capacity to identify with the texture and traditions of national life. George Eliot noted this in 1879. Reflecting on the rise of anti-Jewish attitudes, she sympathized with those who were apprehensive at "what must follow from the predominance of wealth acquiring immigrants, whose appreciation of our political and social life must often be as approximate or fatally erroneous as their delivery of our language."[12] Eliot wrote in the early part of a period when ceremonial practices multiplied, the cult of the monarchy being only the most promiscuous.[13] One effect of these formal affirmations of national identity was growing pressure on groups (such as Jews) whose feelings for the nation were held in question to demonstrate their loyalty. It follows that Jewish approval of Disraeli's belligerent support for Turkey against Russia from 1876 to 1878, if given or imputed from Jewish motives (because of financial investments and the better treatment of their coreligionists under Turkish rule) could be considered as incompatible with their obligations as citizens. Gladstone believed the prime minister's "Jewish feeling" was the key to his policy, and T. P. O'Connor accused Disraeli of subverting national policy to Jewish ends.[14]

The emergence of ideological antisemitism in the late 1870s presented Jews as unassimilable to the nation, was fundamentally based on race, and can be seen as one part of a general tendency. It was not merely a new formulation of an "ancient hatred," as historians and some contemporaries perceived; it also was an attempt to define the nation as so exclusive that Jews were seen not as merely unpatriotic English but as not English at all.[15] Goldwin Smith's criticism of the Jews' conduct over the eastern question was developed most clearly into a critique of Jewish emancipation. "Judaism, like the whole circle of primitive religion of which it is a survival, is a religion of race," Smith argued.[16] This backwardness was predicated on the emergence of a higher, more rational, more universal religion—Christianity. "The affinity of Judaism is not to non-conformity but to caste," he concluded—an inexorable barrier to the development of patriotism.[17]

These arguments did not go unanswered by leading Jews, but their response to the stresses of emancipation was to insist more firmly on the correctness of its premises. Their articles yielded a stark reassertion of the religious definition of the Jewish community and the firm relegation to an antique past of any national aspects of Jewish tradition. Far from yearning for their ancient homeland, English Jews were presented as exemplifying patriotic feeling for the British empire.[18] At the same time, Jewish writers sought to refute the suggestion that "the essential doctrines of the Jewish religion are tribal and stand consequently in direct opposition to the religious and political tendencies of modern civilization."[19] They claimed that departure from tribalism was the achievement of Judaism. In recognizing the existence of one God for all humanity, Judaism had been the great dynamic agent of modern civilization and foundation of both Christianity and Islam.[20]

Yet it also was recognized there were other tendencies in the Jewish past and that Jewish life had emerged only recently from insularity. Claude Montefiore indicated this when he explained that in his essay, "Is Judaism a tribal religion?," Judaism was defined as "the religion of educated Jews in the civilized countries at the present time."[21] The concept of modern Judaism simultaneously constructed another traditional Judaism from which

Anglo-Jewry was said to have long since evolved. However, immigrant Russian Jews came from an empire that had not moved toward either liberalism or rational religion; inevitably the immigrants inhabited this other Judaism. This point was clear each time the Jewish East End was referred to as "the ghetto," for whether the term was intended as a pejorative or sentimental one, the ghetto represented a form of social life that was assuredly premodern.[22]

The vigorous and partly defensive identification of English Jews with patriotism and progress left them vulnerable to the effects of Jewish immigration from empires seen to be underdeveloped politically and intellectually. Therefore it becomes apparent that the apprehension of Anglo-Jewry in the face of Jewish immigration was not simply a matter of class interest. It reflected the niche occupied by the leaders of London Jewry among the propertied classes of the capital as well as the difficulties and pressures they experienced after emancipation in aligning patriotism and Jewishness.

3

To Jewish and non-Jewish observers alike, the streets of Whitechapel appeared as a piece of eastern Europe thrown down in the capital of the world's largest empire. "The feeling is of being in a foreign town," wrote Charles Booth's co-worker George Duckworth.[23] Leonty Soloweitschik richly described the impression of difference that suffused the Jewish East End: the streets decorated with advertisements in Yiddish announcing the arrival of a theater troupe from New York, the services for upcoming religious festivals and a Yiddish newspaper soon to be published. Even the post office printed its instructions in Yiddish.[24] The impression of separateness was intensified by the competition between immigrants and natives in the district's housing market and in the workshop trades—tailoring, boot and shoe making, and cabinet making—in which Jewish workers were concentrated.[25] Immigration thus became bound up with debates over sweated labor and the housing shortage in London.

The problems credited to Jewish immigrants were not limited to the field of social policy. They possessed a political dimension that cut to the heart of Jewish emancipation. This was stated clearly in an 1887 *St James Gazette* article:

Take the colony as it stands. Eliminate the idea that it represents an invasion and treat its members neither as foreigners nor as paupers.

Look at them as citizens, ratepayers, heads of families and trades people. Inquire how far they fulfill the ordinary duties of civilised life as members of a free and independent community. The answer to that question might be given in a single sentence: they never forget they are Jews and that other people are Gentiles. They are a people apart. Long as they may live among us they will never become merged in the mass of the English population.[26]

The problematic interaction of the immigration question with the legacy of Jewish emancipation occurred in social policy, too, and was revealed in the language of public debate. The leading restrictionists insisted that they were indifferent to the religion of the aliens; what was important was that they were destitute.[27] But the Jewish question could not be prevented from intruding by this device; contrary to theoretical prescription, men and women continued to perceive Jews as more than a dissenting religious minority. The everyday perception of the immigrants as Jews—despite the intention to repress it—is illustrated in a characteristic remark, made by an East End insurance agent, who complained that "Christians" in the East End were being swamped by "aliens"—an observation intelligible only after acknowledging that the aliens were the Jews.[28] Criticism of aliens thus spilled into commentary on Jews. It is no surprise that the *Jewish Chronicle*, the principal Anglo-Jewish newspaper, despaired at the "difficulty which the popular mind has in maintaining a distinction" between Jews and aliens.[29]

The political dynamic of the anti-immigration agitation further aggravated the contradictions of Jewish emancipation. As the expanding collectivism of the state added to the consequences of popular suffrage, so the ideals and needs of the nation to which Jews had to conform became increasingly wide. It is no coincidence that the proponents of statutory restriction aligned their cause with that of national efficiency.[30] In 1905, advocating an Aliens Bill that became law, Prime Minister Balfour asserted his belief that "we have a right to keep out everybody who does not add to the strength of the community—the industrial, social and intellectual strength of the community."[31] By opposing the Bill, many English Jews raised the question of whether their loyalties were with the national or the Jewish community. Balfour himself expressed these doubts, as did others outside of Parliament, but less politely.[32]

These conditions of public debate gave urgency to Anglo-Jewish efforts to reduce the gap between the immigrants' behavior and the image of the modern and patriotic Jew. This was especially evident from the early 1890s, as immigration appeared to be a permanent problem and as calls for statutory immigration restriction gained more prominence in Parliament, on the hustings, and in trade unions.[33] Whereas public discourse resisted efforts to establish criteria for the legitimate identification of Jews and the sanitization of their image, there remained another strategy to follow: to guide and discipline the immigrants to erase the most unacceptable aspects of their difference. Underlying these attempts to reform the immigrants' manners and mores was a growing unease at the political consequences of their presence.

From 1893 to 1894, the anglicization of east European Jews was a part of the program of the two Anglo-Jewish institutions that most came into contact with them: the JBG and the Russo-Jewish Committee. The individual most closely associated with the changes of these years was N. S. Joseph. In 1893 he warned that "in ten or fifteen years, the children of the refugees today will be men and women constituting in point of numbers the great bulk of the Jews of England. They will drag down, submerge or disgrace our community if we leave them in their present state of neglect."[34] A partial answer was to develop a more personal, less bureaucratic system of philanthropy in which a central role was played by visitors. Their "great aim" was "by direct influence to improve and anglicize them [their cases] and to render them self-supporting."[35] Significantly, it was only at this stage that optimistic attempts were made to disperse the ghetto and that the Russo-Jewish Committee began to hold English classes; in 1894 it published a Yiddish-English phrase book.

Connected with anglicization was the task of civilizing the immigrants. Here their Russian origins impinged heavily upon their reception in England. As early as 1881 the *Jewish Chronicle* had presented the question of how English Jews were "to aid these brethren of ours towards that higher standard of culture offered by English life."[36] The minister of a North London synagogue expressed a similar evolutionist and modernizing view observing that "Russia today is like Spain of the sixteenth century."[37] This was reflected in the fanatical and ritualistic temper of the immigrants' religion, their jargon (Yiddish), and their customary standard of life. "The Russian Jew—when he first comes here—is often abominably filthy; because he is a Russian, of course, not because he is a Jew," argued David Schloss.[38]

Increasingly the communal leaders placed their hopes in the immigrants' children. Proponents of an Aliens Act were answered with reports claiming that Jewish children in East End schools were "the most desirable citizens, physically, intellectually and in their love for the country in which they dwell."[39] Not only compulsory schooling was intended to effect this transformation. In the 1890s, youth clubs and a Jewish Lads Brigade were established with the aim of developing English virtues among the young. Moral rectitude would follow physical well-being. The Brigade's commander explained that his aim was to "instill into the rising generation all that is best in the English character, manly independence, honour, truth, cleanliness, love of active health giving pursuits. . . ."[40]

In this light, barriers to the children's thorough anglicization were institutions that aimed to reproduce east European Jewish culture. Above all, this threat was posed by the religious schools of the East End. The *hedarim* (small classes taught in a single room) and the *Talmud Torah* schools (large institutions, funded partly by charity, containing up to one thousand children and, like the *hedarim*, educating mostly boys) were attended after day school and at weekends. They were the focus of much discussion at a conference on Jewish elementary education in June 1898. The main paper described *hedarim* as the peculiar products of Russian conditions. Presented thus, the *hedarim* were ripe for modernization and reform. The *melamdim* who taught in the schools were said to be unsuitable "both in their manners and in their method of teaching." Physical conditions in the schools reflected the immigrants' standard of life and primitive values. By 1898 the *hedarim* had become scapegoats for failure to achieve a more far-reaching improvement among the rising generation.[41] The assumptions underpinning this attack were made explicit by the chief rabbi. "It was not correct to speak of a *chedar* in Booth Street Buildings as only two hundred yards from the nearest Board school," he stated "the fact was two hundred years lay between them."[42]

4

For the leaders of Anglo-Jewry, the immigrants' anglicization and their social advancement were closely connected. These goals were yoked together from a radically different political perspective by anarchist and social democratic revolutionaries in the Jewish East End. Central to Jewish history in these decades in eastern Europe, the United States, and in England was the conjuncture that united educated Russian Jewish revolutionaries and the emergent Jewish working class. In the 1880s London was at the center of this development.[43]

The pioneers of the radical press perceived themselves in an educative as well as a political role. *Di poylishe yidl (The Polish Jew)* was the earliest of these newspapers, first appearing in July 1884. It encouraged its readership to learn English, because it anticipated that it would lead to improved relations with English workers and enable east European Jews to read books unavailable in Hebrew or Yiddish. Thus the commitment to Yiddish was pragmatic, and the editors looked forward to a time when the newspaper could be published in English.[44]

The educational intent of *Di poylishe yidl* was not exceptional, and a similar purpose was central to the Jewish revolutionary press throughout this period. Similarly, the stock in trade of socialist and anarchist clubs were English lessons, libraries, reading rooms, and lectures on scientific, literary, and political themes.[45] Organization of the workers and the revolution were conceived of as projects of enlightenment that simultaneously liberated the proletariat and signified progress for humanity as a whole.[46] It was an idea that drew on a social evolutionist current widespread within the revolutionary movement as well as within liberal tradition. For Jews it also drew upon the self-image of the *maskilim*—the enlighteners—as harbingers of westernization among the stagnating and inward-looking Jewish masses.[47] Even within the ghetto, participation in the revolutionary movement was also a means of transcending the ghetto's confines. Trade unionism, cultural progress, and the solution to the Jewish question were brought together in this version of anglicization, with the first element presented as the key.

> Don't stand off from your English comrades. Throw away the asiatic customs you have brought from Russia. Unite in unions and join English unions wherever possible. Don't allow yourselves to be sweated by the bloodsuckers. Live like human beings and demand human wages. In a word become men (at present you are half wild) and citizens. . . . Here are your means; only in this way can the Jewish Question be resolved.[48]

In this context of their belief in the existence of humanly discernible laws of development in nature and society is placed the fierce atheism of many of the revolutionaries. Free thought and the revolution were connected, because the ties and beliefs of Judaism misled the workers to put their faith in God and their hopes in philanthropists rather than in their collective strength.[49] "Before becoming a progressive, a socialist, even a nationalist, simply a civilised person, a European equal with other men, he [a Jew] must first become anti-religious," was a characteristic belief, expressed here by Karl Liberman.[50]

Between the free-thinking propaganda of immigrant revolutionaries and the responses of Anglo-Jewish philanthropists to institutions such as the *hedarim*, there was a striking agreement on the backward origins of the Jewish immigrants and their expression in religious orthodoxy. These views tell us more about the contours of discourse than they do about the responses of the immigrant orthodox to the technological, cultural, and political opportunities of their new environment.

The *Machzike Hadath* was the institution that focused the opinion of the militantly orthodox in the Jewish East End. During 1891 to 1892 the society engaged in a dispute with the communal authorities over the ritual cleanliness of meat slaughtered under the supervision of the latter. An impasse was reached, and the militants responded by building their own slaughterhouse and repudiating the religious authority of the chief rabbi. For £4,500, a chapel was bought and converted to accommodate the expanding needs of the synagogue and the *Talmud Torah* attached to it.[51]

One supporter of ritual slaughter expressed the fundamentalist beliefs motivating the controversy, asserting that "Jews who do not obey Jewish laws have no religious principles."[52] But alongside the principle of unbending religious integrity lay a conflict over anglicization. *Der yidisher ekspres (The Jewish Express)* described the support gathered around the *Machzike Hadath* as a protest against the treatment of Russian Jews as "ignorant beggars, as barbarians who must be civilised through Sabbath sermons, soup kitchens and such like."[53] Against this, the leaders of the *Machzike Hadath* embraced anglicization. At one early meeting the chairman assured the audience that the defenders of Jewish law also intended to be patriotic citizens. He pointed out that the Jew who keeps the dietary laws, "that very Jew knows the tradition 'thou shalt pray for the welfare of the kingdom'."[54] This opinion was confirmed by the synagogue's religious leader, Rabbi Aba Werner, who also expressed his belief that "there is no reason why secular education should alienate Jews from their own literature."[55]

Opposition of Anglo-Jewish prescription was not atavistic even concerning religious education. A meeting held at the Jewish Working Men's Club in response to the Anglo-Jewish educational conference was described by the *Jewish Chronicle* as very large and aggressive by the standards of the Jewish East End.[56] The speakers denounced the religious education English Jews wished to introduce to the Jewish East End and which was said to leave its pupils ignorant. Reportedly, Yiddish was required in the East End partly because immigrant teachers were most comfortable in that language. But defense of Yiddish was a vivid refusal to accept the condescension of English Jews and an indication of the desire to achieve a different accommodation with English society.[57] The speakers did not reject educational reform, however. Eliezer Laizerovich, a journalist for *Der yidisher ekspres*, called for better accommodation and shorter hours in the *hedarim*; Joseph Cohn-Lask, leader of the Union of *melamdim*, claimed that critics underestimated the degree to which changes had taken place.[58] Thus even the militantly orthodox possessed a willing patriotism and an engagement with new forms of learning.

Both Werner and Laizerovich were political Zionists, and *Der yidisher ekspres* consistently supported Herzl's movement. Through political Zionism a view was clearly articulated of Jewish integration within the political system, different from the one promoted by the leaders of Anglo-Jewry. The movement was anathematized inevitably by the communal leaders. Basically, political Zionism was an embarrassment because it appeared to discard the demands of emancipation by claiming for Jews a political identity alongside one of loyalty to the states in which they were subjects.[59] For Zionists, however, this indicated an understanding of Jewish emancipation that did not require the effacement of Jewish interests. During the Boer War, *Der yidisher ekspres*, a consistently Zionist newspaper, combined its support for the British in the war with a Jewish populist viewpoint. The anti-Jewish attitudes expressed at the time by pro-Boer Liberals and anti-alien Conservatives met with a strong response: "the question is not whether Jews think of England as their home now but how England will later regard its Jews; as its own people or as foreigners."[60] This bold statement rejected those relations of power inherent to the conditional acceptance of Jews within the nation that bore so heavily on English Jews.

5

The forms of anglicization urged upon Jewish immigrants by Anglo-Jewish philanthropists, revolutionaries, the orthodox, and Zionists shared elements of analysis and prescription, each welcoming political emancipation and engaging with new forms of knowledge. Despite this confluence, the meaning of anglicization, the shape of the modern world, and the position of Jews within it were subject to contests between widely different programs.

A contextualized understanding of anglicization must at least account for the range of possible transformations that were imagined to lead to this goal and define it. It is a step with interpretative as well as descriptive consequences. In contrast to the view that immigrant life was motivated by traditional concerns, attention has been drawn to the widespread eruption of modernizing ideologies and practices in the Jewish East End. Here an opposition between immigrant traditionalism and western modernity appears as an abstraction. The immigrant colony was the site of a conflict, not between traditionalism and modernity, East European culture and anglicization, but between conflicting conceptions of westernization and "anglicism." Our understanding of anglicization depends upon our view of these conflicts.

Any plausible explanation must account for the decline of religious practice and belief and the general weakness of socialism and anarchism as well as not preclude an understanding of the persistence of fundamentalist Judaism or revolutionary dissent. Thus it is notable that fundamentalist Judaism was a presence among English and foreign Jews in these years. Although the religious temper of Judaism in late Victorian England was generally similar to that of a lackadaisical Anglicanism, a pious minority sustained an uncompromising faith in traditional Jewish belief.[61] Because fundamentalist beliefs and practices constituted a significant presence within Anglo-Jewry, one doubts whether the westernization of Jewish immigrants also necessarily implied secularization. A sociological account of an orthodox Jewish community in New York City in the mid-1950s has concluded that "the urban setting does not necessarily limit or arrest the *Hasidic* way of life; it may even contribute positively to its growth and development."[62]

Undoubtedly, confrontation with new scientific knowledge, technological innovation, and the dynamics of capitalism have presented traditional Jewish beliefs and practices with new challenges. But in view of the persistence of fundamentalist beliefs among a significant minority, an interpretation of secularization among Jewish immigrants as an inevitable consequence of modernity and migration westwards is unpersuasive.[63] Nevertheless, tenets of Jewish religious practice, such as Sabbath observance, did disappear in London. By the 1920s, the Anglo-Jewish ministers were concerned not by the undecorous and ritualistic character of the immigrants' Judaism but by the need to rescue the English-born generation from indifference.[64]

Decline in religious observance can be explained more readily by the attenuated opportunities after emigration to sustain and reproduce traditional beliefs and practices. During their movement away from Russia and Poland, the institutional foundations of Judaism were removed from a close integration with the sources of political and economic power. They were transplanted to a society in which they were forced to compete for the allegiance of their constituency, not only with the *maskilim* and Jewish revolutionaries, as in eastern Europe, but with the conflicting messages of institutions supported by the state and Anglo-Jewry. Compared to the legal powers and financial resources available to day schools, for example (which aimed to turn pupils into their conception of "good English subjects"), the resources of immigrant synagogues were puny.[65] In the Russian Empire the synagogue had enjoyed a compulsory financial subvention from the Jewish community, something it did not enjoy in London. Furthermore, the role of the rabbinate in managing the legal integration of Jews with the state also disappeared. Despite encroachments made by the centralizing administration in St. Petersburg, Jewish communities in Russia retained some legal autonomy, including a large degree of rabbinical control over marriage and divorce.[66] In Britain, by contrast, one of the principal gains on the way to political and legal equality had been the integration of Jews within the general framework of marriage law—an arrangement mediated by the laity, the JBD, not the rabbinate.[67]

Alongside the disposition of political-legal power, religious orthodoxy in London was hobbled by the economic life of the immigrant quarter. In the East End, pious Jews were neither sufficiently numerous nor wealthy to protect themselves from the rhythms of trades that induced Sabbath desecration. Poll's study of the *hassidim* of New York illustrates the significance of these factors in enabling orthodoxy to insulate itself from the disintegrating currents of city life.[68] In East London, by contrast, Sabbath desecration was widespread. In the tailoring trade, much blame was placed on contractors who required complete work to be returned on Saturdays before noon. But even where Saturday was a rest day, the frenetic pace and long hours characteristic of the workshop trade left many workers wanting only to rest.[69] It would be a mistake, however, to overestimate the extent of secularization. Synagogue attendance was not displaced as the common currency of public Jewish expression. In the East End, on the High Holydays, theaters, schoolhalls and meetingplaces, such as the Great Assembly Rooms, were used to accommodate the additional thousands attending services.[70]

The orthodox also were handicapped by the local economy in other respects. The uncertain, fragmented conditions of small-scale production and exchange, which typified the Jewish East End, generated a milieu that made it impossible for immigrant orthodox, revolutionaries, or Zionists to achieve the stability to build a sustained challenge to communal authority, because the financial resources did not exist. Compared to the situation in some eastern European cities and the United States, the Jewish population was not large enough to overcome the debilitating effects of poverty by weight of numbers.[71] Among the orthodox, the *Machzike Hadath* was compelled to return to the communal fold in 1905 when Lord Rothschild and Lord Swaythling cleared its debts of £5,000. The most radical implications of immigrant orthodoxy had been contained because of financial necessity. This outcome is revealing because among the leaders of the *Machzike Hadath* there were individuals from the wealthiest stratum of the immigrant population—traders and merchants who had risen above the workshop trades.[72] In other respects, too, poverty took its toll upon independent initiatives. The Great Garden Street *Talmud Torah*, for example, helped secure its survival by pledging to conduct lessons in English.[73]

The concept of secularization is too large to convey the complexity of these developments. The term describes a general tendency, but the dynamic leading to the decline of traditional Jewish observance and belief is in the contested and specific relations between religious institutions, society, and the state. Thus the persistence of orthodox religious belief is comprehensible, not as a quick contrary to the tendency of social development, but as a reflection of the capacity of minorities to erect structures of social and cultural independence.

Removed from religious orthodoxy, immigrant institutions were similarly weak. Revolutionary newspapers and clubs, for example, endured a hand-to-mouth existence in most of these years. They attained heights of influence in the Jewish East End in 1889 to 1890 and again between 1911 and 1914. In the first period, however, the defeats of new unionism in the Jewish East End led to a powerful reversal. During the latter time, growth was oriented toward the anarchist movement and was destroyed mainly because of repression and internal division during World War I.

Although the challenges emanating from the East End were necessarily ephemeral, the political and economic resources of the Anglo-Jewish elite provided powerful weapons with which to stifle disruptive influences and foster more desirable ones. Yet to explain this effort as an exercise in bourgeois social control and to account similarly for anglicization will not do, first because it takes too narrow a view of what propelled Anglo-Jewish social policy. In the early sections of this essay it was seen that for English Jews the demands of citizenship and patriotism were continuing sources of ambiguity and, at times, discomfort. Their responses to Jewish immigration demonstrated their perturbation. Like the capital's propertied classes, as Englishmen they were vulnerable and in danger of being challenged. More than one relation of power structured the interaction of Englishmen, Jews, and immigrants.

Responses to immigration from within the communal elite were not uniform. One effect of these divisions was to create opportunities for dissident forms of political, cultural, and religious expression. Thus a further problem with the social control model of anglicization is that it overestimates the coherence of elite interventions within the immigrant colony. Political Zionism, for example, benefited from the support of one member of the cousinhood—Sir Francis Montefiore.[74] But the most significant phenomenon was the patronage received by the Federation of Synagogues from Samuel Montagu. The Federation, established in 1887, consisted of sixteen synagogues in the East End. By 1911 it encompassed fifty-one synagogues and six thousand seatholders and was the largest and longest-lived institution in the Jewish East End. The self-governing synagogues of the Federation appealed to Montagu's liberal politics; their religious principles aligned well with his own; and the organization improved his prestige and power base within Jewry. From 1887 until his death in 1912, he supported the organization with loans and donations and was its dominant figure.[75]

In many cases the synagogue officers were drawn from among the workshop masters of the district, and the Federation allowed them to advance their status.[76] To a degree, the Federation allowed the co-option of a section of East End opinion and its leaders. When the *Machzike Hadath* schism occurred, Montagu prevented the Federation's committee from discussing the issue. Moreover, the Federation was an agent of modernization along particular lines: Yiddish was banned from its councils, and, more constructively, Montagu encouraged and provided loans for the replacement of unsanitary places of worship with purpose-built synagogues.[77] But within the East End there was ample support for precisely this combination of orthodoxy, anglicization, and communal loyalty. Under Montagu's leadership, East End residents could secure their synagogues and find a voice within the communal organization, urging it to become more strict in its observance and more democratic in its government.[78]

Not only through the Federation were concessions gained. The leaders of Anglo-Jewry pursued goals that at times contradicted a policy of vigorous anglicization. One was the need for communal unity: something felt keenly as the campaign for an Aliens Act neared fruition. This was the background to the financial and political concessions that persuaded the *Machzike Hadath* to rejoin the official community.[79] Additional compromises were made because of the desire to combat the influence of Jewish revolutionaries. Religious expressions usually regarded as backward, such as the performances of *magidim* (preachers), were patronized because of a desire to divert Jewish workers from the agitators' influence.[80] External factors, including the state's actions, which could have the greatest impact, could also affect the balance of forces in the contest over anglicization. When the Balfour Declaration of 1917 (the most outstanding example) declared the government's support for a Jewish homeland in Palestine, it appeared to contradict official Anglo-Jewish policy and to adjust the terms of Jewish debate in favor of political Zionism.[81] Approval for Yiddish culture from prestigious sources also produced a confusing message over how best to achieve acceptance within gentile society.[82] The abundant concessions, compromises, and contradictions found within Anglo-Jewish responses to immigration never transformed relations between Anglo-Jewry and the immigrants nor did they render British society and politics any more welcoming of a self-conscious and public Jewish presence. But they did provide resources, create niches, and occasionally supply opportunities for expansion to a plurality of immigrant adjustments to their transformed circumstances.

Finally, we should consider the resistance of East End Jews to cultural forms and messages that were not to their liking. From the English working class, reformers met with a selective response at best.[83] Jewish immigrants were not different from the native population in this regard. Efforts to disperse the ghetto floundered upon the need of Jewish immigrants to live near their workplaces, opportunities in the street labor markets, and the support networks they had established.[84] When the political responses of Jewish immigrants were strongly touched, whether in response to the Kishinev pogrom in 1903 or the tailors' strike in 1906, the calls for Jews not to demonstrate publicly were ignored.[85] During World War I, Lucien Wolf, a leading figure within Anglo-Jewry, conceded wearily that most immigrants remained in sentiment a part of their countries of origin.[86] Even among the "rising generation," whose thorough anglicization was advertised by Anglo-Jewish propagandists, the process was only partial and its results not always those intended. In the interwar period, when this generation became influential in the Jewish East End, the visible, occasionally violent response to the campaign of the British Union of Fascists, in contrast to the policy of quietness advocated by the JBD, illustrates the continuing force of radical forms of Jewish self-expression.[87] The same point is apparent from the course of the Zionist movement in the period. In the mid-1920s, the Federation of Synagogues was captured for political Zionism by a new generation that ejected Samuel Montagu's son as the organization's president. Significantly, a central drama in the revolt was the decision to allow Yiddish to be spoken at the Federation's committee meetings.[88] The increased assertiveness of East End Jews in the interwar period—the claims made for Yiddish, the declaration of independence from West End patrons, and the vigorous response to anti-Jewish political movements— was unparalleled between 1880 and 1914. In addition to tendencies toward anglicization, there were others toward a more forceful assertion of Jewish identity in England.

Neither "westernization" nor "social control" adequately conveys the contested and fractured process of anglicization in the Jewish East End. It was framed by the interaction of political, legal, economic, and ideological forces that determined the opportunities available to immigrants as they adjusted to a new environment. Within these limits cultural and political change was shaped by the participants' own perspectives on becoming English. Their actions developed from choices made as they sought to reconcile necessary change with their formation as East European Jews. The conflicts arising from this concerned the boundaries and content of British as well as Jewish identity. At stake were the terms upon which Jews and immigrants might be contained within the national community, just how inclusive that community was to be. Therefore, if ethnic minorities and their factions in contemporary Britain can learn from the Jewish immigrant past, the lesson may be encapsulated within a maxim from the Jewish scholar Hillel, one which appeared often in the immigrant press: "If I am not for myself, who will be? If not now, when?"

Notes

1. I am grateful to George Behlmer, Jennifer Davis, and Linda Pollock for their comments on earlier versions of this paper. J. A. Garrard, *The English and Immigration: A Comparative Study of the Jewish Influx, 1880–1910* (London: Oxford University Press, 1971), pp. 3–10, and K. Lunn, ed., *Hosts, Immigrants and Minorities: The Historical Responses to Newcomers in British Society, 1870–1914* (Folkestone: St. Martin, 1980), pp. 1–8, are two studies that place historical inquiry within the contemporary context.

2. C. Holmes, *Anti-Semitism in British Society, 1876–1939* (New York: Holmes & Meier, 1979), pp. 108–9, 220–34; H. Pollins, *Economic History of the Jews in England* (London: Associated University Presses, 1982), p. 141. See also the comments of the present chief rabbi on "Problems of the Inner Cities," *Jewish Chronicle*, 24 January 1986, pp. 27–29.

3. L. Gartner, *The Jewish Immigrant in England, 1870–1914*, 2d ed. (Detroit: Wayne State University Press, 1960), pp. 166, 241–42, 268.

4. For a discussion of socialization and social control, see F. M. L. Thompson, "Social Control in Victorian Britain," *Economic History Review*, 2d ser. 34, no. 2: pp. 190–92.

5. Bill Williams, "The Anti-Semitism of Tolerance: Middle Class Manchester and the Jews, 1870–1900," in *City, Class and Culture: Studies in Social Policy and Cultural Production in Victorian Manchester*, ed. Alan J. Kidd and K. W. Roberts (Manchester: Manchester University Press, 1985), p. 92. See also Jerry White, *Rothschild Buildings: Life in an East End Tenement Block, 1887–1920* (London: 1980), 174, 257–58.

6. For a more detailed exposition of the demographic impact of Jewish immigration on the East End, see D. M. Feldman, "Immigrants and Workers, Englishmen and Jews: Jewish Immigrants in the East End of London, 1881–1906" (Ph.D. thesis, Cambridge University, 1986), pp. 23–36.

7. T. Endelman, "Native Jews and Foreign Jews in London, 1870–1914," in *The Legacy of Jewish Migration: 1881 and Its Impact*, ed. D. Berger (New York: Brooklyn College Press, 1981), pp. 109–29. Bill Williams, "The Anti-Semitism of Tolerance," gives a different view of why Anglo-Jewry was concerned about English opinion.

8. M. C. N. Salbstein, *The Emancipation of the Jews in Britain: The Question of the Admission of Jews to Parliament* (Rutherford: Fairleigh Dickinson University Press, 1982), pp. 47, 90.

9. The term is Chaim Bermant's. See Bermant, *The Cousinhood* (New York: Macmillan, 1972).

10. Feldman, "Immigrants and Workers," pp. 127–52.

11. Williams, "Anti-Semitism of Tolerance," pp. 75–76. As Gladstone put it, when speaking in favor of Jewish emancipation for the first time, "they [Jews] had discarded many of their extravagant and antisocial doctrines and had become much more fit to become incorporated within the framework of general society." Great Britain, *Parliamentary Debates*, 3d ser. 95, cols. 1285–86.

12. G. Eliot, *Impressions of Theophrastus Such* (London: 1879), p. 346.

13. D. Cannadine, "The Context, Performance and Meaning of Ritual: The British Monarchy and the Invention of Tradition, c. 1820–1977," in *The Invention*

of Tradition, ed. E. Hobsbawm and T. Ranger (Cambridge: Cambridge University Press, 1983), pp. 120–38, and E. Hobsbawm, "Mass-producing Traditions in Europe, 1870–1914," ibid, pp. 263–307.

14. R. T. Shannon, *Gladstone and the Bulgarian Agitation, 1876* (London: Archon, 1963), p. 199; *Times* (London), 20 December 1879, p. 11; T. P. O'Connor, *Lord Beaconsfield: A Biography* (London: 1879), p. 672. A. Ramm, ed.,*The Political Correspondence of Mr. Gladstone and Lord Grenville, 1876–86* (Oxford: Oxford University Press, 1962), pp. 24, 28.

15. Lucien Wolf portrayed the Jews' enemies as irrational spokesmen of a medieval hatred that would fall before the civilizing movement of "modern liberalism." L. Wolf, "A Jewish View of the Anti-Jewish Agitation," *Nineteenth Century,* February 1881, p. 335.

16. G. Smith, "England's Abandonment of the Protectorate of Turkey," *Contemporary Review,* February 1878, p. 618.

17. G. Smith, "Can Jews Be Patriots?," *Nineteenth Century,* May 1878, p. 879, and "The Jewish Question," *Nineteenth Century,* October 1881, p. 499.

18. H. Adler, "Can Jews Be Patriots," *Nineteenth Century,* April 1878, p. 643.

19. C. Montefiore, "Is Judaism A Tribal Religion?" *Contemporary Review,* September 1882, p. 362.

20. Ibid, pp. 364–70; Adler, "Can Jews Be Patriots," pp. 638–40; H. Adler, "Jews and Judaism: A 'Rejoinder'," *Nineteenth Century,* July 1878, pp. 135–40; L. Wolf, "What is Judaism? A Question of Today," *Fortnightly Review,* August 1884, p. 243.

21. Montefiore, "Tribal Religion," p. 361.

22. B. Cheyette, "The Jewish Stereotype and Anglo-Jewish Fiction" (paper in author's possession, 1985); S. Ashheim, "The East European Jew and German Jewish Identity," *Studies in Contemporary Jewry* 1984, pp. 3–25.

23. London School of Economics and Political Science, Booth collection, B351: 49.

24. L. Soloweitschik, *Un proletariat meconnu* (Brussels: 1898), p. 30.

25. This pessimistic view of the immediate economic effects of immigration is argued in Feldman, "Immigrants and Workers," pp. 75–80, 83–89.

26. *St. James Gazette,* 4 April 1887, p. 4.

27. See, for example, *Parliamentary Debates,* 4th ser. 145, col. 721.

28. *Parliamentary Papers* (henceforth *PP*), vol. 9 (1903), *(Royal Commission on Alien Immigration),* vol. 5, pp. 433–36, 829.

29. *Jewish Chronicle,* 8 August 1902, p. 14.

30. G. R. Searle, *The Quest for National Efficiency: A Study in British Politics and Thought* (Oxford: Oxford University Press, 1981).

31. *Parliamentary Debates,* 4th ser., 145 col. 821.

32. *Parliamentary Debates,* 4th ser., 149 cols. 1, 282–83; *Jewish Chronicle,* 15 November 1901, p. 9; ibid., 28 February 1902, p. 19.

33. B. Gainer, *The Alien Invasion: The Origins of the Aliens Act of 1905* (London: 1972), pp. 170–80.

34. *Jewish Chronicle,* 3 February 1893, p. 16.

35. Jewish Board of Guardians, *Annual Report for 1893,* p. 67.

36. *Jewish Chronicle,* 12 August 1881, p. 9.

37. London School of Economics and Political Science, Booth collection, 197: 45.

38. D. F. Schloss, "The Jew as Workman," *Nineteenth Century,* June 1891, p. 99.

39. *Jewish Chronicle,* 28 April 1902, pp. 20–21.

40. Ibid., 23 August 1901, p. 6.

41. Ibid., 17 September 1989, pp. 5–6.

42. Ibid.

43. On this subject, see W. J. Fishman, *Jewish Radicals, 1875–1914* (New York: Pantheon, 1975); E. Mendelsohn, *Class Struggles in the Pale: The Formative Years of the Jewish Workers Movement in Tsarist Russia* (Cambridge: Cambridge University Press, 1970); E. Tcherikover, *Di geshikhte fun der yidisher arbayter bavegung in di faraynikte shtaten*, 2 vols. (New York: YIVO Institute, 1943–1945).

44. *Di poylishe yidl*, 8 August 1884, p. 9.

45. Tcherikover, *Di geshikhte*, pp. 110–11; Fishman, *Jewish Radicals*, chap. 2; R. Rocker, *In shturm* (London: Frei Arbeter Shtime, 1951), pp. 310–12.

46. *Der veker*, 6 June 1893, p. 1.

47. *Di fraye velt*, July 1892, pp. 71–72, presents the self-image of the enlightened socialist intelligentsia laboring among the ignorant Jewish masses.

48. *Der veker*, 28 December 1892, p. 1.

49. *Der arbayter fraynd*, 22–29 March 1889, p. 2.

50. *Di fraye velt*, July 1892, p. 72.

51. B. Homa, *A Fortress in Anglo-Jewry* (London: 1953), pp. 1–54.

52. *Jewish World*, 18 August 1892, p. 4. For an exploration of the world of Jewish fundamentalism, see J. Jung, *Champions of Orthodoxy* (London: 1974). For a statement of its tenets, see the letter from Rabbi Mayer Lerner to Samuel Montagu in the Federation of Synagogues, minute book, 12 July 1892.

53. *Der yidisher ekspres*, 24 July 1901, p. 4.

54. University College, London, Anglo-Jewish archives, minute book of the *Machzike Hadath*, 7 Adar 5651.

55. *Jewish Chronicle*, 9 February 1911, p. 20.

56. Ibid., 22 July 1898, p. 25.

57. *Der yidisher ekspres*, 22 July 1898, p. 4; on the inadequacies of the religious education provided by Anglo-Jewry, see Federation of Synagogues, minute book, 7 April 1891.

58. *Der yidisher ekspres*, 22 July 1898, p. 4, and 29 July 1898, p. 3.

59. S. Cohen, *English Zionists and British Jews: The Communal Politics of Anglo-Jewry, 1895–1920* (Princeton: Princeton University Press, 1982), 47–49.

60. *Der yidisher ekspres*, 2 February 1900, p. 4.

61. On Montagu's Judaism, see Lily H. Montagu, *Samuel Montague First Baron Swaythling: A Character Sketch* (London: n.d.), 18–31; The *Machzike Hadath* also found allies among the Jews of North London, Homa, *A Fortress in Anglo-Jewry*, p. 7. Moreover, even the majority of the elite observed major Jewish holidays, the Sabbath, and dietary laws. See Endelman, "Communal Solidarity Among the Jewish Elite," p. 498.

62. S. Poll, *The Hasidic Community of Williamsburg: A Study in the Sociology of Religion* (New York: Schocken, 1969), p. 254.

63. For an account of English Christianity that criticizes the theory of secularization, see J. Cox, *The English Churches in a Secular Society: Lambeth, 1870–1930* (Oxford: Oxford University Press, 1982). A different view can be found in A. Gilbert, *The Making of Post-Christian Britain* (London: Longman, 1980).

64. See, for example, J. Hertz, "Jewish Religious Education," *Fourth Annual Conference of the Central Committee on Jewish Education* (London: 1924), p. 9.

65. White, *Rothschild Buildings*, p. 167.

66. On the incomplete erosion of Jewish authority and autonomy within the Russian Empire, see S. Dubnow, *History of the Jews in Russia and Poland from the*

Earliest Times Until the Present Day, vol. 2 (Philadelphia: Jewish Publication Society, 1918), pp. 59–61, 195.

67. Salbstein, *The Emancipation of the Jews in Britain,* p. 47; *PP* vol. 21 (1912/13) (*Royal Commission on Divorce and Matrimonial Causes,* vol. 41), pp. 384, 467, 500, 482. For a view asserting the primacy of "God's Law," see University College, London, Anglo-Jewish archives, Gaster papers, bound vol. 18, M. Gaster to C. H. L. Emmanuel, 17 January 1911.

68. Poll, *Hasidic Community,* p. 254.

69. *PP* vol. 19 (1895) (*Report of the Chief Inspector of Factories and Workshops,* 1894, vol. 48); *PP* vol. 15 (1906) (*Report of the Chief Inspector of Factories and Workshops,* 1905), pp. 50–51.

70. Woburn House, London, minute book of the United Synagogue, 6 November 1894; C. Russell and H. Lewis, *The Jew in London* (London: 1900), p. 123.

71. This may help explain differences between London and other lesser centers of immigrant settlement, such as Manchester and Leeds.

72. Greater London Record Office, records of the Spitalfields Great Synagogue, A/S95 35/36.

73. P. L. S. Quinn, "The Jewish Schooling System of London, 1656–1956" (Ph.D. thesis, University of London, 1958), pp. ii, 611.

74. Cohen, *English Zionists,* p. 49.

75. J. Blank, *The Minutes of the Federation of Synagogues* (London: 1912).

76. *Jewish World,* 1 January 1892, p. 3; *Der yidisher ekspres,* 14 January 1903, p. 4.

77. Federation of Synagogues, minute book, 10 November 1891, 8 December 1891, 19 November 1899.

78. Ibid., 16 January 1888.

79. *Jewish Chronicle,* 17 February 1905, p. 28.

80. *Jewish World,* 18 February 1894, p. 6. See also Jung, *Champions of Orthodoxy,* chap. 2.

81. Cohen, *English Zionists,* pp. 291–97.

82. *Jewish Chronicle,* 29 June 1900, p. 18, and 13 July 1900, p. 7.

83. Thompson, "Social Control," passim.

84. In 1911, 83 percent of Russians and Russian Poles in London remained in the East End; that is, the boroughs of Stepney and Bethnal Green. *PP (Census of 1911),* 9, 19.

85. *Jewish Chronicle,* 29 May 1903, p. 14; 26 June 1903, pp. 10–11; and 27 June 1906, p. 9.

86. Memorandum by Lucien Wolf, 31.1.1917, folder 47, YIVO, New York, David Mowshowitch collection, papers of Lucien Wolf.

87. G. Lebzelter, *Political Anti-Semitism in England, 1918–39* (New York: Holmes & Meier, 1978), chap. 2.

88. Federation of Synagogues, minute book, 3 November and 2 December 1925.

6

Natives and Foreigners: Geographic Origins and Jewish Communal Politics in Interwar Vienna

Harriet Pass Freidenreich

"**E**ast is east and west is west and never the twain shall meet." Does this cliché hold true for modern European Jewry? Certainly the theme of western Jews hostilely confronting immigrants from the east plays a prominent role in the historical development of both large and small Jewish communities in Germany, France, England, and the United States, especially during the mass emigration after 1880.[1] To what extent did eastern Jews, commonly known in German-speaking lands as *Ostjuden*, maintain separate subcommunities after moving westward? How long did it take for their leaders to become accepted as part of the Jewish communal leadership in their new homes? To understand some of the complexities in the interaction between eastern newcomers and westernized "natives" within Jewish communal life, we look at Vienna, a crossroads between east and west.

Most of the Jews living in Vienna in the early twentieth century were not native-born Viennese but had come from other parts of the Habsburg Empire. As Marsha Rozenblit has amply documented, several successive migration waves since the mid-nineteenth century shaped the Viennese Jewish community. First came the Czech Jews, from Bohemia, Moravia, and occasionally Silesia. Then came the Hungarians, mainly from western Hungary, including western Slovakia and the Burgenland. Around the turn of the century, Galicians began arriving in large numbers.[2] During World War I an additional influx of Galician refugees streamed into Vienna.

A pecking order developed based on order of arrival, expressing itself in terms of "west" versus "east"—an east-west axis, however, that did not conform to that of standard maps. Farthest to the west were the Bohemians and then, surprisingly, the Hungarians, with the Moravians located closer to the center, trying to balance the two extremes. To these "westerners" we must add their Viennese-born children, the only real "natives," many of whom still shared the old residency status of their parents. The pejorative term *Ostjuden* applied to Jews born in Galicia or Bukovina and those who came from tsarist Russia or Rumania. By the interwar period members of this group, including their children, were often referred to collectively as "foreigners," although their residency and citizenship status usually did not differ significantly from that of so-called "natives." In Vienna as elsewhere, Galician Jews were near the bottom of the informal European Jewish hierarchy.

Rozenblit, in her study of Viennese Jewry before 1914, argues that two Jewish communities coexisted in Vienna: one composed of native-born, Bohemians, Moravians, and Hungarians; the other, a distinct Galician community. She demonstrates that the Galician Jews were more endogamous and residentially concentrated than the other groups. Their special characteristics can be attributed to their more recent arrival, their lower socioeconomic status, and the different cultural baggage they carried. The Poles who had moved to the capital before the late nineteenth century tended to have been more prosperous and urbanized; therefore, they were accepted more rapidly than those arriving in the twentieth century, especially the destitute refugees who flooded the city during the war, many of whom subsequently returned to Poland either voluntarily or involuntarily.[3]

During the interwar period, however, this segregation of Galicians, although still evident, was beginning to break down. Indicative of this trend, at least among the elite, was the increased involvement of Galician leaders in organized mainstream Jewish life in Vienna, as exemplified by the *Kultusgemeinde*. Ascent into leadership was less difficult for those who had come before 1890 or even 1910 than for compatriots who arrived later. Nevertheless, length of time in Vienna was probably less of a factor in their gaining acceptance than a movement within the leadership of Viennese Jewry away from Liberal control toward the Zionists or Jewish Nationalists.

Before World War I, leadership of the *Israelitische Kultusgemeinde Wien* was almost exclusively in the hands of the Liberals, a group overwhelmingly comprised of westerners. Alfred Stern, born in

Vienna, served as communal president from 1904 until his forced retirement in November 1918 at the age of 86.[4] Gustav Kohn, originally from Prague, held the office of first vice-president until his death in 1915,[5] and Stern's second vice-president and temporary successor as president was Benjamin Rappaport, who was born in Galicia in 1844 but arrived in Vienna early enough to be accepted among the ranks of the Liberals. With some exceptions, top Jewish communal leaders tended to have migrated from either Czech or Hungarian lands.

After the war, Liberal leaders continued to be predominantly western, but not necessarily Viennese, in origin. Alois Pick, elected to head the *Kultusgemeinde* for three successive terms from 1920 to 1932, came from Karolinenthal in Bohemia.[6] The three Liberals who served briefly as vice-presidents during Pick's first term were Hungarian Jews by birth. Jakob Ornstein, communal vice-president from 1924 to 1934, hailed from Moravia, as did his successor, Josef Ticho. Of the thirty-nine Liberal candidates in the 1928 *Kultusgemeinde* elections, eleven were Viennese by birth, ten were born in Hungary (including Slovakia and Burgenland), fourteen came from Czech lands (four from Bohemia and ten from Moravia), and four hailed from Galicia[7] (see Table 1).

The Union of Austrian Jews, the Austrian counterpart of the German *Centralverein* which represented the Liberal viewpoint, made Austrian citizenship a prerequisite for membership and described its supporters as "natives" and patriotic Austrians.[8] During most of the interwar period, Jakob Ornstein served as president and Josef Ticho as vice-president of this organization, and eleven of the 1928 Liberal candidates mentioned above served simultaneously on its board of directors.[9] When comparing the data in Table 1 with Rozenblit's, we find that Liberal leaders, and probably members of the Union of Austrian Jews as well, were more likely than the average Viennese Jew to have been born in Vienna (28 percent versus 20 percent), or Hungary (26 percent versus 23 percent), and especially in the Czech lands (36 percent versus 27 percent), but less likely in Galicia or Bukovina (10 percent versus 21 percent) or other locales outside the former Monarchy.[10] The Union leadership, although westerners by origin, had little justification for stigmatizing Galicians as foreigners, because in many cases the ink on their own naturalization papers had just dried. Like most other Viennese Jews, most Liberals were Viennese by adoption, not by accident of birth.

The Galicians did not seriously attempt to integrate themselves into the *Kultusgemeinde* through the Liberal establishment, but instead chose the opposition's route—as supporters of Orthodox parties, Jewish Nationalists, or members of Socialist groups. In the 1928 elections, the only year for which there is complete information concerning birthplace for all candidates, *Ostjuden* made up 70 percent of the Orthodox candidates, 58 percent of the Jewish Nationalists, and 38 percent of the Socialists, as compared with 10 percent of the Liberals[11] (see Table 1 for additional breakdowns). Only within the Orthodox framework, however, does one regularly discover electoral factions composed exclusively of either easterners or westerners, indicating separate religious communities organized on the basis of geographic origins.

By the 1930s Vienna had 104 Jewish houses of worship recognized officially by the *Kultusgemeinde*. Of these, seven were com-

Table 1
Candidates for Communal Office by Place of Birth*

	Liberal		Zionist		Socialist		Orthodox		All
WESTERN JEWS									
Austria									
Vienna	11		4		10		1		26
Provinces	0		1		0		0		1
Subtotal	11	28.2%	5	(13.9%)	10	(31.2%)	1	(3.7%)	27
Hungarian Lands									
Hungary	4		0		2		3		9
Burgenland	3		1		0		1		5
Slovakia	3		1		1		3		8
Subtotal	10	(25.6%)	2	(5.6%)	3	(9.4%)	7	(25.9%)	22
Czech Lands									
Bohemia	4		1		2		0		7
Moravia	10		6		5		0		21
Silesia	0		1		0		0		1
Subtotal	14	(35.9%)	8	(22.2%)	7	(21.9%)	0		29
Total	35	(89.7%)	15	(41.7%)	20	(62.5%)	8	(29.6%)	78
EASTERN JEWS									
Habsburg Empire									
Galicia	4		16		10		11		41
Bukovina	0		1		0		1		2
Subtotal	4	(10.3%)	17	(47.2%)	10	(31.2%)	12	(44.5%)	43
Elsewhere									
Russian Empire	0		2		1		5		8
Rumania	0		2		1		2		5
Subtotal	0		4	(11.1%)	2	(6.3%)	7	(25.9%)	13
Total	4	(10.3%)	21	(58.3%)	12	(37.5%)	19	(70.4%)	56
GRAND TOTAL	39	(100%)	36	(100%)	32	(100%)	27	(100%)	134

*Source: CAHJP, AW, 60/3, Wahlen 1928, lists of candidates for all parties, including place and date of birth.

munal synagogues, sixteen were associational synagogues, 77 were associational prayerhouses, and four were considered private chapels. Six of the seven communal synagogues and thirteen of the associational prayerhouses were Liberal temples, and the remaining 85 houses of worship were all Orthodox "shuls" or "shtiebels."[12] At least fourteen of these, including all the private chapels, can be identified further as Hasidic (all related to Galician dynasties), nine as Zionist, six as Hungarian, five as Polish, and one as Sephardic, and many others were undoubtedly Galician *landsmanshaftn* whose names and self-descriptions did not betray either place of origin or specific orientation. Perhaps 20 percent of Viennese Jewry belonged to the various Orthodox congregations. The two largest Orthodox congregations were Adas Jisroel, known as the Schiffschul, and Beth Israel, or the Polnische schul, which served as the flagship synagogues for the two major Orthodox communities, the Hungarians and Poles, respectively.[13]

Most of the Hasidic rebbes and their followers were recent arrivals and generally remained outside *Kultusgemeinde* politics, but the Hungarians, Poles, and Religious Zionists entered the communal fray, vying to represent Orthodox interests. A separate western Orthodox community, centered on Adas Jisroel, had existed since the mid-nineteenth century. This group, which became identified closely with the Viennese branch of Agudas Yisroel, competed in *Kultusgemeinde* elections for the first time in 1920 and subsequently formed a coalition with their fellow westerners, the Liberals. As far as can be ascertained, most individuals associated with Adas Jisroel leadership circles, including the seven who ran in the 1928 elections, originated from former Hungarian territories. In 1934, after their Liberal allies had lost control over the *Kultusgemeinde*, the Schiffschul community attempted unsuccessfully to secede formally from the larger community.

The Galician Orthodox, however, whether Hasidim, Poles, or Zionists, strongly supported communal unity, at least in principle. Nevertheless, the easterners generally fielded two religious lists in communal elections during the interwar years, one from Mizrachi and the other, calling itself "Apolitical," associated with the modern Orthodox Polnische schul. Leo Landau, president of Beth Israel and its representative on the communal board from 1928 to 1938, tried to bridge the gap between Liberal and Orthodox groups by heading the Federation of Viennese Temple Associations and organizing the Association of Conservative Prayerhouses.[14] Viktor Bauminger, the Mizrachi spokeman on the board from 1924 to 1932, spoke repeatedly on behalf of equality for *Ostjuden* within a united community. "Our Torah," he declared, "recognizes no maps" or geographical boundaries. "There are neither Polish nor Hungarian Jews; there are only Jews, and all Jews, even Viennese Jews, must identify completely with our unified religious community." The Mizrachi credo, he went on to say, was "One God, one People, one Land, one language and one *Kultusgemeinde!*"[15]

Landau and all but one of his seven fellow Apolitical candidates in 1928 had been born in Galicia; the sole exception was from Rumania. About half of the twelve individuals running on the Religious List Mizrachi in 1928 also hailed from Galicia, one person was a native Viennese, and the rest, including Bauminger, came from either tsarist Russia or Rumania.[16] (As evident in Table 1, the Orthodox leaders, and presumably their followers as well, were less likely than the Socialists, Liberals, or Jewish Nationalists to have been born in Vienna.)[17] The *Ostjuden* elected on Orthodox tickets, whether as Religious Zionists or Apoliticals, usually sided with the Jewish Nationalists rather than the Liberals or their Hungarian Orthodox partners, except on specific religious issues. *Landsmen* stick together.

By contrast, Moravians by birth never appeared on religious slates, although such individuals as Josef Ticho and Ernst Feldsberg (both Liberals), Josef Löwy (a Social Democrat), and Desider Friedmann (a Jewish Nationalist) were among the more traditional *Kultusgemeinde* board members in background and orientation. Feldsberg served as trustee of Beth Hamidrash Ohel Abraham, an Orthodox prayerhouse in Alsergrund; Löwy was vice-president of the Orthodox Schönlaterne shul in the Inner City. Such Moravians might speak out on behalf of conservative religious interests but did not officially represent the Orthodox community. The Hungarians and Poles therefore monopolized Orthodox lay leadership within the *Kultusgemeinde*.

Easterners played a somewhat different role among the Socialists active within the Viennese Jewish community than within the three other political camps. In the 1928 elections, thirty-two Socialists ran as the "Electoral Alliance of Jewish Workers," including both Labor Zionists and non-Zionists. The individuals on this slate divided into three roughly equal groups: those born in Vienna (31 percent), Galicia (31 percent), and elsewhere (38 percent), of whom 22% hailed from Moravia, 9% from Hungary and the remaining from Rumania or Russian Poland. It is striking that Socialist candidates were about eight times as likely as Orthodox, more than twice as likely as Zionists, and slightly more likely than Liberals to have been born in Vienna. Although they were significantly less likely than the Zionists or the Orthodox to have come from Galicia, three times as many Socialist candidates as Liberals did so. Socialists were as likely as Zionists to have been born in Czech lands, but less likely than Liberals. Hungarian Jews were definitely underrepresented.[18]

Although it is tempting to speculate that most of the Socialists born in Galicia were Labor Zionists, and the native-born Viennese were more likely to be found among the non-Zionists, the sketchy evidence available does not fully support this interpretation. Of the eleven candidates on the list definitely identified as either Poale Zionists or non-Zionists, three of five Labor Zionists were born in Vienna and the other two came from Galicia and Rumania; three of the six non-Zionists were born in Vienna, two in Galicia, and one in Moravia. Few Jewish Social Democrats became actively involved in the *Kultusgemeinde*, but those who did, especially the Labor Zionists, were younger than their Orthodox or Liberal counterparts or the General Zionists running on the Jewish Nationalist tickets. Many of those born in Vienna undoubtedly had Galician-born parents. Unlike those of Hungarian origin, a disproportionate number of *Ostjuden* and their children supported the Austrian Social Democratic Party, on the one hand, and Labor Zionism, on the other.

The Labor Zionists, Poale Zion, and Hitachdut combined and ran their own list in both the 1932 and 1936 communal elections. An overwhelming majority of their leaders and supporters were of Galician origin. Galician Jews had predominated among the founders of Viennese Poale Zion before the war and also formed the nucleus of Hitachdut after the war. All indications point to a continuation of this trend. Galician Jews also supported the moderately leftist Adolf Stand Club, which was named after a prominent prewar Galician Zionist leader and also competed separately in the 1936 electoral campaign. At the other end of the Zionist spectrum, Galicians largely controlled the Austrian Mizrachi organization.[19] Generally Galician Jews, along with Jews of Moravian origin, inclined more to Zionism than Jews of Hungarian or Bohemian extraction or native-born Viennese. Although there were many of them among the rank and file of the General Zionist, Radical, and Revisionist factions (and less among their leadership), one can assume that *Ostjuden* played a more salient role on the Zionist left and among Religious Zionists in Vienna than in the center or on the right. Because of this eastern dominance, both Labor Zionism and Mizrachi remained relatively weak political forces in the Austrian capital, as well as on the *Kultusgemeinde* board.

The major conflict within the *Israelitische Kultusgemeinde Wien* during the interwar years was not a religious struggle between the Orthodox and the Liberals or a class struggle between the Socialists and the Liberals but the battle between the supporters of Jewish nationalism and their opponents over the nature of the Jewish community and who should control it. At least two separate Orthodox communities coexisted in Vienna: the Hungarian Schiffschul group associated with the anti-Zionist Agudas Yisroel and the western Liberals and the various Galician groups, including the Mizrachi, which supported the Jewish Nationalists. The Socialists also divided into Zionist and non-Zionist factions, generally along east-west lines, although not to the extent of the Orthodox. The primary battleground, however, was between the two middle-class non-Orthodox parties—the Jewish Nationalists and the Liberals. Aside from the ideological debate of whether Jews constituted a separate nationality or merely a religious group, a controversy which does not concern us here, this conflict involved a clash between an older and a younger generation of Jewish leadership, as well as between westerners and easterners.

Among the 134 candidates competing in the 1928 communal elections, 10.4 percent were younger than 40, 33.6 percent were in their 40s, 27.6 percent were in their 50s, 20.9 percent were in their 60s, and 7.5 percent were older than 70 (see Table 2). Among the Liberal candidates, only 20.5 percent were younger than 50, and 15.4 percent were in their 70s. By contrast, 58.3 percent of the Jewish Nationalists were younger than 50 and 5.6 percent were older than 70. Generally, the Socialists were younger than the Jewish Nationalists; the Orthodox were older than the Jewish Nationalists but younger than the Liberals. Among both Socialist and Orthodox candidates, the Zionists on the average were younger than their non-Zionist counterparts. When place of origin is considered, one discovers that those born in the Hungarian or Czech lands, most of whom were Liberals, tended to be older than the *Ostjuden* or the native-born Viennese. Only 35 percent of the Hungarian or Czech leaders were younger than 50; 49 percent of the Galicians, 54 percent of the Russians or Rumanians, and 52 percent of the Viennese were in this lower age category. (The oldest candidate was Wolf Pappenheim, spokesman for the Hungarian Orthodox Schiffschul community, born in Slovakia and older than 80.)[20]

Even more striking than relative ages of candidates for the

Table 2
Candidates by Party, Age, and Region of Birth*

	30s		40s		50s		60s		70s		All
Liberals											
Austrians			3		6		2				11
Hungarians			3		3		1		3		10
Czechs	1				5		5		3		14
Galicians			1		3						4
Subtotal	1	(3%)	7	(18%)	17	(44%)	8	(20%)	6	(15%)	39
Zionists											
Austrians	2		3								5
Hungarians			2								2
Czechs	1		4		3						8
Galicians			8		1		7		1		17
Other			1		1		1		1		4
Subtotal	3	(8%)	18	(50%)	5	(14%)	8	(22%)	2	(6%)	36
Socialists											
Austrians	3		3		3		1				10
Hungarians			1		1				1		3
Czechs			3		2		2				7
Galicians	4		6								10
Other	1		1								2
Subtotal	8	(25%)	14	(44%)	6	(19%)	3	(9%)	1	(3%)	32
Orthodox											
Austrians					1						1
Hungarians	1		1		2		2		1		7
Galicians	1		1		4		6				12
Other			4		2		1				7
Subtotal	2	(8%)	6	(22%)	9	(33%)	9	(33%)	1	(4%)	27
Total	14	(10%)	45	(34%)	37	(28%)	28	(21%)	10	(7%)	134

*Source: CAHJP, AW, 60/3, Wahlen 1928, lists of candidates for all parties, including place and date of birth.

communal board was the age difference among the various parties within the top elected leadership of the *Kultusgemeinde*. Liberals chose their older members as president, vice-president, or executive committee members; Jewish Nationalists, Socialists, and Galician Orthodox chose younger spokesmen for their higher positions (see Table 3A). Liberal Alois Pick was sixty-one years old in 1920 when he assumed the communal presidency, an office he held for 12 years; Jakob Ornstein was 66 when he became vice-president in 1924 and 76 when he resigned. By contrast, Jewish Nationalist Desider Friedmann was only 41 when he was elected vice-president in 1921 and 52 when he assumed the presidency, and Josef Löwenherz was 40 when he became communal vice-president.

   Although the Jewish Nationalists chose younger individuals as
their leading representatives within the *Kultusgemeinde,* they usually did not select *Ostjuden* as their top delegates on the communal
board. Although 42 percent of General Zionists elected to the
Kultusgemeinde during the interwar period for whom place of
origin is known came from Galicia, only one of the four Jewish
Nationalists who served as either president or vice-president originated in Polish territory; the rest came from Moravia. Of the nine
General Zionists on the executive committee for whom birthplace
data are available, one was Galician, five Moravian, and three
Austrian (see Table 3B). Desider Friedman, Robert Stricker, and
Jakob Ehrlich—all born in Moravia—as well as Leopold Plas-
chkes—born in St. Pölten, Austria, of Moravian parentage—became the most prominent leaders in communal, as well as

Table 3
Kultusgemeinde Top Leadership, 1920–38
A) By Age*

	30s	40s	50s	60s	70s	Unknown	All
Praesidium†							
Liberals		2	3	1			6
Zionists	2	2					4
Total	2	4	3	1			10
Executive Committee†							
Liberals		3	2	1	2	5	13
Zionists	1	4	3	1		3	12
Socialists	1	3				2	6
Orthodox	1	1			1		3
Total	3	11	5	2	3	10	34

B) By Place of Birth

	Austria	Bohemia/ Moravia	Hungary	Galicia	Unknown	All
Praesidium†						
Liberals		3	3			6
Zionists		3		1		4
Total		6	3	1		10
Executive Committee†						
Liberals	1	2	4	1	5	13
Zionists	3	5		1	3	12
Socialists	1	1		2	2	6
Orthodox			1	2		3
Total	5	8	5	6	10	34

*Age is calculated upon assumption of office.
†Seven individuals served on both the Praesidium and the Executive Committee
during this period.

internal, Zionist affairs. Whereas men like Isidor Schalit (born in the Ukraine), Leo Goldhammer (born in Rumania) and Oskar Grünbaum (from Galicia), all of whom served as president of the Austrian Zionist Federation during the interwar years, sat on the communal board for brief terms, they never became actively involved. It is difficult to imagine that this policy was not deliberate, although the Jewish Nationalists never would have admitted it publicly.

The major exception to this general unwritten rule was Josef Löwenherz, born in Pivovsznyza, Galicia, who arrived in Vienna in 1919. After becoming a naturalized citizen, Löwenherz was elected to the *Kultusgemeinde* in 1924 and served as the Jewish Nationalist vice-president for three successive terms. When the Jewish Nationalists won the 1932 elections and succeeded in "conquering the community" with the help of the Labor Zionists and Mizrachi, Löwenherz retained his vice-presidency, and Friedmann became communal president. The Union of Austrian Jews insisted that Löwenherz had been passed over for the top job because he was an easterner. In 1935 the Jewish Nationalists appointed Löwenherz to the position of executive director, the *Kultusgemeinde*'s top administrative office. This infuriated the Liberals, who attempted to block the appointment by resigning from the board and appealing to municipal authorities. According to the complaint submitted by the Union of Austrian Jews, someone who had been an Austrian citizen for only fifteen years was not an appropriate choice as the official representative of the Jewish community, whether in an elected or an appointed capacity. The Liberals failed to prevent Löwenherz from assuming his new job, but this dispute provoked internal disgruntlement among the Jewish communal leadership.[21]

As westerners, the Liberal establishment felt threatened by the idea that easterners might take over their community. They had tried to do everything to maintain the prewar status quo. Although the Jewish Nationalists argued in favor of universal suffrage in communal elections, the Liberals consistently attempted to restrict the voting rights of *Ostjuden*. Immediately after World War I, the Liberals pushed through a temporary electoral reform disallowing most noncitizens from voting. At least one Liberal admitted in debate that he and his party opposed admission into the electorate of the recently arrived *Ostjuden* for fear of strengthening the Jewish Nationalists. In the 1920 elections, noncitizens who had been eligible to vote in the last elections in 1912 could continue to be registered voters, but all others who had not yet been naturalized could not vote.[22] This decision resulted in a clear Liberal victory that year, but the restriction was subsequently lifted. After 1924 only the minimal communal tax requirement prevented Jews from voting in elections if they so desired; non-citizens, however, still could not run for communal office.

The Union of Austrian Jews blamed foreigners, i.e., the *Ost-juden*, for causing the shift in power within the *Kultusgemeinde* away from the Liberals and toward the Jewish Nationalists. After the citizenship requirement had been rescinded, in 1928 the Liberals and their Hungarian Orthodox partners retained only half of the seats on the communal board, and after 1932, the Liberals suffered outright defeats.[23] In 1936 the Union list received only 36.5 percent of the overall vote. The Liberals won a majority in only one voting district, the suburb of Floridsdorf, which had few Jews. In their former stronghold, the wealthy Inner City, they attracted 48 percent of the votes. Because they lost the election badly not only in Leopoldstadt and Brigittenau, which were settled heavily by Galician-born Jews, but also in Döbling and Währing and the other suburbs inhabited largely by western or native Jews, it belied the Liberals' assertion that Jewish Nationalist victories were due primarily to the vote of foreigners or even *Ostjuden*.[24] The Zionists went to the trouble of verifying with the police the citizenship of all those who had voted in 1936, discovering that 83 percent (26,430) were Austrians and that of the 17 percent (5,330) who were foreigners, only 7 percent (2,343) were Polish citizens. Less than 45 percent of Austrian citizens' votes went to the Union list.[25] This election proved several points. First, by the mid-1930s, most of the Jews living in Vienna, including those from Galicia, had already become Austrian citizens. Second, although most easterners supported the Jewish Nationalists, many westerners did as well.

The Jewish Nationalist victory in the Austrian capital in the 1930s did not signify a victory of easterners over westerners or foreigners over natives. Instead, it indicated a change of leadership from an older generation representing the status quo to a younger generation promising change. At the helm of the community still sat a Jew of Czech origin, Desider Friedmann from Moravia this time, rather than Alois Pick from Bohemia. Both the Jewish Nationalist vice-president, Robert Stricker, and his Liberal counterpart, Josef Ticho, came from Moravia; Friedmann and Ticho even came from the same hometown, Boskowitz. But all of these individuals were in their fifties, not their seventies. Therefore this shift within the *Kultusgemeinde* leadership was one of age and ideological orientation more than geographic origins.

Galician voters had helped bring the Jewish Nationalists into office and provided much of their secondary leadership. Thus the relative newcomers from Galicia were becoming better integrated into the communal leadership. The *Ostjuden* had better representation in the communal boardroom in the 1930s, not only among the Jewish Nationalists but also among the Socialists and the Orthodox, than they had had twenty years earlier when the Liberals had exercised complete control. But they did not dominate the *Kultusgemeinde*. Only after the *Anschluss* did Josef Löwenherz, already executive director, become appointed president of the Jewish community. The Nazis chose an easterner to head a community that prided itself on its western leadership.

Decreasing segregation of Galician Jewry in Vienna did not necessarily mean that one's birthplace was inconsequential, however; geographical origin continued to influence political behavior within the Jewish community. Based on trends among the leaders, it would appear that one's origins limited where one could comfortably find a political or even a religious home within the *Kultusgemeinde* structure. Hungarian-born Jews gravitated toward the Liberals or, in a minority of cases, toward the Orthodox Schiffschul community, rarely becoming either Jewish Nationalists or Socialists. Jews of Bohemian birth also tended toward the Liberals or the Socialists; they were attracted infrequently to Jewish Nationalist groups or the Orthodox. In contrast with these western Jews, Galician Jews leaned strongly toward the Jewish Nationalists, with the Socialists and their own Orthodox factions as alternatives. Some religious Galicians remained more isolated from the mainstream than the rest. For most *Ostjuden* the Liberals were not an option. Moravians, however, proved the exception. Although westerners, they managed to fit into nearly every camp. Moravians provided much of the leadership for both the Liberals and the Jewish Nationalists and also were well represented among the Socialists. Sometimes they belonged to Orthodox congregations but usually did not lead them. Moravians provided the top spokemen for most major factions and served as the mediators between westerners and easterners. The Viennese-born, depending on parentage, also identified themselves with the different groups, with the exception of the Orthodox. In Vienna, east generally remained east for one generation or more, and although west might not have been west initially, the twain at least began to meet.

During the interwar period, Viennese-born Jews did not provide the leadership for the *Israelitische Kultusgemeinde Wien*. A majority can be considered westerners, with about one-fourth of the individuals elected to the communal board coming from Czech lands, one-fifth from Hungarian lands, and one-quarter being Viennese natives. About 30 percent of the board was comprised of *Ostjuden*, most of whom came from Galicia. All of these men held Austrian citizenship; few could have considered themselves true Viennese, even if they had been born in the Austrian capital. In another generation perhaps both *Ostjuden* and *Westjuden* could have become fully integrated as Jews in Viennese society, but by the time of the *Anschluss*, although they were no longer foreigners, the Jewish communal leadership could not be called natives.

Notes

1. This essay is taken from a larger work in progress on Jewish politics in interwar Vienna. The author gratefully acknowledges support for this project from the American Council of Learned Societies, the Memorial Foundation for Jewish Culture, and Temple University. Studies dealing with this issue include Salomon Adler-Rudel, *Ostjuden in Deutschland 1880–1940* (Tubingen: Mohr, 1959); Steven E. Aschheim, *Brothers and Strangers* (Madison: University of Wisconsin, 1982); Jack Wertheimer, *Unwelcome Strangers* (New York: Oxford University Press, 1987); Paula Hyman, *From Dreyfus to Vichy* (New York: Columbia University Press, 1979); Lloyd P. Gartner, *The Jewish Immigrant in England, 1870–1914* (Detroit: Wayne State University Press, 1960), and Irving Howe, *World of Our Fathers* (New York: Harcourt, Brace, Jovanovich, 1976).

2. Marsha L. Rozenblit, *The Jews of Vienna 1867–1914* (Albany: State University of New York Press, 1983), pp. 13–45.

3. Ibid., pp. 40–45.

4. Central Archives for the History of the Jewish People, Jerusalem (hereafter CAHJP), AW, 744/9, Dr. Alfred Stern, Gedenkrede von Vizepräsident Dr. Ornstein, 29 August 1931.

5. Max Schwager, ed., *Zum Gedächtnis . . . Dr. Gustav Kohn* (Vienna: 1916), pp. 4–5; CAHJP, AW, 734/2, Alfred Stern, eulogy for Gustav Kohn (1915).

6. "Professor Pick 70 Jahre alt," *Die Stimme* (hereafter *DS*) 2, no. 96 (17 October 1929): 3.

7. CAHJP, AW, 60/3, Wahlen 1928, Wahlvorschlag der Wählergruppe "Jüdische Union."

8. Allgemeines Verwaltungsarchiv, Vienna (AVA), BKA-I, 15/4, 310.081–31, Statuten der "Union deutsch-österreichischer Juden" (1920) and Statuten der "Union österreichischer Juden" (1937).

9. "Dr. Jakob Ornstein," *Die Wahrheit* (hereafter *DW*), 50, no. 19 (27 April 1934): 1; Ernst Feldsberg, "Dr. Josef Ticho," *DW* 50, no. 19 (5 May 1934): 5; "Vom Zentralvorstand der 'Union'," *DW* 45, no. 24 (14 June 1929): 12.

10. CAHJP, AW, 60/3, Wahlen 1928, Wahlvorschlag der Wählergruppe "Jüdische Union"; Rozenblit, *Jews of Vienna*, table 2:4, p. 21.

11. CAHJP, AW, 60/3, Wahlen 1928.

12. The seventh communal synagogue belonged to the Association of Turkish Israelites, the Viennese Sephardic Community. Although affiliated with the *Kultusgemeinde* and the recipient of communal subventions, it operated as a

completely separate entity. For information on the Sephardim in Vienna, see N. M. Gelber, "The Sephardic Community in Vienna," *Jewish Social Studies*, 10, no. 4 (1948), and Rudolf Till, "Geschichte der Spaniolischen Juden in Wien," *Jahrbuch des Vereins für Geschichte der Stadt Wien* 5–6 (1946/47): 108–23.

13. This analysis is based on a compilation of information on Viennese synagogues and prayerhouses taken from the following Israelitische Kultusgemeinde Vien Reports: *Bericht der IKGW über die Tätigkeit in der Periode 1912–24* (Vienna, 1924), pp. 16–19; *Bericht der IKGW, 1925–28* (Vienna, 1928), pp. 18–22; *Bericht der IKGW, 1929–32* (Vienna, 1932), pp. 20–25; IKGW, *Bericht des Präsidiums, 1933–36* (Vienna, 1936), pp. 32–35; *Jüdisches Jahrbuch für Österreich, 1932/33 (5693),* 23–41; CAHJP, AW, 289, Verzeichnis der jüdischen Vereine, A) Tempel und Bethausvereine (1938); Hugo Gold, *Die Geschichte der Juden in Wien: Ein Gedenkbuch* (Tel Aviv: Olamenu, 1966), pp. 117–28.

14. Yad Vashem, Jerusalem, 01/244, Leo Landau, Im Wien von 1909 bis 1939 (unpublished memoirs).

15. CAHJP, AW, 71/18, Protokoll der Plenarsitzung vom 29 Dezember 1924; Viktor Bauminger, "Gemeinde und Mizrachi," *DS* 5, no. 250 (20 October 1932): 5.

16. CAHJP, AW, 60/3, Wahlen 1928, Wahlvorschlag der Wählergruppe "Unpolitische Wahlvereinigung" and Wahlvorschlag der Wählergruppe Religiöse Liste "Misrachi."

17. CAHJP, AW, 60/3, Wahlen 1928.

18. CAHJP, AW, 60/3, Wahlen 1928, Wahlvorschlag der Wählergruppe "Wahlvereinigung werktätigen Juden."

19. Meir Henisch, "Galician Jews in Vienna" in *The Jews of Austria*, 2nd ed., ed. Josef Fraenkel (London: Valentine-Mitchell, 1970), pp. 368–73; Rozenblit, *Jews of Vienna*, pp. 96–97.

20. CAHJP, AW, 60/3, Wahlen 1928.

21. "Austritt der 'Union' aus dem Kultusvorstand," *DW* 52, no. 6 (7 February 1936): 1–4; AVA, BKA-I, 15/4, 210.081–31, petition from the Union österreichischer Juden to Magistrat der Stadt Wien, 5 February 1936.

22. CAHJP, AW, 74/6, Protokolle der Plenarsitzung vom 13 März 1919 und 16 März 1919; 26/9, memo from IKG to Magistrat der Stadt Wien, 6 June 1919; *Bericht der IKGW, 1912–24,* 5–6.

23. AVA, BKA-I, 15/4, 310.081–31, petition, 5 February 1936.

24. "Der grosse zionistische Wahlsieg in Zahlen," *Neue Welt* 10, no. 607 (10 November 1936): 1; "Wahlspazierung durch die Bezirke," *DS* 9, no. 596 (13 November 1936): 2; "Wahlresultate in den Gemeindebezirken," *DS* 9, no. 597 (17 November 1936): 4; "Konfessionsgliederung der Bevölkerung Österreichs," *Die Ergebnisse der österreichischen Volkszählung, 2* (1934).

25. "Eine gösartige Legende, *Neue Welt* 12, no. 725 (8 February 1938): 1.

7

Models of Urban Ecology and Their Application to Jewish Settlement in Western Cities

Vivian Z. Klaff

S tudies of immigrant distributions in Western cities have revealed that these minority groups tend to congregate in spatially discrete areas. Considerable importance has been attached to the intensity and spatial pattern of immigrant settlement, particularly in relation to a city's ecology and to social interaction between the immigrant and host populations.

The history of American immigration reflects the Americanization of ethnics but not the abandonment of ethnic identities. The study of space and implications derived from analyzing spatial arrangements contribute to our understanding of social relations in our society. Robert Park felt that the study of spatial form was critical because "most if not all cultural changes in society will be correlated with changes in territorial organization, and every change in territorial distribution . . . affects changes in the existing culture."[1]

Analysis of the spatial patterning of Jewish populations contributes to our understanding of Jewish community development. However, Jewish communities are diverse in religious and institutional affiliation and in ideological perspective as to the degree of integration to be maintained within the wider society. For example, a study by Robert Rockaway pointed to the conflict between German and Russian Jewish immigrants in early twentieth-century Detroit based on religious affiliation associated with socioeconomic level.[2] Although most Western urban Jewish populations have become assimilated structurally into the economic framework of their respective societies, there is ongoing debate on cultural assimilation's impact on the future of Jewish communities. The social analyst, therefore, needs to distinguish among various integration models before the objective analysis of data can be translated into social policy.

The classical ecological approach to the social integration of ethnic immigrant groups is reflected in the "assimilationist" model. In U.S. history, this manifested itself in "Anglo-Saxon conformity" and in social policy emphasis on social proximity and dispersal within the formal institutional spheres as conditions for successful integration.[3] The majority of writings about the impact of residential distribution of racial, ethnic, or minority groups on social integration use the assimilationist model of social integration, an approach traced back to the work of the Chicago school of human ecologists.[4] This perspective is well expressed in Hawley's discussion of spatial patterns' impact on race relations. Hawley maintains that "redistribution of a minority group in the same territorial pattern as that of the majority group results in a dissipation of subordinate status and an assimilation of the subjugated group into the social structure."[5] In his study of ethnic patterns in American cities, Lieberson states "[we] should not call an ethnic group assimilated if they are highly segregated residentially from the remainder of the total population of a given city."[6] K. E. and A. F. Taeuber suggest that a sociological approach to the subject of integration "must view assimilation as a process of dispersion of members of the group throughout the social structure."[7]

This essay reviews the spatial distribution of Jewish populations within urban ecological models, presents what we know about Jewish settlement, and outlines directions for future research. Its basic assumption follows Park's early claim that "social relations are . . . frequently and . . . inevitably correlated with spatial relations."[8]

1. The Research Issue

> If you would know what kind of Jew a man is, ask him where he lives; for no simple factor indicates as much about the character of the Jew as the area in which he lives. It is an index not only to his economic status, his occupation, his religion, but to his politics and his outlook on life and the stage in the assimilative process that he has reached.
>
> Louis Wirth, "The Ghetto"

This statement was written in the 1920s. Although Wirth often misrepresented the sociological implications of spatial patterns because of his ideological viewpoint, the issue he raises is as important today as it was for Chicago in the early twentieth century and for European cities in past centuries. The nineteenth and twentieth centuries have not only brought rapid worldwide population growth but have also seen extensive population movements of people within and across country boundaries. Settlement of large cities by population groups from widely different cultural and socioeconomic backgrounds and their subsequent distribution patterns have been subjects of increasing interest for social scientists.

In many towns of medieval Europe, and more recently of Asia and North Africa, the urban fabric is physically divided into areas referred to as wards and quarters. The pattern of residential differentiation and segregation in the modern city may be less obvious than is generally seen in the preindustrial community, but the absence of walls and other physical demarcation by no means implies any lessening of social differentiation. Similar populations cluster together and come to characterize their areas. Residential differentiation of the urban population takes place. Research indicates that almost any criterion differentiating individuals and groups may become the basis for their physical separation.[9]

Much of the ecological research on ethnic groups implies that there is a special relationship between the minority group and the wider community. T. R. Lee, for example, states that

> . . . residential segregation is basically a spatial phenomenon; but it is one which has economic, social and cultural causes and ramifications. Thus, residential segregation may symbolize and reflect social rejection and social isolation, but it may also reflect the relative economic standing of different groups and their access to power in the community.[10]

In their analysis of the impact of residential segregation on the process of social integration, Marston and Van Valey state: "The question of the residential patterning of racial and ethnic groups is clearly one of the most significant and sensitive problems facing society today."[11] Although research on residential distribution patterns of minority groups is quite extensive, there have been few atttempts to conduct a comparative cross-cultural investigation of a specific group to examine the urban ecology of minority groups. The Jewish group is generally considered an urban population, and study of Jewish populations in different historical and cultural settings can assist us in examining strategies of environmental adaptation used by minority groups.

The task here is to examine the shape of Jewish distribution in cities. Preliminary available evidence, based on a literature review, suggests the following generalizations:

1. Jews traditionally represent a highly urbanized population.
2. Jews traditionally represent a highly centralized population; that is, a community concentrated in the inner areas of cities.
3. Jewish immigrants to the West have begun their stay in highly segregated areas in the inner city but have dispersed in future generations.
4. As Jews become socially upwardly mobile, they tend to move out of immigrant areas, and a process of decentralization occurs.
5. Jews tend to retain their affinity to the inner city more than non-Jews.
6. Jews, when they move out of inner-city areas, tend to reconcentrate in other areas through a process of leap frogging, or of sectorial expansion, rather than expansion in concentric circles.

To examine the above assumptions, this essay, more an overview than a detailed empirical study, focuses on four sets of issues that appear to be crucial in understanding the urban ecology of Jewish populations:

A. Do Jews differ from other ethnic groups in their residential distribution pattern, and to what extent do they differ? The answers to the above questions involve measurement of residential differentiation (segregation).
B. How do they differ? This involves an analysis of how the Jews conform to the models of internal structure of cities and mobility patterns of immigrant populations.
C. Why do they differ? First we need to investigate settlement ideologies as they affect Jewish populations, and second, the determinants and functions of residential differentiation.
D. What are the consequences of specific patterns of residential distribution? This involves investigation of the social, psychological, and institutional consequences of distribution patterns.

2. Research

A. RESIDENTIAL SEGREGATION

Since its inception, urban ecological study has focused on the patterns of residential segregation between groups. Ecological investigations of residential segregation of subgroups (ethnic, social class, religion) have concluded that the residential dissimilarity of subgroups is present in many different cultural settings. Studies using the index of dissimilarity—a summary measure of the divergence between two population distributions—have shown that large proportions of the varying populations constituting cities in the developed world would need to change their place of residence if all were to share the same residential pattern. When there is complete similarity of distribution patterns, the index will be zero; in complete dissimilarity—in which no members of the one population live in any areas inhabited by the other—the index will be 100.[12]

In an analysis of U.S. cities, Taeuber and Taeuber found that the average index of dissimilarity between blacks and whites is 87.3 at the city block level and 79.3 at the census tract level.[13] Subsequent research by Sorensen et al.[14] and Van Valey et al.[15] have demonstrated continued racial segregation in U.S. cities into the 1970s. There also is convincing evidence that residential segregation persists among ethnic immigrant groups in U.S. cities. Lieberson, for example, indicates that in 1950 the average index of ethnic concentration for twelve foreign-born groups in ten American cities was 39.[16] Kantrowitz demonstrates the continued existence of high index values for European migrant groups in New York forty years after the cessation of large scale immigration.[17] Uyeki, in a study of Cleveland that covers sixty years (1910–1970) points out that ". . . correlations suggest historical continuity in the intergroup relationship set down at an early period in Cleveland history."[18] A striking demonstration of the configuration of ethnic and racial residential segregation that exists in American cities can be found in Sweetser for Boston in 1960,[19] a situation reconfirmed by Kantrowitz for 1970 when he states that "segregation between European ethnicities has remained stable or has declined little. . . ."[20]

Studies carried out in a variety of cultural contexts, including Melbourne, Singapore, Prague, Poona [India], Toronto, Tel Aviv, Belfast, London, and Leicester, demonstrate the existence of residential differentiation among population subgroups within large urban areas.[21] There also are many examples of residential segregation of populations classified by socioeconomic variables. The classic work carried out by the Duncans in 1955 demonstrated definite patterns of residential distance among different occupational groups.[22] This research has been replicated and expanded by Uyeki, Simkus, and Bleda,[23] which together present ample evidence for the ecological statement that spatial distance becomes an indicator of social distance.

The classic model of Jewish immigrant residential distribution is the ghetto, representing the segregation of Jewish communities.[24] There are many examples of the Jewish ghetto in eastern and central Europe. (The term *ghetto* originated with the creation of a distinct neighborhood as a means of social control over sixteenth-century Venice's Jewish population.) These areas of extremely high segregation of Jews from non-Jews represent an important phase in Jewish urban ecology. Specific examples can be found in historical data for Warsaw and Rome.[25] There also is evidence that Jewish communities were segregated in the cities of Asia and North Africa.

Historical investigation of Jewish social segregation provides a framework for examining the Jewish communities of modern cities. Most Jews in the cities we will examine have their cultural and demographic origin in eighteenth- and nineteenth-century European cities. Evidence of twentieth-century Jewish residential segregation is sketchy, because of the scarcity of census data on religion and the lack of appropriate statistical techniques to undertake comparative analyses. Data for North American cities suggest that patterns of Jewish clustering have persisted beyond the initial immigrant status. In a study of Chicago's Jewish immigrant population, Wirth stated that "West of the Chicago River, in the shadow of the crowded central business district, lies a densely populated rectangle of tenements representing the greater part of Chicago's immigrant colonies, among them the ghetto."[26] According to Wirth, the ghetto traces its ancestry back to a medieval European urban institution by which the Jews were segregated involuntarily from the rest of the population. In modern times, however, the term *ghetto* does not apply to the place of officially regulated Jewish settlement, but rather to those local cultural areas that have arisen over time, that are selected voluntarily, or that are built up by Jews.[27]

Several studies in the U.S. have found that Jews (after the initial settlement period) moved at a surprising rate from the working class to the middle class, but there was less of a trend toward residential integration. Glazer and Moynihan point out that "Jewish residential concentration is not confined to the immigrant generation or the poor. It is a characteristic of the middle and upper-middle classes and the third generation no less than the second."[28] For example, the Chicago ghetto referred to by Wirth spread westward in the 1930s; the Jewish population then advanced northward to specific neighborhoods in the mid-twentieth century. In a recent study of Jewish residential mobility in Chicago, Jaret concludes that "among Jews the desire to live in close proximity to group members is still strong. Jews tend to live clustered together in residential areas in much greater density than their percentage of the population."[29]

Similar patterns of clustering exist in New York[30] and Boston.[31] Uyeki's 1980 series of index of dissimilarity matrices prepared for Cleveland (1910–1970) shows that the average index of segregation of Russians (a predominantly Jewish group) from other European immigrant groups have (with few exceptions in early years) been consistently the highest of all the intergroup averages. Although there are obvious problems with using Russian foreign stock data as a proxy for Jews because of the aging of the population, the Cleveland data and similar analyses of other large U.S. cities confirm continuing segregative tendencies of Jewish groups.[32]

According to the data presented by Rees, a residentially distinct Jewish community is characteristic not only of the larger American metropolises, but also of much smaller cities:

> In examining the relative levels of assimilation of various ethnic groups, using the index of dissimilarity, the "Anglo Saxon" ethnic groups (British, German and Canadian) appear to be well assimilated, followed by Norwegians, Swedes, Czechs and Irish with slightly lower degrees of residential assimilation. The Southern and Eastern Europeans have higher index values, particularly the Russian group which in almost all cities is composed largely of members of the Jewish faith.[33]

Some data for residential segregation of Jews in non-U.S. cities are also available. Although the Jews accounted for 1.5 percent of Melbourne's population as a whole in 1961, they were concentrated heavily in a small number of areas that had higher percentages than the average. Seventy-five percent of Melbourne's Jewish community lived in neighborhoods that contained only 16 percent of the total city population. In these areas, Jews averaged 7 percent of the resident population.[34] According to Burnley, "In the adjacent local government area of Caulfield there was another high status district, this time in association with an ethnic concentration, that of Jewish persons, more specifically of people from central and Eastern Europe."[35] In Canada, evidence shows that in Winnipeg in 1941, three-fourths of the Jewish population lived in five census tracts in the north end, where they originally settled in the 1880s.[36] Data from a census tract analysis demonstrates that in Toronto significant levels of residential segregation existed in 1961 among European immigrant groups:

> There is a rather low level of segregation between any pair of the five groups originating from northern and western Europe. Those from southern and eastern European origins are more highly segregated not only from the former, but also from each other. The Asiatic, Other and Other European (predominantly Jewish: 60%) are less segregated from the northern and western European groups than those of southern and eastern European heritage.[37]

In addition, the Russian-born immigrants (predominantly Jewish) had the second highest average rates of segregation from all other groups, second only to the Italian. These results confirm earlier work carried out by Rosenberg for the 1951 census and Murdie for the 1951 and 1961 censes.[38]

Data for Johannesburg, South Africa, prepared from research carried out by Dubb and DellaPergola[39] indicate definite areas of Jewish residential concentration. Kosmin has pointed out that "we can see a spreading Jewish population in London over time but it remains surprisingly concentrated and conservative as regards residential movement by regional standards."[40] He also states that

> The borough pattern of residential distribution fits a core-periphery model. The Jewish core in Hackney and Ilford tops out at about 40% of the total population of Jews, and around 4,500 Jews per ward. In Edgware in the 1960s again the Jews were about 40% of the total. This is interesting, since the Jewish proportion in the borough as a whole is 20% in Barnet, 14% in Hackney and 9% in Redbridge. The Jewishness of the average Jew's environment due to such local densities was 24% in Hackney and 17% in Redbridge. The density level was 1.8 times the expected in the inner area of secondary settlement and 2.0 times the expected in the tertiary suburban area. Moreover the Redbridge Jewish population is 94% British-born.

The evidence presented above suggests that Jewish populations, both past and present, differ in their residential distribution pattern from other urban population subgroups. This continued tendency among Jewish populations to maintain separate high mobility and suburbanization calls for further investigation. The question now posed is, Do Jewish populations differ in their distribution patterns from the generally accepted models of internal structure of cities?

B. CHARACTERISTICS OF ECOLOGICAL DISTRIBUTION

The ecological model of social morphology for large industrialized American cities presented in the 1920s by Park and Burgess states that the city center was the watershed for poor immigrants who used secure, dense inner-city neighborhoods close to the city's economic center as their initial point of settlement.[41] In time these immigrant groups moved on and were replaced by new immigrant groups. This concentric zone model suggests that the socioeconomic status of the urban population increases as one moves from the city's center to its periphery. Competing models have been developed that suggest that population and housing characteristics are wedges running from the center to the periphery,[42] or that several nuclei serve as organizing foci for the city's development with subgroups arranged according to concentric or sectorial configurations around each nucleus.[43] (Excellent reviews of the classic models are found in Timms and Herbert and Johnson.[44]) Residential distribution patterns can be analyzed from a static perspective (where do people live?) or a dynamic perspective (how and where do people move?). Ecological models of residential patterns suggest that immigrant groups cluster initially in ethnic inner-city neighborhoods but eventually are absorbed into wider society. In general, industrialized societies in the twentieth century have seen population decentralization, usually known as suburbanization. Racial and ethnic subgroups, however, behave differently in their patterns of physical mobility.[45] Comparative analysis of cities has raised questions concerning the location models. It has been suggested that cities are at different stages of development and that, as they move from preindustrial to industrial, the location model moves from high socioeconomic concentration in the center to the periphery of cities.[46]

Another question is whether different subgroup characteristics are distributed differentially over urban space. For example, there is evidence that in less industrialized cities economic status, family cycle, and immigrant-status of subareas overlap, and in more industrialized cities these variables become more independent. It also has been suggested that some characteristics are distributed according to the zonal model, and others according to the sectorial model (e.g., immigrant ethnic groups in U.S. cities are distributed in a sectorial spatial pattern, and the population characterized by economic status is distributed concentrically).[47] A common settlement pattern of minority groups is to move toward the city's periphery. These centrifugal movements do not necessarily imply a concomitant end of segregation, because segregation patterns re-emerge in new areas. The North American pattern of Jewish residential mobility is outward but concentrated, where new areas are settled, re-establishing Jewish concentrations around new institutions. Despite increasing out-movement, evidence for Western Europe and North America suggests that Jews remain overrepresented in inner areas of cities when compared with the general population.

A recent analysis of approximately twenty European cities shows that in comparison with non-Jewish populations, the Jews are more centralized in the inner areas of these cities, and more specifically in the intermediate ring between the city's center and the outer suburbs.[48] In Prague between 1869 and 1939, the spatial distribution of Jews differed from that of the general population.[49] Although there were decentralization and out-migration from the ghetto after 1859, Jews remained fairly concentrated in the center of town. They did, however, move to newly established middle-class districts of Greater Prague. Jewish households also concentrated in the center of Brussels (66 percent compared with 53 percent of general population).[50] Between 1922 and 1931, Warsaw experienced major decentralizing trends among most of the non-Jewish population but few such trends among the Jews.[51] Few Jews moved to the suburbs, preferring instead to move outside the nucleus of the great ghetto.

In a 1960s study of Providence, Rhode Island, Goldstein and Goldscheider found a central concentration of Jews, but also Jews scattered throughout the suburbs. The general trend in the years 1951–1963 has been "a more general residential integration of the Jewish community into the larger population of the metropolitan areas."[52] A review of the suburbanization ratios of ethnic groups in thirteen U.S. cities between 1950 and 1960 concluded that "Negroes, other non-whites, Russians and Italians are distinctly more concentrated in the central city than is the total population."[53] Using more recent data, Goldstein in a 1981 article notes that in the U.S. Jews are moving to the suburbs at a significant rate, but he leaves open the question of concentration or intracity movement.[54]

A study of Jewish residential mobility in Chicago from 1960 to 1974 reports that the desire by Jews to live in close proximity to group members is still strong.[55] Jews have moved to the suburbs with the rest of the population, but most moves by Jews are *within* a city. Jews moving to suburbs tend to be less concentrated in areas, but still concentrated in blocks along certain streets. Boston data suggest that in the early decades of the twentieth century, the Jewish population was heavily concentrated in the central city.[56] In the late 1950s and early 1960s, however, the Jewish population was dispersed predominantly in the north and west, and by the mid-1970s there had been further decentralization. Large reductions in Jewish population in Boston City had occurred. Little is known, however, about concentration or segregation levels because data is limited. In Cincinnati a study concluded that there is a strong tendency for the Jewish population to move within the same community, but of those moving outward the general pattern is sectorial.[57] The early settlers lived close to the central business district, and Jewish clusters have appeared in a northerly direction over time.

Evidence of decentralization yet maintenance of clustering among Canadian Jews is presented in Driedger and Church's 1974 study of Winnipeg. They point out that Jewish immigrant groups initially formed inner-city concentrations and later moved to suburban locations.[58] Although upwardly mobile in social status, Winnipeg Jews maintained high residential proximity.

The most illustrative and comprehensive study of the residential distribution patterns of Jews has been carried out on Toronto by various researchers. The Canadian census is one of the few reporting population statistics by religion. In addition, the Jewish group is included as one ethnic-origin classification category. Toronto, a large heterogenous city, has a Jewish population estimated in 1961 at sixty-six thousand, approximately 5.4 percent of the metropolitan total. Rosenberg's data from the 1950 census demonstrate that, although the Jews were not isolated in one neighborhood in the early twentieth century, there was a significant concentration in the inner-city downtown area. Within a few years, however, the Jewish population had decentralized to the north.[59] Wider dispersion occurred as population became integrated increasingly in economic and cultural life. As decentralization toward the northern residential suburbs occurred, Jews tended to be more centralized than the total population until 1951, but the 1961 data suggest that Jews were decentralizing rapidly. In 1951 Jews comprised 6.7 percent of Toronto's city population and 2.1 percent of the outer suburbs. By 1961 the percentages were 2.8 percent and 7.2 percent, respectively. According to Murdie, the Jews, unlike the Italians, remained segregated largely by choice to be near friends, synagogues, and grocery stores. The Jews have moved northward in sectorial fashion.[60] An ongoing geo-statistical analysis of Toronto data confirms the clustering of Jewish population in the area leading from the north of the central city into the northern suburbs.[61] Preliminary analysis of data from the 1971 census points to a continued decentralization but clustering trend in a sectorial northerly direction.[62]

Caution is suggested concerning the impact of recent in-migration of a minority group into an area. It is important to differentiate between decentralization of Jewish population and the settlement of Jewish immigrants in peripheral areas. The period of immigration has an impact on the residential distribution pattern of immigrant groups. Decentralization must not be confused with settlement patterns of groups who arrive at different times. New groups may settle in peripheral areas, giving the impression of decentralization.

In summary, (1) Jewish populations are decentralizing in urban areas with expanding suburbs, but at a slower rate than the general population; (2) Jewish population moves tend to be sectorial; and (3) the Jewish population is regrouping in new areas, in which new concentrations of Jewish populations are found.

C. DETERMINANTS OF RESIDENTIAL SEGREGATION

Residential clustering of population subgroups is neither a random nor a nonrational process. Why do these patterns exist? The classic ecological explanation is based on economic competition for space and the trade-off between time and space. Values and many other influences, subjective and objective, also affect decision making, particularly an understanding of settlement ideologies. Both the receiving host society and a particular minority group generally have perspectives on social interaction and on their ideological commitment to this model of interaction.

Most writings about the impact of residential distribution of racial, ethnic, or other minority groups on social integration use the assimilationist model. This model suggests that residential isolation is an important indicator of the lack of assimilation, and minority groups want to assimilate into the mainstream culture of the society. Using this perspective, researchers maintain that the degree of residential segregation is an acceptable indicator of, or a proxy for, assimilation. An ethnically enclosed residential experience insulates a group from important mechanisms of assimilation, limits cross-cultural contacts that affect socialization of the young, and has serious implications for intermarriage, upward job mobility, and the formation of social ties. Segregation restricts social mobility and has negative effects on the psychological development of a segregated group. Thus, the lower the degree of segregation, the greater the likelihood that a group is experiencing assimilation. Desegregation then is likely to result in a dissipation of the subordinate status and assimilation of the subjugated group into mainstream society.

Early studies on immigrant groups and black population in the United States suggest evidence of a distinct ethnic group, and incomplete dispersion of these groups within institutional spheres of society.[63] As social policy, emphasis was placed on social proximity as well as dispersal within the formal institutional sphere as conditions for successful integration.[64] In 1944 Gunnar Myrdal stated, "We assume it is to the advantage of American Negroes as individuals and as a group to become assimilated into American culture, to acquire the traits held in esteem by the dominant white Americans."[65]

Investigation of societies with ethnic minorities reveals, however, that residential segregation persists in most of these societies, and in many situations ethnic group identity has persisted and become more salient.[66] This represents a different model leading to alternate forms of social interaction. In some societies the trend is toward preservation of cultural elements within the national societal unity. Residential segregation is an important element in maintaining this pluralist model of integration because ethnic residential clusters in cities perform several positive functions. Ethnic minority groups also can be seen as interest groups engaged in a struggle with other groups for public resources.

When people are in conflict or feel threatened, segregated areas may perform one of these functions:

People seek each other's company for defense and security, and the community can provide a haven for new immigrants.

Clustering may be the result of a desire to preserve group identity and to provide a complete set of services for members.

Clustering can use the resources of a common territory to gain additional resources and power.

The pluralist model of residential distribution patterns suggests that ethnicity or minority group status can be one of many characteristics on which a territorial group can base solidarity. However, it is difficult to disaggregate voluntary from involuntary forces contributing to segregation. Greeley and Metzger each argue strongly for the positive aspects of ethnic pluralism as a strategy of community adaptation to a new or hostile social environment.[67] But evidence collected by social scientists is quite persuasive that a considerable amount of residential segregation is created and maintained by discriminatory procedures, both legal and informal, that make it difficult for minority groups to settle voluntarily in certain residential areas, involuntarily assigning them to other areas.[68]

In the United States, studies have pointed out that socioeconomic differences among racial groups do not fully explain their residential segregation. Karl Taeuber, in an extensive analysis of the relationship among economic factors and racial patterns of American housing, stated that

> These sample analyses demonstrate that poverty has little to do directly with Negro residential segregation in the Cleveland metropolitan area. They demonstrate that if incomes were the only factor at work in determining where white and Negro families live, there would be very little racial residential segregation.[69]

Hermalin and Farley report that "data from the census of 1970 reveal that economic factors account for little of the concentration of blacks within central cities, their absence from suburbia or the residential segregation of blacks from whites in either cities or suburbs."[70]

There is evidence in New York that residential segregation among European-origin ethnic groups can be explained by socioeconomic status. A number of studies find a clear correspondence between the ordering of occupational categories by general social standing and by residential patterning. Also, the greater the prestige distance between two occupational populations, the less likely they are to nominate each other as friends and the more dissimilar their residential distributions. Areas with high ethnic concentrations also tend to have low economic status. The interpretation of this relationship is more complex, and both ecological and individual characteristics must be considered.

Discrimination and voluntary self-segregation may be two sides of the same coin, difficult to differentiate. When the host society controls the housing market either overtly using segregative settlement policy (e.g., Jews only allowed to live in a certain area) or covertly using institutional barriers (e.g., loans not available to Jews), the consequences are high levels of involuntary separation. The traditional Jewish ghettos in Europe and North Africa are good examples. However, there are many minority groups who, unilaterally or by mutual agreement with the host society, choose to remain segregated. Where do the Jews fit? Bloch points out that after the 1862 emancipation of the Jews in Warsaw, the expected great exodus from the ghetto by law before 1862 did not occur. He suggests that this was due partly to the desire to retain a sense of Jewish community and partly to the hostility of the surrounding population.[71]

In 1971 R. J. Johnson, an influential urban sociologist, wrote that "the Jews are the usually quoted example of a minority group who have chosen to continue to live in ghetto situations."[72] Although Johnson uses Wirth's definition of ghetto, the evidence to support Johnson's claim needs to be reexamined in the light of recent data. Wirth's analysis of the Chicago Jewish ghetto and the population's behavior suggests a gradual process of cultural assimilation, but one in which the Jews leaving the ghetto are followed by others, creating a new concentration.[73]

Finally, one must examine whether Jews are segregated or concentrated because of a desire to be close to their own group, or because of other factors such as socioeconomic status. Studies in North America have found that Jews moved rapidly from working-class to middle-class status. Jewish residential concentration was not confined to the immigrant generation or the poor but characterized the middle- and upper-class and the third generation no less than the second generation.

In a study of Jewish assimilation in Chicago, Rosenthal states

A modicum of Jewish education and voluntary segregation are two parts of a three part device designed to forestall large scale assimilation. The third is residence in a high-status area. . . . Settlement there removes the stigma that is usually attributed to a separate ethnic community. . . . Residence in a high-status area indicates the voluntary nature of the settlement of Jews as well as non-Jews and lifts the burden of alienation from the younger generation in particular.[74]

Referring to Leeds, England, Krausz writes,

> working and middle class Jews do not move to working and middle class areas. The aim is to move to a better area and not a non-Jewish area. The Jew belonging to his own elite appears to be happy living with other members of the Jewish elite.[75]

An extremely interesting question concerns the part that economic status plays in the distribution of ethnic groups. Generally, research findings in the United States suggest that the higher the group's occupational status, the less residentially segregated from native-born whites of native parents. Whether ethnic groups are residentially segregated because of their ethnicity (ethnic status model) or socioeconomic status (class model) is an important research issue.[76] Darrock and Marston found evidence in Toronto of social class segregation within ethnic groups.[77]

Summary data presented by Rees point out that in U.S. cities a major exception to the residence-status relationship is "the Russian group"—the group with the highest educational and occupational status and yet the least residentially assimilated of the European ethnic groups. "A very strong preference for living in a Jewish community among co-ethnics together with some degree of housing discrimination against Jews in the past undoubtedly account for the residential concentration of the Russian foreign stock group in all the urbanized areas. . . ."[78] Concluding their analysis of ethnic differences in the residential search process in Toronto, Gad et al., state that "the Jews, more than Italians, form a close-knit community with strong social, cultural and economic ties, and are motivated to maintain these ties. They are also aware of the location of social contacts and Jewish institutions and take these into consideration in a relocation decision."[79]

Little empirical information, however, is available concerning differential residential distribution of socioeconomic subgroups within the Jewish population of cities. A comprehensive review of the determinants of the distribution patterns, both positive and negative, for the Jewish group is crucial to our understanding of the urban ecology of minority groups.

D. CONSEQUENCES OF RESIDENTIAL DISTRIBUTION PATTERNS

Using the perspective of urban ecology, it has been possible to draw conclusions about the historical development of Jewish populations in urban settings. Although much of the data does not bring us completely up to date, clearly population mobility is increasing, and the Jewish population is part of this dynamic movement reshaping urban communities.

The consequences of residential distribution patterns are complex, involving subjective perceptions of the meaning of territory. It is important, however, for groups to understand the dynamics of settlement patterns. A group may view increased spatial redistribution of its members as successful integration or see the need for a critical mass to maintain viable communal and religious facilities.

Most European Jewish communities, although more concentrated than non-Jewish populations, "face a pattern of location of the main Jewish services and facilities in the central city, and of increasing redistribution of Jews toward the periphery of metropolitan areas, where opportunities for Jewish communal life are poorer."[80] The question emerges of the relative good for the individual versus the good for the community. There is an important connection between territory and institutions. Minority groups often move their ethnic institutions; maintenance of institutions in a new location is crucial to the continuation of residentially segregated areas. Those ethnic groups who maintain a strong identity generally have succeeded in creating and sustaining a comprehensive set of ethnic institutions. Some studies have found that those ethnic minorities with the highest degree of institutional completeness display the highest levels of residential segregation.

The community literature has documented feelings of group identity and has recognized that local communities are viable entities with increasing socialization and political functions. The emphasis that urban ecologists have placed on the processes leading to social integration characterizes the immigrant ghetto, or ethnic village, as temporary, potentially distintegrative, and a barrier to eventual assimilation. Residential proximity increases the probability of social interaction, and persons with similar social positions, values, and expectations tend to locate in close proximity so that group interaction can be maximized and group norms maintained.[81] Over time different residential areas of a city acquire the social characteristics of their residents, and spatial distance indicates social distance.

Some observers of the urban scene have argued that a combination of high personal mobility and modern communication techniques has rendered any territorial constraints on human association obsolete. To proponents of this view, community becomes devoid of territorial content. To ecologists and geographers, location remains a major determinant of interaction patterns and the concept of community is firmly anchored in a territorial base. Technological developments in transport and communications may have lessened territorial constraints, but place of residence is a major factor in allocating life chances and determining interaction patterns. The notion of a territorial base to services (local and other) ensures that locality will continue to be vitally important in the organization of society.

The overall summary points to the Jewish trend of decentralization at an ever-increasing rate combined with the tendency to relocate in areas that are Jewish in character. Thus, although clustering or residential segregation persists, it continues in a diluted form. Concentration does not necessarily reflect isolation, and Jews living in what might be termed a Jewish environment in the suburbs are nevertheless exposed to physical and cultural contact with other groups.

This brief review of residential distribution patterns of Jewish populations suggests that the basis for clustered communities exists. Ecological theory points to the importance of spatial contact in maintaining subgroup identification, and recent research indicates that interest in ethnic group identity is increasing.

Notes

1. Robert E. Park, "The Urban Community as a Spatial Pattern and Moral Order," *Human Communities* (New York: The Free Press, 1952), p. 14.

2. Robert Rockaway, "Ethnic Conflict in an Urban Environment: The German and Russian Jew in Detroit, 1881–1914," *American Jewish Historical Quarterly* 60, no.2 (December 1970): 133–50.

3. R. A. Schermerhorn, *These are Our People* (Boston: Heath, 1949).

4. Robert E. Park and E. W. Burgess, *Introduction to the Science of Sociology* (Chicago: University of Chicago Press, 1970).

5. A. Hawley, "Dispersion versus segregation: apropos of a solution of race problems," Papers of the Michigan Academy of Arts and Letters, 1944, p. 30.

6. Stanley Lieberson, *Ethnic Patterns in American Cities* (New York: The Free Press, 1963).

7. K. E. Taeuber and A. F. Taeuber, "The Negro as an Immigrant Group: Recent Trends in Racial and Ethnic Segregation in Chicago," *American Journal of Sociology* 69, no.4 (January 1964): 375.

8. Park, "The Urban Community," p. 68.

9. M. Lagory and J. Pipkin, *Urban Social Space* (Belmont, California: Wadsworth, 1981).

10. T. R. Lee, *Race and Residence: The Concentration and Dispersal of Immigrants in London* (New York and London: Oxford University Press, 1977), p. 5.

11. W. G. Marston and T. L. Van Valey, "The Role of Residential Segregation in

the Assimilation Process," *The Annals of Political and Social Science* 441 (January 1979): 13–25.

12. O. D. Duncan and B. Duncan, "Methodological Analysis of Segregation Indexes," *American Sociological Review* 20 (1955): 210–17.

13. K. E. Taeuber and A. F. Taeuber, *Negroes in Cities* (Chicago: Aldine, 1965).

14. A. Sorensen, K. E. Taeuber, and L. J. Hollingsworth, Jr., "Indexes of Racial Residential Segregation for 109 Cities in the United States, 1940 to 1970," *Sociological Focus* 8, no.2 (1975): 125–42.

15. T. L. Van Valey, W. C. Roof, and J. E. Wilcox, "Trends in Residential Segregation: 1960–1970," *American Journal of Sociology* 82, no.4 (January 1977): 826–44.

16. Lieberson, *Ethnic Patterns*, passim.

17. Nathan Kantrowitz, *Ethnic and Racial Segregation in the New York Metropolis, 1961* (New York: Praeger, 1973).

18. E. S. Uyeki, "Residential Distribution and Stratification, 1950–60," *American Journal of Sociology* 85 (1980): 401.

19. F. L. Sweetser, *Patterns of Change in the Social Ecology of Metropolitan Boston* (Boston: Massachusetts Department of Mental Health, 1962).

20. N. Kantrowitz, "Racial and Ethnic Residential Segregation: Boston 1830–1970," *The Annals of the American Academy of Political and Social Science* 441 (January 1979): 53.

21. F. L. Jones, *Dimensions of Urban Social Structure: The Social Areas of Melbourne, Australia* (Toronto: University of Toronto Press, 1969); G. Musil, "The Development of Prague's Ecological Structure," in *Readings in Urban Sociology,* ed. R. E. Pahl (New York: Pergamon Press, 1968); Mehta, "Patterns of Residence in Poona (India) by Income, Education and Occupation," *American Journal of Sociology* 73 (1968): 498–508; A. G. Darrock and W. G. Marston, "The Social Class Basis of Ethnic Residential Segregation: The Canadian Case," *American Journal of Sociology,* 76: 1971, 491–510; Vivian Klaff, "Ethnic Segregation in Urban Israel," *Demography* 10 (2 May 1973): 161–84; M. A. Poole and F. W. Boal, "Religious Residential Segregation in Belfast in mid-1969: A Multi-level Analysis," in *Social Patterns in Cities,* ed. B. D. Clark and M. B. Gleave (New York: Academic Press, 1973); D. Phillips, "The Social and Spatial Segregation of Asians in Leicester," *Social Interaction and Ethnic Segregation,* ed. P. Jackson and S. J. Smith (New York: Academic Press, 1981).

22. O. D. Duncan and B. Duncan, "Occupational Stratification and Residential Distribution," *American Sociological Review* 50: 493–503.

23. Uyeki, "Residential Distribution," p. 401; A. A. Simkus, "Residential Segregation by Occupation and Race in Ten Urbanized Areas, 1950–1970," *American Sociological Review* 43 (February 1978): 81–93; S. E. Bleda, "Socioeconomic, Demographic and Cultural Bases of Ethnic Residential Segregation," *Ethnicity* 6 (1979): 147–67.

24. R. J. Johnson, *Urban Residential Patterns* (London: Bell and Sons, 1971).

25. B. Bloch, "Spatial Evolution of the Jewish and General Population of Warsaw: 1792–1939," *Papers in Jewish Demography 1973* (Jerusalem: The Hebrew University, Jewish Population Studies, 1977) and S. DellaPergola, "Urban Geography of the Jews in Rome and in Milan," working paper (Jerusalem: The Hebrew University, Institute for Advanced Studies, May 1981).

26. Louis Wirth, *The Ghetto* (Chicago: University of Chicago Press, 1928), p. 195.

27. See, for example, M. L. Hansen, *The Atlantic Migration, 1607–1860* (Cam-

bridge: Harvard University Press, 1940); D. R. Goldfield and J. B. Lane, *The Enduring Ghetto* (New York: Lippincott, 1973).

28. Nathan Glazer and Daniel P. Moynihan, *Beyond the Melting Pot* (Cambridge: MIT Press, 1963), p. 143.

29. C. Jaret, "Recent Patterns of Chicago Jewish Residential Mobility," *Ethnicity* 6 (1979): 235–48.

30. C. M. Horowitz and L. J. Kaplan, *The Estimated Jewish Population of the New York Area: 1900–1975* (New York: Federation of Jewish Philanthropies, 1959).

31. F. J. Fowler, *A Study of the Jewish Population of Greater Boston* (Boston: The Combined Jewish Philanthropies of Greater Boston, 1977).

32. Kantrowitz, "Racial and Ethnic Residential Segregation," p. 53. See also A. M. Guest and J. A. Weed, "Ethnic Residential Segregation: Patterns of Change," *American Journal of Sociology* 76, no.5 (1971): 1088–1111.

33. P. H. Rees, *Residential Patterns in American Cities: 1960* Research Paper no. 189 (Chicago: University of Chicago, Department of Geography, 1979), pp. 322, 326.

34. Jones, *Dimensions of Urban Social Structure*, passim.

35. I. H. Burnley, *Urbanization in Australia: The Post-War Experience*, (Cambridge: Cambridge University Press, 1974), p. 141.

36. L. Driedger and G. Church, "Residential Segregation an Institutional Completeness: A Comparison of Ethnic Minorities," *Canadian Review of Sociology and Anthropology*, 11, no.1 (1974): 30–52.

37. Darrock and Marston, "The Social Class Basis," p. 496.

38. L. Rosenberg, *The Changes in the Geographic Distribution of the Jewish Population in the Metropolitan Area of Toronto, 1851–1951* (Canadian Jewish Studies, Jewish Community Series, no. 2 1954; and R. A. Murdie, *Factorial Ecology of Metropolitan Toronto, 1951–1961*, Research Paper no. 116 (Chicago: University of Chicago, Department of Geography, 1976).

39. A. A. Dubb and S. DellaPergola, *Geographical Distribution and Mobility*, South African Jewish Population Study, Advance Report no. 9 (Jerusalem: The Hebrew University, Institute of Contemporary Jewry, 1978).

40. B. Kosmin, "The Urban Ecology of London Jewry," working paper (Jerusalem: The Hebrew University, Institute of Advanced Studies, May 1981).

41. E. W. Burgess, "The Growth of the City: An Introduction to a Research Project," in *The City*, ed. Robert E. Park, E. W. Burgess, and R. D. McKenzie (Chicago: University of Chicago Press, 1925).

42. H. Hoyt, *The Structure and Growth of Residential Neighborhoods in American Cities* (Washington, D.C.: U.S. Government Printing Office, 1928), sector model.

43. C. Harris and E. Ullman, "The Nature of Cities," *Annals of the American Academy of Political and Social Science* 242 (1945): 7–17.

44. D. W. G. Timms, *The Urban Mosaic* (Cambridge: Cambridge University Press, 1971); D. T. Herbert and R. J. Johnson, *Spatial Patterns and Form* (New York: John Wiley and Sons, 1976).

45. L. F. Schnore, *Class and Race in Cities and Suburbs* (Chicago: Markham, 1972); B. J. L. Berry and J. D. Kasarda, *Contemporary Urban Ecology* (New York: Macmillan, 1977); and W. H. Frey, "Black Inmigration, White Flight—The Changing Economic Base of the Central City," *American Journal of Sociology* 85, no.6 (May 1980).

46. Schnore, *Class and Race*; A. Hawley, *Urban Society* (New York: Ronald Press, 1971).

47. Murdie, *Factorial Ecology*; H. Carter, *The Study of Urban Geography* (New

York: Crane, Russak, 1972), pp. 241–87.

48. S. DellaPergola, "Toward a Typology of Jewish Population Distribution in European Cities," working paper (Jerusalem: The Hebrew University, Institute for Advanced Studies, 1981).

49. Jan Herman, "The Evolution of the Jewish Population in Prague, 1869–1939," *Papers in Jewish Demography, 1977* (Jerusalem: The Hebrew University, Jewish Population Studies, 1980), pp. 53–68.

50. W. Bok, "Some Socio-Economic Characteristics of the Jewish Population in Greater Brussels," *Papers in Jewish Demography 1977* (Jerusalem: The Hebrew University, Jewish Population Studies, 1980), p. 163.

51. Bloch, "Special Evolution," passim.

52. S. Goldstein and Calvin Goldscheider, *Jewish Americans: Three Generations in a Jewish Community* (Englewood Cliffs: Prentice-Hall, 1965)

53. Rees, *Residential Patterns*, pp. 321–22.

54. S. Goldstein, "The Jews in the United States: Perspectives from Demography," *American Jewish Yearbook,* 81 (1981).

55. Jaret, "Recent Patterns," pp. 235–48.

56. Fowler, *Study of the Jewish Population.*

57. D. P. Varady, S. J. Mantel, Jr., C. Hirtz-Washofsky, and H. Halpern, "Suburbanization and Dispersion: A Case Study of Cincinnati's Jewish Population," *Geographical Research Forum,* no. 3 (May 1981): 5–15.

58. Driedger and Church, "Residential Segregation," pp. 30–52.

59. Rosenberg, *Changes in Geographic Distribution.*

60. Murdie, *Factorial Ecology,* pp. 94–102.

61. R. Bachi and Vivian Klaff, "L'ecologie Urbanie des sous populations," Compte-Rendus du Colloque *Demographie et Destin des sous-populations* (Liege: Association Internationals des Demographes de Langue Francaise, 1981).

62. Vivian Klaff and R. Bachi, "A Geo-statistical Analysis of the Jewish Population of Toronto: 1950–1980," forthcoming.

63. E. G. Hartmann, *The Movement to Americanize the Immigrant* (New York: Columbia University Press, 1948).

64. W. Lloyd Warner and Leo Srole, *The Social Systems of American Ethnic Groups,* vol. 3, Yankee City Series (New Haven: Yale University Press, 1945); Schermerhorn, *These are Our People.*

65. Gunnar Myrdal, *An American Dilemma* (New York: Harper, 1944), p. 919.

66. Glazer and Moynihan, *Beyond the Melting Pot;* W. M. Newman, *American Pluralism: A Study in Minority Groups and Social Theory* (New York: Harper and Row, 1973).

67. A. Greeley, *The Demography of Ethnic Identification* (Chicago: Center for the Study of American Pluralism, University of Chicago, 1974); L. P. Metzger, "American Sociology & Black Assimilation: Conflicting Perspectives," *American Journal of Sociology* 76, no.4 (January 1971): 627–45.

68. A. H. Hawley and V. P. Rock, eds., *Segregation in Residential Areas* (Washington, D.C.: National Academy of Sciences, 1973); D. Pearce, *Black, White and Many Shades of Gray: Real Estate Brokers and their Racial Practices* (Ph.D. diss., University of Michigan, 1976); P. Thigpan, "Blacks in the Housing Market: The Politics of Exclusion," in *The Politics of Housing in Older Urban Areas,* ed. R. C. Mendelson and M. A. Quinn (New York: Praeger, 1976).

69. Karl F. Taeuber, "The Effect of Income Redistribution on Racial Residential Segregation," *Urban Affairs Quarterly* 4 (1968): 12.

70. A. I. Hermalin and R. Farley, "The Potential for Residential Integration in

Cities and Suburbs: Implications for the Busing Controversy," *American Sociological Review* 38 (October 1973): 595.

71. Bloch, "Spatial Evolution," p. 229.

72. Johnson, *Urban Residential Patterns*, p. 273.

73. Wirth, *The Ghetto*, p. 261.

74. E. Rosenthal, "Acculturation Without Assimilation? The Jewish Community of Chicago, Illinois," *American Journal of Sociology* 66 (1961) 275–88.

75. E. Krausz, *Leeds Jewry: Its History and Social Structure* (London: W. Heffer and Sons, 1964), p. 24.

76. Guest and Weed, "Ethnic Residential Segregation," pp. 1088–1111.

77. Darrock and Marston, "The Social Class Basis," pp. 491–510.

78. Rees, *Residential Patterns*, pp. 327, 330.

79. G. Gad, R. Peddie, and J. Punter, "Ethnic Differences in the Residential Search Process," in *The Form of Cities in Central Canada: Selected Paper*, ed. L. S. Bourne, R. D. MacKinnon, and J. W. Simmons (Toronto: University of Toronto Press, 1973), p. 179.

80. DellaPergola, "Toward a Typology."

81. H. Marshall and R. Jiobu, "Residential Segregation in United States Cities: A Causal Analysis," *Social Forces* 53, no.5 (March 1975): 449–60.

8

The Perpetuation and Growth of Sectarian Pluralism: The Case of the Jewish Communities of Boro Park, Brooklyn

Egon Mayer

Pluralism among the Jews of New York City is hardly surprising. Their great numbers, heterogeneity, and density of settlement make that inevitable. Since the 1940s, this pluralism includes a rich blend of sectarian establishments that grew in size and strength beginning in the 1960s—a sociological anomaly that warrants examination.

To appreciate the significance of sectarianism in the present-day New York Jewish community, several words should be defined. According to widely accepted social science usage, religious groups can be classified broadly as *churches* or *sects*. The former seek to accommodate their beliefs, practices, and organization to the secular everyday world. The latter, usually smaller groups, try to ensure the purity of their beliefs, practices, and organizations either through isolation or retreat from the secular world, or through radical transformation of the secular world.

In an insightful essay on "Orthodoxy in American Jewish Life," Charles Liebman suggests that the three main branches of American Jewry can be correctly understood as fitting along various points on the church-sect continuum.[1] Along that continuum the Reform movement is closest to the church type, and the Orthodox is most like a sect. However, as Liebman quickly points out, even among the Orthodox there are many (perhaps, even most) whose style of religion and whose religious institutions fit more with the church than the sect definition. Who, then, are the sectarian Orthodox?

Historically, these sectarian Orthodox were recent immigrants whose attachments to *shtetl* ways made them dogmatically opposed to change in religious beliefs, customs, rituals, and lifestyle. Generally, they lacked secular education, were of low socioeconomic status, and maintained few economic or political contacts with broader American or Jewish society. At the turn of the century on the Lower East Side or in Brownsville, the locus of community organization was the *shtibl* (prayer room) or *bes hemedresh* (study hall), small shops catering to dietary and stylistic requirements, and the densely settled neighborhood in which *landslayt* and family were within easy reach. The social control necessary to perpetuate a sectarian worldview was enforced informally through close family networks, multigenerational acquaintanceships, and commercial ties. These mechanisms operated in a cultural medium of distinctive modes of dress, dialects of Yiddish, forms of prayer and study, home rituals, and legends of rabbinic authority—all of which linked the American community directly to its roots in specific eastern European localities.

As the annals of American Judaism make clear, with the passage of time and the coming of a successive generation of American-born members, sectarian Judaism readily gave way to the more church-like Orthodox, Conservative, or Reform forms. Nevertheless, some sectarian Orthodox communities survived; some have even flourished and grown.

The present essay first describes one New York Jewish community that is home to many such sectarian subcommunities. Second, it accounts for their persistence and growth into the postimmigrant generation. Finally, the essay offers some conjectures about the significance of these subcommunities for Jewish communal life in New York City and elsewhere.

Boro Park: A Jewish Suburb Grows in Brooklyn

The neighborhood and subcommunal organization of Boro Park in the southwest corner of Brooklyn covers approximately twenty street blocks long (39th Street to 60th Street) and about eight avenue blocks wide (10th Avenue to 18th Avenue). It is bounded by Bay Ridge on the west, Flatbush on the east, Bensonhurst on the south, and Kensington and Sunset Park on the north.

During the past sixty years within these narrow geographic coordinates, a Jewish community has evolved that is both a testimonial and a sociological puzzle. It is a testimonial to Jewish survival and American pluralism. It is a puzzle to the sociological understanding of how ethnic-religious minorities are integrated into modern American society.

Before the 1920s, the area contained mostly small farms and country mansions. In many respects Boro Park was typical of the communities in Brooklyn, the Bronx, and Queens that sprang up during the 1920s, following the extending ganglia of the New York City subway system. Contemporary observers have noted that the place name apparently was the creation of two local land developers, William Reynolds and Edward Johnson, who converted many of the local farms into profitable real estate.

What was perhaps atypical about the neighborhood is that from its earliest development it was distinctly Jewish. Its allure to upwardly mobile Jews from the Lower East Side is captured vividly by Michael Gold, in his popular novel, *Jews Without Money:*

> One day we travelled to Borough Park to see the house and lot Zachariah was persuading my father to buy . . . the suburb was a place of half-finished houses and piles of lumber and brick. Paved streets ran in rows between empty fields where only weeds rattled. Real estate signs were stuck everywhere, "Why pay rent? Build your house in God's country."

In a subsequent passage, the fictional Zachariah is urging the author's father to stake his claim to a piece of Boro Park real estate without hesitation.

> "Look Herman, it's the best piece of real estate in Brooklyn. In five years it will be worth double the price. . . . All the refined businessmen are moving here."[2]

Zachariah was correct; many successful Jewish businessmen from the Lower East Side and elsewhere were moving to Boro Park. According to available records, by 1930 the Jewish population of Boro Park was approximately sixty thousand, constituting a little more than 50 percent of the neighborhood.[3] The other half of the neighborhood consisted of Irish at the Bay Ridge end and Italians toward Bensonhurst and Flatbush.

But perhaps most noteworthy about the area even in its first decade of significant Jewish settlement is that within its geographic boundaries, the primary institutional identity of the community was clearly Jewish. The dozens of synagogues and Hebrew schools that were built during the first decades of Jewish settlement were not constructed in the shadow of church steeples or parochial schools. These latter institutions occupied land at the periphery of the boundaries described above. The Hebrew book stores and kosher butcher shops that sprang up along Thirteenth Avenue generally did not abut Italian salumeria or Irish pubs. In short, the Jewish segment evolved into a geographically unified identity within clearly defined boundaries. Although many Jews and Italians lived side by side along tree-lined streets of one- and two-family homes, the dominant community culture was Jewish from the start.

Apart from the Jewishness of the community culture, it is important to note that both Jewish and non-Jewish residents were among the most upwardly mobile segment of their respective groups. Although many were first-generation immigrants, Boro Park was not their first area of settlement. Boro Park clearly was a move upward on the American ladder of success. Consequently, their homes, lawns, shops, and public institutions symbolized material success. For example, Etz Chaim, the first modern Hebrew day school for boys in the community—and one of the first in the United States—was established in 1917 on an imposing lot in a large, equally imposing colonial-style building that had previously housed a country club in the heart of the community.

Other local Jewish institutions, also established during this period, included Temples Emanu-El and Beth-El, The First Congregation Anshe S'fard, the YM-YWHA, Shulamith School for Girls, as well as numerous smaller congregations. Each of these newly established institutions occupied its own separate building, expressly built by the founders. The buildings' cost and architecture proclaimed with equal vigor the particular Jewish commitments of the residents as well as their pride in their Americanness, financial success, and general "modernness."

Consistent with their American middle-class acculturation, even the Orthodox Jews of Boro Park (in the majority then as now) were abandoning the specifically ethnic traditionalism characteristic of immigrant communities such as the Lower East Side. Yiddish was rapidly falling into disuse; the local day schools preferred the use of Hebrew, and synagogue sermons were delivered in English. Although there were numerous *shtibl*-type synagogues in private homes or storefronts in the area, most of the residents belonged to a major synagogue. Services in the latter houses of worship had become decorous and formalized, with officiating rabbis and cantors.

All of these developments tended to wear away ethnic and

ideological distinctions among the Jews of Boro Park, making them increasingly more alike in their beliefs, practices, and life-styles. The most important criterion of demarcation among the various Boro Park Jewry was that among the three Jewish denomi-nations: Orthodox, Conservative, and Reform.

According to the *Jewish Communal Register*, published in 1918 by the Kehilla of New York City, twenty-seven permanent syn-agogues existed in the area at that time. Of these, fifteen were Orthodox, seven Conservative, and five Reform, thus characteriz-ing the Jewish community by what one might call denominational pluralism.

As later scholars, such as Herberg, Sklare, and Glazer, have made clear, that pluralism served as the organizing principle for the successive generations of immigrants and their children.[4] It also provided the means of integration for lower-, middle-, and upper-class Jews. Typically, the Orthodox drew support from those closer to the immigrant generation's experiences, those not yet advanced fully into the middle-class, particularly in education and occupational status. The Conservative gained support from those at least one generation removed from immigrant status, those who had moved fully into the middle-class. Those who were two or more generations past the immigrant experience and who were advancing above middle-class status were attracted to the Reform.

Although the socioeconomic, immigrant, and social class dis-tinctions among these three denominations usually held true, the overarching commitments of all residents to acculturation into American society and to economic advancement cemented the community into a cohesive whole. The cohesiveness and increas-ing homogeneity of Jews in their life-style was undoubtedly fos-tered by close residential proximity to Italian and Irish residents, and in the later decades (from the 1930s on), by shared concerns with anti-Semitism in Europe and activism on behalf of the Zionist cause.

Thus from the latter half of the 1910s through the 1940s, Boro Park evolved into a Jewish suburb—a community with many of the land-use and demographic characteristics of then-emergent suburbs. As in suburbs elsewhere, established Jewish institutions (e.g., congregations, community centers, lodges) increasingly be-gan to serve the large cross-section of the local Jewish community rather than perpetuate particular practices or ideals of any single Jewish subgroup from one locality or region of ethnic "mother country." Even the Orthodox congregations adopted a variety of typically American practices such as sermons in English, leisure time social activities for members and community, social action programs, and less strict separation between the sexes, all of which made them appealing to a wide cross-section of the community. Some of the larger congregations, such as Beth El or Anshe S'fard, made their reputations by hiring world-renowned cantors.

Their Orthodox leadership, as that of synagogues in the Conservative and Reform movements, passed from what Max Weber might have called traditional or charismatic leaders to elected lay leaders and salaried rabbinic professionals. Sectarian Judaism, so characteristic of immigrant areas of first settlement, was clearly waning in Boro Park as it was wherever Jews were forming new communities.

The Revival of Jewish Sectarianism

Refugees from Nazi persecution and, later, survivors of the Holocaust were singularly responsible for the revival of Jewish sectarianism. Orthodox Jews from Frankfurt, Germany, began to establish their own tightly knit enclave in Washington Heights by the end of the 1930s. Others from Austria, Belgium, Hungary, Rumania, and Poland trickled in at the same time, settling in large numbers in Williamsburg, Brooklyn. Reflecting on this period, George Kranzler writes,

> More than any other single factor . . . the rise of the diamond trade was responsible for the greatest material and spiritual boom Jewish Williamsburg has known. . . . As in Belgium, the majority of those engaged in it were Orthodox Jews who brought their skills with them when they settled in New York. Naturally, they attracted their own type of people (into the industry) when they began to open up shops here. . . . People left the garment, fur, tie-making, and other trades which could not offer earnings like those of the diamond business. . . . Many of the older men had been previously religious functionaries, rabbis, teachers, beadles. Now they abandoned the meager salaries of these professions as well as the low status attached to them in the (American) class order in which the successful businessman occupies the top rung of the social ladder.[5]

The influx of extremely religious immigrants from Hungary infused new vigor and variety into the kosher food industry, and equally religiously oriented immigrants from Russia and Poland stimulated the revival of traditional Jewish education and the formation of new *shtiblekh*.

What was striking sociologically about these developments among New York Jewry in the 1930s, 1940s, and early 1950s was that they were taking place primarily among recent immigrants and in older Jewish neighborhoods, such as the Lower East Side, Williamsburg, and Brownsville, which had long been areas of first settlement for new Jewish immigrants. Therefore, there was little reason to expect that such a sectarian revival would outlast the immigrant generation and the movement of their American-born children into areas of second and third settlement.

The Persistence of Jewish Sectarianism

By the early 1960s, however, it was becoming apparent that the new Jewish sectarianism, created by the Holocaust-era immigrants, would not follow the sectarianism of the earlier generations of immigrants. This became most apparent in Boro Park.

According to the best available estimates, in 1960 there were twenty-five yeshivas and about eighty congregations for a Jewish population of approximately sixty thousand in Boro Park. Of these, four major schools and about a dozen major congregations served the needs of the majority. The rest catered to the requirements of much smaller sectarian clusters.

More than twenty years later, the total Jewish population of the area was about 72,250, according to the latest estimate. This population, however, now supports about fifty yeshivas and one hundred and fifty congregations. The names of the latter read like a travelogue through the *shtetlekh* of prewar eastern Europe: Amshinov, Belz, Bobov, Bratzlov, Chust, Debrecen, Ger, Keresztur, Lubavitch, Munkacs, Nyitra, Papa, Rodomsk, Skvir, Szatmar, Temeshvar, Ungvar, Viznitz—but a handful of the community's congregations take their names from the towns in eastern Europe (Hungary-Rumania, Czechoslovakia, and Poland) from which they trace their rabbinic leadership and many of their respective members trace their ancestry.

The largest groups, such as the Bobover, the Szatmarer, the Belzer, the Munkacser, and a few others, have evolved a complete network of organizations including schools, shops, ritual baths, and free-loan societies. These groups now number in the tens of thousands, thus, making Boro Park the sectarian Jewish community *par excellence* in 1982. More than half its population belongs to one or another of the hasidic *shtiblekh*, which have proliferated in the area since the mid-1960s. Schoolage children, who represent approximately 30 percent of the local population, attend the numerous yeshivas associated with some of the larger hasidic groups. Long established communal yeshivas (so-to-speak non-sectarian) have suffered continuous decline in the past decade or two. The oldest one, Etz Chaim, founded in 1917, closed its doors in 1979. Others, such as the Shulamit school for Girls and Yeshiva Toras Emes, have survived through vigorous recruitment from outside of the immediate neighborhood.

Profile of Sectarian Boro Park

A 1982 survey of 375 randomly selected households in Boro Park provides additional information on its demographic features.[6] The current Jewish population, 72,250, is greater than it was in the 1930s. This number, however, must be seen against the backdrop of significant Jewish population decline from the 1950s through the 1960s which, according to 1970 census-based estimates, was about fifty thousand. In the 1982 survey, 38 percent of respondents indicated that they moved to Boro Park sometime during the previous fifteen years, many arriving from Israel, Russia, and Rumania. Whereas in 1970 the proportion of foreign-born in the community was 34 percent, survey figures indicate that in 1982 the foreign-born adult population was about 43 percent.

Significantly, as in earlier decades, Boro Park still serves as a second area of settlement for large numbers of upwardly mobile Orthodox Jews, many of whom are immigrants. The Jews moving to the community during the past fifteen years, however, are quite different from their counterparts who had moved there earlier. Among those who moved to the community before the mid-1960s, most described themselves as Orthodox, about 25 percent described themselves as Conservative or Reform, and only about 10 percent described themselves as Hasidic. Among those who have moved to the community during the past fifteen years, about 70 percent still define themselves as Orthodox, but now about 25 percent describe themselves as Hasidic, and only 5 percent describe themselves as Conservative or Reform. Given the much higher birth rate among the self-described Hasidic, the hasidic population of the community includes at least half of Boro Park's Jewry.

Thus, the 1970s and 1980s have witnessed an increasing hasidic presence in Boro Park, a phenomenon that has gone hand-in-hand with dramatically increased birth rates when compared either to earlier Boro Park or to Jewish communities elsewhere. Earlier residents had an average of 2.8 children per household, and about 17 percent had five or more children. Among those who have moved to the community during the 1970s and early 1980s, there were an average of 3.4 children per household, and 26 percent had five or more children. About five thousand babies are delivered annually at the Maimonides Medical Center on 48th Street and 10th Avenue.[7] According to hospital spokesmen, this is about double the rate for any other hospital in New York City.

This pattern of population growth has accompanied the proliferation of yeshivas and *shtiblekh* under sectarian auspices. Interestingly, this growth pattern also has had a tremendous effect on the local housing market. Boro Park has become one of the most ambitious centers of residential real estate activity in the city during the past five years. "Land prices have soared as contractors buy old frame houses on side-streets off the main avenues, demolish them, and build new two-family and three-family houses (on the same lots). Dilapidated walk-ups have been bought and rebuilt as cooperative apartments selling for $80,000 to $130,000."[8] The pressure on land values and house expansion is only partly fueled by the sheer growth of the local population. It is also, and perhaps even more importantly, fueled by the desire of various hasidic group members to live as close as possible to their *rebbes* and *shtiblekh,* as well as other family members. Thus by 1982 sectarian Judaism had moved successfully from first areas of settlement to a second area of settlement, and from the immigrant generation to the second and even third generation—although 13 percent was foreign-born.

Close observation of this community also suggests that sectarian Judaism has found a way to blend the commitments to particularistic survival with participation in the economy and politics of the metropolis. Community residents are still employed heavily in the jewelry trades and the manufacture and sale of dry goods. However, many of the American-born children and grandchildren also work in retail and wholesale merchandising (particularly small electric and electronic appliances), computer programming, local construction, civil service bureaucracies, and community service.

Community leaders also have become sophisticated in the ways of New York's ethnic politics. Given the cohesiveness of each subcommunity under its own sectarian leadership, many local rabbis and institutional administrators have become figures to be courted by aspirants for elected office. In addition, since 1973 the Council of Jewish Organizations of Boro Park has served as an umbrella organization for most of the sectarian subcommunities, helping them individually and collectively to attract government support for such programs as CETA, youth services, housing, home energy asistance, and resettlement of Russian immigrants. These activities have made many of the leaders of the sectarian Jewish subcommunities in Boro Park significant players in Brooklyn and New York area politics. These activities also have confirmed to all of sectarian Jewry that one can remain legitimately within one's chosen worldview and life-style and also be an active and respected participant in New York's political and economic life.

The Significance of Boro Park

The perpetuation and growth of sectarian Judaism in Boro Park during the past two decades contrasts sharply with the adaptation strategies of all earlier generations of America's Jews. It also controverts prevailing sociological wisdom concerning the adaptation of immigrant ethnic-religious minorities to the mainstream of American culture and society. For both these reasons it is a noteworthy example. Social scientists are challenged by it to ponder the limits of acculturation as a necessary prerequisite to integration into the dominant society.

The vitality of the rigorously Orthodox community in Boro Park comports with a larger theoretical perspective developed recently by scholars of contemporary Jewish Orthodoxy. Social scientists Charles Liebman and Menachem Friedman each have turned what may be called the "modernity hypothesis" on its head. Classical social theorists anticipated the decline of national, ethnic, and religious loyalties with the advance of industrialization and Western culture. In opposition to this perspective, powerful sectarian religious communities have managed not merely to persist but to thrive under modern conditions.

In his treatment of "Religious Extremism," Liebman credits various aspects of modernity for the ascendancy of Orthodox *rejectionists*, his term for the more insular Orthodox. "Economic prosperity [to take but one feature of modernity] . . . permitted the establishment of an elaborate educational network providing intense socialization to rejectionist values."[9]

Menachem Friedman, in his study of Israel's rigorously Orthodox communities, *haredim*, focuses on other aspects of modernity. He notes

> While the [modern] city provided easy opportunities for Haredim in certain spheres of business, at the same time the Haredim became the almost exclusive suppliers of services and accessories connected with religious practice. These factors made it possible to decrease the tension between the anti-economism of the yeshiva and the pragmatic values of the economy. . . . In the setting of the big city, the haredi ghetto provides a solid territorial base for various subgroups in the community. It enables the Haredim to maintain an independent culture which can borrow selectively elements from the surrounding culture, and to maintain a large measure of internal social control.[10]

All of these processes and more have been at work in Boro Park. Affluence, intensive education and socialization, occupational specialization, and territorial concentration have served to invigorate and fortify sectarian Orthodoxy in Boro Park. These factors emerge not despite the modern, industrialized society, but because of it.

Notes

1. Charles S. Liebman, "Orthodoxy in American Jewish Life," *American Jewish Year Book* 66 (1965): 21–98.

2. Michael Gold, *Jews Without Money* (New York: Horace Liveright, 1930), pp. 155–56, 158.

3. See my book, *From Suburb to Shtetl: The Jews of Boro Park* (Philadelphia: Temple University Press, 1979), for documentation.

4. Will Herberg, *Protestant, Catholic, Jew: An Essay in American Religious Sociology* (New York: Doubleday, 1955); Marshall Sklare, *Conservative Judaism: An American Religious Movement* (New York: Schocken, 1972); Nathan Glazer, *American Judaism* (Chicago: University of Chicago Press, 1957).

5. George Kranzler, *Williamsburg: A Jewish Community in Transition* (New York: Philipp Feldheim, 1961), pp. 54–55.

6. Egon Mayer, *The Boro Park Community Survey, 1982–1983* (New York: Council of Jewish Organizations of Boro Park, 1983), pp. 6–14.

7. *New York Times*, 21 May 1982.

8. Ibid.

9. Charles Liebman, *Deceptive Images* (New Brunswick, N.J.: Transaction, 1988), pp. 35–36.

10. Menachem Friedman, "Haredim Confront the Modern City," *Studies in Contemporary Jewry* vol. 2, ed. Peter Y. Medding (Bloomington: Indiana University Press, 1986), p. 93.

Part III
Personal Perspectives on Modern Jewish Communities

9

Some Days Are More Important: A Memoir of Immigrant New York, 1903–1913

Samuel Golden

Introduction

DEBORAH DASH MOORE

When he was in his sixties and still actively involved in the business he had built, Samuel Golden sat down in his Riverside Drive apartment to dictate his memoirs. Looking out of windows facing the Hudson River, Golden imagined his life as a Jewish Horatio Alger. Born into poverty on the Lower East Side, Golden rose steadily in the printing business until he reached the graciousness of Riverside Drive. Although he was the child of immigrant parents, his life story fits neither the typical second-generation saga nor the myth of Horatio Alger. Elements of both characterize his past, yet neither provides a ready lens with which to view his life.

Like most second-generation Jews, Golden could have anticipated a home environment sustaining his ambitions. The earnings of two older brothers born abroad contributed to the family income; hence, Samuel might have looked forward to the typical Jewish path of upward mobility through education. Instead, his mother's incapacitation disrupted this plan, and, before he reached the age of bar mitzva, Golden experienced a dislocation as profound as if he had been reborn as an immigrant, but one with a sure knowledge of English.

At this point in Golden's life story, elements of the Alger myth appear. The Horatio Alger adventures describe a worthy, poor, young man who makes his fortune through ready wits, pluck, drive, and a heavy dose of luck. Samuel Golden possessed the first three, as well as an exceptional oratorical ability that charmed many he met and produced the required dose of luck. His adolescence is studded with the paternalistic interest of strangers who decided to help. But Golden later took pains to repay the help, and as an adult often tried to assist other worthy young people in similar difficult straits.

This assistance illustrates how networks of personal charity worked, even in an age when philanthropy was becoming systematized and institutionalized. Aid rendered by the department store magnate Edward Blum of Abraham and Straus was marked by a noblesse oblige and genuine concern that belies the standard portrait of German Jews' coolly correct charitable behavior toward their east European brethren. Yet Blum was prompted by a crucial letter of introduction that reflects Jewish involvement in New York City machine politics. Golden's story reveals the impact on him of two New York City Jewish elites rarely viewed together and suggests the power of ethnic ties over mere political affiliation. In contrast, the aid given by the family where Samuel boarded underscores a more typical combination of altruism and self-interest that characterized immigrant patterns of assistance.

The link between politics and religion appears vividly in the memoirs. Both involve passion for the spoken word, the vision of a better society, and a vital sense of shared identity. Neither is reductive, exclusive, or constraining. Golden never describes contradictions between his commitment to socialism and his desire to become a successful capitalist. Nor does one sense a fundamental conflict between Golden's adherence to Judaism and his devotion to social justice. Historians often seek a logical coherence in Jewish politics, ideology, religion, and occupational activity that this individual account subverts.

The narrative breaks off as Golden's adolescent years end, shortly after he lands a printing job. In 1917 he married despite her father's objections, Bella Lasker, a Brownsville public school teacher. Deciding to become a printing salesman, Golden hired at his own expense an assistant bookkeeper to allow him to get away from the office. In 1920 he started his own printing company. Although he soon specialized in printing posters and playbills for the theater, he also used the company to support political causes he valued, such as women's suffrage.

In 1920 Golden returned to school to learn how to draw so he could translate visual ideas into sketches for his printing clients.

"Instead of trying to get business by pleading for an opportunity to quote prices, I would generally present 'ideas' that promoted the new plays and books my customers announced for the future," Golden recalled. "In this way, I believed I avoided just being a peddler," and became instead a "creative printer." Although this pragmatic rationale prompted him to turn to art, the classes he took with Harry Wickey at Wickey's 23rd Street studio introduced him to the world of artists and inspired his life-long passion to bring America's art to its people.

Bringing art to the American public initially meant upgrading the quality of theater poster design. In 1924 Golden bought a printing plant and established Artcraft Lithograph and Printing Company. The plant employed nonunion workers when Golden acquired it, but he soon invited leaders of the printers union to unionize the workers. Artcraft became a leading theatrical printer, not only because of Golden's fascination with the theater, but because of his innovative decision to house under one roof all elements involved in printing, from original art work to final proofs. Collections of his posters, window cards, and souvenir books are housed in the Library of Congress, the Museum of the City of New York, and several university libraries.

Golden's expanding world of artists, theater producers, and managers collapsed during the depression and his business declined drastically. New ventures in theatrical producing failed—especially a play he coproduced with David Boehm, *Sing High, Sing Low*. Golden's earlier involvements in off-Broadway productions had succeeded, including a play, *Precedent*, based on the Tom Mooney case, written by his younger brother Israel. Golden suffered financially and emotionally, withdrawing from active business life for two years. His family included two children, Irene and Allen, both born in the 1920s (a first-born son died as an infant). Responding to these financial hardships, his wife returned to teaching, now at the high school level. The family moved from one Brooklyn apartment to another, each move reflecting Golden's varying fortunes.

After his withdrawal period, and supported by friends and family, Golden started over again in the mid-1930s, building a printing business that brought fine art to millions in their own homes. Golden and artists including Adolph Dehn and Rockwell Kent developed the American Artists Group, a company offering fine art to the American public. Returning to a historic use of printing as an inexpensive medium of artistic reproduction, Golden experimented with reproducing art at popular prices and selling it in such unconventional places as bookstores and department stores. Art critics hailed the large series of unsigned black and white prints, lithographs, etchings, and woodcuts, created by more than thirty young American artists produced by the American Artists Group. These inexpensive prints prefigured the popular art posters and art reproductions of a later period. Golden also applied his commitment to fine art to greeting cards and experimented with printing a small series of silk scarves designed by artists. Artists received royalties for their work and retained possession of the originals. The innovative approach quickly achieved solid success and raised artistic and technological standards in the greeting card field. The greeting cards especially reached a large public that was reluctant to spend $2.75 on an art print. The cards often were framed by those who appreciated their artistic beauty.

During the postwar decades, Golden expanded the American Artists Group's printing ventures into book publishing. He published a substantial series of monographs on individual American artists, containing reproductions and brief autobiographical statements, several volumes on technique, and major autobiographies by such artists as Jerome Myers, Harry Wickey, and Guy Pene du Bois. Although not successful commercially, his publishing activity reflected a reverence for books and the world of artists. Throughout his life, Golden hungered for the learning associated with books and school that he had never satisfied. Events that disrupted the normal contours of the life of a second-generation American Jew prevented him from fulfilling his intellectual ambitions, although he attended night classes and completed the Regents high school course.

Golden never lost his love of oratory and his willingness to seek out good speakers irrespective of their creed. While still in his teens, he walked to Temple Emanu-El to hear Judah Magnes preach. Later, during his Brooklyn decades, he heard other rabbis, especially Nathan Kraus and Stephen Wise, valuing their political and religious stands. He avidly attended the sermons of John Haynes Holmes, sometimes taking his children with him to the Community Church to listen to the pacifist preacher. After moving to Riverside Drive in 1939, Samuel and Bella became strong supporters of Mordecai Kaplan. They joined the Society for the Advancement of Judaism and became adherents to the Reconstructionist movement. Undoubtedly Kaplan's oratorical skills, as well as his philosophy of Judaism, appealed to Golden.

Dictating his memoirs represented for Golden a synthesis of the spoken and written word, two forms of communication he loved. But the process also involved a measure of pain, self-reflection, and self-criticism, and these color the recollections that survive. The project was cut short by Golden's sudden death on 22 April 1963 at age 67.

Some Days Are More Important

SAMUEL GOLDEN

The purpose of this memoir is to report the busy life of a first-generation American fortunate enough to enjoy life from a cultural and economic level. Another reason for attempting to create this record is to compensate for the feeling that I not only didn't know any grandparents, but doubted very much whether I ever really had any anywhere. Now that I'm a grandpa myself, I have a notion that some of the things I have lived through may give my children and grandchildren some insight as to what things were like when I was young at the beginning of this century.

Instead of lamenting what has passed or worrying about things that are not yet, I regard every morning as a fresh challenge to learn something new, to encounter something entirely new, to try to think some good or do some good—and so to make each day count as an important addition or segment to a useful life. I regard every day as the next play in any game, as the decisive one. I realize, however, that there are some days that are more important than others. Those are the days we never forget. Those are the days that are important because they are the days when we start along an entirely new road, open doors that often change the direction of our life.

*   *   *

As I awoke I had a feeling that there was something very strange about this very hot July morning. It felt very different from any other morning. Like so many other early summer mornings, it was hot and humid and the only things stirring were flies who, since all the windows were wide open, seemed to take possession of the house.

There was no such thing as air-conditioning in 1903, and on Monroe Street between Scammel and Jackson on the Lower East Side even window screens were luxuries that few in the neighborhood could afford. Flies and mosquitoes, no matter where you turned, were everywhere. It seemed to me that we got more than our fair share of these pests in our home. Now I realize that there was a very good reason why the flies were so particularly partial to us. It never occurred to me at the time that the stables in the backyard of our house were to a large extent the really big attraction for the flies.

To cope with these constant annoyers, half a dozen swatters and several tightly folded newspapers were strategically placed around the house so that no matter where you sat, stood, or lay, you could stretch out, pick up one of the swatters or one of the newspapers, and fight your enemy. And there were battalions of flies on every side, no matter where you turned. Another effective method in reducing the population of flies and mosquitoes was to catch them on streamers of sticky flypaper that were suspended from all the gaslight chandeliers and hung on door knobs and the like. These gummy streamers, with their sickening oversweet smell, were suspended all around the house, in every room, and it was all one could do not to walk into or lean up against one of these streamers and have it stick to you. Heaven help you if your hair brushed against it!

This was the first morning that when I awoke I was not able to see my mother cleaning, cooking, straightening things, and hustling around the place. Not until this morning did it ever occur to me that there was any other place that my mother could be but in the house when we got up in the morning. In a few minutes after I awoke, my father came into the house. He looked worn and tired. He told us at once that he had left very early in the morning with my mother and my little sister and had taken them to the hospital.

My little sister was the youngest child and the only girl in our family. I had two older brothers who were born in Russia and were seven and eight years older than I, and the two younger brothers before my sister arrived. From birth she was a very beautiful and delicate child and looked very much like my mother.

During this terribly hot summer siege, my mother did everything to make my little sister comfortable, but that still meant that the most she could do was to move her cradle as close as possible to the window in front of the fire escape on which some of us boys slept. Three or four days ago my sister took sick, and yesterday she began vomiting and became very sick. Everybody in the house was forgotten while a doctor came back and forth several times the first day, and at least two or three times the next day. There was general agreement that my sister's condition was getting worse, and that some specialists had to be brought in. I have no idea of where the money came from. I remember seeing two or three doctors standing around in a huddle.

My mother didn't come home all day and night. Father left again in the morning. Both returned late in the afternoon.[1]

* * *

The day my mother left Russia was a very important day for me, since I was the first in my family to be born on American soil. My father arrived in this country some time in 1887 and then seemed to have forgotten all about his wife and my two older brothers left in Russia. One of them hadn't been born when he left Russia. Though both my parents came from religious homes, time and circumstances made mother a very orthodox and a strictly religious woman, while my father, though not irreligious, was not a pious observer of religious customs and holidays. My father always maintained that he had a very hard struggle and didn't want to bring the family over until he could comfortably support them.[2]

When my mother arrived in America, my father was running a little delicatessen store on Carmine Street in lower New York.[3] To my mother's consternation and surprise, she discovered it was not only not kosher, but ham and pork were being sold, and the store was open on her Sabbath, Saturday. This was something she could not possibly reconcile herself to, and as the legend came down, whether true or not, she did everything she could to get my father out of this business. For as many years as I knew my father, he would tell how he was well on the way to becoming a successful businessman until my mother arrived and did everything she possibly could to have him give up a *trefe* business and stop working on Saturday.

Many a time I heard the painful subject brought up, embroidered differently each time, but always my father would blame mother for having accomplished within less than a year what it took him nearly seven years to build up. Though it may have been the custom and took a lot of money to bring a family from Europe, he never spent much time explaining why he left my mother for seven years. She probably would have remained there for a longer time if it weren't for some of her relatives in Russia who felt that they ought not to wait any longer and found a way to send her and my brothers to her husband in the United States.[4]

As I look back now, I know that we were very poor. The only memories, however, that I have of poverty were periodic unemployment seasons during which my father earned no money. During such times, slowly but surely the food we ate underwent a complete change. Tastier dishes disappeared and the menu eventually consisted almost entirely of bread, butter, herring, and potatoes. The happiness of my childhood was hardly affected by this change of menu because there were many religious holidays which mother celebrated by doing all kinds of extra baking and cooking of special holiday foods, like *taglach*, for the festive table.

No matter what mother would do without, the only thing that she insisted must never be interrupted was our religious and Hebrew education. Day in and day out, after a regular school day, we had to spend from one to two hours with a rabbi learning how to write and read Yiddish and Hebrew and studying the Bible. On Saturdays, Jewish holidays, and Friday nights, we would be taken to the synagogue. It was a special treat on Saturday mornings when my father took me to the Educational Alliance[5] on East Broadway to hear Dr. Radin deliver a sermon.[6] This was my first contact with oratory, and I know that Dr. Radin must have been very effective because he created in me an appetite that kept me running for many, many years to hear ministers, rabbis, priests, and political candidates.

Coupling politics with religion came naturally in my life. Growing up on the East Side, my two older brothers were attracted to the Socialist movement. I can remember them hanging a picture of Karl Marx which, within a few hours was not only removed from the wall, but completely destroyed by my mother when she learned that Marx wasn't only the leader of the Socialist movement, but a *geshmatered* Jew (which meant that he denied the fact that he had been born a Jew). The facts were not exactly the way mother said they were, but that didn't stop her from destroying the second and third pictures that my brothers hung before they gave it up as a lost cause.

The heat and intensity of this conflict between my brothers and my mother naturally aroused an interest on my part in socialism and politics. I early became aware that the world didn't offer everybody an equal opportunity, and I was hardly twelve years old when I was beginning to make speeches, getting all excited about making the world a better place for my grandchildren. I was very young when I read Gustavus Myers's *History of American Fortunes*.[7] After that, I was sure that anybody who in any way supported the capitalist system was necessarily cruel, wicked, and corrupt.

I remember marching in a parade that was organized to register a protest against President Theodore Roosevelt[8] for trying to prejudice the American public against the labor leaders Moyer, Haywood, and Pettibone as "undesirable citizens."[9] They were being blamed for the murder of a former governor of Idaho because they tried to organize the much exploited miners and workers in the western part of the country. Nothing was too brutal in this struggle. If it had not been for the quick mobilization of all liberal, labor, and socialist forces, the frame-up of Haywood and Pettibone would have succeeded.[10] This case brought into prominence young Clarence Darrow,[11] who defended the indicted labor leaders, and William Borah,[12] district attorney of Boise, Idaho, at the time. After a long trial, Haywood and Pettibone were exonerated and one of the principal conspirators, Harry Orchard, went to prison.[13]

When I was young, the Ludlow massacre[14] made the name of Rockefeller[15] anathema to anybody who had the slightest concern about his fellow human beings. Hence, my early training religiously and politically prepared me for some exciting scraps that I got into as the years passed.

I should have elaborated on the fact that my mother's resentment of socialism was not due to opposition either to its philosophy or to the personality of Karl Marx. It was due more to the fact that my oldest brother Meyer, who had been very religious and a good student on his way to becoming a rabbi, had a complete change of heart. He abandoned everything with which he was vitally concerned until now that dealt with the study and observance of religion. I have been told that Meyer was an exceptionally brilliant student and was well advanced in the study of Talmud when he was still in Russia. When he arrived in this country, it took him only one year to complete and graduate from public school, after which he was immediately admitted to Rabbi Isaac Elchanan Theological Seminary.[16] The very same earnest, intense, and complete absorption in the Talmud and the Torah and his preparation for becoming a rabbi was reversed, and he spent considerable time attacking the religious teachings he profoundly believed in before. Thus my mother's opposition to everything connected with Karl Marx and socialism meant opposition to everything responsible for making an atheist of her son who was well on his way to becoming a rabbi, had he not absorbed the new social ideas.

* * *

When I was very young and saw my mother form a committee of two or three women or join such a committee, I knew that some neighbor in our house or nearby was in dire circumstances. Early one Sunday morning I remember Mrs. Lenick and Mrs. Cohen opening the door and asking my mother to step out into the hallway. When she returned she said in Yiddish, "Don't leave the house until I come back. Take care of Izzy and Davey and see if you can get the dishes washed that are in the sink. I will be gone for about a half an hour and see that everything is all right when I come back."

I realized from the way my mother measured the handkerchief in the palm of her hand that she was on her way out on another mission to collect some money for somebody that needed it more than we did. The idea of two or three women going together was to reassure anybody they approached that there was a real need, and yet not to have to disclose for whom the money was being gathered. The anonymity of the recipient was more important than anything else.

*   *   *

There were several days in the year that you never could forget. None it seems was more picturesque than the day before Passover week. There wasn't a sidewalk on any street that wasn't piled high with every conceivable kind of *chometzdika* food and rubbish that had been found in every Jewish home. It all had to get outside. Passover compelled a thorough spring cleaning, because there must be nothing *chometzdik* left in the house during Passover. *Chometz* included anything that in any way had come in contact with the ordinary, everyday, leavened bread. Every dish, pan, and utensil that was used during the year had to be put away for a week and another set of dishes had to be used during the Passover holiday when unleavened *matzos* replaced ordinary bread and rolls.

One of the most exciting rituals of the year was the search through the house for any *chometz* in every corner of every room. The ceremony usually started with father gathering his family and saying, "Now, let us go on a search for *chometz*, and make sure that there isn't a crumb of it left anywhere in this house. We must do this so that tomorrow night we can begin celebrating the Passover." Every member of the family, with lighted candles in his hands, fell into a procession following the father of the house. He generally carried a little brush or whisk broom and a large wooden or metal spoon, and when anyone found any bread crumbs, they were brushed into the spoon. When the search was finished, to make sure that no *chometz* would fall out, the spoon was thoroughly secured and bound with cloth. Then everyone watched as the bandaged spoon was taken out to the street and thrown into the blazing community bonfire.

There was nothing quite as dramatic in preparation for other holidays, yet there was something memorable about the Rosh Hashana and Yom Kippur holidays. Parents would buy new clothes for their children so that they would be all dressed up when they went to the synagogue on the High Holy days.

I must have been eight or nine years old, dressed up and on my way for the first evening service of Rosh Hashana ushering in the new year holiday. We lived on Monroe Street on the mostly Jewish Lower East Side. However, when you crossed Cherry Street, where there were few Jews, you had to be on your lookout. On this particular night, a group of boys out for a little fun, surrounded me. As I looked around, it seemed as if every one of the boys had an egg in his hand. They didn't throw any at me. They just tried to slip eggs into all of my pockets—on the right side and the left side, the vest pocket and any pocket they could get at. As soon as they had shoved several eggs into my pockets, they began smacking and slapping at the pockets until they were sure that the eggs were completely crushed.

You can imagine what it meant to wait for the Rosh Hashana holy days to get a suit, only to have it ruined before you even were able to show it to everybody in the synagogue! When they left me, my pockets were dripping. Instead of proceeding to the synagogue, I tearfully ran back home.

The purchase of a new suit was an annual event of the greatest significance. There would be conversation for weeks about the day that father would take us to Canal Street to buy us new clothes. Rosh Hashana either coincided with the reopening of the schools or came a little earlier or later. The new clothes, however, were only worn for the first time so as to be shown off during the holidays at the synagogue. The clothes' subsequent wear at school and everywhere else was only incidental to their holiday display.

My father didn't just go to one store and buy me a suit. There was trading to be done. There was no such thing in those days as a price label that really meant what it said. In order to get an idea of how the market was running, my father would go in and out of half a dozen stores. One he usually left for near the end was Joseph Marcus's store on Canal Street, the biggest store on the street. Mr. Marcus would stand at the door, a short man with a big gray mustache who would always give my father a very enthusiastic greeting and then would be the one with whom father generally made his final trade as we would begin going out of the store. Mr. Marcus was not only the most successful clothier on Canal Street, but before he died, president of the, at that time, all-powerful Bank of the United States.[17]

The market or asking price was only the point from which bargaining started. A suit marked $15 meant to my father that he'd start by offering half, many times coming very close to what he actually had to pay. Before a purchase would be made, you generally went out of the store several times only to be brought back by either the boss or a puller-in. Everybody would, as he made an offer, say that this was the last and final offer and he couldn't possibly do better. Then the merchant would swear that he'd be losing money making the sale at the price my father would offer. However, many a time I saw my father stand his ground and make his purchase at a considerably lower price.

* * *

It is very difficult for me to place exactly whether it was 1905 or 1906 that we moved up to Harlem from the East Side. I think we moved because it was no longer possible for all of us to live in the small Monroe Street apartment. In addition, my older brother Harry had completed a business course and was working, as was my brother Meyer. I know that I was sad the day we moved because of severance of affiliations with boys in the neighborhood and the school I went to. I seemed to be moving into an entirely new world.

Late in the afternoon, after the moving van had unloaded all of our things at our new home on the east side of Park Avenue on 98th Street, my father said, "Before we begin setting things up, let's go out for a walk and see what our new neighborhood looks like." It was probably four or five o'clock in the afternoon. Within a couple of minutes after I had walked out of the house with my father, a group of young boys surrounded us and before I could look around, I saw my father's hat being thrown into the gutter. My father had a beard, and we probably were the first Jews to live on 98th Street east of Park. As I bent down to pick up my father's hat, I was struck with a heavy stick across the face and almost immediately was covered with blood. I had a deep cut at the top of my nose.

This was my first awareness of anti-Semitism. Only within the proverbial "stone's throw" was a thoroughly Jewish community. The mistake my father made was to rent an apartment on the east side of the Park Avenue tracks instead of going to the west side. There were bridges across the tracks at 90th and 100th streets but not at 98th Street. All one had to do was to cross over the tracks and immediately you were in the middle of a Jewish community.[18]

We probably remained on the wrong side of the tracks for a year, maybe a little more, and then moved into the heart of Harlem, on 106th Street between Madison and Park. One of the first things my mother did when we moved to Harlem was to find a Hebrew teacher for me. I also managed to find a number of friends. It was here that my affiliation with things political began. We started going around to the headquarters of the Socialist Party on Madison Avenue between 103rd and 104th Streets. It wasn't very long before we organized a young Socialist Club that later grew to be the national organization known as the Young Peoples Socialist League (YPSL).

On any possible occasion, without coaxing, I would get up and deliver a speech or get into a debate, so that I was continually embroiled in one argument after another. One of these speeches or something I did attracted the attention of an elderly gentleman named Edgar Edgerton, who felt that somebody with my talent ought to be given special training in public speaking. I thought I already was getting first-hand instruction because I would go a good long way if there was a chance to hear a good speaker. Any orator held me spellbound, whether a national figure like a Debs,[19] or a Bryan,[20] or merely a capable stump speaker who by one trick or another could manage to interest his audience.

However, Mr. Edgerton insisted on paying for a course in public speaking at the Rand School,[21] in those days in a brownstone on East 19th Street. The teacher of the class was Professor George R. Kirkpatrick, a famous Socialist orator and debater, and who, on one occasion, was candidate for Vice-President on the ticket headed by Eugene V. Debs.[22]

I attended classes which were held on Sunday afternoons. Each week after the first three or four lectures, two members of the class were assigned subjects on which they had to deliver a five-minute talk. I wish that I could remember the subject he assigned to me on the Sunday afternoon I was to be the speaker. I do remember, however, that as I stood up and started delivering my speech, I kept walking from one side of the platform to the other and felt that I was commanding the undivided interest of my audience all the way.

When I was through, Professor Kirkpatrick started by saying that he thought I had organized my talk very well and that some of the points I had made were quite good. However, the important criticism he wanted to stress was the fact that I distracted the attention of my audience by continually walking back and forth. Standing up straight, he indicated how, within an area of three feet, he could sway, or lunge, go up and down, charge sideways, in all directions, and bring all kinds of gestures into play. "You can use all the gestures you want," he said, "but stay within that three feet." Instead of being completely demolished, when Professor Kirkpatrick was through, I told him that I had listened to Eugene Debs talk for over an hour and a half at the Hippodrome and that from the moment he started he walked from one end of the platform to the other, which ran from 43rd to 44th Street; and yet, if one dropped a pin, you would have heard it because Debs had so completely commanded the undivided attention of his audience.

I felt I had delivered a telling argument and that my professor would not know how to meet it. Without thinking for a moment, Professor Kirkpatrick got up and said, "If you must imitate great men, try to imitate them in their greatness, not in their weakness. Eugene V. Debs would probably have been a great orator even if he stood on his head because he was a genius and his devotion, sincerity, and concern for his fellowmen made him the great and compelling orator that he was. Don't imitate great men in their weaknesses because that's easy. Anybody can do that. Try to find out and imitate what it is that makes them great. Anybody can move from one place to another, but that will never make an orator great. It's his head, not his heart that does that."

The first political campaign I remember was 1904, when Theodore Roosevelt was the Republican Party presidential candidate against Alton B. Parker. It seemed as if political meetings were going on at every corner. In many cases there would be two or three on one corner, and it was very noticeable that neither a Socialist nor a Republican would dare set up a platform or a truck from the back of which an orator could plead his cause. The corners with the saloons were completely Tammany Hall property.

I remember one Socialist standing on the back of the truck and beginning an address, when all of a sudden a rather good-looking—shall we call him son?—came forward and said, "Shake, brother, I'm with you." The Socialist orator, surprised, extended his hand, only to have it yanked and find that he was in the gutter and really in quite a mess.

However, there were plenty of courageous men and women who just couldn't be daunted. Those were the years when J. G. Phelps Stokes,[23] John Spargo,[24] Robert T. Hunter,[25] Meyer

London,[26] Morris Hillquit,[27] Algernon Lee,[28] William Mailly,[29] and men like Ben Hanford[30] and Abe Cahan[31] of the *Jewish Daily Forward* were carrying on a fight that would brook neither intimidation nor physical danger.

Speechmakers on political corners were always subject to listeners' heckling. When I was making speeches, we were subject to interruption by any policeman who felt that he didn't want you to hold a meeting. You had to meet the whims and caprice of the individual policeman on the corner in order to hold a meeting. That was why the Socialist Party in those days informed all members that the guarantee of free speech could not be denied by a policeman and that it was not necessary to obtain a permit for a meeting unless there was some good reason to believe that it might result in a disturbance or create noise in an area where it was prohibited, like a hospital. However, there was no reason why one couldn't step up on a stump and deliver a talk on a busy business corner.

With all of that, the Young Socialist League arranged for a meeting at the corner of 116th Street and Lenox Avenue on Tuesday, 11 August 1908, and I was to be one of the speakers. After I was on the platform for five or six minutes, a policeman came over and wanted to talk to me. Knowing that would break up the meeting, I asked one of the boys on the committee, standing alongside the platform, to talk to the policeman and see just what he wanted. While the policeman was explaining that he wanted us to shut up shop, the crowd had grown. I imagined that he realized that any attempt to stop the meeting would be difficult, and that the best thing he could do was to forget the matter. That's the way it seemed to me. But what he actually did when he left our meeting was to call a riot squad to help him break up the meeting. The first group of about seven or eight policemen arrived. But by this time there was an audience of over a thousand people hanging on to everything I was saying. I am quite sure the crowd liked me and would have come to my help. A call went in for more police.

When the second squad arrived and an officer came up to me and told me that I was under arrest, I at once decided to stop the meeting. I told the audience to please disperse peacefully because the meeting was being stopped by the police. The kindliness and decency I was to encounter from that moment definitely was most surprising. It shook my prior belief that all opposition to socialists or socialism was necessarily corrupt, inhuman, and cruel.

Instead of loading me into a police wagon, the police took me by subway to the 125th Street station and there booked me on a charge of disorderly conduct. When the officer who booked me learned that I was only twelve and a half years old, he could not send me to the Tombs[32] downtown, but had an officer take me down to the Gerry Society,[33] which I think was located on Madison Avenue somewhere in the neighborhood of 23rd Street. There the man in charge, a very nice person, was very sorry and concerned to think that I would probably have to spend the night in the Gerry Society. He asked me whether there was any way by which he could reach some member of my family by telephone.

Of course, we did not have any telephone in our home, and so the search was made to locate the nearest public pay station. Finally, a call was put in to a drugstore at the corner of 106th Street and Madison Avenue. Though it was ten o'clock at night, whoever answered the phone volunteered to run up to my home and get somebody to answer the phone. In a very little while I heard the officer in charge at the Gerry Society talking to my brother Meyer. The officer told my brother that if my brother would come down immediately, he would be able to take me home under his custody, with the assurance that I would be in court the next day.

The hour was getting late and the officer told me that he left at eleven o'clock. But when eleven o'clock came, he had become involved in a discussion with me and said that he would stay until my brother arrived. So instead of being thrown into the dungeon, at about eleven-thirty, I walked out of the place and went home with my brother. The next morning and afternoon all of the papers carried the story of my arrest. The shading was different, depending upon the political complexion of the newspaper.

On Wednesday morning, 12 August, I went down to the Children's Court, located on Second Avenue somewhere in the neighborhood of 12th Street, and waited until my name was called. Far from being frightened, I think that I was hoping to become a martyr for the cause and help to bring about a new social order. If I had come before a justice who would have been less considerate and less understanding in handling a young twelve-year-old, everything would have been different. I might have been convinced that nowhere in the world except among the socialists was there any decency and that all successful Republicans and Democrats were corrupt and dishonest. Martyrdom, however, was denied to me by a wise judge and I became infinitely more tolerant of people who differed with my political beliefs.

The *New York Herald* on Thursday, 13 August 1908, published the account under the heading "Boy Orator Shines in Juvenile Trial. Samuel Goldstein, aged twelve makes effective plea in Children's Court."[34] The third and fourth headings read: "Speaks on Socialism, Judge May courteously discharges young Demosthenes whose street oratory attracted the police." The full report follows:

> Samuel Goldstein, a socialistic clown, has just experienced that victorious clash with the police which makes for enviable distinction in the set in which he orates. So ably did the embryo Demosthenes plead his cause yesterday in the Children's Court that Judge Mayo discharged him in an address which borders on the apologetic.
>
> The persuasive youth had been the center of a gathering at Lenox Avenue and 116th Street the night before and had necessitated the aid of reserves to get him to the police station, not that Samuel himself was obstreperous. On the contrary, the boy was a model of deportment and policeman O'Brien who made the arrest said as much in a few well-chosen words, appreciative of Samuel's gentility of bearing.
>
> "I asked him if he had a permit to speak," said the policeman. When the boy orator replied that he had not, O'Brien set out to make the arrest. This was an ambition not easily realized, for from all accounts the gathering rivalled a Polo Ground attendance in numbers. And everybody protested against haling [sic] the child socialist off to the dungeon keep. However, Samuel was finally landed. He is neat, brown-eyed and intelligent, and not a bit embarrassed in any sort of company.
>
> Judge Mayo frowned as he heard the testimony and asked Samuel—and by the way, no one would dream of addressing this young speaker as Sam—"Surely your political creed does not advocate special privileges? Why should you be allowed to speak without a permit and others be required to take out a license? You have as much right to air your opinions as I have, but the law says that you must go about it in the legal way and obtain a permit."
>
> "If Your Honor pleases," answered Samuel readily, "I did not know that there was any infraction of the law. It was not my meeting. I was simply an invited speaker and as such I did not understand that it was necessary for me to ask for a permit. In fact, as the Socialist party is recognized politically, I was informed no special permit was required."
>
> The judge nodded in appreciation of the plea, and said that he took a great deal of pleasure in discharging Samuel. He added personal encomiums that Samuel probably will treasure for many a day.
>
> "Thank you, Judge," said Samuel.
>
> "Entirely welcome," said the Judge.
>
> "Good day, Judge."

"Good day, Samuel. Call again; that is, I trust that I may see you another time and another place."

This kind and considerate treatment opened an entirely new world to me, and ever since I have been an infinitely more tolerant person with those whose opinions I was positive were absolutely wrong.

* * *

The summer of 1908 not only proved to be an eventful one but a tragic one for me. Aside from my Socialist activities, I, like Jewish boys of my age, was looking forward to my bar mitzvah sometime in October. But that was not to be, because my boyhood and youth came to an abrupt and sudden end one hot August night. A quick succession of events uprooted me, forced me to become self-reliant and grow up as best I could.

For a time I thought that I was in some way—if not in every way—responsible for what occurred. It was a hot night, and a number of people were sitting on the steps of the stoop where we lived. The conversation, while it touched everything, was mostly devoted to the achievement of the children. I was annoyed and reported to my mother how my father talked deprecatingly of my older brothers while all of the other neighbors were bragging about the accomplishments of their children. My report was thoroughly honest, but I later learned, it was not necessary to tell everything that one hears. All the truth can be too much.

When my father came into the house, a heated argument ensued between him and my mother. Though it was very late at night, my mother walked out of the house; when she came back early the next morning, she was a thoroughly sick woman. She was agitated. I was too young to understand what it was all about. Now I know that it may have been a nervous breakdown, change of life, or mental upset. No attention was given to these, especially then.

Within a couple of days, my brother Harry took my mother to see the famous and old Professor Jacobi.[35] After examining my mother, he told her in my brother's presence that she had a very aggravated case of diabetes and that if she took very good care of herself, she could probably live a half a year or a year.

That was the final blow. After that it wasn't long before she left the house and began making her peace morning, noon, and night with God. And the unfortunate thing is that instead of ever suffering from diabetes, she lived for some fifteen years completely upset by the whole thing. When one gets older, one realizes that such a storm must have been brewing for a long time before it happened. But at the time I thought all of this was due to the arrogance and stupidity of a world-renowned physician who told her what he thought was the truth but which was everything else but that.

When our home was broken up, I probably had to bear the brunt more than any other of my brothers. My two older brothers were nineteen and twenty-one and quite able to take care of themselves and support my mother because they were working. My two younger brothers who remained and stayed with my father, were only eight and ten.

I was a big boy for my age and could easily be taken for fourteen or fifteen. Before I was able to get a job, however, I learned what it meant to sleep in parks and in the subway. In the subway the trick was to change at some double station before coming to the end of the line. One night I overslept and went all the way to the last station at 180th Street. When I attempted to walk from one side of the platform to the other, a policeman stopped me. In spite of my plea that I had overslept my station and didn't have any money with me and only wanted to get back, I was told that the only way I could do so was to get out and pay another nickel. It was a rainy night and the only thing I could do was just go downstairs, stand in the rain, and ask somebody to give me a nickel, the price of a fare, because I didn't have one. I remember that I must have looked pretty honest to the man who gave me ten cents, and upon my request gave me his name and address so that I could send the money back to him, which somehow or other, I did a few days later.

It was difficult to find a job during the summertime and I watched all the ads. I would do anything to get to a place way ahead of time if there was a job, only to find that somebody had gotten there before I did. I tried to sell newspapers but discovered that I was encroaching upon somebody's territory and was told to leave before I got into trouble.

"No experience necessary." To make sure that nobody would be following on my heels, I took the sign along with me and came up and said, "Here's the sign and here I am. I think I can fill the job since you say 'no experience of any kind is necessary'." The first thing that happened was I was asked why I brought the sign along with me. "Well, I thought since I was going to answer it, I would use it as a sort of credential." That sort of started me off on the wrong foot. However, I managed to get a job starting at eight o'clock in the morning until six o'clock at night for $2.50 a week. The shop produced leather novelties sold at various resorts, little pocketbooks with the names Adirondacks or New York City or something like that embossed on them. Aside from sweeping up the place, I brought up whatever supplies came in, and they very often consisted of large barrels of paste or bundles of hides and leather, and just about all kinds of things.

In those days we had no elevator. There was just a great big hole and strong pulleys up at the roof and you pulled everything up on heavy ropes. It was not unusual to read every once in a while of somebody falling right through these holes from the third, the fourth, or the fifth floor, because all that protected you was a kind of a ledge that you stood at as you pulled the ropes. When the package arrived at your floor, you swung at it and moved it in.

I was so anxious to please that I not only did the dirty work, but I asked whether I could stand at the bench and paste together some of the cardboard with the leather that made up most of the articles they were selling. I was getting along fine, I thought, and after some four or five weeks, I asked one of the bosses for a raise. "Oh," he said, "that's alright, next week you'll get $3.00." When my next pay envelope came around, it still only contained $2.50, so I went over and asked my boss whether he had forgotten about the raise he promised me. "Oh, no," he said, "I had to take it up with my partner and my partner just wouldn't approve of my giving you anymore than you are getting. That's all there is." That's the way things were sometimes in 1909. I needed the job too badly to take any chance and continued to work for this salary until their season was over. Then I discovered that I was working on a seasonal job.

After taking on several odd jobs that paid anywhere from two to two and a half dollars, I finally got a job in the stockroom of Ruble and Company at 96 Fifth Avenue. As I ran back and forth from the stockroom to the shipping tables with coats and suits, I often wondered if it would ever be possible for me to continue my interrupted studies. While I was working, on several occasions I went back for a little while and stayed with my father, who had moved from Harlem to Brownsville. For some reason that I can't clearly remember, I again had to leave my father's home and boarded with strangers.

One day as I was going over to the stock table, I saw a man standing with the head shipping clerk. He asked me whether I had my working papers, and if I did, did I have them with me. It was at this point that I lost my job. It wasn't possible for me to have any working papers because I don't think I was much more than thirteen or thirteen and a half at the time. And you had to be at least fourteen to get your working papers.

To meet this crisis, I remembered that one of the nicest men I had ever met was a rabbi-turned-politician, who, in the fluke election of 1907 was elected to the Board of Aldermen from Harlem. His name was Bernhard Goldschmidt.[36] Many a time in a goodnatured way he would stop and listen to me delivering a fiery oration denouncing everybody but the Socialists and the Socialist candidates. When the meeting was over, he would pat me on the back and say that it was just too bad that I couldn't say something nice about him. Now that I was in trouble, it occurred to me that maybe I could in some way get his help.

Although he was no longer a member of the Board of Aldermen, he told me that Alexander Drescher,[37] who represented the Brownsville section, was a very good friend of his and that he would go down to the Board of Aldermen and ask him to do something for me. Within a couple of days, he gave me a letter to Alexander Drescher, who in turn told me that he had spoken to Mr. Edward C. Blum,[38] President of Abraham & Straus, and that if I would present the letter he was giving me to Mr. Blum, he would probably be able to help me.

In spite of the fact that Edward C. Blum was head of a great department store, it was no more than three or four minutes after I had given the reception clerk the letter that he came out and sat down alongside me. I told him my tale of woe, and he asked me how long it would take me to complete my public school education and how much I needed to live per week. I told him that it was hard for me to say how long it would take me to complete my public school education but I would, if I got some help, go and talk to the principal at Public School 109 and tell him that it was my hope that since there were still the months of November, December and January, I could do enough work to make it possible for me to enter the graduating class in February. If I were able to do that, I would undoubtedly be able to complete my course by the end of June.

When I told him that I would probably need two dollars a week to live on, he said, "I will give you three dollars a week. Here is six dollars and you come back here every second week and I will give you the money." I lost no time in going to see Mr. Oswald Schlockow,[39] who was then the principal of P.S. 109. And after telling my story, he rang for Miss Lenkowsky to come down to see him. He proceeded to explain that even though I hadn't been in the 7th or 8th year classes, he felt that I could probably cover enough ground and that if she would take a little special effort to tell me what I ought to do besides the work that was being done in the classroom, I would undoubtedly be worthy of being sent on to the graduating class at the term's end.

As I came into Miss Lenkowsky's class, I was put alongside a boy named Abraham Bernstein. When the class was let out I asked him whether he had any idea where I might be able to find some lodging for as long as I went to school. He at once said that he was quite sure that even though there were five children in his parents' family, that they would be able to squeeze me in some corner or other. And that, of course, was all that I needed. I paid two and a half dollars a week and had a whole half dollar left for myself for candies and books and pencils, and the like.

With Miss Lenkowsky's assistance, I was able to keep right up with the class and read the things that I had missed in the seventh year. Mr. Edward C. Blum, on every occasion when I came back to his office at Abraham & Straus would come out, talk to me, ask me how I was getting along, and give me six dollars to take care of me for the next two weeks.

Only on one occasion during the nine months that I visited his office did he fail to see me, and that was a day that he was out of town, but he left the money for me with his secretary. When I called on him for the last time, about the middle of June, and told him that I would be graduating at the end of the month, in addition to the six dollars, he gave me fifteen dollars so that I might buy myself a suit, shoes, and hat, and wished me all kinds of luck.

I clearly remember that as I stood at the corner of Dumont and Sackman Streets after the graduating exercises wondering what I was going to do now, Mrs. Bernstein, with whom I had been living, and who had been at the graduation to see her own son graduate, tapped me on the shoulder, and said, "What are you worrying about? After all, you're not Atlas. You don't have to carry the whole world on your shoulders. Come on, forget all about it and let's go home and have lunch."

All I needed was this reassurance because I believed that with public school graduation, I would no longer be barred from continuing my studies at the higher level, if and when I could find a way to do so. While it took me several years before I could accumulate all of the money that I needed to pay back the loan, eventually I did it.

During the nine or ten months that I attended P.S. 109, I became acquainted with a number of boys who played important parts in the school's self-government. After I was only in the school for about three months, there was a general election and Alexander Kaiser, who was running for Governor, insisted that I run for Chief Justice, which was probably the second highest office in the school. Despite the fact that I had only been around for a little while, I was overwhelmingly elected and began to dispense justice in disputes between boys and against offenders of the peace and order within our school building. My ability to campaign came in very handy. I also had an idea that being a Chief Justice was a pretty good way to start on the road to a regular career, which maybe I could manage somehow, some way, some time in the future.

Several months back at school had whetted my appetite for more education. It seemed to me that if only I could find how to learn stenography, typewriting, and bookkeeping, I could earn my living the way one of my older brothers did and at the same time continue studying. When I went up to one of the business schools in Brownsville to find out what would be necessary and how much it would cost, I soon discovered that there had to be some way I could earn some money while I was going to school. The bright idea that I could probably go around soliciting customers for the school occurred to me and worked very well. In return for the training I was getting, I would go to homes from five or six o'clock until ten o'clock in the evening. That was the time to see the fathers and mothers of boys and girls who were likely prospects for a business school education.

At the school I went to, on Sunday afternoons there used to be a public forum. Brownsville was so anxious for learning and training that there must have been half a dozen forums of one kind or another going on, and there was one at this school every Sunday afternoon at three o'clock. After I had probably been connected with the school for two or three months, one of the speakers was Don C. Seitz, well known in the newspaper world and general manager of the *New York World*. The subject dealt with the importance of a free press, and when he was finished, there was the usual period of questions. I, of course, didn't miss the opportunity of asking him how free and independent the newspapers of the day were. After spending several minutes answering my question, he asked, "Have I answered your question satisfactorily, young man?" I answered, "Well, I wasn't going to say anything but since you questioned me, I must say that I still feel that the particular issue I raised has not quite adequately been met." He continued talking for about four or five minutes and said, "Young man, you're the kind of man that ought to think actively about being in the newspaper world. It is men like you that we are trying to train and I hope that when this meeting is over, you will come over and see me." This began an important new chapter.

When the meeting was over, Mr. Seitz said to me, "Can you come down to see me some morning during the coming week?" Since I was going to school, I told him that I couldn't quite do it without interrupting the studies I had undertaken in stenography and typewriting. So he said, "If you will come in to see me some afternoon, let's make it Wednesday at three or four o'clock, I will be very happy to see what I can do for you."

When I came to Mr. Seitz's big office on the main floor of the Pulitzer Building at 62 Park Row, he told me that he could easily arrange it so that for a while I could work nights, and continue my studies I had undertaken, and earn some money and get into the swim, so to speak, before I was completely finished with my courses. What a windfall this was! It no longer was necessary for me to spend the evenings going from one home to another trying to sell parents the advantages of a business course.

I spent several years working for the *New York World*, running copy from the editorial room to the composing room and subsequently covering some little stories. Then I was moved into the business department, and finally to the classified advertising department. Mr. Seitz had a kind of fatherly interest in me and tried to see that I got a glimpse of all things around. Many events happened during the exciting couple of years that I was with the *New York World*, but none more exciting than the note I found one morning asking me to see Mr. Seitz.

When I appeared in his office, he told me that there was no sense for me to stay on at the *New York World* any longer. "Now," he said, "with schools of journalism, the only men that will get a chance to get into the editorial departments are college graduates. Your chances in the business department are as good as they are for anybody else, but you are right up to a point today where the next man ahead of you has been with us for nearly fifteen years. In fact, you're making more money than he is because you somehow or other manage to get a story or two in and collect as much from the editorial department as you do from your own job. Hence, unless somebody resigns or dies or the man over you moves up, you are locked in and just can't go anywhere. Now you're much too young to find yourself in such a position and I would like you to try to find a job elsewhere."

I knew that Mr. Seitz had my interest at heart as if he were my own parent, but I needed the job so badly that I said to him, "Mr. Seitz, my hope was that if I were here for a very long time, I might some day do as well as some of the people who have become important here, and after all, even though you say you've been here forty years, you haven't done so badly yourself." He burst out into laughter and then pulled open a drawer on the righthand side from which he took out a card. "You see this card? This means that I have an honorary continued membership in Typographical Union #6, of which I was a member when I went to work for Mr. Pulitzer as the foreman of his night composing room. This card always gave me the feeling that if everything else went wrong, I could still go back into the composing room and set type. Now you haven't got either a trade or a profession and to merely find yourself in some groove in this place and to wait for a decent one for years is something that I do not think you ought to do. So,"—and here he took the memorandum pad that was on his desk—"I'm writing that six months from today, if you are still here, you will be fired. Now go out and try to locate something that will offer you a future and something that you will enjoy doing."

At the time, this seemed like a terrible blow, but as the years rolled on, I have come to realize that he certainly had my interests at heart. There were many exciting days during my employment at the *New York World*. A few stand out against the general run of excitement that carried on from day to day: the sinking of the Titanic[40]; the campaign of 1912 when Theodore Roosevelt was running against Wilson and Taft[41]; the murder of Rosenthal[42] and the whole cleanup of the Police Department with the activities of District Attorney Whitman[43]; and the death of Joseph Pulitzer,[44] which at once was felt throughout the Pulitzer Building and made quite a difference in what the *New York World* was to become. Somehow or other, being in the middle of these things gave one a sense of importance, and among my young friends, the mere fact that I could say that I was on the *New York World* carried a lot of weight. It made me aware that somehow or other, people were impressed by labors regardless of just what one did or how good the performance was.

Now that I knew that I was to spend only six months on the *New York World*, I began looking at everybody that came into the office, weighing the possibilities of finding a job with them. There were two kinds of customers who appeared in our office every day. One was a group of classified agency owners who placed advertising that they had received for the classified columns. The other group was rather crude looking, heavily jowled, big paunches, who seemed to make their money easily but had a hard time dragging the bills out of their pockets. The first man that came in after I saw Mr. Seitz was a man by the name of Hornsby who ran an agency called the Chelsea Advertising, located in midtown. Within a couple of days, I had struck up enough of a relationship for him to ask me to join his Agency whenever I decided to leave the *World*. Instead of waiting, I would make my move very quickly, and I arranged to leave the *World* within a couple of weeks.

I found the job in a classified advertising agency full of petty detail. Not being at my strongest on petty detail, I began to think what other things I might do. I remembered how the employment agency men used to come in and insert ads which ran something like this: "Men for railroad construction work. No experience necessary. Come prepared to leave at once," and then followed the name of the agency. The men that I had met—all of them were very successful. It was the kind of a sure thing that you could make a million dollars if you went into the business, and so I began to investigate. I discovered that the best possible location for that kind of an agency at that time was on Fourth Street between First Avenue and Avenue A. I was beginning to make plans to rent a store when one of the men working along side of me in the Chelsea Agency insisted upon being a partner of mine and wanted to do it on a fifty-fifty basis, with him investing as much money as I. Not only the confidence that he displayed, but the very fact that he was a much older man than I, reassured me that I was on my way towards success, even though events later surprised me.

I discovered that in order to run an agency, you had to get a license from the city. When I got that, I discovered that there were certain records to be kept. So I rented the store, and I bought the furniture, and I got the license, and I got all the necessary recordbooks, and then proceeded to put in an ad the way all the others read. On the Monday morning that I ran the advertisement, a number of men came in. I asked them to wait, and it wasn't until there were about a dozen of them that it occurred to me that I had no idea what I was going to do with them because I had made no arrangement to place them with anybody. Under the circumstances, I telephoned one of the men whom I used to meet over the counter of the *World* and told him that I had a dozen men and he at once volunteered to say that he would come up to get them and that we would split the fee. Thank God he got the men, even though he never gave us any money.

I at once discontinued the ad that was to run all that week and started out going to various railroad employment offices to find out whether they would take any men that we could supply. Far from being welcome, I discovered that something was already known about our being in the field and that they would have none of us. Finally, in desperation, I went down to the Erie Railroad and when I saw the man, pleaded and begged him to take some of our men. He was a middle-aged man who, taking a fatherly interest in me, told me that it was just too bad that I hadn't made my arrangements before I opened the store. He told me how the people in other agencies on the block had complained about my getting right in the middle and said that if any of our men were taken, they would not supply any to the Erie. Under the circumstances, all I could do was to realize that I had come a cropper but I hadn't the slightest idea of what I should do. So I went home and stayed in bed for a couple of days and finally decided that I had certainly pulled a terrific boner and that my career in the employment agency business was over. The only good thing that came out of this experience was that in all of the undertakings I went into after that, I knew that I had to be sure somebody wanted my service, or would use my service, and I never proceeded on a plan unless I knew my advance and had some idea of how I would retreat if everything wasn't the way I imagined it would be.

Now I decided that the thing to do was to bone up on my bookkeeping, shorthand,and typewriting, which I had more or less forgotten during my years in the *New York World*. Throughout a whole summer, morning, noon and night, I was either taking dictation, practicing on a typewriter, or going to school and preparing myself for some inside clerical job. I had a hankering interest in printing and directed all of my energies toward getting into the printing business. I finally got a job with a firm called Fleming and Revele on West 19th Street. They were small printers in a large color printing plant, which in those days did the best work for such magazines as *Harper's*, all of the Conde Nast full-color and highly-illustrated magazines. After assuming control of the office affairs, on the chance now and then of going into the composing room, I struck up a friendship with Mr. Revele, who was in charge of the plant. He told me that if I wanted to learn how to set type, I could, when the day was done, come in and set up anything I wanted to, provided that before I left, I had again distributed the type so that the place was left exactly in the condition as when I started.

I was getting along very well with everybody when one day I got a telephone call from a man who was in the ruling and binding business and he said that he would like me to meet him at luncheon. When I did, he explained to me how a fellow named Lair, who had worked with Fleming and Revele when they were with the Daily Press, decided to leave the Daily Press and to invest some money with Fleming and Revele so that he would become the office manager. This, of course, meant that while I was out of a job, he was sure that I could get the job that Lair was leaving. An appointment was made for me to meet the Davey Brothers, and the first thing that surprised me was that it was located in the basement of the Stephen Merritt Burial and Cremation Company.

Notes

1. The sister died. Samuel was seven years old and grew up with four brothers.

2. The six years of separation between a husband and his wife and family were neither typical nor unusual. They suggest deep strains in the marriage that immigration to America only heightened.

3. Carmine Street is located on Manhattan's west side in Greenwich Village. In the 1890s the Carmine Street area contained a mixed population of blacks, and Irish and Italian immigrants. After the turn of the century, the neighborhood became primarily Italian.

4. The initiative shown by the relatives was unusual and demonstrated their concern that the mother not become an *agunah*, an abandoned wife.

5. In 1889 several Jewish organizations sponsoring cultural activities on the Lower East Side amalgamated to form the Hebrew Institute. Four years later, reorganized and renamed the Educational Alliance, "an Americanizing, educational, social and humanizing" institution, it became nonsectarian. After the turn of the century, the Alliance modified its antagonism to Yiddish and Judaism, sponsoring Yiddish lectures and the People's Synagogue. But Orthodox Jews continued to see the Alliance as a bastion of Reform, and immigrant radicals saw it as a tool to silence social protest through Americanization.

6. Adolph Moses Radin (1848–1909), born in Lithuania, came to Elmira, New York, as a rabbi in 1886. There he also served as a visiting chaplain to the State Reformatory and pioneered in working with Jewish inmates. In 1890 he moved to a New York City congregation and became a chaplain for all the prisons in New York City and Brooklyn. His work with immigrants brought him to the pulpit of the People's Synagogue of the Educational Alliance in 1905.

7. This was first published in 1911, when Samuel was fifteen. Gustavus Myers (1872–1942) was part of a group of journalists and intellectual leaders of

the Socialist party in New York City. Myers left the Socialist party in 1917 because he supported American participation in World War I.

8. Theodore Roosevelt (1858–1919) became president after William McKinley's 1901 assassination and won a second term in 1904 on the Republican ticket. On 2 April 1907, Roosevelt attacked labor leaders awaiting trial in Boise, Idaho, by making public a letter that stated that a railroad magnate was "at least as undesirable a citizen as Debs, or Moyer, or Haywood." Debs responded by attacking Roosevelt, and the public quarrel drew attention to the proceedings in Idaho. The parade in support of the labor leaders took place on 4 May 1907. About twenty thousand people from the Lower East Side marched up to Grand Central Palace to hear speeches.

9. William D. ("Big Bill") Haywood (1869–1928) led the Western Federation of Miners (1896–1908). In 1901 he joined the Socialist party and presided over the 1905 Chicago convention that gave birth to the Industrial Workers of the World (IWW). An advocate of syndicalist trade unionism and a revolutionary style that included violence and sabotage, Haywood was one of the few labor leaders to be admired by both workers and intellectuals. In 1918 he and other IWW leaders were arrested and convicted for their outspoken opposition to America's entry into World War I. Sentenced to twenty years in prison, he jumped bail while awaiting appeal and fled to the Soviet Union in 1921.

Charles H. Moyer, president of the Western Federation of Miners, and George F. Pettibone, a former union member who was a small Denver retailer and good friend of union officials, were abducted with Haywood and charged with conspiring to kill the former governor of Idaho, Frank R. Steunenberg, in 1906.

10. Haywood and Pettibone stood trial separately in 1907 after languishing in jail for a year. After each was acquitted, the charges against Moyer were dropped.

11. Clarence S. Darrow (1857–1938) was admitted to the bar in 1878. In 1887 he moved to Chicago and became a junior partner in the law firm of John Peter Altgeld. He was serving as counsel for the Chicago and North Western Railroad when Eugene Debs and the American Railway Union were held in contempt of court for striking. Because he sympathized with labor's cause, Darrow quit his job to defend them. In 1902 he represented the United Mine Workers in the Pennsylvania anthracite strike. His successful defense of Haywood in 1907 secured his reputation as an outstanding trial lawyer who supported organized labor.

12. William E. Borah (1865–1940) started his political career as a pro-silver Republican supporter of William Jennings Bryan in 1896. He entered the Senate from Idaho in 1907 as a Republican and an admirer of Theodore Roosevelt, and he remained a senator for the rest of his life. He was a special prosecuting attorney in the case of the murder of Idaho's former governor. A fine orator, Borah blended support of such domestic reforms as the income tax, the eight-hour day, and social security, with a dedicated defense of isolationism.

13. Harry Orchard, a drifter and former member of the Western Federation of Miners, tried twice to shoot Steunenberg, who had been governor of Idaho and the bitter opponent of the WFM in the Coeur d'Alene strikes of 1899. Orchard killed Steunenberg on 30 December 1905 by planting a bomb at his home. Orchard was encouraged to confess that he was only a hired hand, which provided grounds to arrest Haywood and Moyer on conspiracy charges.

14. The Ludlow Massacre occurred in 1914 when militia fired on striking miners and their families at a Colorado tent camp. The unprovoked attack was

authorized by the John D. Rockefeller subsidiary, Colorado Fuel and Iron Company.

15. John D. Rockefeller (1839–1937) started his business career with a petroleum refinery. In 1870 he organized Standard Oil Company of Ohio. Within a decade an alliance of forty firms under Standard Oil controlled 90 percent of the petroleum industry. The Standard Oil Trust was declared illegal by the Supreme Court in 1892, and it became a holding company until separated forcibly in 1911. Rockefeller amassed an enormous fortune through investments.

16. Rabbi Isaac Elchanan Theological Seminary, founded in 1897 as an institution for advanced study of Talmud, attracted primarily immigrant youth. The first advanced yeshiva in the United States, it merged with Yeshiva Etz Chaim (an elementary school) in 1915. Meyer was among the first students enrolled. In 1906 and 1908, student protest over the lack of secular studies led to a reorganization of the school's administration and some secular studies were introduced. Subsequently, RIETS became one of the component schools of Yeshiva University but remained devoted to the traditional teaching of Talmud and codes.

17. Marcus got his start in banking by setting up a cashier's desk in his store. People trusted him because he was known as an honest man. The Public National Bank, with Marcus as president, and then the Bank of the United States grew out of these modest beginnings. In the early 1930s when the Bank of the United States suffered a spectacular collapse, repercussions were felt throughout the Jewish immigrant community.

18. From 1900 to 1910, about eighty-thousand Russian Jews migrated to Harlem, making it the second largest concentration of immigrant Jews in the United States. Migration of Russian Jews to Harlem supplanted Irish and Germans, who had predominated. The area west of Lexington Avenue in Harlem, where Samuel later moved, contained more upwardly mobile segments of Russian Jews.

19. Eugene V. Debs (1855–1926), labor leader and socialist, charismatic speaker progressively radicalized, entered politics through the Brotherhood of Locomotive Firemen, a craft union, then left to create an industrial union, the American Railway Union, and finally helped found the IWW as the union arm of the Socialist party. During the 1894 Pullman Strike, Debs was imprisoned for contempt of court and there converted to socialism. By 1901 he organized the Socialist Party of America. He edited a Kansas Socialist weekly and ran for president five times between 1900 and 1920. He opposed U.S. entry into World War I and was indicted and sentenced to ten years in prison under the Espionage Act. He ran for president from jail, however, and received 920,000 votes. Presiding Harding commuted his sentence in 1921. Debs remained a Socialist when the Communists split.

20. William Jennings Bryan (1860–1925) was a powerful Democratic political leader from Nebraska. In 1896 his "Cross of Gold" speech in favor of silver and agrarianism won him his party's nomination for president. He ran again in 1900 but lost a second time to McKinley; a third presidential bid also failed. In 1901 he established the *Commoner* as an outlet for his opinions. His support for Woodrow Wilson in 1912 made Wilson appoint him Secretary of State. He remained a leading Democratic reformer, but in the 1920s Bryan identified with Prohibition, the Ku Klux Klan, and the crusade against evolution.

21. The Rand School of Social Science, founded in 1906, offered courses in public speaking, English grammar and composition, socialist theory and history, stenography, and American history and government. It was one of the early

institutions in the field of worker education, "a bridge between the intellectuals and the rank and file."

22. George R. Kirkpatrick (1867–1937), a vigorous antiwar speaker and pamphleteer and a teacher at the Rand School, ran for vice president on the Socialist ticket in 1916, the year Debs was not the candidate for president.

23. J. G. Phelps Stokes (1872–1960) was a millionaire Socialist, educated at Yale and Columbia. In 1905, his marriage to Rose Pastor, a Jewish immigrant, drew widespread attention. He ran for the Board of Alderman in 1905 on the Municipal ownership ticket and served as president of the Intercollegiate Socialist Society (1907–17). In 1917 he withdrew from the Socialist Party because he supported American participation in World War I. His subsequent biography reads like that of a conservative millionaire.

24. John Spargo (1876–1966) wrote many popular books on Socialism. *The Bitter Cry of the Children*, written in 1906 with Robert Hunter, focused public attention on the exploitation of child labor. Spargo led the right wing of the Socialist Party until World War I when he supported American participation in the war. Born in England, Spargo came to the United States in 1901 and worked as a journalist. In 1909 he moved to Vermont, and after leaving the party he became increasingly conservative, supporting Calvin Coolidge in 1924.

25. Robert T. Hunter (1874–1942), a Socialist and a reformer, tried since his college days to improve the lot of the masses. He entered the settlement movement at Hull House, Chicago, was a resident of Toynbee Hall, London, and became the head worker at University Settlement in New York City in 1902. His book, *Poverty*, published in 1904, stirred public controversy with its claim that 12 percent of the population of prosperous America were poor. Hunter joined the Socialist party in 1905 and ran for several state offices. He chaired the first New York Commission for the abolition of child labor. In 1914 he left the Socialist Party and became increasingly conservative.

26. Meyer London (1871–1926), born in Poland, came to the United States in 1891. He followed his father into radical politics and joined the Socialist Party of America. Admitted to the bar in 1898, he gave legal counsel to many unions, especially in the needle trades, and helped formulate the Protocol of 1910. In 1914 he was elected to the House of Representatives from the Lower East Side and was reelected in 1916 and 1920. He opposed American entry into World War I and tried to protect the civil liberties of dissenters.

27. Morris Hillquit (1869–1933), born in Latvia, came to the United States in 1886. He quickly became involved in radical politics and helped to organize the United Hebrew Trades in 1888. He led the revolt against Daniel DeLeon that created the Socialist Party of America. He favored working with unions and was identified with the moderate wing of the Socialists. Although he ran for political office many times, his 1917 campaign for New York City mayor on a peace platform attracted the most attention. He opposed Communist efforts to take over the party in the 1920s.

28. Algernon Lee (1874–1954) was president of the Rand School from 1909 until his death. A Socialist leader and editor of *The Daily Call* in New York City, he was a Socialist alderman (1918–21). A pacifist, he opposed American entry into World War I. He sided with the moderate Socialists when the party split in 1934 and subsequently favored American participation in World War II.

29. William Mailly (1871–1912) was born in Pittsburgh but grew up in Scotland. He returned to the United States in 1888 and worked as a coal miner. His involvement in the labor movement led him into journalism, and by 1906 he

was editor of *The Socialist* of Toledo, Ohio. In 1903 he became national secretary of the Socialist Party but declined reelection to return to journalism, including writing drama criticism.

30. Benjamin Hanford (1861–1910) was a Socialist party leader, running with Debs for vice-president in 1908. Born in Cleveland, he came to New York City in 1897 and worked as a printer for several newspapers. He ran for governor many times on the Socialist ticket.

31. Abraham Cahan (1860–1951), editor, author, and Socialist, often is linked with the *Jewish Daily Forward,* the Yiddish paper he founded in 1897 and edited until his death. Born in Lithuania, Cahan came to America in 1882 with the first wave of Jewish immigrants. He wrote for Pulitzer's *New York World* and Lincoln Steffen's *Commercial Advertiser* in the 1890s before returning to Yiddish journalism. Cahan also authored several novels, the best known is *The Rise of David Levinsky* (1917). Cahan stood intellectually and emotionally at the confluence of three worlds: the Jewish, the American, and the Russian Socialist.

32. The Tombs was the name given the Men's House of Detention in Manhattan.

33. The Gerry Society was the nickname given to the Society for the Prevention of Cruelty to Children, founded by Elbridge Gerry, in 1875 in New York City. Gerry, a wealthy reformer had been working with the Society for the Prevention of Cruelty to Animals when he discovered an abused child and realized that there were more laws protecting animals than children. He served as president from 1879 to 1901. The Society paid special attention to children performing on the stage and those working in the streets, often having them arrested for violating the child labor laws.

34. Samuel later changed his name from Goldstein to Golden.

35. Abraham Jacobi (1830–1919) founded American pediatrics. Born in Germany, he was studying medicine when the 1848 revolution erupted. Jacobi became involved, was imprisoned, and escaped to the United States in 1853. In 1860 the first chair in pediatrics was established for him. He wrote extensively on children's and women's diseases and helped organize the children's ward at Mount Sinai Hospital.

36. Bernhard Goldschmidt (1858–1922), born in Russia, came to the United States in 1876. A rabbi, he served as superintendent of the Hebrew Convalescent Home. From 1912 to 1914 he was the Republican representative to the Board of Aldermen.

37. Alexander S. Drescher (died 1928) came to the United States from London as an infant after the death of his father. He went into real estate and politics in Brownsville. As a Democrat, he fought for public bathhouses at Coney Island, advocated the extension of the subway to Brownsville, and pushed for the creation of Betsy Head Park in Brownsville. While engaged in civic work, he went to law school at night and entered the bar in 1914. He served as an alderman between 1910 and 1911 and 1916 and 1917, when he was defeated by the Socialist candidate, although Drescher was running on both the Republican and Democratic tickets.

38. Edward C. Blum (1863–1946) was born in Manhattan but returned to Germany as an infant with his mother when his father died. Educated in Europe, Blum returned to New York in 1885 for a position in an importing business. In 1896 he joined the staff of Abraham & Straus, after his marriage to Florence Abraham. He was a partner in the firm until 1920 when he became first vice president and then president in 1930. Blum was active in Jewish and cultural philanthropies in Brooklyn.

39. Oswald Schlockow (1874–1954) was the first Jewish principal of a public school in Brownsville. Born in Germany, he immigrated to New York in 1882, graduated from City College, and received a Ph.D. from New York University. He taught at P.S. 22 in Manhattan before becoming principal of P.S. 109 in 1902. In 1918 he left for P.S. 50, became district superintendent in 1928, and assistant superintendent for Brooklyn in 1936.

40. The Titanic sank on 16 April 1912. The newspapers carried banner headlines of the event.

41. The presidential campaign of 1912 was particularly exciting because it was a three-way race. The Democrats nominated Woodrow Wilson, who shaped a creed called the "New Freedom," although the Democratic and Republican platforms were nearly identical. The Republicans nominated President William Taft, rejecting Theodore Roosevelt's bid. Roosevelt was nominated by the Progressive ("Bull Moose") Party and called his creed the "New Nationalism." With the Republicans split, Wilson won. Debs, running on the Socialist ticket, polled the largest Socialist vote to date.

42. Herman Rosenthal, a notorious Jewish gambler, was gunned down in Times Square the evening before his grand jury appearance and three days after *The New York World* achieved a coup in publishing on 13 July 1912 an affidavit by Rosenthal chronicling his business dealings with Lieutenant Charles Becker, head of the police department's antigambling strong-arm squad.

43. District Attorney Charles Whitman blamed the police department for Rosenthal's murder by using confessions of gamblers who said they plotted the murder and hired the thugs at Becker's command. Elected as a regular Republican in the 1909 Fusion victory, Whitman pledged to expose vice and hoped to use the trial to further his political ambitions. The Rosenthal affair made front page news for 41 consecutive days. All but Becker and one hired thug were Jews.

44. Joseph Pulitzer (1847–1911) was born in Hungary and came to the United States at age 17 to serve in the Union Army. After the war he went to St. Louis and worked as a reporter. In 1871 he bought an interest in a paper, became managing editor, and then sold back shares at a vast profit. He moved to New York in 1883 and bought *The World*. His innovations in journalism—promotion, sensationalism, sympathy for labor—made his papers extraordinarily popular and successful.

10

Passover in the Mea Shearim and Geula Neighborhoods of Jerusalem

Samuel C. Heilman

To feel the onset of a Jewish holy day in Jerusalem, the best place to go—I learned during my year of wanderings—is Mea Shearim. Here life throbs to a beat that begins at the dawn of tradition and winds its way to the present moment through eternal yesterdays. Here the preparations for the ancient festivals, carried on in ways that echo the past, give order to life and meaning to existence.

At each holy day, the rhythm of the beat changes and so does the melody of preparations. Here, where the sound of the shofar blows through the air from every other alley, I witnessed the sounds and silences preceding the Days of Awe. Later, at *Sukkot*, I saw these streets filled with vendors selling palm and myrtle branches, citrons, and willows in anticipation of their use in the rituals of the season. On corners and empty lots, boards and rods used in the construction of the *sukkah*, the booth in which the devout would take their meals (and some even slept) during the coming seven days, were everywhere. During the festival, the verandas and courtyards bustled with activity as entire families ritually reenacted the transient life of the Israelites during the forty-year sojourn through the wilderness to the Promised Land. For these traditional Jerusalem Jews, their actual wandering over, all that remained was an endless replay. As I watched it, it seemed to me that in their scrupulous attachment to the tradition, the Jews who each year rebuild their *sukkah*, that symbolic temporary dwelling, precisely as they did the year before and who also reassembled their palm branch, citron, myrtles, and willows were celebrating the victory of tradition over transience, of stability over impermanence.

But if *Sukkot* was a dramatic reenactment of the Jewish victory over impermanence, Passover (or *Pesach*, as it is called in Hebrew) was a celebration of more fundamental survival. The exodus from Egypt that it recalled was the sunset of enslavement and the dawn of Jewish peoplehood, a testament of the everlasting vitality of God's covenant with father Abraham, the beginning of the triumphal return to the land, and the necessary prelude to the acceptance of the Torah (that last event to be celebrated seven weeks later during the *Shevuot* holy day).

"In each generation," wrote the author of the Haggada, the document of redemption that Jews reread at the annual Passover Seder, the ritual meal that serves as the centerpiece of the holy day celebration, "a person is required to see himself as if he were going out of Egypt." Commenting on this, the rabbis explained that each Jew must recount the event as a personal experience, for "not only our forefathers did the Holy One, May He be Blessed, redeem but also we ourselves, all of us alive today."

How does one reenact the sense of anticipation, anxiety, and preparation that must have absorbed all those awaiting Passover on the fateful night generations earlier? Perhaps there is first the imaginative and spiritual leap backward, the plumbing of ancient narratives and the exploration of talmudic exegeses—the recitation of the Haggada. "And whoever elaborates the story in greater detail," the rabbis proclaimed, "he shall be praised."

In the weeks before Passover, the alleys and streets of Mea Shearim and nearby Geula are filled with tables holding hundreds of editions of the Haggada for sale. In one printed for children, each Israelite leaving slavery is illustrated in the likeness of an eastern European hasid, complete with beard, earlocks, and caftan. In another are the commentaries of a revered sage set in harmony with the text. A third contains not only the narrative but a compendium of Passover laws whose ritual complications have filled the hours of thousands of scholars and yeshiva students. A fourth depicts the story of the exodus with photographs of artifacts discovered in archeological digs (these for the outsiders who come to shop in the neighborhood). The incarnations of the text appear to be endless.

And at each of these tables stand men—the women never shop for these holy books—perusing new editions, reviewing old ones, comparing pages and reading through the small print of obscure commentaries, as if preparing for the imaginative leaps they will soon be asked to lead on the night of the seder. The street becomes one great academy of learning. Those who peruse the books find ways of displaying their scholarship through their choice of books to peruse. Young yeshiva boys are especially prominent here, conspicuously losing themselves in the fine print of a thick text that they hold in such a way that passers-by will see them at study. A boor looks through a picture book; a scholar plumbs a commentary or codex.

Passover reaches its climax at the *seder*, and at the heart of that ritually ordered meal meant to arouse the memory of that first night of liberation generations earlier is the *matza*. In their haste to leave the darkness and death that Egypt had become, the Israelites rushed out of their homes and in packing their provisions for the journey into the wilderness, did not have time to allow their dough to leaven and rise. Therefore in perpetuity—in commemoration of that paradigmatic impulsive act to follow without hesitation in the path toward which their God directed them— their offspring would forever after during all the days of Passover not eat anything that had leavened, eating instead the flat bread, the *matza*, their forebears had prepared and then eaten on that night. Although this bread of affliction had been eaten hurriedly on that first Pesach by people still smitten by slavery, the freed children of slaves would eat it luxuriously, extending their meal by discussions of the miraculous transformation of their destiny. And, while the priestly order still ministered at the Holy Temple, they would bring the Pascal lamb as a sacrifice, which unlike other such offerings to God, they would eat with *matza* and bitter herbs (to recall the bitter life of slavery).

The rabbis spent generations articulating the details of the *matza*. To some, it was necessary to watch the wheat from the time of harvest to assure that no liquid touched the grains and began the leavening process. When preparing the dough during rolling and baking, they maintained a scrupulous watch on all materials used to be sure that no leavening would begin, however accidentally. From this began the practices attached to the making of *matza*.

In Mea Shearim, the baking, carried on for weeks in anticipation of the festival, brings life to deserted bakeries and labor to boys otherwise engaged in the study of Talmud and other venerated tests. Fingers that normally roll across black and white columns of text now roll dough.

To see the process, I visited one such *matza* factory with my friend and guide Yisrael, the woodturner.

"Every eighteen minutes," he explained, "every item in the

place—rolling pins, bowls, even the sticks on which the matza is put into the oven—are exchanged for new ones."

"Why eighteen minutes?"

"That is the time it takes for dough to become *hametz*."

Eighteen was a number replete with Jewish mystical significance because transposition of the letters that signify it spells *chai*, the Hebrew word for life. I had no idea how long the leavening process took, but the calculation that it was precisely eighteen minutes seemed to me to be the product of one of those imaginative leaps that the rabbis had always been able to make and which those who believed in their authority had been willing to accept.

"Look," Yisrael said as we entered the tiny factory across the street from his workshop. "Each step takes another expert." He said this last word, "expert," in English and gave a little giggle.

But he was right about the steps in the process being clearly defined. At the back of a long hall were boys who made up the dough in deep round bowls that were exchanged for new ones every eighteen minutes. Completing their job, they spilled the dough onto a narrow table covered with paper sheets that were also removed after eighteen minutes.

Next to the table stood five boys, each holding a long thick metal rod—something like an oar handle—that was hinged to the table in such a way as to allow it to be raised and lowered or pushed back and forward. Underneath it was a wad of dough that was being kneaded in this way. Up and down and then from side to side, the rod went.

"Why the rod?" I asked.

"So that from now on as few hands as possible will touch the dough. Who can tell what moisture, dirt, or *hametz* is on them?"

Like the bowls and table covers, every eighteen minutes these rods would be exchanged for others while the first set were cleaned and buffed. When the time to switch rods came, a nervous energy overtook the boys as they rushed to another corner to bring in the replacements.

With the kneading complete, the dough was made into long salamilike rolls and placed on the edge of another table. Here a man with a long knife, its blade gleaming from all the buffing it received in between operations, cut the roll into a series of small disks, each of which was handed to another boy who used a smooth, steel rolling pin to roll it out into a thin, circular wafer. These were passed—thrown like a pizza, really—to a third table where a bearded hasid ran over them with a spiked brass wheel and made holes that allow the *matza* to bake to its crisp final form with a minimum of rising and bulging. When he had rolled over five, he placed them gingerly across a long wooden pole that rested atop the table but also reached through to another room where it was held at its far end by another hasid.

As soon as the five wafers were folded across the pole, it was raised and put into the open hearth oven where in a single deft movement the wafers were unfolded and laid on its red-hot floor. While the now empty pole was given to a young boy standing near the back wall whose job was to buff it clean and prepare it for reuse. The man who had loaded the wafers into the oven took a long wooden spatula and withdrew the freshly baked *matza*. He then shoveled these over to the last man in the line who carefully loaded the crisp disks on their edges into the boxes which awaited them. At about $15 a kilo, they were sold almost as quickly as they were packed.

"The further along in the line you are," Yisrael told me, "the more you make."

"So those at the oven make the most?"

"Twelve dollars an hour—but who can last more than a few hours in front of the heat?"

"Will we buy some now?" I asked, already imagining the hard bites I would take on that night of the seder. In keeping with custom, I had not tasted *matza* for a month before the holy day; that way on the evening of the celebration, the taste would be fresh and exciting to the senses.

"We'll order, and if we're lucky, we'll get our share next week. Of course," he added, "you can come back on the eve of the holy day and bake your own *mitzva* matza, but I don't advise it."

The rush of all those wishing to reenact the experience of the baking on that Passover eve would be crushing, and only the hearty or those with connections to the owner of the bakery would have the opportunity. There were even some groups who rented the bakery for a few hours. Outsiders need not apply.

But there is more to preparing for Passover than baking or buying *matza*. For this seven-day celebration, also called the festival of spring, tradition decreed that all leavening must be rooted out of the house, banned from one's possession. Therefore, before the holy days, in Mea Shearim and the other domains of tradition, spring cleaning becomes a ritual and religious duty. Dishes, pots, and other utensils that may have come in contact with and absorbed leavened food must be put aside or scoured;

sales in new dishes for Passover are extraordinary. Sidewalks are filled with displays of pots, pans, dishes, plastic racks, glasses, and everything even remotely associated with food. At the tin-smith's, special cutouts are made to cover the stovetop. Passover dishes may be placed on these shells without the risk of their contacting even a microscopic morsel of leavening, *hametz*. For those for whom this purchase is too expensive, others sell long sheets of industrial strength aluminum foil to cover a counter or stovetop.

Living in an age when pots and utensils were acquired only once in a lifetime, the rabbis stipulated that metal, if dipped in boiling water inside of which are red hot stones, that, as it were, "double" the boiling, could be made kosher for Passover. Accordingly, on several corners of Mea Shearim, one discovers huge cauldrons atop fires, filled with red hot stones. The hiss of the water and the rumble of the rocks tumbling about in vats fill the air and add to everyone's sense of anticipation. Pesach is coming to a boil.

"How much for all these?" a man asks showing his pots and utensils to a man who has set up one set of cauldrons. After a quick glance, the boiler quotes a price.

"Agreed."

The entire bundle is placed into a metal basket and dipped into the boiling vat of water. In a flash, it is lifted and lowered into a vat of cold water. The two dips over, the owner hands over his bills to the soaked hands of the boiler and takes back his now kosher-for-Passover pots and utensils, dripping his way home.

All during the year there are vegetable markets throughout the neighborhood. During the weeks and days preceding Passover, however, the produce in them changes noticeably; and vegetables that normally are not sold in bulk or at all make an appearance in the stalls. Above all others stand the potatoes, overflowing the sidewalks and plugging the alleys. When leavened dough is off limits, the Jews of Mea Shearim and others like them begin to eat potatoes. They make them mashed, baked, and fried. They make paste out of them, and some have even managed to make starchy rolls that look as if they were made from dough but once tasted reveal the potato baked into their heart.

Then, too, there are the eggs. Boiled, scrambled, mixed with *matza*, or even dropped into chicken soup, they appear on Pesach plates day after day. In the square just outside of the woodturner's shop, the station wagons and trucks from the egg farms park and, setting out hundreds of cartons of flats, sell to all comers. In principle all eggs are kosher, but those with a blood spot are not. Holding eggs up to the sun as if she could thereby see through the shells and discover the spots inside, a young woman patiently examines each egg of the sixty she has chosen to take home.

The bitter herbs with which each Jew at the seder must recall the bitter experience of slavery take a variety of forms. Some say romaine lettuce is the desirable form, but only if the leaves are without the tiny bugs that sometimes inhabit them. While his wife examines the eggs, a husband, sliding his black hat back on his head and sitting on a sack of potatoes, searches the lettuce to find a few leaves that will suffice for his observance of the commandment. He pores over the leaves with the same attitude of deliberation that he might use on another occasion to pore over a page of the code of law.

Some eat a horseradish in fulfillment of the bitter-herb obligation. They believe they are genuinely able to cry as their enslaved antecedents did only by biting into the sharp white root that brings tears to their eyes and a lump to their throat. This white vegetable, never available during the rest of the year, suddenly becomes a staple of the market.

Parsley, parsnips, celery, carrots—all these enable the Jew during the seder to dip a vegetable into salt water or vinegar, an act steeped in symbolism and mystery and which traces its origins to the time of the Second Temple. Carrying handfuls of each, shoppers of Mea Shearim display the customs of their family as they fill their marketing sacks.

And then there are the feathers. On the night before the seder, the house must be ritually and symbolically searched for all leaven, making certain that the Passover will be ushered into a totally cleansed house and that the free man will be different from the slave. With candle in hand, the head of the household searches each corner of the house, finding the last morsels of bread left out to be found. Using a feather, he must brush the crumbs into a wooden spoon and then drop them into a bag.

Among the butchers of the neighborhood there is now a bustling market for feathers. Boxes stand before each shop, and for a few shekels the shopper chooses the firmest and most robust-looking feather, which will be burned after its use with the remaining *hametz* until they both become "like the dust of the earth."

On the morning before the *seder*, Jews stand over small bonfires, watching all the *hametz* they ritually collected the night before burn. Silently, the smell of burning bread fills the air. In empty lots, park corners, and little hillocks, where the bonfires announcing the new moon once burned, Jews now stand watching as its prohibitions turn into ashes and dust. Smoke arises into the air in narrow plumes while Passover drops over Jewish Jerusalem and the season of redemption begins.

Glossary

Deborah Dash Moore

Agudas Yisroel: Anti-Zionist Orthodox party.

Alsergrund: Vienna's ninth district.

Angestelite: People who work in an office for a fixed salary. The term includes government bureaucrats, clerks, salesmen, and managers in private enterprise.

Brigittenau: Vienna's predominantly working-class twentieth district.

College of Notables: Twenty-five wealthy lay leaders chosen by the French government in each consistorial district to elect the members of the local consistory.

Consistory: The governmentally recognized communal institution of French Jews, established by Napoleon.

Dobling: Vienna's nineteenth district, known for its villas.

Floridsdorf: Vienna's twenty-second district, an outlying suburb.

General Zionists: Middle-of-the-road bourgeois Zionists.

Gymnasium (plural, *Gymnasien*): Elite secondary public schools in German-speaking Central Europe. Designed for children from ten to eighteen years of age, these schools emphasize the Greek and Latin classics, history, literature, and foreign languages. To attend university, students must complete the gymnasium curriculum.

Hametz: Leaven. Fermented dough made from primary grains forbidden during Passover.

Heder (plural, *Hedarim*): A small, traditional Jewish religious school that taught Hebrew, Bible, and introductory rabbinic literature. Literally, a room.

Hitachdut: Labor Zionist organization, more moderate than Poale Zion.

Inner City: Vienna's affluent first district.

Israelitische Kultusgemeinde: Literally, the Jewish religious community. All Jews in Central Europe were required by law to be members of the local Jewish community and pay taxes to it. These communities provided the religious, philanthropic, and Jewish educational needs of the Jews of the city.

IKG: Abbreviation for Israelitische Kultusgemeinde.

Khevra kadisha: Burial society.

Landrabbiner: Title applied in Germany to the government-recognized rabbi with civic authority over an entire political region.

Landsmanshaftn: Organizations of immigrants from the same town or district.

Landsmen: People from the same town or district.

Leopoldstadt: Vienna's predominantly Jewish second district.

Maskil (plural, *Maskilim*): An adherent to the Jewish enlightenment.

Mea Shearim: Hassidic Orthodox Jewish neighborhood in Jerusalem.

Melamed (plural, *Melamdim*): Teacher.

Memorbuch: Name given by German Jews to books read on anniversaries that contained memorial prayers, lists of martyrs and communal benefactors, and other historical material.

Minyan (plural, *Minyanim*): Prayer quorum of ten adult men.

Mitzva: Literally, commandment. A biblical injunction that can be positive or negative.

Mizrachi: Religious Zionist party.

Ostjuden: Jews from Eastern Europe, a somewhat pejorative term.

Poale Zion: Labor or Socialist Zionist party.

Polnische schul: Beth Israel, known as the Polish synagogue, a large Galician congregation.

Radical Zionists: Subgroup of General Zionists, slightly left of center.

Revisionist Zionists: Members of right-wing Zionist group.

Schiffschul: Adas Yisroel, the main Hungarian Orthodox synagogue in Vienna.

Shekel: The official membership dues of the World Zionist Organization. Before World War I, the shekel was worth one German mark or 1.20 Austrian kronen. Currently, the shekel is the basic unit of Israeli currency.

Shtibl (plural, *Shtiblekh*): Small synagogue or prayer room.

Shul: Synagogue.

Sukkot: Jewish harvest festival, Feast of Booths, celebrated each fall after the New Year holiday.

Talmud Torah: A traditional elementary school for Jewish learning, usually for poor Jews.

Wahring: Vienna's wealthy eighteenth district.

Yeshiva (plural, *Yeshivot*): Traditional academy of higher Jewish learning.

Contributors

Several of the essays in this volume were, in earlier versions, papers submitted for a conference held 21–23 March 1983 at the Graduate Center, City University of New York.

STEVEN M. COHEN, professor of sociology at Queens College, the City University of New York, has also taught at Brandeis University, The Hebrew University, Yale University, and the Jewish Theological Seminary of America. His books include *American Modernity and Jewish Identity* (1983) and *American Assimilation or Jewish Revival?* (1988). He is coauthor of two recent books: *Cosmopolitan Parochials: Modern Orthodox Jews in America* and *Two Worlds of Judaism: The Israeli and American Experiences*.

DAVID M. FELDMAN teaches at Christ's College, Cambridge University. His doctoral thesis is "Immigrants and Workers, Englishmen and Jews: Jewish Immigrants in the East End of London, 1881–1906."

HARRIET PASS FREIDENREICH is associate professor of history at Temple University in Philadelphia. Her previous publications include *The Jews of Yugoslavia: A Quest for Community* (1979). She is currently completing a book on Jewish politics in interwar Vienna.

SAMUEL GOLDEN (1896–1963), born Samuel Goldstein, was a second-generation immigrant and a lifelong New Yorker. Committed equally to socialism and capitalism, Golden was at various times a printer, theater poster designer, orator, producer, and book publisher.

SAMUEL C. HEILMAN is professor of sociology at Queens College, the City University of New York. His publications include *A Walker in Jerusalem* (1987), *People of the Book: Drama, Fellowship, and Religion* (1983), *The Gate Behind the Wall* (1985), and *Synagogue Life: A Study in Symbolic Interaction* (1976).

PAULA E. HYMAN is Lucy Moses Professor of Modern Jewish History at Yale University. She is the author of *From Dreyfus to Vichy: The Remaking of French Jewry, 1906–1939* (1979) and coeditor of *The Jewish Family: Myths and Reality* (1986). This essay is drawn from her current study, *Jews into Frenchmen: Emancipation, Acculturation, and Tradition in Nineteenth Century Alsace*, publication forthcoming.

SAMUEL D. KASSOW is professor of history at Trinity College. He is the author of *Students, Professors and the State in Tsarist Russia, 1894–1917* (1989). He contributed "Community and Identity in the Interwar *Shtetl*" in *The Jews of Poland Between Two World Wars*, eds. Yisrael Gutman, Ezra Mendelsohn, Jehuda Reinharz and Chone Shmeruk (1989). His current work includes a study of Vilna Jews, 1915–1922, and "The Search for Civic Culture in Tsarist Russia."

VIVIAN Z. KLAFF is associate professor of sociology at the University of Delaware at Newark. He specializes in urban ecology, with a particular emphasis on racial and ethnic residential patterns. In 1981 he was a Fellow at the Institute for Advanced Studies of the Hebrew University in Jerusalem. He is completing work on a book on the use of computer software to teach demography.

SHULAMIT S. MAGNUS is director of the Department of Modern Jewish Civilization at the Reconstructionist Rabbinical College. Her essay is drawn from her doctoral thesis, "Cologne: Jewish Emancipation in a German City, 1798–1871," Columbia University, 1988.

EGON MAYER is professor of sociology at Brooklyn College, the City University of New York. His publications include *Love and Tradition: Marriage between Jews and Christians* (1987) and *Conversion among the Intermarried* (1987). This essay reflects a return to the subject of his first book, *From Suburb to Shtetl: The Jews of Boro Park* (1979).

DEBORAH DASH MOORE, professor of religion at Vassar College, was research director of the YIVO Institute for Jewish Research and dean of the Max Weinrich Center for Advanced Jewish Studies. Her books include *At Home in America: Second Generation New*

York Jews (1981) and *B'nai B'rith and the Challenge of Ethnic Leadership* (1981).

MARSHA L. ROZENBLIT is associate professor of history at the University of Maryland-College Park and the author of *The Jews of Vienna, 1867–1914: Assimilation and Identity* (1983).

Index

DATE DUE

		MAY 1 3 1999
NOV 1 5 1992		
NO 09 '92		MAY 2 ? 1999
FEB 0 7 1995		JUN 2 8 2000
FEB 2 8 1995		
MAR 1 3 1995		
FEB 0 6 1996		
FEB. 0 6 1996		
APR 2 1 1998		
MAY 1 2 1998		
MAY 0 6 1998		
RENEWALS 362-8433		

DEMCO 38-297

Affordable Locksmith

CUSTOMER'S ORDER NO.	DATE
	5/23/16

NAME: Michelle @ Flaksmith

ADDRESS: 103 N. Corby

CITY, STATE, ZIP: Cottage 60010

SOLD BY | CASH | C.O.D. | CHARGE ON ACCT. | MDSE. RETD. | PAID OUT

Charge on acct. [X]

QUAN.	DESCRIPTION	AMOUNT	
1	Service Call	15	—
4	Re-keys	60	—
5	Total →	275	—
6			
7			
8			
9			
10			
11			
12			

RECEIVED BY

THE JEWS OF MOSCOW, KIEV AND MINSK

The Jews of Moscow, Kiev and Minsk

Identity, Antisemitism, Emigration

Robert J. Brym
Professor, Department of Sociology
and Centre for Russian and East European Studies
University of Toronto

with the assistance of
Rozalina Ryvkina
Professor
All-Russian Centre for Public Opinion
Research, Moscow

Editor
Howard Spier
Head of Central and East European Department
Institute of Jewish Affairs
London

NEW YORK UNIVERSITY PRESS
Washington Square, New York

in association with the
Institute of Jewish Affairs

For Rhonda, Shira, Talia and Ariella

First published in the U.S.A. in 1994 by
NEW YORK UNIVERSITY PRESS
Washington Square
New York, N.Y. 10003

in association with the
Institute of Jewish Affairs
79 Wimpole Street
London WIM 7DD
Great Britain

Library of Congress Cataloging-in-Publication Data
Brym, Robert J., 1951–
The Jews of Moscow, Kiev, and Minsk : identity, antisemitism,
emigration / Robert J. Brym with Rozalina Ryvkina.
p. cm.
Includes bibliographical references and index.
ISBN 0–8147–1226–6. — ISBN 0–8147–1230–4 (pbk.)
1. Jews—Russia (Federation)—Politics and government. 2. Jews–
–Ukraine—Politics and government. 3. Jews—Belarus—Politics and
government. 4. Jews—Former Soviet republics—Identity. 5. Jews–
–Former Soviet republics—Migrations. 6. Antisemitism—Former
Soviet republics. 7. Former Soviet republics—Ethnic relations.
I. Ryvkina, Rozalina Vladimirovna.   II. Title.
DS135.R92B78 1994
305.892'4047'09049—dc20   94–9893
                                                                  CIP

Printed in Great Britain

Table of Contents

List of Tables

List of Figures

List of Photographs

Foreword

It is indisputable that in the republics which comprise the former Soviet Union Jewish culture and Judaism are undergoing an unprecedented renaissance, Jews are free to pursue virtually any career they wish, links with world Jewry and Israel proceed without obstacle and, to all intents and purposes, emigration is free. It must be emphasized that these are great and historic gains for the Jews of the former Soviet Union, for Israel and for the Jewish people as a whole.

At the same time, the fact that there is a considerable downside to this felicitous situation cannot be ignored. The shift towards a Western-style market economy in the republics of the former Soviet Union (as well as in Moscow's former satellite countries) has, as is well known, been accompanied by enormous difficulties. Most prominently perhaps in Russia and Ukraine, large sections of the population have been demoralized by an economy verging on hyper-inflation and falling living standards, social divisions have widened, and crime has grown inexorably. In addition, many Russians are deeply alarmed at their country's declining international status.

From a specifically Jewish point of view, the state-backed anti-Zionist campaign of the Brezhnev period, with its antisemitic excesses, has been replaced, in Russia, by a considerable grass-roots antisemitic movement mainly, but not entirely, on the fringe of society.

Given the grave instability experienced by Russia combined with its long tradition of authoritarianism, there are those who believe that the best the country can hope for in the medium and long term is some sort of benevolent autocracy. At the time of writing—on the occasion of Russia's first fully free parliamentary elections and a referendum on President Yeltsin's draft constitution—it has become clear that the far-right Liberal Democratic Party of Vladimir Zhirinovsky will play a substantial role in the new parliament. There can be no clearer illustration of the volatility of life in the CIS which Professor Brym rightly underlines.

As Professor Brym points out, this is "the first book based on an *in situ* survey of a representative sample of Jews in the Commonwealth of Independent States". The survey in question was conducted in the three

Slavic republics—Russia, Ukraine and Belarus—between February and April 1993. Professor Brym is also at pains to place the results of the survey in their social and historical context. Just a few short years ago the very idea of conducting a survey in these republics was unthinkable—like so much else in the countries of the post-Communist Soviet Union. Nevertheless, while the means the author employs to reach his conclusions may be novel, it is legitimate to enquire whether his findings tell us much we did not already know.

I must confess that I, and perhaps many others, have certain reservations about the value of surveys of this type. For example, do they really represent more than a snap-shot of what someone happens to be thinking at a specific moment and in certain circumstances and do respondents always give a frank answer? Also I have reservations about "sociological jargon". Having said that, I find it difficult not to be impressed by Brym's methods and the conclusions he reaches.

In the following pages Brym himself alludes to scepticism of this type. It must be said, however, that he is scrupulous in steering as clear as he possibly can of what he himself has described as "sociologese". Not only is there a refreshing absence of "jargon" in the book but Brym's language could not be less tendentious. The fairly large number of tables and charts inevitable in a work of this nature also have been reduced to the greatest possible simplicity.

The fundamental questions Brym asks in this work are the following: Precisely how many Jews are we talking about? What is the extent of their Jewishness? What factors account for variations in strength of Jewishness? How serious do they perceive the threat of antisemitism to be? How many of them are likely to emigrate and how many are likely to remain? Where are those emigrating likely to go?

Professor Brym and Professor Ryvkina asked some very valid questions and some of the results they have come up with are extremely interesting, even intriguing. To my mind, the single most important contribution to our knowledge of Jews in the three Slavonic republics—where the Jewish population of the former Soviet Union mainly resides—are the figures Brym puts forward in connection with the long disputed question of the actual size of the Jewish population. As of the beginning of 1993 there were 1,144,000 Jews in the former USSR, of whom 435,000 were in Russia, 389,000 in Ukraine, and 92,000 in Belarus, a total of approximately 916,000 (roughly 139,000 in Moscow, 85,000 in Kiev, and 31,000 in Minsk). Brym's method of calculation seems to me utterly convincing. Moreover, he completely discounts wishful thinking as well as the opinions of those who, he tells us, have a vested interest in exaggerating or playing down the figures. One suspects that the figures he comes up with are the most precise which can be attained at the present time.

On several of the other matters investigated, many of them a matter of sharp dispute between CIS-watchers, Brym sheds considerable light. On the issue of Jewish identity, for example, only about a third of Brym's respondents said they wished to be involved in the Jewish community. Similarly, on the subject of antisemitism, over 70 per cent of his respondents expressed fear of anti-Jewish activities.

In regard to the process of emigration, Brym does not hesitate to make prognostications for the future—as he himself acknowledges, a highly risky endeavour given the uncertainty which surrounds the future of these republics. Thus Brym's extremely rough projections suggest that from 1994 to 1999 just over 480,000 Jews will emigrate from the former USSR. Of these between 204,000 and 275,000 will go to Israel, and between 276,000 and 368,000 will go elsewhere. Brym also estimates that in the year 2000 less than half a million Jews will remain in the territory of the former USSR and those who do remain will for the most part be old, highly assimilated and swifly diminishing in number.

These are important conclusions which need to be taken seriously. In addition to the academic interest such research entails, there is also of course important material here for those who make policy in such matters—not only in relation to the likely numbers of emigrants, their characterization and their possible destinations but also—and not not least important—those who are likely to remain indefinitely where they are. It is very much to be hoped that attention will be paid by such persons to the results achieved by the painstaking research and dispassionate analysis demonstrated in this book.

Howard Spier

Preface

During a trip to Moscow in 1989 I was struck by an outlandish idea: might it be possible to conduct a public opinion survey in the USSR? At first I was sceptical. I needed to find competent collaborators in Moscow, establish reliable lines of communication with them and convince funders that a public opinion survey could be executed in the Soviet Union and yield meaningful results. For two years I failed on all three fronts. Then, in 1991, as the Soviet Union disintegrated, things began to fall into place for me.

These apparently contradictory events were connected. The disintegrating Soviet Union allowed more travel abroad for its academics, more involvement in international professional organizations, more exposure to Western scientific and humanistic literature—and the complement for Western academics. As a result of these sorts of contacts I met some Russian social scientists of the first rank—Dr Nikolai Popov of the All-Russian Centre for Research on Public Opinion (VTsIOM) in Moscow, Dr Andrei Degtyarev of the Department of Political Science and Sociology of Politics at Moscow State University, Professor Vladimir Yadov of the Institute of Sociology of the Russian Academy of Sciences, and Professor Rozalina Ryvkina of VTsIOM.

Professor Iadov and Dr Popov supplied me with reports on current survey research in the former USSR that I have used profitably in preparing this book. I conducted my first modest survey in Russia with Dr Degtyarev in October 1992. Some of the results of that survey were published in *Slavic Review* in 1993 and are reprinted in Chapter Four with the permission of the American Association for the Advancement of Slavic Studies. After Professor Ryvkina and I had established a collegial relationship I wrote an Introduction to a report on the refugee crisis in Russia by her and Rostislav Turovskiy. Part of that Introduction is reprinted in Chapter 2 with the permission of York Lanes Press, York University, Toronto. Most of this book, however, is based on a survey conducted with the assistance of Professor Ryvkina between February and April 1993. By means of personal visits, fax machines and electronic mail I have kept in very close touch—indeed, nearly daily contact—with Professor Ryvkina and my other collaborators for eighteen months. It has been an extraordinarily exciting experience both intellectually and personally. I am deeply indebted to my collaborators, and most especially of course to Professor Ryvkina. She has worked with diligence, efficiency and creativity to overcome what at times seemed insurmountable problems.

In Canada, Professor Robert E. Johnson, Director of the Centre for Russian and East European Studies at the University of Toronto, helped the progress of my research immeasurably by generously subsidizing my visit to Moscow and the visits of Professor Ryvkina, Dr Popov and Dr Degtyarev to Toronto. I am also extremely grateful to the Social Sciences and Humanities Research Council of Canada, which supplied the bulk of the funding for this project, and to the Humanities and Social Sciences Committee of the University of Toronto for supplementary financial assistance.

From London, Dr Howard Spier of the Institute of Jewish Affairs gave me encouragement and bibliographic help. With a firm but always friendly editor's hand, he made a number of useful suggestions for improving the manuscript.

I also wish to express my thanks to three Israeli friends—Professor Baruch Kimmerling and Professor Michael Shalev of the Department of Sociology and Social Anthropology at the Hebrew University of Jerusalem and Professor Ephraim Tabory of the Department of Sociology at Bar-Ilan University. Professors Kimmerling and Shalev provided instant and invaluable bibliographic assistance and Professor Tabory made some good suggestions for improving the questionnaire.

It is with much sadness that I must recall the support and advice which my friend, the late Professor Sidney Heitman of Colorado State University, gave me in the early stages of this project. This book is less than it could have been because it was written without the benefit of Sid's criticisms.

Most authors seem to be afflicted with stoic family members who gladly allow them to spend endless hours buried away in isolated thought. I suffer no such misfortune. My wife and three children have done their utmost to ensure that I understand clearly what is more important and what is less important in life. My debt to them is without limit. I dedicate this book to them as a symbol of my thanks and love.

RJB
Toronto, August 1993

1 The Scope of the Study

The Jews of the former Soviet Union have frequently been the subject of intense controversy. Especially during the past two-and-a-half decades, a period which may be said to have begun with the Six Day War in the Middle East, they have provoked unprecedented attention. How many of them are there? How strongly do they identify themselves as Jews? How do their patterns of identification, belief and practice vary from one category of the population to the next? Will they leave or will they stay? If they leave, where will they go? What types of Jews are most likely to emigrate? How do they perceive antisemitism in their countries? Will they be persecuted or will they enjoy new freedoms? If the latter, will they undergo a cultural revival undreamed of under Communism or will they assimilate and cease to exist as a community? These are among the chief questions that have enlivened discussions of Jews in the republics now known as the Commonwealth of Independent States. They are the questions I examine here. They have sparked debate for intellectual reasons and because they have serious policy implications not only for the CIS countries but also for Israel, the United States and some other countries such as Germany.

Too little fact has informed this debate. Expectations have therefore been dashed more than once. In 1984 it seemed to many analysts that the emigration of Soviet Jews was at an end for the foreseeable future. Yet by 1989 the rate of emigration had reached an unprecedented level. In 1989 many people expected a million Soviet Jews to emigrate to Israel in the next three years. In the event, 39 per cent of that number arrived. In 1990 pogroms were expected by some circles in Russia. None materialized. Unforeseen, singular events—the rise of Gorbachev, the collapse of Communism, the Gulf War—obviously played a large part in confounding people's expectations. The surprises might not have been so great, however, if analysts had been less emboldened by ideological certainty and better able to survey the actual intentions, perceptions, motivations and fears of Jews in the region as well as the degree to which they were rooted in their social circumstances.

Until very recently, such surveys were out of the question. Freedom

1

to conduct surveys of public opinion in the Soviet Union dates only from the late 1980s. Local expertise was also lacking. Tatyana Zaslavskaya, one of the top sociologists in the former Soviet Union and an advisor to Gorbachev, remarked in *Pravda* in 1987 that "Soviet sociology is sociology without sociologists."[1] Nor could Western sociologists immediately hope to undertake surveys themselves. The terrain was unknown and the pitfalls many. Finally, most of the Western individuals and organizations that could have funded survey research on Soviet Jews were justifiably sceptical of its success.[2]

All this is now beginning to change, as this book testifies. The main survey on which this book is based was funded by a grant from the Social Sciences and Humanities Research Council of Canada.[3] Professor Ryvkina and I designed the questionnaire with the assistance of Dr Leonid Kosals of VTsIOM. Professor Ryvkina designed the sample and organized the field work. She was assisted by Dr Leonid Kosals and she consulted with Professor A. V. Superanskaya. I analyzed the data and wrote the book, taking into account Professor Ryvkina's critical comments on the first draft. The result of this effort is the first book based on an *in situ* survey of a representative sample of Jews in the Commonwealth of Independent States (CIS).

Due to financial considerations I had to limit the survey to the Jews of Moscow, Kiev and Minsk, the capital cities of Russia, Ukraine and Belarus respectively. The Jews in those three cities account for approximately 28 per cent of all Jews residing in the three Slavic republics of the CIS (see Table 1.1). I strongly suspect that my findings are generalizable to all Jews living in the larger cities of the three republics but I cannot test my suspicion until I conduct more extensive sampling at some future date. I am, however, confident that within known limits my findings are generalizable to the Jews of the three capital cities because of the way the sample was selected.

In the autumn of 1992 Professor Ryvkina contacted Professor A. V. Superanskaya, a leading linguist in Moscow who specializes in the study of Jewish surnames. Professor Superanskaya drew up a list of the 405 most common Jewish surnames in Russia, Ukraine and Belarus (see Appendix A). The list was given to the police offices in Moscow, Kiev and Minsk which are responsible for keeping computerized records of all city residents. The head of the police office in each city was paid to have his computer generate at random a list of 1,110 households with family surnames corresponding to those on the list of 405.

Dr Kosals then selected every third household from each of the police lists—334 from Moscow and 333 from each of Kiev and Minsk. An

Table 1.1
Jewish Census Population (1989) and Sample Size

	Russia	Ukraine	Belarus	Total
population	550,000	487,000	112,000	1,149,000
% of total Jews	48	42	10	100

	Moscow	Kiev	Minsk	total
est. population	175,500	107,000	39,500	322,000
% of republic Jews	32	22	35	28
% of Jews in 3 cities	54	33	12	100
actual interviews	334	333	333	1,000
weighted interviews	545	332	123	1,000
weighting factor	1.63	1.00	0.37	—

Source for republic population data: Sidney Heitman, "Jews in the 1989 USSR census", *Soviet Jewish Affairs*, vol. 20, no.1, 1990, 23-30.

alternative list of the remaining addresses was also compiled. If, after three attempts, it was not possible to interview anyone in a household from the first list, a household from the alternative list was selected at random.

Interviewing was conducted between 3 February and 17 April 1993 by 102 trained interviewers, sixty-one of whom were Jewish. If only one adult was at home the interviewer tried to interview that person. If more than one adult was at home the interviewer asked to interview the person in the household who was eighteen years of age or older and had had the most recent birthday. That was done in order to randomize the selection of individuals within households. If it was not possible to interview the selected person at the time of initial contact or at some future date the interviewer obtained some minimal information about the selected person's social characteristics and drew a new household from the alternative list. This procedure was repeated if necessary.[4]

The interviewers continued in this way until 1,000 Jews had been interviewed in the three cities. A total of 1,207 actual contacts were made to obtain the 1,000 interviews; 207 contacts refused to participate in the study. Thus the response rate was a very high 83 per cent. Because of the randomization procedures followed, I am confident that the 1,000 respondents are representative of the Jewish populations of Moscow, Kiev and Minsk.[5]

The questionnaire is reproduced in Appendix B. It consists of 157 questions that were answered by respondents and twenty-three questions that were answered by interviewers. The interviews were conducted on a face-to-face basis in the respondents' homes, about half of them beginning between 5:00 pm and 8:00 pm and the other half scattered throughout the day. The interviews lasted anywhere from 10 to 120 minutes, depending on how many questions were answered and on how much time was required to explain questions to respondents. Over two-thirds of the interviews took between 30 and 60 minutes. On average, each interview lasted 36 minutes.

As can be seen in Table 1.1, Moscow Jews constitute about 54 per cent of Jews in the three cities, Kiev Jews about 33 per cent and Minsk Jews the remaining 12 per cent. In order to draw accurate inferences about the Jewish populations of the three cities as a whole I was obliged to weight the replies given by respondents to take account of that distribution. Thus each Moscow interview was "counted" 1.63 times, each Kiev interview once, and each Minsk interview 0.37 times.

One can be confident that the results reported below are accurate plus or minus 3.1 per cent at the 95 per cent confidence level. This means that if one were to draw twenty random samples of 1,000 people each, and report results from each of those twenty samples, nineteen of them would be at most within 3.1 per cent of the results I report.

In order to appreciate fully the significance of the survey results it is necessary to place them in social and historical context. The following chapter provides that background as briefly as possible. Because of the survey's topicality, and in the interest of getting the survey results published while they are still fresh, I decided not to take the time to paint an elaborate socio-historical portrait. Instead the following chapter draws a sketch that accentuates only two issues. I first explain why ethnic distinctiveness persisted and even became accentuated in the Soviet era. I then describe the position of Jews in Soviet and post-Soviet society and some of the dilemmas they face.

NOTES

1   Tatyana Zaslavskaya, "*Perestroyka* and sociology", *Pravda*, 6 February
     1987. See also Rozalina Ryvkina, "From civic courage to scientific demon-
     stration", *Soviet Sociology,* vol. 28, no. 5, 1989, 7-23; Robert J. Brym, "So-
     ciology, *perestroika*, and Soviet society", *Canadian Journal of Sociology,*
     vol. 15, no. 2, 1990, 207-15.

2   The only exception of which I am aware is the American Jewish Committee,
     which has funded research on antisemitism since 1989. See Lev D. Gudkov
     and Alex G. Levinson, *Attitudes Toward Jews in the Soviet Union: Public
     Opinion in Ten Republics* (New York: American Jewish Committee, 1992);
     L. Gudkov and A. Levinson, "Attitudes towards Jews", *Sotsiologicheskiye
     issledovaniya*, no. 12, 1992, 108-11; James L. Gibson and Raymond M.
     Duch, "Anti-semitic attitudes of the mass public: Estimates and explanations
     based on a survey of the Moscow oblast", *Public Opinion Quarterly*, vol. 56,
     1992, 1-28. For a good up-to-date synopsis of problems of survey research
     in the CIS see Michael Swafford, "Sociological aspects of survey research in
     the Commonwealth of Independent States", *International Journal of Public
     Opinion Research*, vol. 4, no. 4, 1992, 346-57.

3   In addition, I will refer to the results of a telephone poll of 946 non-Jewish
     adult Muscovites which I conducted in October 1992 with the assistance of
     Professor Andrei Degtyarev of Moscow State University. For methodologi-
     cal details see Chapter 4.

4   Nearly three-quarters of interviews were conducted on the first try, nearly 11
     per cent on the second, and just over 8 per cent on the third. In order to
     verify that interviews were being conducted as reported, administrators at
     the branches of the All-Russian Centre for Public Opinion Research
     (VTsIOM) in each city made random telephone checks on just over 12 per
     cent of the respondents.

5   Jews by any criterion who Slavicized their surnames are not found either in
     our sample or in the 1993 population estimates given in Chapter 3. Are they
     Jews? Consider the following anecdote, related by Aleksandr Burakovsky,
     Chairman of the Kiev Sholem Aleichem Society, in 1992. Burakovsky re-
     lates that during business trips to the Russian city of Chelyabinsk, where
     many Ukrainian Jews fled the Nazis, "I see young men with Jewish features,
     and I ask them, and their names are Ivanov and Petrov, good Russian names.
     And I ask them about their parents and their grandparents, and they're all
     Ukrainian." See Steven Erlanger, "As Ukraine loses Jews, the Jews lose a
     tradition", *The New York Times,* 27 August 1992.

2 The Jews in Soviet and Post-Soviet Society

THE PERSISTENCE OF ETHNICITY IN THE SOVIET ERA[1]

Lenin believed that nations first emerged during the transition from feudalism to capitalism and that under Communism they would eventually fuse. Following the Revolution, however, the Bolsheviks took over an enormous country with over a hundred recognized national or ethnic groups[2] at various levels of economic development. They concluded that Soviet reality demanded the creation of a federal state with fifteen national republics and many smaller divisions (autonomous republics, autonomous regions and national districts), each associated with a particular ethnic group.

It was not until the Brezhnev era that some Soviet social scientists proclaimed the realization of Lenin's dream. A new community, "the Soviet people", had allegedly been forged out of the ethnic mixture inherited from the Tsars. Here is what some of the Soviet Union's leading students of ethnicity wrote at the time:

> The natural social and economic integration of the peoples of the USSR is closely associated with their political integration within the framework of a single federal state which represents the organic harmony, and not simply a conglomerate of national-administrative units. The Programme of the CPSU points out that as social construction continues, the boundaries between the Union republics continue to lose their former significance. These fundamental changes signify that the national question, as inherited by the socialist state from the past epoch, has been resolved completely, finally and irrevocably.
>
> Socio-economic and socio-political changes in the USSR have resulted in a new historical community, the Soviet people. . . . [3]

Wooden phrases notwithstanding, there was an element of truth in these claims. After 1917 a growing proportion of the Soviet population learned to speak Russian. Economic inequalities between the myriad national groups diminished. Regionally, economies were unified and placed

6

under central control, while homologous stratification systems crystallized. A country-wide educational system and curriculum were established. Monopolistic mass media broadcast uniform "truths". Remarkable national achievements, such as victory in World War II, galvanized the people and unified them against a "common enemy". Other accomplishments, such as the national space programme, served as a focus for their pride. Common lifestyles were adopted by many citizens, regardless of their ethnic origin. Some members of the national groups most recently incorporated into the USSR resented Sovietization. But to a degree—in some cases, to a large degree—people *did* come to think of themselves as part of "a new historical community, the Soviet people".

Contrary to the claims of the late Brezhnev era, however, the "national question" was not "resolved completely, finally and irrevocably". Far from it. The great paradox of ethnicity in the Soviet Union was that alongside the abovementioned integrative and assimilative pressures, precisely opposite forces throve. This was because ethnicity was used as one of the most important criteria by which people were recruited to higher educational institutions, professional and administrative positions and political posts.[4]

Soviet nationality policy was developed as a means of securing the loyalty of the professional classes in the republics to the political centre and thereby preventing ethnic separatism. Members of ethnic groups residing in their own national republics were given special privileges; elite and professional recruitment was based partly on territorial-ethnic principles. Those residing outside their designated homelands (e.g. Russians in Estonia, Uzbeks in Kyrgyzstan) and especially those without designated homelands (e.g. Jews, ethnic Germans)[5] came to be permanently disadvantaged as a matter of state policy.

The system of territorical-ethnic recruitment first took shape as early as the 1930s. A corollary of Stalin's heretical decision to create "socialism in one country" was the need for iron discipline. This entailed purging all regional elites and replacing them with indigenous Party loyalists. Around the same time, Stalin instituted the internal passport system. Although originally conceived as a mechanism for preventing peasants from escaping collective farms, internal passports soon became the administrative means by which ethnic recruitment was carried out. Each person over the age of fifteen was obliged to carry an internal passport listing, among other things, his or her nationality. Over the years, and especially as attempts were made to invigorate growth in underdeveloped regions, ethnicity became critically important in determining where and what one would study and where and

at what one would work. Soviet federalism made ethnicity one of the most
salient bases of social mobility and immobility.

The following tables help substantiate the argument presented above.
In 1979 Rasma Karklins, an American political scientist, conducted a survey in West Germany of 176 ethnic German immigrants from the Soviet
Union.[6] Among other questions, she asked her respondents what criteria
were in their opinions most important in facilitating access to higher education. The results varied by the respondent's region of origin. As Table 2.1
shows, however, nationality was perceived to be the overwhelmingly important criterion in Kazakhstan and the four republics of Central Asia and
very important indeed in Russia and the three Baltic republics. Nationality
was far and away the single most frequently mentioned criterion perceived
to determine access to higher education in all republics.

Karklins also participated in the 1983 Soviet Interview Project,
which involved a survey of Soviet immigrants in the United States, over 83
per cent of whom were Jews.[7] Among other questions, each respondent was
asked who in his or her republic was treated best in terms of access to
political positions, jobs, and higher education—Russians or members of the
titular nationality (Ukrainians in Ukraine, etc.). Table 2.2 gives the results
for the 924 respondents who answered the question. Only among respondents from Latvia and Belarus did fewer than 40 per cent think that members
of the titular nationality were favoured in recruitment to political positions,
jobs and higher education. In Ukraine, Georgia and Armenia the corresponding figure was in the neighbourhood of 50 per cent. In the remaining
republics—Russia, Kazakhstan, the four republics of Soviet Central Asia,
Lithuania, Estonia and Moldova—a huge majority was convinced that titular nationality mattered above all else in determining the allocation of political positions, jobs and places in the system of higher education.

Part of Table 2.3 illustrates in broad strokes the consequences of
these policies. Column 1 gives the proportion of people in each republic
who were members of the titular nationality in 1989, the year of the last
Soviet census. Column 2 gives the proportion of people in each republic's
administrative-managerial cadres who were members of the titular nationality in 1989. Subtracting the numbers in column 2 from the corresponding numbers in column 1, we see that in nine of the fifteen republics the
titular nationality was overrepresented among administrative-managerial
personnel (as indicated by the plus signs in column 2). In five other republics the degree of underrepresentation (indicated by the minus signs
in column 2) was small—an average of 1.7 per cent. Only in tiny, agricultural Moldova were members of the titular nationality significantly

Table 2.1

*Criteria Mentioned as Facilitating Access to Higher Education, Soviet German
Immigrants in West Germany, by Region, 1979 (in per cent; n=176)*

	Russia	Baltic	Central Asia	Kazakhstan	Other
nationality only	33	39	68	82	50
nationality and					
other factors	17	4	12	7	11
other factors only	50	57	20	11	39
total	100	100	100	100	100

Source: Rasma Karklins, *Ethnic Relations in the USSR: The Perspective from Below* (London: Unwin Hyman, 1986), 64.

Table 2.2

*Perceptions of Nationalities Treated Best, Soviet Immigrants in USA, by Region,
1983 (in per cent; n=924)*

	Political positions		Jobs		Higher education	
	Russians	titular	Russians	titular	Russians	titular
Azerbaydzhan	4	87	4	83	4	92
Russia	88	88	81	81	84	84
Lithuania,						
Estonia	7	83	8	56	7	76
Kazakhstan,						
Central Asia	4	76	1	71	3	71
Moldova	20	68	11	77	5	61
Georgia,						
Armenia	11	63	4	52	5	43
Ukraine	27	52	20	51	27	47
Latvia	40	35	32	20	45	28
Belarus	35	32	21	31	29	25

Source: Adapted from Rasma Karklins, "Nationality policy and ethnic relations in the USSR" in James R. Millar (ed.), *Politics, Work, and Daily Life in the USSR: A Survey of Former Soviet Citizens* (Cambridge UK: Cambridge University Press, 1987), 305-7.

Table 2.3
Ethnic Heterogeneity in the Soviet Republics, 1989

	proportion titular nationals of total republic population	proportion titular nationals of total administrative-managerial personnel in republic (over- or underrepresentation in parentheses)		proportion non-republic residents of all titular nationals (millions in parentheses)	
Russia	81.5	77.3	(- 4.2)	17.4	(25.3)
Ukraine	72.7	79.0	(+ 6.3)	15.3	(6.8)
Belarus	77.9	77.7	(- .2)	21.2	(2.1)
Moldova	64.5	49.8	(-14.7)	16.0	(.6)
Lithuania	79.6	91.5	(+11.9)	4.7	(.1)
Latvia	52.0	63.1	(+11.1)	4.9	(.1)
Estonia	61.5	82.2	(+20.7)	6.2	(.1)
Georgia	70.1	89.3	(+19.2)	4.9	(.2)
Armenia	93.3	99.4	(+ 6.1)	25.7	(1.1)
Azerbaydzhan	82.7	93.8	(+11.1)	14.3	(1.0)
Kazakhstan	39.7	39.5	(- .2)	19.7	(1.6)
Uzbekistan	71.4	67.6	(- 3.8)	15.3	(2.6)
Turkmenistan	72.0	71.8	(- .2)	7.0	(.2)
Tadzhikistan	62.3	66.3	(+ 4.0)	24.7	(1.0)
Kyrgyzstan	52.4	55.1	(+ 2.7)	11.8	(.3)

Sources: Adapted from John P. Cole and Igor V. Filatotchev, "Some observations on migration within and from the former USSR in the 1990s", *Post-Soviet Geography*, vol. 33, no. 7, 1992, 440, 444; L. L. Ribakovsky and N. V. Tarasova, "Migration processes in the USSR: New phenomena", *Sotsiologicheskiye issledovaniya*, no. 7, 1990, 40.

underrepresented (by 14.7 per cent). On average, titular nationalities were overrepresented by nearly 5 per cent in their republics' administrative-managerial personnel. This is remarkable, especially given the underdeveloped state of Soviet Central Asia and Kazakhstan seventy years earlier. Clearly, the territorial-ethnic basis of recruitment had worked well. It had served as a mechanism for allocating privilege and indulgence.[8] Of course, it therefore necessarily served also as a mechanism for allocating underprivilege and resentment. As a result, and despite more than seven decades of Sovietization, ethnic identity was prominent and smouldering on the eve of the collapse of the Communist system in 1991. This was especially evident in the case of the Jews.

THE JEWISH DILEMMA[9]

Under the Communist regime, the Jews were at first a privileged minority to some degree. In a country still consisting largely of illiterate peasants, they were relatively urbanized and educated. In a country whose new rulers were intent on excluding, expelling and killing many members of the old educated classes on grounds of disloyalty, they were disproportionately faithful to the new regime, which many of them saw as their salvation from discrimination and pogroms. In a country whose dominant idea was equality they were viewed by some officials as members of a persecuted minority who deserved special advantages. For all these reasons the Jews advanced quickly in the new Soviet hierarchy.

By 1926 the social structure of the Jewish community had altered considerably. In 1897 a plurality of the Jewish labour force, fully 31 per cent, consisted of merchants, nearly all of them economically marginal. Twenty-nine years later merchants constituted only 12 per cent of the labour force. The proportion of agricultural workers had quadrupled. The proportion of salaried nonmanual workers had more than doubled. Between 1926 and 1935 the number of manual workers tripled.

Jews were particularly attracted to occupations demanding high levels of education. By 1970 they were by far the most highly educated group in the USSR. Some 239 out of every 1,000 Jews over the age of ten had a university education in that year. That compares with a mere 62 out of 1,000 for the entire population and 155 out of 1,000 for Georgians, the second-ranked group. In 1973, when the Jews represented only about 1 per cent of the population, they comprised nearly 2 per cent of university students in the USSR, over 6 per cent of all scientific workers, nearly 9 per cent of all scientists, and 14 per cent of all Doctors of Science (the equivalent of a full professorship in North America). In absolute terms, the only ethnic group with more Doctors of Science than the 2 million Jews were the 130 million Russians. In Moscow, the intellectual capital, Jews comprised nearly 14 per cent of all scientists and over 17 per cent of all Doctors of Science. This extraordinary profile is reflected in Table 2.4, which shows the educational and occupational attainment of the respondents in my sample. Fewer than a tenth of the respondents are manual workers.

Over two-thirds have at least some university education. Six per cent have earned a PhD or higher.

These figures demonstrate that within two generations of the Revolution the Jews of the Soviet Union had been transformed from a destitute and persecuted minority, comprising mainly economically marginal merchants and artisans in Ukraine and Belarus, into the country's most highly educated and urbanized ethnic group, a plurality of whose members had

Table 2.4
Respondents by Education and Occupation

education	frequency	per cent
less than 7 years	3	0
7-8 years	10	1
9-11 years	131	13
professional-technical school	39	4
technical school	140	14
at least some university	615	62
PhD	51	5
Doctor of Science	9	1
total	998	100

occupation	frequency	per cent
manual worker	56	9
teacher	51	8
government service	44	7
private manager	96	15
entrepreneur	30	5
scientist	49	7
engineer	207	32
physician	35	5
lawyer	8	1
free professional	40	6
government administrator	38	6
other	3	0
total	657	101

Note: Percentages do not necessarily total 100 due to rounding.

moved to the Russian heartland. The fact that, practically speaking, possessed no territory of their own[10] initially operated to their advant. they were a facile group whose members could easily be mobilized by the regime to play special modernizing functions in a country initially lacking intellectual resources.

The price for this unprecedented upward social mobility was the virtual destruction of Jewish culture. In 1913 Lenin wrote that anyone who supported the idea of Jewish national culture was an enemy of the proletariat. That attitude did not preclude state support for elements of culture that were (according to the Bolshevik formula) national in form but socialist in content. Consequently, throughout the 1920s those modes of Jewish political and cultural expression which supported the regime were tolerated and even fortified—Yiddish-language newspapers, public schools, proletarian theatre, literature and art, Jewish Sections of the Communist Party, Jewish soviets, and so forth. All these institutions were directed at enforcing pro-Communist tendencies in the Jewish community—and at eliminating Judaism and Zionism from the Jewish cultural repertoire. Thus despite state support for Jewish proletarian culture, thousands of Jewish schools and synagogues were closed in the 1920s.

By 1930 Stalin had initiated a policy of homogenizing all politics and culture and harnessing them to the single aim of building socialism in one country. His campaigns against various deviations from the Party line and the ensuing purges touched many national groups. They affected Jews disproportionately because they were so heavily involved in Party affairs. In addition, most official Jewish institutions were shut down by 1938. The brief flowering of Jewish proletarian culture was over.

The strength of Jewish cultural life in the Soviet Union was briefly invigorated in 1939-40. Under the terms of the Molotov-Ribbentrop pact the Soviet Union annexed the Baltic states and parts of Poland and Romania together with their large Jewish populations. There were now more than 5 million Jews in the USSR and 60 per cent of them had no experience of the homogenizing effects of more than two decades of Soviet rule. However, only half the Jews in the Soviet Union survived the Nazi genocide machine. And due mainly to rural antisemitism, the Jews from the western territories who remained alive after World War II tended to migrate to the larger cities of the region and to Russia proper. There assimilative processes operated in full force.

From 1946 to 1953 Stalin launched a series of campaigns against the Jews who, although never named directly, were singled out by means of codewords—"rootless cosmopolitans", "bourgeois nationalists", "plotters against Stalin" and the like. The remaining fragments of organized Jewish life were now swept away and the community's leading cultural figures shot or sent to die a slower death in remote prison camps.

A crusade against "economic criminals", initiated by Khrushchev in 1961 and lasting three years, had unmistakable antisemitic overtones. And a sustained battle against "international Zionists" was waged by Brezhnev's regime in the wake of the Arab-Israeli war in 1967.

State-sponsored antisemitism became more intense when it was expedient for the regime and less intense when it served no useful purpose. But underlying the emergence of state-sponsored antisemitism in the first place was the simple reality that the Jews did not fit into the grand scheme of Soviet nationality policy, with its emphasis on the proportional representation of titular nationalities in administrative, professional and scientific positions. The central leadership judged that social stability could be bolstered if Jewish professionals were replaced by members of the titular nationalities, thus securing the fealty of the latter and preventing their involvement in republic nationalisms.

As early as the 1930s some replacements became available. Stalin initiated the widespread educational upgrading of *vydvizhentsy*, or workers "from the bench", and their recruitment to precisely the sorts of jobs in which Jews figured prominently. Khrushchev proudly noted that the Soviets had "created new cadres" and explained that "[i]f the Jews now want to occupy the top jobs in our republics, they would obviously be looked upon unfavourably by the indigenous peoples."[11]

But it was really only in the period 1967-71 that large numbers of Jews began to wonder whether they and their children had any future in the USSR. Many memoirs and systematic studies from that period show that Jews began to face sharply restricted educational and professional opportunities at that time. Here is just one contemporary example of the operation of ethnic quotas. In 1979 there were 47 non-Jewish and 40 Jewish student applicants to the Mechanics and Mathematics Department of Moscow State University. The non-Jews had won 26 mathematics Olympiads, the Jews 48, yet 40 non-Jews and only six Jews were accepted into the Department.[12] These and similar circumstances were repeated countless times, especially in the better schools and institutes. This is one of the most important reasons why some Jews began to consider the difficult process of emigrating. Their lives in the Soviet Union were based on their ability to achieve professional excellence. When opportunities to excel professionally were restricted, they felt that there was no future for them in the USSR.

The anomalous position of the Jews in the structure of Soviet nationality relations was the most fundamental reason for the emergence of the emigration movement. But it was not the only reason. The United States of America and other Western governments began to use whatever influence they could muster, including trade sanctions, to encourage the Soviet authorities to permit some Jews to leave. Isreal's victory in the 1967 Six Day War stimulated a feeling of pride, defiance and Zionist activism among some Soviet Jews. The "anti-Zionist" ideological and political campaign, with its antisemitic excesses, launched by the regime to counter the philosophy and practice of emigration convinced many Jews that they no longer had a place in Soviet society and that they should abandon all hope of political and cultural reform. Thus the emigration movement grew in response to a unique conjuncture of structural circumstances, precipitants and motivations.

The emigration movement began haltingly in 1966 and in earnest in 1971. Until 1977 most of the emigrants were inspired to leave by Zionist and religious motives. Most of them came from peripheral areas where assimilation was less widespread, notably the Baltics, Moldova, western Ukraine, western Belarus (all of which fell under Soviet rule only after World War II) and Georgia. Most of the emigrants went to Israel. By 1977, however, a change in the nature of the movement was signalled by the fact that, for the first time, more than half the emigrants chose to go to the United States and other Western countries rather than Israel. Thereafter, most Jews left for less ideological and more pragmatic reasons—to enjoy political and cultural freedom, to escape the burden of being a Jew in the Soviet Union, to join family members, to ensure a secure future for their children and, especially from the end of the 1980s, to flee political instability and economic ruin. A growing proportion of emigrants now came from the Russian heartland and eastern Ukraine and Belarus: they were relatively assimiliated Jews whose families had lived under Communism since 1917, who had passed through the Soviet education system and who thought of Russian culture as their own.

Indeed, many relatively assimilated Jews—Ted Friedgut refers to them as the "silent majority"[13]—decided not to emigrate at all. They tried their best to accomodate themselves to the realities of the Brezhnev years and the new uncertainties of life under Gorbachev and Yeltsin. Many were simply confused about who they were and what they should do. One contemporary lamented:

Who am I now? Who do I feel myself to be? Unfortunately, I do not feel like a Jew. I understand that I have an unquestionable genetic tie with

Jewry. I also assume that this is reflected in my mentality, in my mode of thinking, and in my behavior. But this common quality is as little help to me in feeling my Jewish identity as similarity of external features— evidently, a more profound, or more general, common bond is lacking, such as community of language, culture, history, tradition. . . .

I am accustomed to the color, smell, rustle, of the Russian landscape, as I am to the Russian language, the rhythm of Russian poetry. I react to everything else as an alien. . . .

And nevertheless, no, I am not Russian, I am a stranger today in this land.[14]

The marginality that characterizes the Jews of the region, their uncertainty as to where they belong, their cultural and geographical suspension, as it were between East and West, has made them ideal political pawns. In the Cold War era they were used (if I may mix metaphors) as bargaining chips in US-Soviet relations. In the swift economic and political decline that has characterized the CIS over the past few years, antisemites have cast them as devious and powerful conspirators against the once-mighty empire. Israeli officials have been inclined to give high estimates of their numbers and distort their motives for emigrating. Many Jews in Israel and the West perceive tremendous potential in the region for a revival of Jewish culture and have generously donated personnel and resources to facilitate that rebirth. Clearly, these and other groups have strong vested interests in characterizing the Jews of the region in one way or another. The desire to sort out competing depictions is sufficient justification for wanting to listen systematically to what the remaining Jews of the region have to say about themselves. In my judgement, the survey results reported in the following pages represent one of the most finely tuned listening devices available to date.

Let us now turn our attention to three of the questions which the survey can help answer. How many Jews now live in Russia, Ukraine and Belarus? How Jewish are they? Which factors determine variations in the degree of Jewishness typically found in different categories of the population?

NOTES

1. This section is a slightly revised version of Robert J. Brym, "From 'the Soviet people' to the refugee crisis in Russia" in Rozalina Ryvkina and Rostislav Turovskiy, *The Refugee Crisis in Russia*, Robert Brym (ed.), P. Patchet-Golubev, trans., (Toronto: York Lanes Press, 1993), 1-4.

2. I use the terms ethnicity and nationality interchangeably here.

3. J. Bromley *et al.*, *Present-Day Ethnic Processes in the USSR* (Moscow: Progress Publishers 1982 [1977]), 269-70.

4. Victor Zaslavsky and Robert J. Brym, *Soviet-Jewish Emigration and Soviet Nationality Policy* (London: Macmillan, 1983).

5. Birobidzhan, the officially designated Jewish autonomous region near China, is largely a fiction. Only 0.6 per cent of Soviet Jews lived there in 1989. See Felix Ryansky, "Jews and Cossacks in the Jewish Autonomous Region", *Refuge*, vol. 12, no. 4, 1992, 19-21.

6. Rasma Karklins, *Ethnic Relations in the USSR: The Perspective from Below* (London: Unwin Hyman, 1986).

7. Rasma Karklins, "Nationality policy and ethnic relations in the USSR" in James R. Millar (ed.), *Politics, Work, and Daily Life in the USSR: A Survey of Former Soviet Citizens* (Cambridge UK: Cambridge University Press, 1987), 305-31.

8. This is not to suggest that ultimate power ever resided in the hands of the titular nationalities. Slavs, and Russians in particular, dominated the central apparatus and were nominally second-in-command in all republics.

9. The following sketch is based mainly on Mordechai Altshuler, "The Jewish Community in the Soviet Union: A Socio-Demographic Analysis" (Jerusalem: Magnes Press, Hebrew University of Jerusalem, 1979) (in Hebrew); Jonathan Frankel, "The Soviet regime and anti-Zionism: An analysis" in Yaacov Ro'i and Avi Beker (eds.), *Jewish Culture and Identity in the Soviet Union* (New York and London: New York University Press, 1991), 310-54; Yehoshua A. Gilboa, *The Black Years of Soviet Jewry, 1939-1953*, translated by Yosef Shachter and Dov Ben-Abba, (Boston: Little, Brown, 1971); Zvi Gitelman, *Jewish Nationality and Soviet Politics: The Jewish Sections of the CPSU, 1917-1930* (Princeton: Princeton University Press, 1972); Solomon M. Schwarz, *The Jews in the Soviet Union* (Syracuse NY: Syracuse University Press, 1951); and Zaslavsky and Brym.

10. See note 5.

11. "Meetings between representatives of the French Socialist Party and Soviet leaders (1956)" in Benjamin Pinkus (ed.), *The Soviet Government and the Jews 1948-1967* (Cambridge UK: Cambridge University Press, 1984), 58.

12. Moscow Helsinki Monitoring Group, *Discrimination Against Jews Enrolling at Moscow State University, 1979*, Document 112 (n.p.: 5 November 1979, mimeograph).

13. Theodore Friedgut, "Soviet Jewry: The silent majority", *Soviet Jewish Affairs*, vol. 10, no. 2, 1980, 3-19.

14   Larisa Bogoraz, "Do I feel I belong to the Jewish people?" in Aleksandr
      Voronel, Viktor Yakhot and Moshe Decter (eds.), *I am a Jew: Essays on
      Jewish Identity in the Soviet Union* (New York: Academic Committee on
      Soviet Jewry and Anti-Defamation League of B'nai B'rith, 1973), 63-4.

3 Identity

HOW MANY JEWS LIVE IN RUSSIA, UKRAINE AND BELARUS?

Estimates of the number of Jews in the former Soviet Union range from about 3 million to well under 1 million.[1] The low estimates are based on a strict interpretation of census returns. The high estimates are based on the assumption that an enormous number of Soviet citizens concealed their Jewish roots under the Soviet regime. Presumably, those people are now free to identify as Jews and, increasingly, do just that. In my judgement, neither estimate is accurate although census figures are much closer to the mark.

Three more or less well-known facts need to be reviewed before I offer my own population estimate.

▪ Like all citizens of the former Soviet Union over the age of fifteen, Jews are still required to hold an internal passport listing, among other things, the bearer's nationality, or what in the West is known as ethnicity. All children whose parents are Jewish according to their internal passports are themselves automatically registered as Jews. They cannot normally change their nationality designation, even as adults. In the survey on which this study is based, only 3 per cent of respondents said they had ever changed the nationality designation in their internal passports. Sixteen of the thirty cases involved a change to Russian nationality, ten to Jewish nationality and two each to Ukrainian and Belarusian.

▪ At the age of sixteen the child of a mixed marriage must choose one parent's nationality as his or her own. Research conducted during the Soviet period shows that adolescents chose the non-Jewish nationality in more than 90 per cent of cases. The number of children who made that choice is large, partly because the rate of ethnic intermarriage has been high and is getting higher. According to 1979 census figures, 47 per cent of Russian Jews lived in ethnically heterogeneous families. The corresponding figure for Ukrainian Jews was 33 per cent and for Belarusian Jews 29 per cent.[2]

19

According to 1988 marriage registration statistics, the percentage of mixed marriages in all marriages involving at least one Jewish spouse was 63 per cent in Russia, 45 per cent in Ukraine and 40 per cent in Belarus.[3] In my 1993 survey, the weighted proportion of ever-married respondents reporting a non-Jewish spouse is 60 per cent—61 per cent in Moscow, 58 per cent in Kiev, and 52 per cent in Minsk.

▪ Censuses were taken on an irregular basis in the Soviet Union. In principle, they presented Jews with an opportunity to deny their national origins. However, in the 1970s researchers in Israel sought to determine whether Soviet Jewish immigrants concealed their Jewish identity from Soviet census-takers. They discovered that people registered as Jews in their internal passports tended virtually unanimously to declare Jewish as their nationality in the census.[4] It is therefore commonly assumed that census figures are a good indicator of the number of passport Jews.

In the light of these facts, what can one make of the high and low estimates of Jewish population size? The high population estimates are generally based on the Israeli Law of Return, which offers immediate citizenship to all first or second generation offspring of Jews—defined as the offspring of Jewish mothers or converts—and to members of their households. Some demographers suggest that although the 1989 census counted 1.45 million Jews in the USSR, the actual number is more like 2.9 million if one takes into account "peripheral Jews"—non-Jewish spouses and the children and grandchildren of Jewish mothers who did not have their offpsring registered as Jews in their internal passports.

This estimate may be credible, but it is not very useful. An anthropologist once wrote that if any two people are chosen at random from the planet then on average they will be thirty-second cousins. This may underscore the common origins of all humanity but it does not greatly help us to understand geopolitical conflict among nations today. Analogously, inflated estimates of the number of Jews in the CIS may be of academic or political interest but if one is interested in ascertaining how many Jews are likely to become part of a functioning Jewish community or to emigrate it is necessary to be more realistic.

The plain fact is that many spouses of Jews have no interest in Jewish culture and no interest in leaving their country. Most children and especially grandchildren of Jewish mothers who did not have their offpsring registered as Jews are completely assimilated into Russian culture and also prefer to stay. That is evident from a recent study conducted by the Israeli

Ministry of the Interior. The Ministry issues identification cards to new citizens. It defines a Jew as anyone who was born to a Jewish mother, converted to Judaism, or can present a valid document issued by a legitimate civil authority testifying to the bearer's Jewish nationality. Between October 1989 and February 1991 only 6.4 per cent of 180,754 Soviet immigrants to Israel were not Jews, so defined.[5] While the proportion of non-Jews among all emigrants is somewhat higher (see below), these figures show that only a small minority of the 1.45 million or so peripheral Jews have so far emigrated and suggest that few will do so in the future. Since the main advantage of re-identifying oneself as a Jew is emigrating, far fewer are likely to become involved with the Jewish community in the CIS.

Population estimates at the low end adhere closely to census figures. They thereby ignore the undeniable tendency of some first-generation children of mixed marriages who are registered as non-Jews to re-identify as Jews. This, too, strikes me as untenable. Even under circumstances more stable than those which have characterized the region over the past few years, ethnicity is a somewhat plastic feature of one's identity, especially for people who do not associate very strongly with any one ethnic group.[6] Ethnic identity may change when circumstances and opportunities warrant it and, like members of all other ethnic groups, Jews in the former USSR have to a degree been influenced by pragmatic considerations in choosing their ethnicity. Thus when it was clearly disadvantageous to be registered as a Jew in one's internal passport on account of restricted education and employment opportunities, the children of mixed marriages tended overwhelmingly to register as non-Jews. In contrast, one big advantage has been bound up with Jewish ethnicity since the beginning of the emigration movement: many Jews have been able to obtain a one-way ticket out of the country. Hence the well-known Russian quip that defines a Jewish wife as a means of transportation. Some children of mixed marriages who were registered as non-Jews at the age of sixteen are now declaring that they are Jews.[7] Some of them emigrate. I estimate that in the last few years 15 per cent of all emigrants who declared themselves Jewish were in fact not Jewish according to their internal passports.[8]

If the possibility of emigration has inflated the number of self-proclaimed Jews in what is now the CIS, then by how much? Surveys can help answer that question. In selecting a sample of Jews to be interviewed for this study I decided to cast a wide net with fine mesh. I included in my sample only those people who said they were registered as Jews in their internal passports; *or* who said that their mothers or fathers were so registered; *or* who said they had a Jewish identity or a mixture of Jewish and some other ethnic identity. The sample thus contains Jews defined by diverse criteria. Some of the respondents are marginally Jewish. Some of them are not registered as Jews in their internal passports.

This is what makes it possible to estimate how many Jews lived in Russia, Ukraine and Belarus in 1993. Assume that the 1,000 people in my sample represent the broadest credible definition of the Jewish population in those three countries. Since 6 per cent of the respondents said they were registered as Jews in their internal passports and 31 per cent said that they were not (see Table 3.1), we can calculate that the internal passport criterion underestimates the maximum size of the Jewish population by 46 per cent (31/69). Of course, this refers only to the Jewish population of Moscow, Kiev and Minsk. Most of the rest of the former USSR—smaller centres in the Slavic republics, Moldova, the Baltic republics, and Central Asia—has been less affected by assimilation. If these other centres were included in the sample the underestimate would undoubtedly be smaller, perhaps 35 per cent.

If we knew how many people in the entire population were registered as Jews in their internal passports, we could add 35 per cent to that number to arrive at a rough estimate of the size of the Jewish population, very broadly defined. Fortunately, as we have seen, there exists an accurate estimate of how many people were registered as Jews in their internal passports in 1989. It is found in the census of that year. The way to estimate the size of the Jewish population in Russia, Ukraine and Belarus in 1993 is thus clear: (1) Find the Jewish population size according to the 1989 census; (2) Subtract 85 per cent of the number of emigrants from 1989 to 1992 inclusive (all those registered as Jews); (3) Subtract the population loss during that period due to causes other than emigration, notably the excess of deaths over births; (4) Inflate that figure by 35 per cent.

According to the 1989 census, the Jewish population of the entire USSR was 1,449,000.[9] Some 623,000 people who declared themselves as Jews emigrated from 1989 to 1992 inclusive. Assuming that 85 per cent of the emigrants were registered as Jews in their internal passports, this outflow brought the Jewish census population down to 919,000. In the 1980s the rate of population decline due to factors other than emigration was 2.0 per cent.[10] Assuming that the rate did not change in the early 1990s, this brought the census population down to 848,000 by 1993. Adding 35 per cent to that figure, we arrive at a rough 1993 estimate of 1,144,000 people in the entire territory of the former USSR who identified themselves as Jews, were registered as Jews in their internal passports, or who had at least one parent who was so registered.

In 1989 38 per cent of all Soviet Jews lived in Russia, 34 per cent in Ukraine and 8 per cent in Belarus. Assuming that those proportions remained constant until 1993, the Jewish population of Russia in 1993 was 435,000. For Ukraine the figure was 389,000 and for Belarus 92,000. Thus a realistic estimate of the maximum size of the total Jewish population in the three countries in 1993 is approximately 916,000. Applying the same logic to the three cities surveyed, in 1993 there were roughly 139,000 Jews in Moscow, 85,000 in Kiev and 31,000 in Minsk (see Table 3.2).

Table 3.1
Respondents by Nationality According to
Internal Passports (in per cent)

Jewish	69
Russian	22
Ukrainian	7
Belarusian	1
other	1
total	100

Table 3.2
Estimated Number of People Registered as Jewish, with At Least One Parent
Registered as Jewish, or Jewish Self-Identity, 1993

Russia	435,000	of which Moscow	139,000
Ukraine	389,000	of which Kiev	85,000
Belarus	92,000	of which Minsk	31,000
subtotal	916,000		
rest of former USSR	228,000		
total	1,144,000		

HOW JEWISH ARE THEY?

Now that we have a better idea of the size of the population about which I wish to generalize, I must emphasize that Jewish or any other ethnicity involves more than just identity. It also comprises a bundle of related beliefs and practices.[11] Accordingly, each respondent was asked nearly two dozen questions about his or her Jewish identity, beliefs and practices. The responses to those questions are presented in Table 3.3. Where data on roughly comparable items are available, the results of American and Canadian surveys conducted in 1989 and 1990 are set alongside the CIS results.[12] They help keep the CIS results in perspective.

What do all these numbers mean? Do they add up to a revival of Jewish communal life or a community in decline? The absence of comparable data from an earlier period makes it impossible to answer that question conclusively. However, several relevant observations are possible. First, any reasonably knowledgeable observer would have to be surprised that the values of three indicators of Jewish involvement are so high. The proportion of Jews who at least occasionally read the Jewish press (42 per cent) is higher than the comparable proportion in the USA (33 per cent). The proportion who celebrate Passover (42 per cent), while substantially less than the figures for North America (76 per cent for the USA and 92 per cent for Canada), is still remarkably high given the suppression of Judaism in the Soviet Union for so many years. (The popularity of Passover may be related to the frequently drawn parallel between the Biblical exodus from Egypt and the modern emigration movement.) And the fact that fully 73 per cent of Jews in Moscow, Kiev and Minsk express the desire to have more contact with Jewish culture must surely suggest that some potential for communal revival exists in those cities.

On the other hand, the data show a disturbing discrepancy between belief and practice, or between what Zvi Gitelman analagously calls "passive" and "active" Jewish identity. In his words:

> For most Jews, passive Jewish identity is associated with passive involvement with Jewish culture. For a minority, passive identity turns into active identity, which, in turn, leads to attempts to live actively as cultural Jews, whether defined religiously, linguistically, artistically, or in other ways. . . . Active culture is developed by minorities, but the size of those minorities and the ratio between active and passive identity vary with the fluctuations in Soviet conditions: in times of great pressure, such as 1948-53, the proportion of active identifiers, and

Table 3.3
Indicators of Jewishness Moscow/Kiev/Minsk, USA and Canada (in per cent)

question		Moscow/ Kiev/Minsk	USA	Canada
	general ideological statements			
q70.	Wants Jewish cultural revival	95		
q62.	Wants Jewish religious development	78		
q47.	National identification Jewish or Jewish and other	75		
	average	83		
	specific ideological statements			
q69.	Too little contact with Jewish culture	73		
q68.	Too little contact with other Jews	35		
q72.	Prefers that Jews marry other Jews	26		
q108.	Feels that Israel is the historical motherland of the Jewish people	24		
q56.	Plans to learn Hebrew or Yiddish	20		
q158.	Thinks of living in Israel as very important or important	19	13	21
	average	33		
	behavioural statements			
q65.	Often or occasionally reads Jewish press	42	33	60
q60.	Celebrates Passover	42	76	92
q44.	Spouse's nationality Jewish	40		90
q61.	Attends synagogue often or occasionally	33	50	67
q67.	Do you belong to Jewish community?	27		
q58.	Celebrates Jewish New Year	17		
q59.	Celebrates Day of Atonement	16	64	77
q73.	Bringing up children with Jewish traditions	16		
q57.	Celebrates Jewish Sabbath	10	26	54
q50.	Speaks Yiddish well or moderately well	8		37
q63.	Participates in Jewish organization	6	24	31
q64.	Member of Jewish organization	5	37	47
q49.	Speaks Hebrew well or moderately well	2		25
	average	20		

the amount of overt cultural activity, decline. In times of relative relaxa-
tion, such as the mid-1970s, active identity and culture grow, especially
if external forces feed them.[13]

   Surely the Jews of the region are now experiencing the greatest re-
laxation of state pressure against them since 1917. What then is the ratio of
active to passive Jews or, as I would prefer to put it, how large is the
discrepancy between belief and practice? In order to answer this question I
divided the questionnaire items in Table 3.3 into three categories—general
ideological statements (what the Americans call "motherhood issues"),
specific ideological assertions, and declarations about actual Jewish practice. One immediately notices the very large proportion of respondents who
agree with "motherhood issues". Nearly everyone wants a Jewish cultural
revival to take place in their country and over three-quarters of the respondents would like to witness the invigorated development of Judaism.
   Before concluding that this demonstrates a vast untapped potential
for Jewish cultural rebirth in the Slavic republics of the CIS, however, one
should bear in mind an important fact. Ever since polling has been conducted in the region, researchers have discovered that enormous proportions of the population agree with general principles that are in vogue.
For example, nearly everyone—from die-hard Stalinists to Thatcherite
conservatives—endorsed *perestroyka* in 1988. What they meant by *perestroyka* is, however, a different matter. Pollsters had to ask more specific
questions about political and economic beliefs and practices before meaningful divisions of opinion emerged from their data.[14]
   The same principle applies here. When respondents were asked about
specific beliefs, the proportion choosing the more Jewish response dropped
precipitously and large divisions of opinion materialized. For example,
while 95 per cent of the respondents expressed the desire for a Jewish
cultural revival, only 26 per cent said that it was important for Jews to
marry other Jews. In general, the proportions dropped still further when
respondents were asked about Jewish practice, such as whether they were
bringing up their children in line with Jewish traditions (16 per cent) and
whether they belonged to a Jewish organization (5 per cent). The average
proportion of respondents giving a Jewish response on the three general
ideological statements was 83 per cent. For the six specific ideological
assertions, the average was only 33 per cent. For the thirteen declarations
of Jewish practice, the average dropped to 20 per cent.
   Fewer than a fifth of Jews in Moscow, Kiev and Minsk have a working knowledge of Hebrew or Yiddish, belong to or participate in a Jewish

organization, have a Jewish upbringing, are giving a Jewish upbringing to their children, or celebrate the Sabbath or the High Holy Days. Moreover, with the single exception of reading the Jewish press, the participation rates of the respondents in all Jewish activities are well below the corresponding rates for the 5,500,000 Jews in the USA and far below the corresponding rates for the 370,000 Jews in Canada. In absolute and comparative terms, and speaking here only of group averages, these results indicate that the cultural and organizational infrastructures of the Jewish communities of Moscow, Kiev and Minsk embrace only a small fraction of the Jewish population. Specifically, only 27 per cent of the respondents feel that they are part of the Jewish community. I conclude that while there is a suprisingly widespread desire for a reanimation of Jewish life in Moscow, Kiev and Minsk, it is doubtful whether more than a third of the population wants to become personally involved.

Group averages always mask internal variations, and it is important to know which categories of the population are most inclined to give Jewish responses to the questionnaire items. It augurs well for Jewish communal life in the CIS if the respondents who are most actively involved in the community are likely to remain in the population in the near future. If, on the other hand, the most Jewish respondents turn out to be those who will soon leave the community—in particular, the elderly and emigrants—then its future is bleaker.

WHAT DETERMINES JEWISHNESS?

In order to answer this question I first constructed an index of Jewishness by combining twenty of the items listed in Table 3.3 and then dividing the index into high, medium and low values.[15] I selected cutoff points so that about a third of the sample falls into each of the three values. Table 3.4 shows how Jewishness varies by city, age and a host of other variables. Only relationships that are likely to occur by chance less than once in twenty times are shown; eleven of the fourteen relationships are likely to occur by chance less than once in 1,000 times.

Table 3.4 offers some obvious findings and some surprises. Consider first that level of education is not listed as a statistically significant predictor of Jewishness. A number of researchers, including L. M. Drobizheva and Zvi Gitelman, have emphasized that "the more educated strata are more likely to have more links to their ethnic groups than others. It is precisely more educated people who are more aware of membership in a

Table 3.4
Jewishness by Correlates (in per cent; n in parentheses)

		Jewishness		
question	low	medium	high	total
q5. city				
Moscow	38	33	29	100 (544)
Kiev	33	34	33	100 (333)
Minsk	12	31	57	100 (123)

chi-square = 47.79, d.f. = 4, sig. = .000, tau-c = .142

q8. age				
18-29	41	25	33	100 (182)
30-39	30	37	33	100 (153)
40-49	37	33	30	100 (215)
50-59	31	37	32	100 (284)
60+	28	32	41	100 (167)

chi-square = 15.91, d.f. = 8, sig. = .043, tau-c = .065

q48. exposure to Jewish culture in upbringing				
great	4	12	85	100 (26)
moderate	7	24	71	100 (102)
weak	19	37	44	100 (273)
negligible	46	34	20	100 (582)

chi-square = 179.36, d.f.=6, sig. = .000, tau-c = -.341

q74. emigration plans				
yes	16	28	56	100 (288)
no	43	35	22	100 (572)

chi-square = 107.81, d.f.=2, sig. = .000, tau-c = -.357

q42. father's passport nationality				
Jewish	28	35	37	100 (800)
other	56	26	19	100 (200)

chi-square = 57.56, d.f.=2, sig. = .000, tau-c = -.196

q43. mother's passport nationality				
Jewish	21	37	42	100 (698)
other	61	24	14	100 (303)

chi-square = 162.32, d.f.=2, sig. = .000, tau-c = -.382

Table 3.4 (cont'd)
Jewishness by Correlates (in per cent; n in parentheses)

q44. spouse's passport nationality

Jewish	27	31	42	100 (408)
other	38	34	28	100 (592)

chi-square = 22.88, d.f. = 2, sig. = .000, tau-c = -.158

q45. respondent's passport nationality

Jewish	21	37	42	100 (684)
other	60	25	15	100 (317)

chi-square = 150.62, d.f. = 2, sig. = .000, tau-c = -.373

q123. personally suffered antisemitism

yes	20	38	41	100 (553)
no	48	29	23	100 (328)

chi-square = 77.01, d.f. = 2, sig. = .000, tau-c = -.288

q130. fear antisemitism

very much	20	34	45	100 (297)
not very much	32	36	33	100 (385)
not at all	50	26	23	100 (270)

chi-square = 64.65, d.f. = 4, sig. = .000, tau-c = -.219

q40. occupational satisfaction

satisfied	40	31	28	100 (478)
wants higher	26	37	37	100 (380)

chi-square = 20.07, d.f. = 2, sig. = .000, tau-c = .153

q41. opportunities for upward mobility

yes	42	30	28	100 (178)
no	31	34	35	100 (629)

chi-square = 7.43, d.f. = 2, sig. = .024, tau-c = .081

q162. political system in 1-2 years

freer	39	33	27	100 (142)
same	33	32	35	100 (342)
less free	26	33	42	100 (240)

chi-square = 11.05, d.f. = 4, sig. = .026, tau-c = .107

q163. confidence in own future

yes	47	26	27	100 (162)
no	29	36	35	100 (701)

chi-square = 19.32, d.f. = 2, sig. = .000, tau-c = .106

community of fate."[16] They apparently based their conclusion on casual observation and/or data drawn from non-random samples of Jews. One inference that may be drawn from my survey is that education does *not* influence Jewishness. Less educated Jews are as likely as more educated Jews to have high levels of Jewish identity, belief and practice; being "more aware of membership in a community of fate" is not a luxury (or a burden) unique to the highly educated.[17]

City of residence, in contrast, does have a statistically significant effect on level of Jewishness. It is well known that Jews in the western part of the former Soviet Union are less assimiliated than those in eastern Ukraine and Russia proper because the western territory was incorporated in the USSR only after World War II. "Heartlanders" have had three decades more exposure to Communism than those on the periphery, which is why they are less Jewish. But even Kiev and Minsk, which have (with the exception of the World War II period) been under Russian control since the early years of Soviet rule, contain populations that are more actively involved in Jewish life than are the Jews of Moscow. There are two reasons for this. First, many Moscow Jews are descendants of people who arrived in the city from the western part of the USSR in the years immediately following the Revolution. Many of them were already quite highly assimilated when they arrived. In contrast, Jews from Kiev and especially Minsk are more likely to have arrived later from small centres in the region and to have been less assimilated when they migrated. Indeed, the families of many Jews in Kiev and Minsk left their villages for the city only after World War II. Second, Moscow is a larger and more cosmopolitan centre than Kiev; and Kiev is a larger and more cosmopolitan centre than Minsk. Assimilative pressures probably vary accordingly.

Table 3.4 also shows that people who are sixty years of age and older, and who were therefore more exposed to Jewish culture in their youth, are today more involved in Jewish life than people under the age of sixty, who have had less exposure to Jewish culture. Older Jews are more likely to have had religious or ethnically involved parents. Many secular Jewish institutions functioned until the 1930s. The impact of Jewish schools, theatres, publishing houses and newspapers is still evident among the older generation of Jews in Moscow, Kiev and Minsk.

The last finding may surprise observers of the Jewish scene in the CIS who believe that a widespread revival of Jewish culture is gripping the younger generation. There *is* a revival. However, it is not sufficiently extensive to show up in the survey data. The proportion of respondents between the ages of eighteen and fifty-nine who demonstrate high levels of Jewishness is nearly constant at 30 to 33 per cent. This is not an encouraging finding. In the next decade or two natural demographic processes will eliminate many of the people who are most actively involved in Jewish life in the three cities—those sixty years of age and older.

With the exception of the collapse of the Communist regime, the single most important event for Jews in the region in the past quarter-century was the onset of the emigration movement. As noted above, the very existence of the movement encouraged many people who previously had no connection with the community to redefine themselves as Jews. The data presented in Table 3.4 are certainly consistent with that interpretation. There is a strong association between planning to emigrate, on the one hand, and, on the other, demonstrating strong Jewish patterns of belief and high rates of community participation.[18] Here again we confront a discouraging indicator of communal longevity: the most "Jewish Jews" are planning to leave. Aleksandr Burakovsky, Chairman of the Kiev Sholem Aleichem Society, may have exaggerated only a little when he stated in 1992 "Twenty more years, and the Jews will be gone."[19]

The data also support the view that the persistence of Jewish identity, belief and practice has been encouraged by the internal passport regime. As we saw in Chapter 2, ethnicity was an important factor which helped determine the allocation of students to institutions of higher education. Ethnic quotas were also used to earmark personnel for managerial, professional and scientific positions. The internal passport regime was the administrative mechanism by which the system of ethnic recruitment was implemented. Its unintended consequence was to maintain the salience of ethnicity in general and Jewish ethnicity in particular. Little wonder, then, that in 1993 we should discover higher levels of Jewishness among people who are designated as Jews in their internal passports and whose mothers, fathers and spouses are also so designated.

In the aftermath of World War II Jean-Paul Sartre remarked that "it is the anti-Semite who creates the Jew."[20] Notwithstanding the one-sidedness of his argument, it does contain an element of truth, as Table 3.4 shows. Respondents who have personally suffered from antisemitism and respondents who fear antisemitism are more likely to express high levels of Jewishness than those who lack such experiences and anxieties. This argument is given additional, indirect support by the data on the age distribution of Jewishness. In general, the proportion of people expressing low levels of Jewishness varies inversely with age: younger Jews are more likely to express low levels of Jewishness than older Jews. The only exception is the

30-39 age cohort. Respondents in that age cohort are somewhat less likely to display a low level of Jewishness than expected. That may be because people in that age cohort were in their formative years during the especially virulent and protracted "anti-Zionist" campaigns of the late 1960s to early 1980s.[21]

Finally, Table 3.4 demonstrates that high levels of Jewishness are significantly related to a series of factors indicating a pessimistic outlook on one's future prospects in Moscow, Kiev and Minsk. Research conducted in the USA shows that, in general, ethnicity is reinforced among people who feel that they cannot advance on their individual merits.[22] Especially if they believe that discrimination against their ethnic group is an important reason for their blocked mobility, people tend to view their individual interests as identical with their group interests. They are then inclined to seek collective, ethnic means of improving their situation. These generalizations hold for the Jews in Moscow, Kiev and Minsk. The most Jewish Jews in those cities tend to express dissatisfaction with their current occupations, believe that they have few opportunities for upward occupational mobility, judge that the political system will give them fewer freedoms in the next year or two and in general hold a pessimistic outlook on their future in their country. Respondents who are less Jewishly involved tend not to be so occupationally and politically discouraged. They are therefore more inclined to seek individual rather than ethnic-group means of improving the conditions of their existence.

Table 3.4 lists all the variables in the questionnaire that are statistically significantly related to level of Jewishness. The list is informative, but only to a degree. The main trouble with it is that it gives us no idea of the *magnitude* of the *independent* effect of each variable on Jewishness. By "magnitude" I refer to the fact that each variable discussed above may weigh more or less heavily in determining how Jewish the respondents feel and act. Knowing exactly what causal weight to attach to each variable would represent an advance in our knowledge. By "independence" I refer to the fact that the effects of some variables on Jewishness may be wholly or partly explained by other variables. For example, age is significantly associated with Jewishness. But older people also tend to have had a more Jewish upbringing—and the nature of one's upbringing is also significantly associated with Jewishness. When one takes into account the causal weight of upbringing, how much causal effect is left for age? These and related questions can be answered by multiple regression analysis.

Table 3.5 presents a multiple regression of Jewishness on all of the variables listed in Table 3.4.[23] The standardized slopes (betas) listed in column 3 indicate the magnitude of each variable's independent effects compared to the magnitude of the other variables' independent effects.

We see from Table 3.5 that the single most important determinant of Jewishness is the degree to which one was exposed to Jewish culture during one's upbringing. Planning to emigrate has 72 per cent of the effect of upbringing in determining level of Jewishness. Having a mother with a Jewish passport designation and having a spouse with a Jewish passport designation exert, respectively, 50 and 44 per cent of the effect of upbringing on level of Jewishness. The remaining four variables--whether one personally experienced antisemitism, whether one's father has or had a Jewish passport designation, whether one fears antisemitism and one's city of residence--each exert between 28 and 31 per cent of the effect of upbringing on Jewishness.[24] Age and factors associated with perceptions of blocked mobility do not appear in the table because their effects are totally accounted for by these other variables.

Table 3.5
Multiple Regression of Jewishness

question	slope (b)	standard error	standardized slope (beta)	t
q48-Jewish upbringing	4.18	.33	.36	12.58
q74-emigration plans	4.92	.57	.26	8.62
q43-mother's passport	3.56	.62	.18	5.73
q44-spouse's passport	2.90	.54	.16	5.36
q123-experience antisemitism	1.95	.57	.10	3.44
q42-father's passport	2.29	.76	.10	3.16
q130-fear antisemitism	1.27	.35	.11	3.63
q5-city size	1.32	.39	.10	3.35

intercept = -37.85; n = 731; adjusted R^2 = .42

SUMMARY

About three-quarters of the people in my sample do not feel that they are connected to the Jewish community and about two-thirds of them do not wish to have any more contact with Jews. Many respondents are prepared to state rather vaguely that they would like to have more contact with Jewish culture, but when it comes to specifics the numbers fall sharply. Stated in absolute terms, there are roughly 255,000 Jews in the three cities but only about 85,000 of them are now, or are likely soon to become, part of the Jewish community in any meaningful sense. To this one must add the observation that Jewishness is stronger among those with emigration plans and among older respondents. Thus many of the 85,000 actual and potential community members will leave or die in the near future. On the basis of the information in hand one cannot be very optimistic that in ten or twenty years the cultural revival undoubtedly taking place in the region will engulf any more than a small minority of the Jews in Moscow, Kiev and Minsk.

Several factors emerge from my analysis as the main sources of Jewish identity, belief and practice in Moscow, Kiev and Minsk. They include Jewish upbringing, the possibility of emigration, the passport regime, antisemitism and city of residence. Taken together, these factors explain a very respectable 42 per cent of the variation in Jewishness among the respondents.

In terms of its causal weight, antisemitism ranks only fourth on this list of five factors. Arguably, however, it is the most volatile force on the list. Some commentators feel that the long history of antisemitism in the region, combined with the current economic and political instability of the CIS, could cause antisemitism to spread and Jewish identity to be strengthened as a result. In order to shed light on this question I will next analyze Jewish perceptions of antisemitism and the strength and distribution of antisemitic sentiment in the general population.

NOTES

1   One cannot treat seriously an estimate of 5 million recently proferred by Dmitri Prokofiev, Israel Radio's Moscow correspondent. He cited a report from the "demographic centre of the Russian parliament" showing that "millions of Jews are only now emerging after 70 years in the communist closet." Professor Ryvkina checked with eight of the leading demographers, ethnographers and sociological experts on Jewish problems in Moscow, including one who is connected to the Russian parliament. None had ever heard of this report—or, for that matter, of the "demographic centre of the Russian parliament". See *Canadian Jewish News*, 29 April 1993.

2   Zvi Gitelman, "Recent demographic and migratory trends among Soviet Jews: Implications for policy", *Post-Soviet Geography*, vol. 33, no. 3, 1992, 142.

3   Mark Tolts, "Jewish marriages in the USSR: A demographic analysis", *East European Jewish Affairs,* vol. 22, no. 2, 1992, 9.

4   Mordechai Altshuler, *Soviet Jewry Since the Second World War: Population and Social Structure* (New York: Greenwood, 1987), 18-19, 22-3.

5   Sergio DellaPergolla, "The demographic context of the Soviet *aliya* [emigration to Israel]", *Jews and Jewish Topics in the Soviet Union and Eastern Europe*, winter, 1991, 49-50.

6   See, for example, Stanley Lieberson and Mary Waters, "Ethnic groups in flux: The changing ethnic responses of American whites", *Annals of the American Academy of Social and Political Science*, no. 487, 1986, 79-91.

7   Recall that a third of the respondents who said they had changed their nationality registration switched *to* Jewish.

8   A study of emigrants headed to the West in the years 1976-79 found that over 19 per cent of them were non-Jews according to their passport registration. However, many of them were spouses of Jews according to passport registration. See Victor Zaslavsky and Robert J. Brym, *Soviet-Jewish Emigration and Soviet Nationality Policy* (London: Macmillan, 1983), 52-5. As noted in the text, recent Israeli research found that the proportion of non-Jews by passport registration who emigrated to Israel was 5.8 per cent, although rising slightly over time. *Izvestiya* reported in 1990 that some 35 per cent of Soviet immigrants to Israel were Russians or members of other non-Jewish nationalities but I have seen no evidence to substantiate this claim. See G. F. Morozova, "Refugees and emigrants", *Sociological Research*, vol. 32, no. 2, 1993, 93. In the light of these considerations, 15 per cent seems a credible estimate.

9   Sidney Heitman, "Jews in the 1989 USSR census", *Soviet Jewish Affairs*, vol. 20, no. 1, 1990, 23-30. Figures are rounded to the nearest thousand.

10   This is my calculation based on census figures. Altshuler, *Soviet Jewry . . .* , 30, 236 made comparable estimates before the results of the 1989 census were available.

11   Steven M. Cohen, *American Modernity and Jewish Identity* (New York and London: Tavistock, 1983).

12   The North American data are from Jay Brodbar-Nemzer *et al.*, "An over-
      view of the Canadian Jewish community" in Robert J. Brym, William
      Shaffir and Morton Weinfeld (eds.), *The Jews in Canada* (Toronto: Oxford
      University Press, 1993), 43, 46, 48, 61. Question-wording varied in the sur-
      veys. The Canadian figure for mixed marriage is for Toronto only but earlier
      studies have shown that Toronto is extremely close to the national figure.

13   Zvi Gitelman, "The evolution of Jewish culture and identity in the Soviet
      Union" in Yaacov Ro'i and Avi Beker (eds.), *Jewish Culture and Identity in
      the Soviet Union* (New York and London: New York University Press,
      1991), 8.

14   Richard Pipes, "The Soviet Union adrift", *Foreign Affairs*, vol. 70, no. 1,
      1991, 80.

15   All statistical analysis was conducted using SPSS-PC version 4.0. I first sub-
      stituted missing values on all 22 items with the means of those items. I then
      standardized the 22 items and ran a reliability test. The test revealed that
      items 70 and 62 scaled poorly with the other items. They were therefore
      dropped from the scale. The remaining 20 items yielded a healthy
      Cronbach's-alpha reliability coefficient of 0.804. I added up the standard-
      ized scores of the 20 items to create the index of Jewishness. The range of
      the scale is from -37.25 to 14.63, with low negative scores indicating high
      levels of Jewishness. For greater intuitive appeal, the trichotomized version
      of the scale was coded so that a high score indicates a high level of
      Jewishness.

16   Zvi Gitelman, "The evolution . . . ", 7-8. Research based on random samples
      of American Jews has also failed to find any such relationship. See Steven
      M. Cohen, 82-3.

17   Specifically, chi-square is not large enough to allow me to reject the hypoth-
      esis at the .05 probability level that the distribution of Jewishness by educa-
      tional level is due to chance (chi-square = 17.38, d.f. = 10, sig. = .07).

18   It is highly likely that there exists a reciprocal relationship between
      Jewishness and emigration plans—each contributes to causing the other—
      but in order to keep my presentation straightforward I will not attempt to
      construct a structural equation model that reflects such complex causal rela-
      tions.

19   Steven Erlanger, "As Ukraine loses Jews, the Jews lose a tradition", *The
      New York Times*, 27 August 1992.

20   Jean-Paul Sartre, *Anti-Semite and Jew*, trans. George J. Becker (New York:
      Schocken, 1965 [1948]), 143.

21   Jonathan Frankel, "The Soviet regime and anti-Zionism: An analysis" in
      Ro'i and Beker, 348-9; Ludmilla Tsigelman, "The impact of ideological
      changes in the USSR on different generations of the Soviet Jewish intelli-
      gentsia" in Ro'i and Beker, 70.

22   Michael Hechter, "Group formation and the cultural division of labor", *Ame-
      rican Journal of Sociology*, vol. 84, 1978, 293-318.

23   Here and throughout the book I use the stepwise regression technique.
      At each step in this procedure, the independent variable not in the equa-
      tion which has the smallest probability of F is entered if that probability is
      sufficiently small. SPSS-PC default values are retained. In order to keep my

1 Hebrew class in Minsk (with picture of Lenin still hanging on wall).

2 Lone Jew in front of Babi Yar holocaust memorial, near Kiev, Ukraine.

presentation simple I do not consider whether variables not included in the final equation have indirect effects.

24   A hugely disproportionate number of the leaders of the Jewish community in the region are men. These results suggest, however, that Jewish mothers are the unrecognized heroines of the community, playing nearly twice as important a role as Jewish fathers in causing respondents to develop Jewish identities, beliefs and patterns of practice.

4 Antisemitism

ANTISEMITISM AS A REACTION TO POST-COMMUNISM[1]

Imagine a country in which only 12 per cent of the adult population are satisfied with their lives, 71 per cent find it a financial strain even to clothe their families, 61 per cent report a deterioration in living standards over the past three months, 67 per cent report a decline in the political situation over the same period, and 41 per cent think that the country runs a high risk of complete anarchy. In the same country, only 13 per cent of adults trust the head of state—3 per cent fewer than distrust him—while 71 per cent express little or no trust in the parliament and 57 per cent express little or no trust in the government. Meanwhile, a mere 2 per cent of the adult population belong to a political party or movement and 53 per cent believe that mass disturbances, anti-government riots and bloodshed are likely to break out. That was the situation in Russia in March 1993 according to a country-wide public opinion poll of 2,000 people conducted by the Institute of Sociology of the Russian Academy of Sciences.[2] The poll and others like it show that in Russia, Ukraine and Belarus there is widespread despair, pessimism and political mistrust but no widely perceived economic and political alternative to the status quo. It also suggests potential danger. As Václav Havel recently put it:

> In a situation where one system has collapsed and a new one does not yet exist, many people feel empty and frustrated. This condition is fertile ground for radicalism of all kinds, for the hunt for scapegoats, and for the need to hide behind the anonymity of a group, be it socially or ethnically based. . . . It gives rise to the search for a common and easily identifiable enemy, to political extremism. . . .[3]

Or in the words of Nikolai Popov, one of Russia's leading public opinion pollsters, "people . . . seem ready to support political demagogues or opportunists . . . who promise the quick salvation of the country, and a way out of the economic chaos."[4]

38

In this volatile context the question of antisemitism—its level, social distribution, and possible political uses—takes on special significance. Antisemites have often blamed Jews for the ills of their societies. The former Soviet Union has a long tradition of antisemitism and the largest combined number of Jews and people with negative attitudes towards Jews of any region in the world. The potential for casting Jews in their traditional role of scapegoat thus appears large.

ANTISEMITISM AND PUBLIC OPINION POLLS

Despite the obvious significance of the subject, survey data on antisemitism in the region are meagre. In a 1991 overview of the subject, Gitelman was able to cite only two survey-based studies.[5] The first study reviews the results of a December 1988 telephone poll of 1,006 randomly-selected Muscovites and an April 1989 telephone poll of 1,000 randomly-selected Muscovites.[6] These polls provide evidence that people with negative attitudes towards Jews tend to be older, less educated people with lower socioeconomic status who share various anti-Western, authoritarian and Russian nationalist opinions. They suggest that people who give "undecided" responses tend to be "closet" antisemites. On that basis it was concluded that about a third of Muscovites hold a set of beliefs that include negative attitudes towards Jews.

The second study was conducted in February-March 1990. It was based on a small random sample of 504 Muscovites. The researchers asked respondents numerous questions about their attitudes towards Jews during in-home, face-to-face surveys. They concluded that negative attitudes towards Jews were concentrated among less educated people whose financial condition was deteriorating and who opposed democratization. However, the level of antisemitism discovered by the researchers was less than they expected, probably because they arbitrarily decided that the large number of "uncertain" responses necessarily indicated neutrality rather than a cover-up of negative attitudes.[7]

Since Gitelman's article was written, the results of a third study of antisemitism in the former Soviet Union have been published. L. D. Gudkov and A. G. Levinson conducted a large survey of nearly 8,000 randomly-selected people in Russia, Ukraine, Belarus, Latvia, Lithuania, Estonia, Moldova, Azerbaydzhan, Georgia, Kazakhstan and Uzbekistan under the auspices of VTsIOM, the Moscow-based All-Russian Centre for Public Opinion Research, in October 1990 and March 1992.[8] They asked a wide range of questions concerning respondents' attitudes towards Jews. The authors judged that in these republics a "feeling of tolerance [towards Jews] remains predominant."[9] Because the findings I am about to report lead me to quite different conclusions, I will discuss the Gudkov-Levinson survey in detail in the context of my own data analysis below.

Between 9 and 11 October 1992 I conducted a brief telephone poll in Moscow with the assistance of Professor Andrei Degtyarev of the Department of Political Science and Sociology of Politics at Moscow State University. The poll consisted of seventeen questions, two of which dealt with Jews. The interviewers had one to one-and-a-half years of interview training and experience. The survey was based on a randomly generated list of 1,060 residential telephone numbers in metropolitan Moscow. Interviews were completed with 989 respondents, yielding a very high 93 per cent response rate. Once Jews and respondents under eighteen years of age were deleted from the data set, 946 respondents remained. They are the respondents I analyze here. The maximum margin of error for a sample of this size is ±3.2 per cent, nineteen times out of twenty.

Telephone polls in Moscow are able to tap the opinions of just over three-quarters of the population. The rest have no telephones in their places of residence. Young couples, people living in recently constructed buildings and recently settled neighbourhoods, migrant workers and refugees are necessarily underrepresented in telephone surveys. Individuals living in communal apartments are also less likely than people living in single-family apartments to be interviewed in a telephone poll because many residents share a single telephone in communal apartments and only one respondent per telephone was allowed. These factors introduce unknown biases in estimates of distributions. In order to control for some of those unknown biases, I weighted the sample to match the age and gender distributions of the Moscow population according to the 1989 census. Strictly speaking, however, findings about the proportion of people expressing an attitude should be understood to apply only to people with telephones in their places of residence. On the other hand, sample bias does not usually affect relationships among variables: one may be reasonably confident that the relationship found between, say, income and antisemitism is accurate within sampling error.

Before reporting the results of the survey I must emphasize three points that will help place the findings in social context. First, when I discuss antisemitism I refer only to negative attitudes towards Jews, not to a highly articulated ideological system. There are some Muscovites who are antisemites in the strict ideological sense, people for whom anti-Jewish beliefs constitute a worldview. Such people represent only a small minority of the city's population. A much larger proportion simply hold negative attitudes towards Jews, as we will see. Second, although negative attitudes towards Jews are widespread in Moscow, contradictory trends are also evident. Among some categories of the population tolerance towards Jews is growing. Nonetheless, the data show that negative attitudes towards Jews are common. Finally, Jews are not the most disliked ethnic group in Moscow. A survey of 1,009 Muscovites conducted at the end of 1992 showed that various groups of so-called *chernye* (blacks) are least liked. Azeris are the most disliked ethnic group in Moscow, followed by Chechens, Gypsies, Georgians, and Armenians. Jews rank above the *chernye*—but well below Slavic groups such as Ukrainians.[10]

THE FREQUENCY OF ANTISEMITIC ATTITUDES IN MOSCOW

With these qualifications in mind, I begin by reporting the distribution of responses to a question regarding belief in the existence of a global plot against Russia organized by "Zionists" (i.e. Jews). The myth of an international Jewish conspiracy as manifested in the Tsarist secret police forgery *The Protocols of the Elders of Zion* has become an established element in the ideological makeup of hardcore antisemites the world over. Hardcore antisemites constituted roughly 3 per cent of the US population in 1981 and 4 per cent of the Canadian population outside Quebec in 1984.[11] If, in the Russian context, one is prepared to view hardcore antisemites as people who are inclined to agree that an international Jewish (or "Zionist") plot against Russia exists, then Table 4.1 suggests that the corresponding figure in Moscow is much higher—and Moscow, it must be remembered, is among the more liberal areas of Russia.[12] Specifically, 18 per cent of the respondents agreed or were inclined to agree that a global "Zionist" plot against Russia exists. Of course, the atmosphere of rapid economic decline and political instability that characterizes Russia today is a natural breeding ground for conspiracy theories. Many such theories coexist, and belief in a "Zionist" plot is not necessarily the most widespread of them.[13] Our respondents may have been reacting to the word "plot" as much as to the word "Zionist". That said, the proportion of Muscovites open to the possibility that a "Zionist" plot is responsible for Russia's predicament is very high by North American standards.

Nearly a quarter of the respondents said that they were "undecided" as to whether a "Zionist" plot against Russia existed. Do such responses

Table 4.1
"Do you believe that there is a global plot against
Russia organized by 'Zionists'?"

	frequency	per cent
yes	128	14
inclined to agree	39	4
undecided	229	24
inclined to disagree	53	6
no	492	52
total	940	100

indicate real indecision and neutrality or do they mask the attitudes of antisemites who simply do not want to express their opinions openly? The answer to this question is critically important. If the "undecideds" are in fact antisemites, then one is entitled to reach the shocking conclusion that negative attitudes towards Jews engulf more than 40 per cent of Muscovites.

Table 4.2 suggests that such an alarming conclusion is *not* warranted. Respondents were asked whether they preferred the old or new political order and whether they held the West responsible for Russia's crisis. For both items clearly reactionary responses were possible. I reasoned that if the "undecideds" on the "Zionist" plot question tended to prefer the old political order and held the West responsible for Russia's crisis at least as much as did those who expressed belief in the existence of a "Zionist" plot, then that would constitute evidence for the view that the "undecideds" are in fact closet antisemites. As Table 4.2 shows, however, the percentage of those who prefer the old order and of those who blame the West for Russia's crisis both decline smoothly as one moves horizontally across Table 4.2 from the "yes" to the "no" column, with "undecided" squarely in between.

Although the "undecideds" really do appear to be a neutral category between "yes" and "no", one should bear in mind the substantive meaning of my finding. Nearly a quarter of adult Muscovites are undecided on the question of whether there exists an international "Zionist" conspiracy.

Table 4.2
Belief in Global "Zionist" Plot against Russia by Reactionary Attitudes
(in per cent; n in parentheses)

	yes	inclined to yes	undecided	inclined to no	no
		belief in global plot			
political preference					
old	58	53	45	26	25
other	42	47	55	74	75
total	100 (119)	100 (32)	100 (199)	100 (47)	100 (448)
West responsible					
yes	70	46	21	10	7
other	30	54	79	90	93
total	100 (128)	100 (39)	100 (229)	100 (53)	100 (492)

Together with the fact that nearly 18 per cent of the city's adult population have decided that such a conspiracy *is* probably afoot, it suggests that over 40 per cent of Moscow's adult population are open to this antisemitic canard.

The respondents were asked a second question about Jews—whether they had ever witnessed an infringement of Jewish rights. Table 4.3 sets out the responses to that question. Perhaps surprisingly, fewer than a fifth of the respondents said they had witnessed such an infringement; over three-quarters denied they had, and nearly five per cent were undecided. Here again we are confronted with a quandary: do the "never" and "undecided" responses indicate genuine ignorance of discrimination against Jews? Or do they suggest a refusal to view Jews as victims since Jews, as every antisemite knows, can only be advantaged. The evidence favours the latter interpretation, as Table 4.4 makes clear. Those who claim never to have witnessed an infringement of Jewish rights or to be undecided on the issue are more likely than others to believe in the existence of a global

Table 4.3
"Have you ever witnessed an infringement of the rights of Jews?"

	frequency	per cent
often	69	7
sometimes	114	12
never	712	76
undecided	45	5
total	940	100

Table 4.4
Witnessing Infringement of Rights of Jews by Reactionary Attitudes
(in per cent; n in parentheses)

	infringement of rights		
	often	sometimes	never
global plot			
yes	16	18	19
don't know	14	10	26
no	70	73	56
total	100 (69)	101 (114)	101 (711)
political preference			
old	23	26	37
other	77	74	63
total	100 (62)	100 (108)	100 (632)
West responsible			
yes	14	17	20
other	86	83	80
total	100 (69)	100 (114)	100 (712)

Note: Percentages do not necessarily add up to 100 due to rounding.

"Zionist" plot against Russia, to prefer the old political order, and to believe that the West is responsible for Russia's crisis. The fact that over 80 per cent of Muscovites claim ignorance of any violation of Jewish rights cannot therefore be taken as an indication of the absence of such violations since many of these people adhere to a set of reactionary ideas that includes negative attitudes towards Jews.

ANTISEMITIC ATTITUDES IN THE CIS

How can I reconcile my more dismal conclusion with the view of Gudkov and Levinson, noted above, that tolerance towards Jews predominates in Russia and other republics of the former Soviet Union? Quite easily: my standard of comparison apparently differs from theirs. Consider some of Gudkov's and Levinson's findings, reproduced in Table 4.5. The percentage of respondents who expressed negative attitudes towards Jews varies by attitude and by republic. By North American standards, however, all the proportions are large. For example, depending on republic, between 34 and 68 per cent of Gudkov and Levinson's respondents opposed Jews marrying into their families. Polls conducted in the USA in 1981 and in Canada in 1984 show that the comparable figure for both North American countries was only 10 per cent. In Canada 21 per cent of respondents opposed blacks marrying whites; in the USA the figure was 33 per cent.[14] Thus Gudkov's and Levinson's data convince me that there is considerably more opposition to Jewish-non-Jewish intermarriage in the former Soviet Union than there is opposition to black-white intermarriage in the USA. In general, the percentages in Table 4.5 portray a level of animosity against Jews that exceeds black-white animosities in the USA. Gudkov and Levinson are entitled to regard this as "tolerance", but most North Americans employ a different vocabulary to describe such a situation.[15]

Figure 4.1 uses an unpublished republic-by-republic breakdown of the fourteen questions in Table 4.5 to construct a graph of the incidence of antisemitism by republic. It shows the average percentage of respondents in each republic who gave negative responses to Gudkov's and Levinson's fourteen questions about Jews in 1992. (Georgia was not polled in the 1992 wave of their study.) Of most interest here are the relative positions of Russia, Ukraine and Belarus. While Russia and Ukraine rank near the bottom of the scale, Belarus ranks near the top. If I concluded on the basis of the Moscow telephone survey that antisemitic attitudes are wide-

Table 4.5
Attitudes Towards Jews in Ten Soviet Republics, March 1992 (in per cent)

percentage of respondents who . . .	range	mean
do not approve of Jews as workers	33-55	44.0
are unwilling to work in the same group with Jews	23-38	30.5
maintain that Jews avoid physical work	65-75	70.0
maintain that Jews value making money and profit above human relations	40-53	46.5
are not willing to have a Jew as their immediate boss at work	47-57	52.0
think it is necessary to limit the number of Jews in leading positions	19-33	26.0
are reluctant to see a Jew as president of their republic	53-76	64.5
maintain that Jews do not make good family men	35-56	45.5
have non-positive perceptions of neighbourliness of Jewish families	26-48	37.0
are unwilling to have Jews as members of one's family	34-68	51.0
do not support equal opportunity for ethnic group members to obtain work	17-35	26.0
do not support equal opportunity for ethnic group members to attend educational institutions	15-34	24.5
often have negative feelings towards Jewish parties and organizations	25-45	35.0

Source: Adapted from L. D. Gudkov and A. G. Levinson, "Attitudes towards Jews", *Sotsiologicheskiye issledovaniya*, no. 12, 1992, 109.

Note: Scores for each republic were not reported by the authors. Thus in calculating the mean, republics could not be weighted for population size.

spread in that relatively liberal city, one is obliged to conclude from the Gudkov and Levinson survey that the situation is even more dire in Belarus and most of the rest of the former USSR.

Figure 4.1
Level of Antisemitism in Ten Former Soviet Republics, 1992 (in per cent)

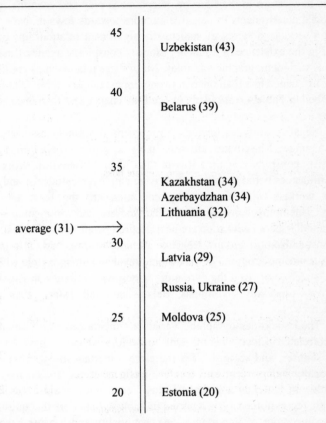

Source: Gudkov and Levinson, unpublished data.

Note: This figure shows the mean per cent of respondents who gave negative responses to fourteen questionnaire items concerning Jews. The overall average is based on republic means, not individual scores.

THE SOCIAL DETERMINANTS OF ANTISEMITISM

Let us now return to the Moscow telephone survey and examine some of the social determinants of negative attitudes towards Jews in that city. Table 4.6 sets out a series of statistically significant relationships between belief in the existence of a global "Zionist" conspiracy against Russia and various sociodemographic variables. All of these relationships are likely to occur by chance less than once in twenty times; the first three relationships described in Table 4.6 are likely to occur by chance less than once in 1,000 times.

Negative attitudes towards Jews are most strongly associated with age. Younger Muscovites are less likely to express belief in a global "Zionist" conspiracy against Russia than older Muscovites. Work status also influences belief in this issue. Private employers, students, and white-collar workers with a university education are the least antisemitic groups. Unemployed people, blue-collar workers, and white-collar workers with middle-school education are next. Retired people and homemakers are the most antisemitic groups. Negative attitudes towards Jews also increase in lower income groups. They are more prevalent among people who work in the state sector. And they are more widespread among non-Russians in Moscow—especially Ukrainians, Belarusians, and Tatars—than among Russians.

The socio-demographic variables mentioned are themselves intercorrelated. Elderly people tend to be less educated, have particular work statuses, and so forth. It is therefore important to ask what are the statistically independent and combined effects of the sociodemographic variables on belief in a global "Zionist" conspiracy against Russia. The multiple regression analysis reported in Table 4.7 answers that question. In descending order of importance, age, nationality and income have independent effects on antisemitic belief.[16]

Belief in the existence of a global "Zionist" conspiracy against Russia is also correlated with other attitudes, as can be seen in Table 4.8. All of the relationships reported in Table 4.8 are likely to occur by chance less than once in 1,000 times. We already know that Muscovites with negative attitudes towards Jews are more inclined to believe that the West is responsible for the crisis in Russia, to prefer the old political system, and to deny witnessing any infringements of Jewish rights. Table 4.8 also demonstrates that people with negative attitudes towards Jews are more likely to expect living conditions to be the same or worse in five years. Moreover, and somewhat ominously, people with negative attitudes towards Jews are

Table 4.6

Socio-demographic Correlates of Belief in Global "Zionist" Conspiracy against Russia (in per cent; n in parentheses)

| | belief in "Zionist" conspiracy | | |
	yes; inclined to think so; undecided	inclined to think not; no	total
age			
<31	32	68	100 (232)
31-59	38	62	100 (490)
60+	61	39	100 (218)
chi-square = 46.47, d.f. = 2, p<.001; tau-c = -0.213			
work status			
employer, student, white collar/ univ	32	68	100 (361)
unemployed, worker white collar/ middle	43	57	100 (333)
retired/ homemaker	56	44	100 (246)
chi-square = 34.64, d.f. = 2, p<.001; tau-c = -0.204			
monthly income in roubles			
<3,000	50	50	100 (450)
3,000-10,000	36	64	100 (395)
>10,000	32	68	100 (95)
chi-square = 20.73, d.f. = 2, p<.001; tau-c = 0.152			
sector of employment			
state	42	58	100 (443)
mixed	29	71	100 (41)
private	29	71	100 (129)
chi-square = 8.46, d.f. = 2, p<.025; tau-c = 0.104			
gender			
male	38	62	100 (402)
female	45	55	100 (538)
chi-square = 5.46, d.f. = 2, p<.05; tau-c = -0.074			
nationality			
Russian	40	60	100 (826)
other	49	51	100 (35)
Ukr/Bel/Tat	59	41	101 (78)
chi-square = 11.12, d.f. = 2, p<.005; tau-c = -0.067			

Note: Percentages do not necessarily add up to 100 due to rounding.

somewhat more likely than people with positive attitudes towards Jews to express willingness to protest their dissatisfaction openly by taking part in strikes, demonstrations, boycotts and even by destroying property. Specifically, among people who are prepared to protest actively their dissatisfaction with declining living conditions, 53 per cent believe in, or are undecided about, the existence of a global "Zionist" conspiracy against Russia, while 47 per cent are inclined to deny the existence of such a plot. In contrast, among those who are *not* prepared to protest declining living conditions openly, 35 per cent believe in, or are undecided about, the existence of a "Zionist" conspiracy and 65 per cent are inclined to deny the existence of such a plot.

Table 4.7
Multiple Regression of Belief in Global "Zionist" Conspiracy against Russia on Sociodemographic Variables (weighted results)

variable	slope (b)	standard error	standardized slope (beta)	t
age	-0.27	0.04	-0.20	-6.09
Russian/ other	0.50	0.14	0.11	3.54
income	0.14	0.06	0.07	2.09

intercept = 4.04; n = 938; adjusted R^2 = .06

The multiple regression analysis summarized in Table 4.9 may be interpreted to suggest the "distance" between belief in a global "Zionist" conspiracy against Russia and various attitudes that are independently and statistically significantly related to that belief at the .05 probability level. Blaming the West for Russia's ills is very strongly associated with belief in a "Zionist" conspiracy. In addition, preference for the pre-Gorbachev political order and belief that women's proper role is in the home rather than in the paid labour force are significantly and independently associated with belief in the conspiracy theory.[17] The evidence thus suggests that some large categories of Moscow's population hold attitudes that are authoritarian, xenophobic, illiberal on social issues and, of course, antisemitic.[18] Given the prevalence of negative attitudes towards Jews in the city, and the even greater prevalence of negative attitudes towards Jews elsewhere in the former USSR, the Jews of the region have reason to be anxious.

Table 4.8
Attitudinal Correlates of Belief in Global "Zionist" Conspiracy against Russia (in per cent; n in parentheses)

	belief in "Zionist" conspiracy		
	yes; inclined to think so; undecided	inclined to think not; no	total
West responsible for Russian crisis			
yes	68	32	100 (426)
no	21	79	100 (515)
chi-square = 216.66, d.f. = 1, p<.001; tau-c = 0.471			
political preference			
old system	55	45	100 (455)
new system	26	74	100 (390)
chi-square = 74.30, d.f. = 1, p<.001; tau-c = 0.291			
expected living conditions in 5 years			
same/worse	47	54	101 (401)
better	30	70	100 (242)
chi-square = 19.09, d.f. = 1, p<.001; tau-c = -0.161			
protest if living conditions worsen			
yes	53	47	100 (215)
no	35	65	100 (560)
chi-square = 25.85, d.f. = 1, p<.001; tau-c = -0.161			
witnessed infringement of rights of Jews			
often/ sometimes	28	72	100 (183)
undecided/ never	46	54	100 (755)
chi-square = 18.65, d.f. = 1, p<.001; tau-c = -0.111			

Note: Percentages do not necessarily add up to 100 due to rounding.

Table 4.9
Multiple Regression of Belief in Global "Zionist" Conspiracy against Russia on Attitudinal Variables

variable	slope (b)	standard error	standardized slope (beta)	t
West responsible	0.46	0.03	0.52	16.72
political preference	0.17	0.05	0.11	3.36
women's role	0.19	0.08	0.07	2.37

intercept= 1.49; n = 794; adjusted R^2 = 0.33

JEWISH PERCEPTIONS OF ANTISEMITISM

The survey of Jews in Moscow, Kiev and Minsk asked a battery of questions concerning perceptions of antisemitism. Not surprisingly in light of the findings summarized above, over 95 per cent of Jews responded "yes" when asked if they believed that antisemitism existed in their country.

Those who answered "yes" were also asked "What are the main manifestations of antisemitism in your country today?" Interviewers did not prompt respondents with a list of possible answers; they could reply in any way they wished. Respondents were, however, asked to rank their replies, that is, to state their opinion of the main manifestation of antisemitism, the second most important manifestation and so forth. Table 4.10 sets out their first choices.

Table 4.10
Jewish Perceptions of Main Forms of Antisemitism (first choice in per cent)

	frequency	per cent
q118-people hostile	326	38
q119-nationalist organizations	212	25
q117-state policy	197	23
q120-articles in press	84	10
q121-people envious	40	5
total	859	100

Nearly 40 per cent of the respondents regard hostility on the part of ordinary people as the main source of antisemitism in their country today. A quarter of them think that the main source of antisemitism lies in the threat of nationalist organizations such as Pamyat and Otechestvo. About the same proportion view state policy as the main source of antisemitism. A tenth of the respondents perceive the nationalist press—publications such as *Molodaya gvardiya* and *Literaturnaya Rossiya*—as the chief manifestation of anti-Jewish feeling. And 5 per cent of them mention popular envy as the most important source of antisemitism in their country today.[19]

The only real surprise here concerns state policy. Russia, Ukraine and Belarus no longer have a state-sponsored policy of discrimination against Jews. That nearly a quarter of the Jews in the three cities nonetheless believe the state to be the main locus of anti-Jewish discrimination probably indicates a combination of three things. First, some individual state officials presumably continue to discriminate against Jews in employment and in other spheres of life despite the abandonment of state-backed antisemitism. Second, since historical memories die hard, some Jews who feel disadvantaged are likely to attribute some or all of their disabilities to their Jewish origin, whether or not this is objectively justifiable. Blaming state authorities for blocking their mobility and making their professional lives unsatisfying is probably a sort of historical reflex for some Jews. Third, in all three cities, and in Moscow in particular, mass anti-Jewish demonstrations are held, antisemitic signs are posted and an active nationalist-fascist press publishes articles and cartoons worthy of *Der Stürmer*. The Ukrainian and, especially, Russian and Belarusian states do little to combat these openly antisemitic acts. Reluctance to put active antisemites out of business by passing tough laws banning the propagation of ethnic hatred and enforcing those laws by means of a police crackdown is perhaps viewed by some Jews as a form of state antisemitism. Just how important each of these three factors is cannot, however, be ascertained on the basis of the available data.

Examining city-to-city variations reveals that antisemitism is perceived differently and takes different forms in different places. Consider Figure 4.2. It shows the proportion of respondents in each city who (1) believe that antisemitism exists; (2) fear antisemitism very much; (3) say they feared antisemitism very much six or seven years ago; (4) feel that pogroms are likely or certain to break out; and (5) have personally experienced antisemitism. Notice that about 5 per cent more Muscovites than Kievans and Minskers believe that antisemitism exists. Roughly 15 per cent more Muscovites than Kievans and Minskers believe that pogroms are likely or certain to break out. And approximately a third more Muscovites than Kievans and Minskers say they feared antisemitism very much six or seven years ago.

It would, however, be mistaken to conclude on the basis of this last batch of figures that Moscow is a more antisemitic city than Kiev and Minsk. After all, Figure 4.2 also shows that the proportion of Moscow Jews who fear antisemitism very much has been cut by more than half since the advent of Gorbachev so that today there is no inter-city difference in the level of fear. In addition, about 10 per cent more Minskers than Muscovites and Kievans have actually experienced antisemitism personally.

Why should more Moscow Jews feel that antisemitism exists and that they are likely to be attacked? Why should they hold such opinions despite experiencing by far the largest drop in fear of antisemitism and personally experiencing substantially less antisemitism than Minsk Jews? Figures 4.3 helps solve this puzzle. It shows the proportion of respondents in each city who ranked each form of antisemitism first. The Moscow profile is strikingly different from that of the other two cities. Moscow Jews are much

Figure 4.2
Perceptions of Antisemitism by City (in per cent)

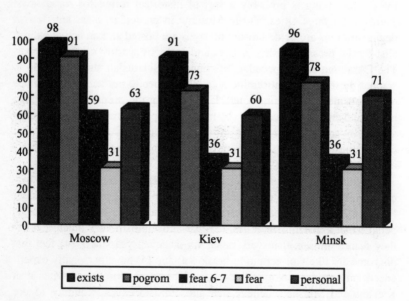

more likely than Jews from Kiev and Minsk to believe that the main manifestation of antisemitism may be found in the activities of nationalist organizations and the nationalist press. That is undoubtedly because Moscow
has a more active anti-Jewish press and larger and better-organized anti-
Jewish organizations than Kiev and Minsk. Thus between August 1991 and
August 1992 antisemitic materials appeared in twenty-two newspapers and
five journals published in Moscow. Some of this material is exported to
Kiev and Minsk, where antisemitic literature is produced on a far smaller
scale.[20] The hysterical nationalist press makes Moscow Jews feel that antisemitism is more widespread in their country. Rabidly nationalist organizations make Moscow Jews feel that they are more open to attack. If Moscow
Jews have nonetheless experienced the greatest decline in fear of antisemitism over the past six or seven years, that may be attributed to the
cessation of anti-Jewish activities on the part of the Russian state. Moscow
is no longer the font of state-backed antisemitism, as it was in the pre-
Gorbachev years. That has clearly brought most relief to the Jews located
closest to the source of the problem.

Figure 4.3
Forms of Antisemitism by City (first choice in per cent)

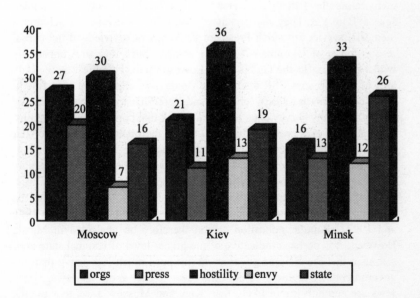

If Moscow ranks first in the perception of what might be called or-ganized group antisemitism then the view is most widespread in Minsk that antisemitism still resides chiefly in state practice. Over a quarter of Minsk Jews hold that opinion compared to fewer than a fifth of Kiev Jews and a sixth of Moscow Jews. Finally, Kiev ranks significantly ahead of the other two cities in the perception that antisemitism is based mainly in the popula-tion at large. Some 49 per cent of Kiev Jews think that the main locus of antisemitism lies in popular hostility towards, and envy of, Jews, compared to 45 per cent of Minsk Jews and 37 per cent of Moscow Jews.

I conclude that one cannot properly speak of a given locale being simply more or less antisemitic than another. Antisemitism is multi-dimen-sional, taking different forms in different places.[21] To be sure, popular hos-tility towards, and envy of, Jews is perceived as the main source of anti-semitism in Moscow, Kiev *and* Minsk. To that degree, educational and inter-communal programmes aimed at enlightening and liberalizing non-Jews are desperately needed in all three cities. But it is also evident that a distinctive policy mix is required to combat antisemitism in different cities.

In Kiev the government and the leading opposition movement, *Rukh*, have been most effective in combatting the organized-group and official forms of antisemitism. They have also taken meaningful steps to re-educate the public. For example, in 1991 officials participated in ceremonies com-memorating the fiftieth anniversary of the Nazi massacre of Ukrainian Jews at Babi Yar. They also organized a series of public events, including a memorial service in which President Kravchuk acknowledged the partial responsibility of Ukrainians for the massacre. Such measures apparently work: according to the Gudkov and Levinson poll, Ukraine was the only area of the former USSR apart from Moldova to experience a decline in hostility towards Jews between 1990 and 1992.[22] History, however, is long. According to my survey data, Kiev Jews think that popular hostility against them is more of a problem than do Jews in the other two cities. Popular education is still needed in Kiev more than elsewhere.

We learned from Figure 4.1 that Belarus suffers from a considerably higher level of popular antisemitism than either Ukraine or Russia. Indeed, the Gudkov and Levinson survey shows that Belarus registered one of the largest *increases* in antisemitic feeling in the former USSR between 1990 and 1992.[23] Popular education cannot therefore be neglected in Minsk. However, it is perhaps indicative of the higher level of residual state anti-semitism that the Belarus government has been much less active than the government of Ukraine in re-educating its citizenry about the Jews. Minsk Jews are certainly more likely than Kiev and Moscow Jews to view the

Belarusian state as still rife with antisemites. Therefore, a thorough housecleaning of antisemitic officials seems more needed in Minsk than in the other two cities.

Between 1990 and 1992 the level of antisemitic hostility among Russia's population remained just about constant. In Moscow, however, group antisemitism is especially prominent. There, political control of highly active and organized antisemitic Russian nationalists is needed more than in Kiev and Minsk.

SOCIODEMOGRAPHIC VARIATIONS

Fear is the only dimension of antisemitism in Figure 4.2 that does not vary from city to city: in Moscow, Kiev and Minsk, 31 per cent of Jews express a great deal of apprehension about antisemitism. Let us now examine the social bases of their fear.[24]

Table 4.11 establishes that a host of factors are related to fear of antisemitism on the part of Jews. These factors fall into four groups:

■ First are what might be called vulnerability factors. Jews who are most frightened of antisemitism tend to be middle-aged, female and employed in white-collar jobs the security of which is no longer assured now that the market is beginning to take slow root and the huge government bureaucracy is being inexorably cut back. They also tend to have a low standard of living and earn low incomes.[25] Indeed, the people with the highest unemployment rate in the general population share many of these characteristics.[26] So far at least, manual workers, government administrators and people who own or manage private businesses—"others" in the crude occupational breakdown of Table 4.11—tend not to be threatened as much by unemployment, especially if they are men.[27]

■ Second are factors indicating dissatisfaction with one's economic prospects. Fear of antisemitism is associated with discontent concerning income and opportunities for upward mobility, with low expectations concerning one's standard of living in one to two years and with a general lack of confidence in one's future.

■ Third are actual experiences of antisemitism. Fear of antisemitism is related to claiming that one witnessed antisemitism during the past year in one's place of work, in one's neighbourhood, in the mass media and in state policy.

Table 4.11
Fear of Antisemitism by Correlates (in per cent; n in parentheses)

question	fear of antisemitism			
	very	not very	not at all	total
q7-sex				
male	21	43	36	100 (483)
female	41	38	21	100 (469)
chi-square = 50.90, d.f. = 2, sig. = .000, tau-c = .247				
q8-age				
18-29	15	40	45	100 (170)
30-39	32	39	29	100 (142)
40-49	35	43	22	100 (205)
50-59	38	39	24	100 (277)
60-90	31	42	27	100 (159)
chi-square = 42.3, d.f. = 8, sig. = .000, tau-c = .125				
q17-occupation				
white collar	35	43	22	100 (403)
other	19	39	42	100 (217)
chi-square = 33.42, d.f. = 2, sig. = .000, tau-c = .234				
q20-income satisfaction				
satisfied	19	43	37	100 (172)
not satisfied	35	39	25	100 (428)
chi-square = 17.07, d.f. = 2, sig. = .000, tau-c = .162				
q25-opportunity satisfaction				
satisfied	27	39	35	100 (202)
not satisfied	36	43	21	100 (264)
chi-square = 11.85, d.f. = 2, sig. = .003, tau-c = .161				
q29-total income				
low	35	41	24	100 (287)
medium	32	45	23	100 (258)
high	27	38	36	100 (288)
chi-square = 15.64, d.f. = 4, sig. = .004, tau-c = .096				
q38-standard of living				
satisfied	24	36	40	100 (198)
not satisfied	35	41	25	100 (671)
chi-square = 19.34, d.f. = 2, sig. = .000, tau-c = .128				

Table 4.11 (cont'd)
Fear of Antisemitism by Correlates (in per cent; n in parentheses)

question	fear of antisemitism			
	very	not very	not at all	total
q39-expected standard of living				
better	20	36	45	100 (160)
same	28	47	25	100 (233)
worse	40	37	33	100 (372)
chi-square = 42.09, d.f. = 4, sig. = .000, tau-c = .178				
q41-upward mobility opportunities				
yes	22	37	41	100 (170)
no	35	41	24	100 (613)
chi-square = 20.71, d.f. = 2, sig. = .000, tau-c = .140				
q163-confidence in own future				
yes	18	31	51	100 (155)
no	38	41	21	100 (673)
chi-square = 62.26, d.f. = 2, sig. = .000, tau-c = .211				
q133-witness antisemitism at work				
none	25	41	34	100 (536)
little	44	37	20	100 (166)
lot	53	27	21	100 (42)
chi-square = 32.60, d.f. = 4, sig. = .000, tau-c = .146				
q134-witness antisemitism in neighbourhood				
none	29	40	31	100 (734)
little	37	43	20	100 (158)
lot	55	34	12	100 (38)
chi-square = 20.73, d.f. = 4, sig. = .000, tau-c = -.091				
q135-witness antisemitism in mass media				
none	20	32	48	100 (234)
little	29	48	24	100 (367)
lot	42	42	15	100 (300)
chi-square = 86.64, d.f. = 4, sig. = .000, tau-c = -.243				
q136-witness antisemitism in state policy				
none	26	40	35	100 (486)
little	35	45	20	100 (192)
lot	50	30	21	100 (104)
chi-square = 33.92, d.f. = 4, sig. = .000, tau-c = -.154				

Table 4.11 (cont'd)
Fear of Antisemitism by Correlates (in per cent; n in parentheses)

question	fear of antisemitism			
	very	not very	not at all	total
Jewishness scale				
high	42	39	19	100 (324)
medium	33	44	39	100 (311)
low	19	38	43	100 (318)

chi-square = 64.65, d.f. = 4, sig. = .000, tau-c = -.219

• Last, fear of antisemitism is strongly related to strength of Jewishness: those with higher levels of Jewish identification and practice tend to fear antisemitism more. This suggests that the most Jewish Jews may be predisposed to perceive antisemitism and regard it as problematic.[28]

Table 4.12 reduces this long list of factors to only five variables that continue to exercise independent and statistically significant effects when entered into a regression equation. At least one variable comes from each of the four groups of factors isolated above. In short, middle-aged and less assimilated women who lack confidence in their own future are most likely to be frightened by antisemitism, particularly when they witness such outrages in the mass media.

Table 4.12
Multiple Regression of Fear of Antisemitism

question	slope (b)	standard error	standardized slope (beta)	t
q135-wit. media	.22	.03	.22	6.80
q7-sex	.34	.05	.22	6.87
Jewishness scale	.01	.003	.17	5.28
q163-conf. future	.35	.07	.17	5.38
q8-age	.08	.02	.14	4.54

intercept = 3.77; n = 786; adjusted R^2 = .217

SUMMARY

Not all Jews in Moscow, Kiev and Minsk regard antisemitism as a problem. Five per cent of them think that antisemitism does not even exist in their countries. A significant number of respondents think that it is *not* mainly nationalist groups and politicians who are behind the spread of antisemitism. Thus interviewers confronted respondents with the statement "The view is becoming widespread that antisemitism exists in your country. In your opinion, who has an interest in spreading this view?" Respondents were asked to rank their responses but they were not presented with a predetermined set of possible answers. Table 4.13 shows that a sixth of the respondents think that it is principally Jewish, Israeli and Western individuals and organizations who wish to spread the idea that antisemitism exists in their country. Finally, 29 per cent of the people in my sample say that they are "not at all" frightened of antisemitism.

Table 4.13
Parties Interested in Antisemitism (first choice in per cent)

question	frequency	per cent
q147-nationalist parties	326	43
q141-political opposition	141	19
q142-certain govt. officials	61	8
subtotal	528	70
q146-Israel, USA & oth. West.	41	5
q143-Jews in country	32	4
q144-Jew. orgs. from ex-USSR	29	4
q145-Jew. orgs. abroad	23	3
subtotal	125	17
q148-misc'l. other responses	98	13
total	751	100

All of these are minority opinions. The evidence assembled in this chapter demonstrates that the great majority of Jews recognize anti-semitism as a serious issue. The perceived dimensions of the problem vary by urban and national context. For example, Jews think that antisemitism is more an issue of popular hostility in Kiev than in Moscow and Minsk, more a problem of state policy in Minsk than in Kiev and Moscow, and more a question of organized anti-Jewish groups in Moscow than in Kiev and Minsk. But over 30 per cent of Jews in each city are very frightened of antisemitism and another 40 per cent are somewhat frightened. Particularly for women; people in their thirties, forties and fifties; less assimilated Jews; and those who regularly witness anti-Jewish excesses in the media, life is thus rendered extremely unsettling. In fact, as we will learn in the next chapter, the experience and fear of antisemitism are so intense and wide-spread that they are important factors prompting many Jews to want to leave their country.

This chapter also presents ample evidence that Jewish perceptions are solidly founded in reality. Many Russians and Ukrainians and propor-tionately even more Belarusians dislike Jews. Certainly the proportions in-volved are very considerably higher than in the West and amount to noth-ing like a situation of what Westerners commonly refer to as tolerance. This does not mean that many Jews are in imminent danger of being at-tacked by organized mobs or that the Slavic CIS states are systematically discriminating against Jews. On the other hand, as a group of Russian soci-ologists correctly concluded in a review of recent surveys, "there are no signs at the present that the influence of nationalist and ethnocentric ideas will diminish in the near future, and that consequently the significance and role of interethnic relations will decline as a factor in social tension."[29] Or as Arthur Hertzberg recently stated, the "recurrent fear everywhere in the former USSR is that the worsening economic situation might bring with it an anti-Semitism increasing to serious proportions."[30] As a result, most Jews in the region are in the historically familiar position of being caught between two worlds, feeling tremendous ambivalence about what, if any-thing, they should call home.

NOTES

1   This section is a revised version of Robert J. Brym and Andrei Degtyarev, "Anti-semitism in Moscow: Results of an October 1992 survey", *Slavic Review*, vol. 52, no. 1, 1993, 1-12.

2   A. Komozin (ed.), *Monitoring: The 1993 Russian Citizens' Opinion Poll Results* (Moscow: Institute of Sociology, Russian Academy of Sciences, 1993).

3   "The post-Communist nightmare," *The New York Review of Books*, 27 May 1993.

4   Nikolai P. Popov, "Political views of the Russian public", *The International Journal of Public Opinion Research*, vol. 4, no. 4, 1992, 330.

5   Zvi Gitelman, "Glasnost, perestroika and antisemitism", *Foreign Affairs*, vol. 70, no. 2, 1991, 155-6. A more detailed report on one of these studies was published after Gitelman's article was written. See James L. Gibson and Raymond M. Duch, "Anti-semitic attitudes of the mass public: Estimates and explanations based on a survey of the Moscow oblast", *Public Opinion Quarterly*, no. 56, 1992, 1-28. In addition, a few surveys of perceptions of antisemitism among Jewish community leaders in Russia and among Russian Jewish immigrants have been conducted. See Alexander Benifand, "Jewish emigration from the USSR in the 1990s" in Tanya Basok and Robert J. Brym (eds.), *Soviet-Jewish Emigration and Resettlement in the 1990s* (Toronto: York Lanes Press, York University, 1991), 38-41.

6   Gibson and Duch. I discuss this issue at greater length below.

7   Robert J. Brym, "*Perestroika*, public opinion, and *pamyat*", *Soviet Jewish Affairs*, vol. 19, no. 3, 1989, 23-32.

8   L. D. Gudkov and A. G. Levinson, "Attitudes towards Jews", *Sotsiologicheskiye issledovaniya*, no. 12, 1992, 108-11.

9   *Ibid.,* 111.

10   Vladimir Zotov, "The Chechen problem as seen by Muscovites", *Moskovsky komsomolets*, 12 January 1993.

11   Geraldine Rosenfield, "The polls: Attitudes toward American Jews", *Public Opinion Quarterly,* no. 46, 1982, 443; Robert J. Brym and Rhonda L. Lenton, "The distribution of antisemitism in Canada in 1984", *Canadian Journal of Sociology,* vol. 16, no. 4, 1991, 411-18. Here, hardcore anti-semites are defined as those scoring in the bottom 25 per cent of a scale indicating positive or negative feelings towards Jews. Eight per cent of Americans and 10 per cent of Canadians outside Quebec had negative feelings towards Jews, i.e., they scored in the bottom half of the scale. The American figures come from a 1981 Gallup poll. I calculated the Canadian figures from the 1984 Canadian National Election Study.

12   V. B. Koltsov and V. A. Mansurov, "Political ideologies in the *perestroyka* era", *Sotsiologicheskiye issledovaniya,* no. 10, 1991, 32 ; V. Yadov *et al.,* "The sociopolitical situation in Russia in mid-February 1992", *Sociological Research*, vol. 32, no. 2, 1993, 7; L. A. Sedov, "Yeltsin's rating", *Ekonomicheskiye i sotsialnye peremeny: monitoring obshchestvennogo mneniya,* Informatsionny byulleten, Intertsentr VTsIOM (Moscow: Aspekt Press, 1993), 15.

13   John F. Dunn, "Hard times in Russia foster conspiracy theories", Radio Free
      Europe/ Radio Liberty Special Report, 23 September 1992.

14   Ronald D. Lambert and James E. Curtis, *"Québécois* and English Canadian
      opposition to racial and religious intermarriage, 1968-1983", *Canadian Eth-
      nic Studies,* vol. 16, no. 2, 1984, 44, note 9.

15   Gudkov and Levinson asked a question about a global "Zionist" conspiracy
      too. Within sampling error, their finding for the proportion of Russians who
      agree that a "Zionist" plot exists is nearly the same as my finding for Mos-
      cow. I am grateful to the authors for supplying some of their unpublished
      data to Andrei Degtyarev.

16   Together these variables account for only 6 per cent of the variation in
      antisemitic belief. R-square is sensitive to the distribution of cases across
      categories of the independent variables. If few cases fall into some catego-
      ries of the independent variables, then the upper limit of R-square decreases.
      In the present case, this occurs with income and nationality. The low R-
      square does not therefore necessarily weaken my argument.

17   Rhonda L. Lenton, "Home versus career: Attitudes towards women's work
      among Russian women and men, 1992", *Canadian Journal of Sociology,*
      vol. 18, no. 3, 1993, 325-31.

18   As Sonja Margolina recently put it, "[t]he equation of 'Jews' and the 'West'
      in the sense of agents of modernization remains until today one of the great
      ideological clichés of premodern consciousness in the East.", Sonja
      Margolina, *Das Ende der Lügen: Rußand und die Juden im 20. Jahrhundert*
      (Berlin: Siedler Verlag, 1992), 8. For a similar conclusion regarding Slo-
      vakia see Zora Bútorová and Martin Bútora, "Wariness towards Jews as an
      expression of post-Communist panic: The case of Slovakia," *Czechoslovak
      Sociological Review,* Special Issue, no. 28, 1992, 92-106.

19   A few respondents gave other responses which I do not consider here. On
      the Russian far right see, for example, *Nationalities Papers,* Special Issue on
      Pamyat, vol. 19, no. 2, 1991.

20   *Antisemitism World Report 1993* (London: Institute of Jewish Affairs, 1993),
      100-102, 104.

21   I tried to create a uni-dimensional scale measuring the intensity of Jewish
      perceptions of antisemitism but failed. No matter what combination of ques-
      tionnaire items I used in the scale I could not achieve a Cronbach's-alpha
      reliability coefficient greater than .465. This strongly suggests that percep-
      tions of antisemitism are not uni-dimensional.

22   *Antisemitism World Report 1992* (London: Institute of Jewish Affairs, 1992),
      68. See, however, *Antisemitism World Report 1993,* 104.

23   *Antisemitism World Report 1992,* 68.

24   For a more technical justification for examining a single dimension see note
      21.

25   In general, however, the income of Jews is above average. For example, the
      average income in Moscow in February-March 1993 was 11,625 roubles
      per month, *Sotsialno-ekonomicheskoe polozhenie rossiyskoy federatsii v
      yanvare-marte 1993 goda,* Ekonomichesky obzor no. 4, Goskomstat Rossii
      (Moscow: Respublikansky informatsionno-izdatelsky tsentr, 1993), 145. All
      the Moscow Jews in my survey were interviewed in those two months. Their

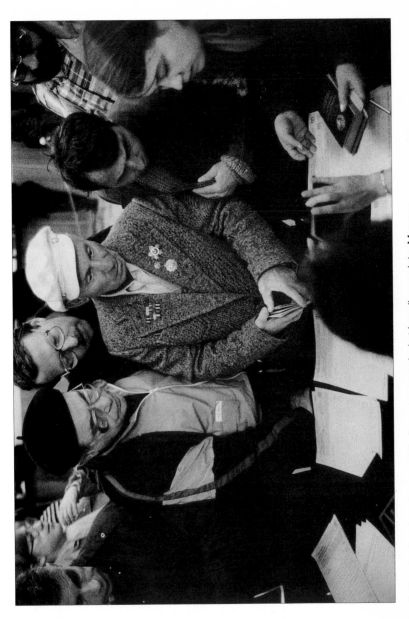

3 Russian immigrants present their papers on arrival at Israeli consulate, Moscow.

4 Kiev airport, departure.

average monthly income was 27,218 roubles, more than two and a third times above the city average. This difference appears *not* to be the result of Jews being more involved in the private sector than non-Jews (Mordechai Altshuler, "Jews and Russians—1991", *Yehudei brit ha-moatsot* (The Jews of the Soviet Union), vol. 15, 1992, 33). Thus 28 per cent of non-Jewish respondents in the October 1992 survey I conducted with Andrei Degtyarev worked at least partly in the private sector, compared to 29 per cent of Moscow Jews in the February-April 1993 survey I conducted with Rozalina Ryvkina. The income difference between the two groups appears to be mainly due to the different occupational structure, higher educational attainment and seniority of Jews. Note also that the *median* income for Moscow Jews was only 13,800 roubles per month. This implies that there are relatively few extremely wealthy Jews who pull up the mean. Although the median income for the general population is unknown, the difference between Jewish and population medians is undoubtedly far less than the difference between the means.

26   In the general population, however, it is the young who are most vulnerable to unemployment. For details on the social composition of the unemployed see Sheila Marnie, "How prepared is Russia for mass unemployment?", Radio Free Europe/Radio Liberty Special Report, 11 November 1992. On the special case of scientists see the results of a poll conducted among 300 Moscow scientists during the summer of 1991 as reported in Nikolai Popov, Roussina Volkova and Vadim Sazonov, "Unemployment in Science: Executive Summary" (Moscow: VTsIOM, 1991).

27   In Table 4.11 I collapsed a more detailed occupational breakdown.

28   I suspect that there is a reciprocal relationship between Jewishness and fear of antisemitism but I have not explored that possibility here so as to avoid technical complications.

29   V. O. Rukavishnikov *et al.,* "Social tension: Diagnosis and prognosis", *Sociological Research,* vol. 32, no. 2, 1993, 58.

30   Arthur Hertzberg, "Is anti-semitism dying out?", *The New York Review of Books*, 24 June 1993.

5 Emigration

THE SIZE AND DIRECTION OF THE EMIGRATION MOVEMENT, 1966-93

Sometime in mid-1993 the millionth Jew emigrated from the former USSR in the twenty-five years since 1968. During that period fewer than two-thirds of the emigrants settled in Israel. Over one-third settled elsewhere, mostly in the USA.

Those are rounded figures. Beneath their smooth contours lies more than a quarter-century of high political and human drama which has been recounted in precise detail by a host of participants and analysts. My intention here is not to provide yet another narrative account of the emigration movement. Rather, I will focus on just two themes. First, I will show that the development and demise of Soviet society, and the actions of the main parties involved in the emigration drama, caused enormous variation from year to year in both the number of Jews who left and in their choice of destinations.[1] Second, I will analyze data from my survey of Jews in Moscow, Kiev and Minsk, as well as from other sources, in order to hazard a prognosis of the future of the emigration movement.

Figure 5.1 tells the first part of the story in graphic form. It shows the number of emigrants who went to Israel and the number who went to the West each year from 1971 to 1993.[2] Table 5.1 helps make sense of the graph by dividing the history of the emigration movement into seven periods. Each period is characterized along three dimensions—the annual number of emigrants, the trend in the annual number of emigrants, and the annual proportion of emigrants who went to the West.

The emigration movement emerged out of a confluence of circumstances, the most fundamental of which I discussed in Chapter 2. Because of the social location they occupied, and the nature of Soviet nationality policy, the Jews had become redundant to the labour requirements of the Soviet federal state. From a broad point of view this was merely a variation on an old historical theme. The Jews migrated in large numbers to Eastern Europe when, beginning in the fifteenth century, the mercantile functions

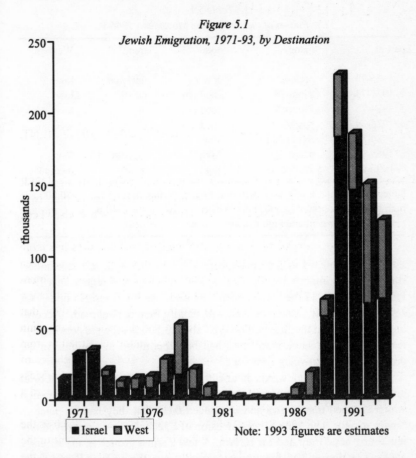

Figure 5.1
Jewish Emigration, 1971-93, by Destination

■ Israel ■ West   Note: 1993 figures are estimates

they performed in the feudal economies of Western Europe became redundant. And they migrated in even larger numbers from Eastern Europe to North America under analogous circumstances four hundred years later. In a sense, major Jewish migrations have always heralded world-historical change. This was no less the case from the mid-1960s onwards than it was one or five centuries earlier.

The first phase of the emigration movement may be dated from the mid-1960s, when it had already become more difficult for some Jews to gain admission to the better institutions of higher education, find good jobs and obtain promotions. As one Soviet commentator noted only a few years later, "[t]he tasks confronting the system of people's education have been fulfilled and overfulfilled. . . . The national economy is close to

Table 5.1
The Phases of the Emigration Movement, 1966-93

period	name	total	trend	Western
1. 1966-70	prelude	low	unstable	low
2. 1971-73	Zionist 1	medium	up	low
3. 1974-75	Zionist 2	medium	down	low
4. 1976-79	post-Zionist	medium	up	medium
5. 1980-88	repression	low	"U"	high
6. 1989-91	panic	high	inverted "U"	low
7. 1992-93	decline	high	down	medium

Notes: For "total", low means 0-10,000 emigrants, medium means 11-70,000 and high means more than 70,000. For "Western", low means 0-40 per cent, medium means 41-65 per cent and high means more than 65 per cent.

saturation in regard to diploma specialists."[3] In this light one can understand the logic underlying Alexei Kosygin's much quoted remark in a 1966 Paris interview: "[T]he way is open", he said, "and will remain open" for Jews in the USSR to be reunified with family members abroad.[4] Accordingly, in 1966 and the first half of 1967 about 3,500 Jews were permitted to leave—about the same number as had been permitted to emigrate in the preceding eighteen years combined.[5]

The Arab-Israeli war in June 1967 brought an abrupt end to that brief policy change. It was replaced by a state-initiated "anti-Zionist" campaign which shocked many Jews and convinced them that they had no place in Soviet society. The 1968 Soviet invasion of Czechoslovakia destroyed any remaining hope they had for reform. A few Zionist groups in the recently annexed territories had functioned secretly since World War II and some new Zionist circles had been inspired by Israel's victory in the 1967 war. They now began to press urgently for the right to emigrate. That gave the regime added incentive to let Jews leave: emigration could serve as a safety valve for the release of Zionist dissidents. In 1970 the "Regulations on Entry into the USSR and Exit from the USSR" were revised to add fees and charges to the emigration process in anticipation of a substantially increased outflow, which began in earnest the following year. Nearly 13,000 Jews were permitted to emigrate from the USSR in 1971 on the pretext that they were being permitted to join family members abroad. That was over 25 per cent more than during the entire period 1948-70.

The second phase of the emigration movement stretched from 1971 to 1973. It was characterized by steadily increasing numbers of emigrants, the virtually unanimous selection of Israel as a destination and what from a later vantage point can be recognized as moderate annual emigration rates—roughly, between 13,000 and 35,000 emigrants per year. The movement's third stage differed in only one respect: between 1974 and 1975 the annual emigration rate declined to about 13,000.

This was the first of three cycles in the rate of emigration, each of increasing amplitude. The annual rate of emigration first peaked in 1973 and bottomed out in 1975, then crested again at a higher rate in 1979 and dropped to an even deeper trough by 1986, then reached its highest-ever point in 1990 and began to fall thereafter and until the time of this writing (August 1993).

It is tempting to view these fluctuations as a reflection of the cordiality of ties between the USA and the USSR/CIS.[6] Some analysts have thus argued that the first peak in emigration was preceded by a general warming of relations in the early 1970s—the period of *détente*. During that era the USA offered the USSR trade credits and Most Favoured Nation status in exchange for more Jewish emigration. Presumably, the first trough in the emigration rate was precipitated by Soviet anger over the collapse of trade talks between the two countries.

By the same reasoning, the peak of the second cycle was preceded by the Soviet Union giving way to US pressure, signing the Helsinki Final Act in 1975 and thereby pledging to make travel and emigration easier for its citizens. In contrast, the rapid fall in the rate of emigration after 1979 was due to the chilling of US-Soviet relations in the wake of the Soviet invasion of Afghanistan and the imposition of martial law in Poland.

Finally, the enormous surge in the emigration rate after 1988 was supposedly a reflection of *perestroyka*, the collapse of Communism and the new friendship that emerged between the USA and the CIS.

While superficially appealing, this "barometer thesis" is flawed, both logically and empirically. Specifically:

▪ It ignores the fact that the emigration movement began around 1966, several years before the *détente* era and the improvement of relations between the superpowers.

▪ It incorrectly assumes that the USA was able to exert substantial influence over Soviet domestic policy. The plain fact is, however, that in no year did Soviet-US commerce ever amount to more than 10 per cent of Soviet trade with the West. Also, whenever the USA tried to use trade sanctions to control Soviet behaviour the Soviets simply turned to Germany, Japan or Canada for Western goods.[7] If anything, what the collapse of trade negotiations in 1974 demonstrates is that the USA *lacked* leverage with the USSR. Negotiations broke down because the USA was demanding what the Soviets saw as too many human rights concessions in exchange for more trade. More generally, the breakdown confirms that the Soviet Union "never, not even in the times of its greatest weakness, permitted concessions in its internal regime to become the object of diplomatic negotiations."[8]

▪ Although the emigration rate started to rise again in 1976, Soviet-American relations were deteriorating on many fronts. This was the period when Soviet and Cuban forces invaded Angola, when the USSR intervened militarily in the Horn of Africa and when protracted SALT negotiations seemed to be getting nowhere.

▪ Only by some perverse logic would the USSR have decided to cut emigration in response to American condemnation of the 1979 invasion of Afghanistan, the imposition of trade sanctions and the boycott of the 1980 Moscow Olympics. Would it not have made elementary good sense to allow more Jews out in order to curry favour with the USA and mitigate American fury?

▪ Some commentators argue that the volume of US-Soviet trade is a good indicator of the warmth of relations between the two countries. If so, it is revealing that between 1971 and 1987 there was no statistically significant relationship between the annual volume of US-Soviet trade and the annual rate of Soviet Jewish emigration.[9]

▪ The rise in the emigration rate after 1988 was undeniably connected to *perestroyka* and the collapse of Communism. Whether the growing friendship between the USSR/ CIS and the USA had any bearing on the course of the third emigration cycle is, however, far from clear. After all, the emigration rate began to fall rapidly again after 1990, but US-CIS relations remained cordial.

On the basis of these considerations I conclude that the warmth of USSR/CIS-US ties has not been the principal influence on the rate of emigration, although it has undoubtedly had some influence. Rather, emigration rates seem to respond most sensitively to two internal factors— (1) ongoing debates at the highest levels of the USSR/ CIS leadership about labour-force requirements, which have fluctuated from one decade to the next; and (2) emigrants' perceptions of, and preferences among, emigration opportunities, which have fluctuated in accordance with the social composition of the emigrants and the immigration policies of Western states.

The importance of emigrants' perceptions and preferences can be seen most vividly if we reconsider the post-1973 slump in the emigration rate. Interestingly, by dividing the emigration wave into two components— emigrants headed to Israel and those headed elsewhere—we see that there was a steady *increase* in the number of emigrants headed elsewhere from 1974 to 1980 and a more or less steady increase in the *proportion* of Western-bound emigrants straight through to 1988 (see Figure 5.1). The mid-1970s slump was actually a decline only in the number of Israel-bound emigrants.

After 1973 fewer emigrants chose to go to Israel partly because the initial pool of Zionist and religious activists had already left the USSR. Later emigrants tended to be more assimilated and less interested in living in the Jewish state. That was partly reflected in the regional origins of the emigrants. From 1966 to 1973 the great majority of Soviet Jewish emigrants came from peripheral regions where Jews were less assimilated, such as the Baltic republics, Moldova, Georgia, western Ukraine and Belarus. After 1973 the proportion of emigrants from Russia, eastern Ukraine and Belarus, where Jews were more assimilated, grew steadily. Surveys conducted at the time revealed a corresponding shift in emigrants' motives for leaving. While many pre-1974 emigrants tended to say that they were leaving due to ethnic discrimination and the desire to live in the Jewish state, post-1973 emigrants tended to express more universalistic and pragmatic motives such as wanting to live in a democracy or in a country where they could enjoy freedom of cultural expression and a higher standard of living. Also important in causing the shift away from Israel as a destination was the 1973 Arab-Israeli war, which underlined the dangers of living in the Middle East. Finally, it soon became apparent that countries other than Israel, especially the USA, were prepared to accept immigrants from the Soviet Union. As this knowledge spread, and as Soviet Jews established a foothold in countries other than Israel, the rate and proportion of Soviet Jewish emigrants bound for countries other than Israel rose.[10]

In 1980 the emigration rate again began to plummet. This was, I believe, due mainly to perceptions of changing Soviet labour-force requirements by a leadership intent on rescuing the Soviet system from itself.[11] Growing problems with the command economy had been evident since the late 1950s and feeble attempts at reform had been made on several occasions, most notably during the Khrushchev era. In the early 1980s, however, the leadership made a last-ditch effort to prevent further declines in productivity and the standard of living—but all within the rigid framework of the Communist system. *Within the limits of the Communist system*, one of the more serious problems they faced was a large and growing labour deficit. This had direct implications for emigration policy.

Arkady Shevchenko spent twenty years in the Soviet Foreign Ministry before defecting to the USA. He is therefore well qualified to speak on the question of emigration policy. In his 1985 memoirs Shevchenko noted that in the Soviet leadership

[a]t any given moment those who protest the loss of skilled technical manpower may have an edge over those who think it possible to obtain Western concessions by clearing the country of a resented minority. At another time the majority view can change. All that is certain is that the issue is a troublesome one that can generate different responses whenever it is raised.[12]

In the early 1980s hardline Communists who feared the loss of technical manpower won out. Labour shortages had become especially acute in the European part of the USSR, where the overwhelming majority of Jews resided. Experts estimated that between 1985 and 1990 the size of the working-age population in the non-Muslim areas of the USSR would actually decline.[13] From the point of view of the Communist leadership, the emigration of substantial numbers of highly trained Jews from precisely those areas threatened with the greatest labour shortages hardly seemed like a good idea under the circumstances. The "back-lash accusing the leadership of provoking a deplorable drain of scientific, cultural, academic and moral capital" predicted by Peter Reddaway was at hand.[14]

This background allows us to make sense of a Central Committee letter on the "Jewish question" that was read at closed Party meetings in 1979. The circular, reported in a *samizdat* journal, emphasized the need to make admission to jobs and higher education somewhat *easier* for Jews while, at the same time, stepping up "anti-Zionist" propaganda and making emigration more difficult.[15] The anti-emigration campaign continued until the advent of Gorbachev. As Theodore Friedgut remarked:

Brezhnev's focus on domestic economic problems was inherited by Andropov, who turned it into a campaign of discipline, eradication of corruption and restoration of a work ethic. The anti-emigration atmosphere was needed for this campaign too. The Jews had to be shown that emigration was out of the question, at least for the coming years, and that in their own interests, as well as those of the Soviet economy, they should live normal Soviet lives.[16]

Some concern over labour shortages extended into the *perestroyka* era. Thus in 1987 a "very senior Soviet official" told the Vice-President of the Canadian Jewish Congress that the advocates of *perestroyka* placed a premium on the technical and managerial jobs for which Jews were especially well trained, as a result of which the authorities were increasingly reluctant to let many more Jews leave.[17] By the late 1980s, however, that had become the minority view.

Most analysts came around to the opinion that serious labour dislocations would result from dismantling the central planning apparatus, rolling back price subsidies, scaling down the bloated state bureaucracy, ending Central Bank subsidies to inefficient industries and passing bankruptcy laws. For example, in 1988 Vladimir Kostakov, Director of the Economics Research Institute, GOSPLAN SSSR, projected that between 1986 and 2000 labour productivity would increase 15 to 25 per cent faster than national income. This meant that 13 to 19 million fewer Soviet workers would be needed in material production by the end of the century. Meanwhile, in *Pravda* it was estimated that administrative and managerial cadres would shrink by 50 per cent or more, leaving an additional 9 million people out of work. Kostakov expected that surplus labour would be absorbed by increasing the size of the pensioned population, offering more generous maternity leave, encouraging full-time rather than part-time education, shortening the working week and expanding the service sector. But even before the collapse of Communism in 1991, most Russian commentators recognized that, at least in the short-to-medium-term, widespread unemployment was a much more likely scenario than the growth of a Swedish-style welfare state.[18]

The panic emigration following 1988 ought to be viewed in the clear light of these structural circumstances. In the period 1989-91 many CIS Jews feared that antisemitic pogroms would break out. Economic ruin and political instability, including ethnic warfare and a coup attempt, acted as additional incentives to leave. The final years of the Communist regime and the disintegration of the USSR witnessed a general liberalization of which emigration policy was one part. Certainly all of these factors contributed heavily to the unprecedented flow of emigrants from the USSR/ CIS. Nevertheless, what made the massive emigration possible in the first place

was that the leaders of a society moving away from central planning fore-
saw the danger of massive labour surpluses. They apparently regarded emigration as one means of easing the burden.

Israel was eager to welcome all new arrivals. Ironically, the USA and
other Western countries were not. Much had changed in twenty years. The
West had promoted freedom of movement when the world economy was
vibrant and the influx of immigrants from the Soviet Union was relatively
modest and stretched over a couple of decades. But in the midst of a deep
recession and tight budgets the task of absorbing a million or more Jews
from the USSR—and, potentially, many more non-Jews—was simply out
of the question.[19] In October 1989 the USA imposed new regulations deny-
ing Soviet Jews automatic refugee status and thereby restricting their influx. Thereafter it became apparent that the USA was prepared to allow
only about 40,000 Soviet Jews to enter annually.[20] As a result, the proportion of emigrants "choosing" to go to Israel shot up once again. In September 1989 97 per cent of Soviet Jewish emigrants chose *not* to go to Israel.
Once the American restrictions were imposed that proportion fell to about
20 per cent and remained at that level until 1991.

The year 1992 marked the beginning of the last phase of the emigration movement listed in Table 5.1. While the number of emigrants going
to countries other than Israel more than doubled over the 1991 figure, the
number going to Israel fell by more than half. As a result, the proportion of
emigrants choosing not to go to Israel rose above the 50 per cent level
again and the total rate of emigration dropped substantially; the projected
1993 total was just over a third of the 1991 total. The panic was subsiding.

Several circumstances changed the mood of CIS Jewry, causing
drops in the emigration rate and the proportion choosing to go to Israel.
The predicted pogroms did not occur. The August 1991 *putsch* was a failure. For some Jews in the region the collapse of the Communist system
held out the promise, however faint, of a better life. Meanwhile, for all its
efforts, Israel found it extremely difficult to absorb the third of a million
new immigrants who arrived on its shores in just two years—a feat proportionate to expecting the USA to house and find jobs for about 16 million
arrivals in the same period or Germany to cope with over 6 million immigrants. Letters from Israel to friends and relatives in the USSR/CIS were
very discouraging.[21]

Indeed, what is surprising is that the 1992 emigration figure broke
the 100,000 mark at all. It did so partly due to a quite unexpected development. Suddenly, quietly and defying all apparent logic, Germany increased
its intake of CIS Jews to over 2,000 a month.[22] Here was a country facing a

flat economy and the mammoth task of modernizing former East Germany. Its open-door immigration policy burdened it with absorbing hundreds of thousands of ethnic Germans from Russia and other asylum-seekers from Eastern Europe annually. Germany had, moreover, to manage increasingly violent anti-immigration sentiment together with an angry backlash on the part of Turkish *Gastarbeiter* and sympathetic native Germans. In this context it is difficult to understand why CIS Jews should have suddenly been so welcome. The only possible explanation is that they served a useful ideological function, allowing the German government to assuage war guilt and demonstrate the absence of racism in its ranks.[23] In any case, in 1993 Germany passed restrictive asylum laws, its economy remained stagnant and the mood of sections of its population remained ugly. It is therefore doubtful that the immigration of CIS Jews will continue for much longer at the 1992 level.

In view of these recent developments—declining emigration rates since 1990, serious absorption problems in Israel, restricted immigration opportunities in the USA, a likely downturn in immigration opportunities in Germany—it seems worthwhile asking what will become of the emigration movement in the near future. How many Jews still want to leave the CIS? Why? What are the social determinants of their decisions to stay or leave and, in the latter case, to choose one country over another? We may now return to the survey of Jews in Moscow, Kiev and Minsk in order to shed light on those questions.

HOW MANY WANT TO LEAVE?

Under certain circumstances virtually every Jew in the former USSR would emigrate. One can speculate what those conditions might involve—complete economic and political anarchy combined with widespread antisemitic violence at home, wide-open immigration regulations combined with abundant job opportunities in the West and Israel. In reality, however, none of those conditions exists. For all the troubles suffered by Russia, Ukraine and Belarus—hyperinflation, declining production, rising crime rates, environmental degradation, intense political conflict between reformers and conservatives, comparatively high levels of anti-Jewish feeling—most Jews in my sample intend to stay put. Specifically, when asked whether they plan to emigrate, 57 per cent of the respondents answered "no", 14 per cent said "don't know" and 29 per cent replied "yes". Fourteen per cent of the respondents said they planned to emigrate to the USA. Only

8 per cent said they planned to emigrate to Israel. Seven per cent expressed the intention to leave for other countries and 2 per cent had not decided where they would go (see Table 5.2, columns one and two).

Table 5.2
Emigration Plans of Respondents and Jewish Population of Former USSR

	respondents		former USSR (est.)	
	frequency	per cent	frequency (in '000s)	per cent
not planning to emigrate	572	57	538	47
don't know	141	14	160	14
planning to emigrate to				
Israel	78	8	183	16
USA	136	14		
Canada	23	2		
Australia	17	2	→ 263	23
Germany	13	1		
other	3	0		
don't know	18	2		
total	1,001	100	1,144	100

Note: Column 1 adds up to 1,001 due to weighting.

Unfortunately, one cannot mechanically manipulate these figures to arrive at a precise estimate of the Jewish emigration potential of the entire territory of the former USSR. Strictly speaking, my survey data entitle me to generalize only about the Jews of Moscow, Kiev and Minsk, who comprise 28 per cent of the Jews in Russia, Ukraine and Belarus. Roughly speaking, however, it is difficult to imagine that figures for the rest of Russia and the other large cities of Ukraine (Kharkov and Odessa) would differ much from those in the first two columns of Table 5.2; the socio-demographic profile of Jews in these other areas is quite similar to the profile of Jews in the three cities where my sample was drawn.[24] I estimate, therefore, that the findings in the first two columns of Table 5.2 hold approximately for 55 per cent of Jews in the former USSR.[25]

As far as the remaining 45 per cent of the Jewish population are concerned, one can state with certainty that their emigration potential is higher than that reflected in the first two columns of Table 5.2 and that a larger proportion of them wish to emigrate to Israel. As we will see below, strength of Jewish identity varies proportionately with emigration potential and with propensity to choose Israel as a destination; and there are proportionately more Jewish Jews living outside Russia and the large cities of Ukraine. The proportions involved are, however, unknown. My guess—and I state emphatically that this is only a guess—is that the emigration potential of the rest of the CIS is similar in proportionate terms to that of Minsk alone (for which see Table 5.6, panel 1). I thus assume that 35 per cent of these other Jews are not planning to emigrate, 15 per cent of them do not know whether they will emigrate, 25 per cent of them intend to move to Israel and 25 per cent intend to move to countries other than Israel or are not sure where they will go.

Combining my approximate estimate for 55 per cent of the population with my much more speculative estimate for the remaining 45 per cent, I arrive at the conclusion that, in the first quarter of 1993, about 47 per cent of the Jews in the former USSR (538,000 people) were *not* planning to emigrate (see Table 5.2, columns three and four). Fourteen per cent (160,000 people) were unsure, 16 per cent planned to go to Israel (183,000 people) and 23 per cent (263,000 people) planned to go to other countries or did not know where they would end up.

Although all these figures are based partly on educated guesswork, one's confidence in them increases when they are placed alongside the results of two independent estimates. The first comes from a newspaper poll conducted in Moscow by Professor Ryvkina in December 1991.[26] Ryvkina had a questionnaire printed in *Yevreyskaya gazeta*, a Jewish newspaper with a circulation of 25,000-30,000 published in Moscow. Ninety-three self-selected experts in Jewish affairs completed questionnaires. They estimated that 61 per cent of Jews would emigrate from the USSR. That is 8 per cent above my estimate of the number of people in the former USSR who are planning to emigrate plus those who are still unsure whether they will emigrate. The 1991 poll was based on a small sample and was conducted during the panic emigration of the very early 1990s, when expectations concerning the number of Jews likely to leave the region were temporarily inflated. Nonetheless, the results of the poll are in line with the results of my survey.

Second, in my survey, respondents were themselves asked to estimate how many Jews would emigrate from the former USSR. The respondents were not experts in Jewish affairs but they tended to be highly educated and had the great virtue of being able to assess the situation "on the ground", as it were. Of the 86 per cent who ventured an opinion, 11 per cent said that "nearly all" CIS Jews would emigrate, 58 per cent answered "a majority", 24 per cent said "half" and 7 per cent replied "a minority". If "nearly all" means 90 per cent, "a majority" means 60 per cent, "half" means 50 per cent and "a minority" means 20 per cent, then the average estimate of my respondents is 58 per cent—5 per cent above my estimate for the number of people in the former USSR who are planning to emigrate plus those who are still unsure whether they will emigrate. I conclude that both independent estimates are in line with my own. Statistically speaking, one can be 95 per cent confident that the difference between my estimate, on the one hand, and both Professor Ryvkina's and my respondents', on the other, is due to chance.[27]

Of course, all estimates can easily be turned upside down by unforeseen developments, as students of Soviet and CIS society know better than most. Moreover, there is a difference between planning to go to a particular country and actually arriving there; United States immigration quotas may, for example, force some emigrants who would otherwise wind up in the USA to go to Israel.[28] Much depends also on what the "don't knows" eventually decide to do. That said, the best information available suggests that Natan Sharansky, among many others, was wrong when he wrote in 1992 that "millions [of Jews] are on their way" out of the former USSR.[29] So was Israeli President Ezer Weizmann, who claimed on Israeli television on 29 June 1993 (Channel 1) that 2 million Jews in the CIS were ready to emigrate. There are no millions. If conditions remain what they are today, and even in the unlikely event that all the "don't knows" elect to emigrate, it seems that as of 1993 about 606,000 more Jews plan on leaving the former Soviet Union. In the equally unlikely event that all the "don't knows" elect to go to Israel, that country can expect at most about 345,000 more Jews to arrive from the former USSR, a figure well below most current Israeli projections, which still speak of close to a million new arrivals between 1993 and 2000.[30] (Another set of estimates of immigration to Israel and elsewhere, based on a projection of current trends, is offered in the concluding section of this chapter.)

WHY DO THEY WANT TO GO?

The foregoing analysis raises a number of subsidiary issues. Why do so many Jews plan to leave the CIS? What keeps so many Jews there? Why do so few plan to go to Israel? Respondents were asked questions about all these issues. Their answers reveal some interesting patterns.

Table 5.3
Reasons for Wanting to Emigrate (first three choices)

	frequency	per cent
q77-for the sake of children's future	176	24
q75-to improve standard of living	129	18
q80-no expected improvement in situation	128	17
economic subtotal	433	59
q76-political instability	103	14
q78-fear of antisemitism and pogroms	99	13
q79-fear of violence	41	6
ethnic-political subtotal	243	33
q81-to keep family together	59	8
total	735	100

The 429 respondents who said they were planning to emigrate were asked to review a list of seven options and select their three chief motives for wanting to leave. Their responses are not quite as enlightening as they could have been because, due to oversight, the list did not include options indicating cultural or ethnic affinity with the West and with Israel (which I strongly expect would have been infrequently selected in any case). Basically, Table 5.3 shows that Jews are motivated to leave more for economic reasons (59 per cent of responses) than for reasons of antisemitic persecution, general fear of violence and political instability (33 per cent) or family reunification (8 per cent). One certainly can-not conclude on this basis that, in general, Jewish emigrants from the CIS are refugees. The data do suggest, however, that a large minority of them could be so defined without any stretching of the Western legal definition.

Respondents were also asked what ties them to their country. They were allowed to choose up to three options from a fixed list of nine. Table 5.4 details their responses. It reveals a pattern nearly the reverse of Table 5.3. One may infer that economic ties keep only a small minority of respondents rooted in their country while familial and especially cultural ties, broadly defined, loom large. Thus while only 12 per cent of responses

Table 5.4
Ties to One's Country (first three choices)

	frequency	per cent
q100-accustomed to it	715	29
q106-closely connected to culture	438	18
cultural subtotal	1153	47
q103-unwilling to leave relatives	375	15
q104-unwilling to leave friends	303	12
familial subtotal	678	27
q99-have a good job here	114	5
q102-hope to increase standard of living here	100	4
q101-hope to establish business here	67	3
economic subtotal	281	12
q107-old age, weak health	195	8
q105-hope for political stability here	157	6
total	2464	100

indicate the importance of economic ties, 27 per cent suggest that family ties prevent Jews from emigrating and 47 per cent of responses suggest that cultural affinity is the most important factor keeping them where they are.

Finally, let us consider why respondents planning to leave for the West do not select Israel as their destination. Up to three choices were permitted from a fixed list of seven options.[31] As Table 5.5 shows, cultural reasons were the most frequently chosen (31 per cent of responses). That is, people planning to leave the CIS often choose to go to countries other than Israel because they would find it too difficult to live in an atmosphere of Jewish culture or to learn Hebrew. Economic reasons for choosing a country other than Israel follow closely in importance (29 per cent). Indeed, the lack of good jobs in Israel is the single most frequent justification for deciding to go to other destinations. Thus when respondents who chose other destinations were asked whether they would go to Israel if they could

Table 5.5
Reasons for Not Wanting to Emigrate to Israel (first three choices)

	frequency	per cent
q85-difficulty of living in Jewish culture	90	18
q88-Hebrew too difficult to learn	68	13
cultural subtotal	190	31
q83-not enough good jobs there	143	28
q84-fear of losing business here	5	1
economic subtotal	148	29
q87-few friends and/ or relatives in Israel	96	19
q86-Arab-Israeli conflict and war threat	71	14
q90-too old or weak	34	7
total	507	100

secure a job comparable to the one they currently hold, fully 31 per cent per cent said "yes" (78,000 people in population terms). Other reasons for choosing a destination other than Israel include having too few friends and/ or relatives in Israel (19 per cent of responses), the Arab-Israeli conflict and the threat of war (14 per cent), and being too old or weak to live in Israel (7 per cent).

I conclude that while Jews who are planning to emigrate are motivated mainly by economic factors, Jews who do not want to emigrate are motivated principally by cultural affinity for their homeland. Meanwhile, among those planning to leave for the West, a combination of economic and cultural factors dissuade them from choosing Israel as a destination. These findings should interest Jewish policy-makers outside the CIS. Cultural predispositions are more difficult to change than economic opportunities and altering each would have different effects. Specifically, investing to create more good jobs in Israel would have a marked impact on shifting the flow of CIS emigrants from the West to Israel but would not substantially increase the number of Jews leaving the CIS. Increasing the number of departures would require, above all else, a long-term campaign aimed at a cultural reorientation to which most CIS Jews do not appear amenable (see Chapter 3).

DETERMINANTS OF MIGRATION PLANS

Now that we have a sense of approximately how many Jews wish to leave the CIS, where they wish to settle, and why they wish to leave, we can examine the social factors underlying their emigration plans. In order to simplify my presentation I combined two questions concerning emigration plans—"Do you intend to emigrate from the country?" and "To which country are you planning to immigrate?"—into a single indicator. In the combined version of these questions there were four possible response categories: (1) No, I do not plan to emigrate; (2) I do not know whether I will emigrate; (3) I plan on emigrating to the West; (4) I plan on emigrating to Israel. Table 5.6 sets out the list of factors that are statistically significantly associated with migration plans at the .05 probability level. Let us quickly sift through the numbers.[32]

The proportion of Jews planning to emigrate increases as one moves from Moscow to Kiev to Minsk; from older to younger age categories; from married and widowed people to never-married, separated and divorced individuals; from people with no children living abroad to people with one, two or more children living outside the country; from retired to employed individuals to homemakers to unemployed people to students; and from people who have no friends or relatives abroad to those who do. It is thus evident that the weaker one's social attachments to one's country—as determined by youth, lack of marital ties, and lack of employment ties—and the stronger one's social attachments abroad—as measured by number of family and friendship ties outside the country—the greater the propensity to leave.

The picture is more complicated when one shifts attention to the proportion of Jews planning to emigrate to Israel. The relationships listed above hold for some variables (city, number of children abroad, having friends and relatives in Israel and, somewhat suprisingly, having friends in the USA) but they are considerably weaker or non-existent for other variables. Consider age. While 61 per cent of the respondents between the ages of 18 and 29 said they plan on emigrating, that figure falls to 22 per cent for respondents 60 years of age and older. Clearly, emigration is mainly for the young. Meanwhile, 10 per cent of the respondents between the ages of 18 and 29 plan to emigrate to Israel, little different from the 8 per cent of people 60 years and older who expressed the same intention. Israel is nearly as likely to attract older immigrants as younger ones. A similar story can be told for marital status, work status, having friends and relatives in countries other than Israel and having relatives in the USA:

Table 5.6
Correlates of Emigration Plans (in per cent; n in parentheses)

		emigration plans				
		no	don't know	West	Israel	total
q5-city						
	Moscow	63	15	16	6	100 (535)
	Kiev	56	12	23	9	100 (329)
	Minsk	41	17	25	18	101 (119)
	chi-square = 37.19, d.f. = 6, p = .000; tau-c = 0.127					
q8-age						
	18-29	39	22	29	10	100 (177)
	30-39	52	19	23	6	100 (151)
	40-49	59	16	18	8	101 (210)
	50-59	62	12	19	8	101 (279)
	60-90	78	6	9	8	101 (166)
	chi-square = 65.23, d.f. = 12, p = .000; tau-c = -0.160					
q10-marital status						
	never married	48	22	23	8	101 (143)
	married	60	14	20	7	101 (680)
	separated/ div.	49	12	22	17	100 (94)
	widowed	75	10	5	10	100 (66)
	chi-square = 34.29, d.f. = 9, p = .000; tau-c = -0.027					
q13-number of children abroad						
	0	60	15	19	7	101 (892)
	1	44	13	26	19	102 (69)
	2+	28	15	31	26	100 (11)
	chi-square = 22.16, d.f. = 6, p = .001; tau-c = 0.053					
q14-work status						
	retired	69	7	14	11	101 (196)
	employed	58	17	18	7	100 (653)
	homemaker	50	12	35	4	101 (38)
	unemployed	44	4	41	12	101 (29)
	student	36	28	30	6	100 (54)
	chi-square = 50.99, d.f. = 12, p = .000; tau-c = 0.081					
q19-work satisfaction						
	yes	61	15	16	7	99 (474)
	no	51	14	27	9	101 (135)
	chi-square = 8.44, d.f. = 3, p = .038; tau-c = 0.083					

Table 5.6 (cont'd)
Correlates of Emigration Plans (in per cent; n in parentheses)

	no	don't know	West	Israel	total	
			emigration plans			

q21-sat. with work conditions

	no	don't know	West	Israel	total
satisfied	63	17	15	6	101 (427)
not satisfied	49	16	26	9	100 (188)

chi-square = 14.74, d.f. = 3, p = .000; tau-c = 0.133

q22-sat. with managers at work

satisfied	63	18	14	6	101 (497)
not satisfied	41	6	39	14	100 (88)

chi-square = 47.18, d.f. = 3, p = .000; tau-c = 0.150

q23-sat. with colleagues at work

satisfied	60	17	18	6	101 (593)
not satisfied	33	19	28	20	100 (25)

chi-square = 12.71, d.f. = 3, p = .005; tau-c = 0.051

q24-sat. with post

satisfied	60	17	16	6	99 (486)
not satisfied	54	10	27	9	100 (115)

chi-square = 10.74, d.f. = 3, p = .013; tau-c = 0.063

q25-sat. with opportunities for advancement

satisfied	62	18	15	5	100 (211)
not satisfied	55	14	21	10	100 (271)

chi-square = 8.39, d.f. = 3, p = .036; tau-c = 0.104

q40-sat. with occupational position

satisfied	68	13	14	5	100 (470)
not satisfied	46	17	27	10	100 (370)

chi-square = 43.46, d.f. = 3, p = .000; tau-c = 0.231

q92-family or rels. in Israel

yes	52	17	20	11	100 (584)
no	69	9	18	4	100 (363)

chi-square = 35.60, d.f. = 3, p=.000; tau-c = -0.166

q93-family or rels. in US

yes	50	15	27	9	101 (510)
no	68	13	11	8	100 (434)

chi-square = 42.16, d.f. = 3, p = .000; tau-c = -0.183

Table 5.6 (cont'd)
Correlates of Emigration Plans (in per cent; n in parentheses)

	no	don't know	West	Israel	total
		emigration plans			

q94-family or rels. in other Western country

	no	don't know	West	Israel	total
yes	50	19	24	7	100 (205)
no	61	12	18	8	99 (714)

chi-square = 11.07, d.f. = 3, p = .011; tau-c = -0.062

q95-friends in Israel

	no	don't know	West	Israel	total
yes	52	15	23	10	100 (633)
no	70	14	13	4	101 (337)

chi-square = 35.92, d.f. = 3, p = .000; tau-c = -0.185

q96-friends in US

	no	don't know	West	Israel	total
yes	50	14	26	10	100 (560)
no	69	15	10	6	100 (408)

chi-square = 49.48, d.f. = 3, p = .000; tau-c = -0.208

q97-friends in other Western country

	no	don't know	West	Israel	total
yes	51	17	26	7	101 (295)
no	62	13	17	9	101 (669)

chi-square = 16.82, d.f. = 3, p = .001; tau-c = -0.086

q108-feeling about Israel

	no	don't know	West	Israel	total
hist. motherland	40	18	25	17	100 (197)
eminent state	57	14	18	11	100 (144)
like other states/ no att.	62	14	19	5	100 (511)

chi-square = 41.77, d.f. = 6, p = .000; tau-c = -0.150

q123-personally suffered antisemitism

	no	don't know	West	Israel	total
yes	51	14	25	10	100 (539)
no	69	13	14	4	100 (326)

chi-square = 34.27, d.f. = 3, p = .000; tau-c = -0.196

q162-political system if 1-2 years

	no	don't know	West	Israel	total
freer	60	18	15	7	100 (142)
same	58	14	17	11	100 (334)
less free	50	11	32	8	101 (236)

chi-square = 23.95, d.f. = 6, p = .001; tau-c = 0.079

Table 5.6 (cont'd)
Correlates of Emigration Plans (in per cent; n in parentheses)

		emigration plans			
	no	don't know	West	Israel	total
q163-confidence in own future					
yes	68	13	10	9	100 (161)
no	56	13	22	8	99 (684)
chi-square = 12.71, d.f. = 3, p = .005; tau-c = 0.077					
Jewishness scale					
low	75	13	11	2	101 (329)
medium	61	16	20	3	100 (327)
high	39	14	28	19	100 (326)
chi-square = 135.88, d.f. = 6, p =.000; tau-c = 0.283					

Note: Percentages do not necessarily add up to 100 due to rounding.

none of these factors exerts a discernible impact on one's tendency to emigrate to Israel.

Apart from the sociodemographic factors just discussed, Table 5.6 shows that three other sets of social forces affect respondents' migration plans. The first set relates to various facets of one's work environment. Note that it is job dissatisfaction as a professional issue, not as a pecuniary concern, that drives people to emigrate. Thus migration plans have nothing to do with actual income levels or levels of satisfaction with earnings. Respondents are, however, more inclined to plan to emigrate if they are dissatisfied with colleague and management relations at work, with actual working conditions, with their posts and with opportunities for advancement. In general, CIS Jews are extraordinarily dedicated to their jobs. The inability to achieve professional and intellectual fulfillment drives many of them out of the country. Note also that professional frustration also tends to increase respondents' propensity to choose Israel as a destination, although to a lesser degree than it affects the decision to leave in the first place.

A third set of factors influencing migration plans concerns Jewishness and the experience of antisemitism. It is the more Jewish Jews and those who have personally experienced antisemitism who are more inclined to plan to emigrate and to choose Israel as a destination.

Finally, being pessimistic about the prospects for democracy in one's country and lacking confidence in one's personal future are associated with planning to emigrate. These attitudes do not, however, increase the likelihood of choosing Israel as a destination.

Many of the variables in Table 5.6 tell us virtually the same thing. For example, age and marital status are similarly related to emigration plans and they are also related to each other (young people are more likely never to have been married and old people are more likely to be widows or widowers). Does age have an effect on emigration plans independent of the effect it shares with marital status? Which other variables have such independent effects and how strong are they? Table 5.7 presents a multiple regression analysis that answers these questions, eliminating redundancy and reducing the information in Table 5.6 to more vivid and informative proportions.

Table 5.7
Multiple Regression of Emigration Plans

question	slope (b)	standard error	standardized slope (beta)	t
sociodemographics				
q8-age	-.16	.02	-.21	7.29
q13-# child. abroad	.39	.09	.13	4.44
q96-friends USA	.21	.06	.10	3.65
q5-city size	.10	.04	.07	2.55
Jewish factors				
Jewishness scale	.04	.003	.33	11.08
q123-fear antisem.	.18	.06	.08	2.81
work factors				
q40-occ. satisfaction	-.21	.06	-.10	-3.31
q23-coll. relations	-.38	.18	-.06	-2.15

intercept = 1.92; n = 1,001; adjusted R^2 = .25

At least two variables from three of the four blocs isolated above exert a statistically significant and independent effect on emigration plans. The bloc of four sociodemographic variables—age, number of children living abroad, city of residence and friendship ties in the USA—exerts the greatest causal impact on emigration plans. Next is the bloc of two Jewish factors—Jewishness and fear of antisemitism. Indeed, the scale of Jewish identity and practice is by far the single most important determinant of emigration plans. The bloc of two work-related factors exerts less than 40 per cent of the causal weight of the Jewish factors. Listing each variable in order of importance, one's propensity to emigrate and to choose Israel as a destination is associated with relatively high levels of Jewish identity and practice, comparative youth, having more rather than fewer children abroad, having friends in the USA, being dissatisfied with one's work, fearing antisemitism, living in Minsk rather than Kiev and in Kiev rather than Moscow, and being dissatisfied with collegial relations at work.

EMIGRATION PROJECTIONS, 1994-99

In ending this chapter I want to engage in what may well prove to be a foolhardy exercise. I want to project the rate and destination of Jewish emigration from the CIS until the end of the century. The reader should be under no illusion about what these projections mean. *They are not predictions.* Rather, they merely extrapolate from current trends in the emigration movement and certain of my survey results, which are themselves based in part on educated guesswork. Specifically, Table 5.8 makes two assumptions: (1) The average annual decline in the rate of emigration was 18 per cent in the period 1990-93. I assume that this trend will continue to 1994. From 1994 to 1999 I assume that the emigration rate will drop at a rate of 10 per cent per year, reflecting the diminishing pool of potential emigrants. (2) About half the emigrants went to Israel in 1992 and 1993, but the survey-based estimates in Table 5.2 suggest that this figure will drop to one-third at the most. In Table 5.8 I assume that the proportion drops evenly to one-third by the end of the century.

Bearing in mind the important qualifications introduced above, Table 5.8 gives an extremely rough idea of how the emigration movement may develop until the end of the century. In brief, it suggests that the annual number of emigrants going to Israel may drop from about 51,000 in 1994 to about 20,000 in 1999, for a total of about 204,000 over the six-year span. The annual number of emigrants going to countries other than Israel may decline more gradually from about 51,000 in 1994 to about 41,000 in 1999, for a total of about 276,000. Table 5.8 also gives somewhat higher and less realistic maximum figures. My best guess, therefore, is that somewhere between 204,000 and 275,000 CIS emigrants will go to Israel between 1994 and 1999. Between 276,000 and 368,000 of them will go to other destinations. This will not spell the end of the Jewish community in the former USSR. It will, however, mark the end of one of its most important chapters.

Table 5.8
Projected CIS Emigration, 1994-99 (in '000s; per cent in parentheses)

	Israel	West	total
1994	51.3 (50.0)	51.3 (50.0)	102.5 (100.0)
1995	43.4 (47.0)	48.9 (53.0)	92.3 (100.0)
1996	35.7 (43.0)	47.3 (57.0)	83.3 (100.0)
1997	29.1 (39.0)	45.6 (61.0)	74.7 (100.0)
1998	24.9 (37.0)	42.4 (63.0)	67.3 (100.0)
1999	20.0 (33.0)	40.5 (67.0)	60.5 (100.0)
total	204.4 (42.5)	276.0 (57.4)	480.6 (99.9)
maximum	275.0	368.0	481.0

Note: The maxima are calculated from Table 5.2 minus 1993 emigration figures. The maximum total does not equal the sum of its components because each maximum is calculated independently on the assumption that it contains all the "don't knows". Some other totals do not equal the sum of their components due to rounding.

NOTES

1   In this section I draw on Robert J. Brym, "The changing rate of Jewish emigration from the USSR: Some lessons from the 1970s", *Soviet Jewish Affairs*, vol. 15, no. 2, 1985, 23-35; Robert J. Brym, "Soviet Jewish emigration: A statistical test of two theories", *Soviet Jewish Affairs*, vol. 18, no. 3, 1988, 15-23; Victor Zaslavsky and Robert J. Brym, *Soviet-Jewish Emigration and Soviet Nationality Policy* (London: Macmillan and New York: St. Martin's, 1983); and Tanya Basok and Robert J. Brym, "Soviet-Jewish emigration and resettlement in the 1990s: An overview" in Tanya Basok and Robert J. Brym (eds.), *Soviet-Jewish Emigration and Resettlement in the 1990s* (Toronto: York Lanes Press, York University, 1991), xi-xxii. Also useful was Laurie P. Salitan, *Politics and Nationality in Contemporary Soviet-Jewish Emigration, 1968-89* (New York: St. Martin's, 1992).

2   Data sources for 1971-1991: "Immigration data—1991", in *Yehudei brit ha-moatsot* (The Jews of the Soviet Union), vol. 15, 1992, 188; for 1992: Sidney Heitman, "Jewish emigration from the former USSR in 1992", unpublished paper (Fort Collins CO: Department of History, Colorado State University, 1993). The 1993 data are projected from figures for the first ten months of the year. I estimate 1993 arrivals in countries other than Israel and the USA at about 15,000.

3   Igor Bestuzhev-Lada, "Social problems of the Soviet way of life", *Novy mir*, no. 7, 1976, 215.

4   "Kosygin on reunion of families and national equality (1966)" in Benjamin Pinkus (ed.), *The Soviet Government and the Jews 1948-1967* (Cambridge UK: Cambridge University Press, 1984), 78.

5   In addition, under the terms of the Soviet-Polish Repatriation Agreement (1957-59), about 14,000 Jews had been permitted to return to their native Poland.

6   Robert O. Freedman, "Soviet Jewry and Soviet-American relations" in Robert O. Freedman (ed.), *Soviet Jewry in the Decisive Decade, 1971-80* (Durham, NC: Duke University Press, 1984), 38-67; "Soviet Jewry as a factor in Soviet-Israeli relations" in Robert O. Freedman (ed.), *Soviet Jewry in the 1980s: The Politics of Anti-Semitism and Emigration and the Dynamics of Resettlement* (Durham NC: Duke University Press, 1989), 61-96; Marshall I. Goldman, "Soviet-American trade and Soviet Jewish emigration: Should a policy change be made by the American Jewish community?" in Robert O. Freedman (ed.), *Soviet Jewry in the 1980s . . .* , 141-59.

7   Gary Bertsch, "US-Soviet trade: The question of leverage", *Survey,* vol. 25, no. 2, 1980, 66-80.

8   Richard Lowenthal, "East-West *détente* and the future of Soviet Jewry", *Soviet Jewish Affairs*, vol. 3, no. 1, 1973, 24.

9   Brym, "Soviet Jewish emigration . . . ". The relationship beyond 1987 is not known because the analysis has not been updated.

10   Zaslavsky and Brym, 49-51, 121-2; Zvi Gitelman, "Soviet Jewish emigrants: Why are they choosing America?", *Soviet Jewish Affairs*, vol. 7, no. 1, 1977, 31-46.

11   At the time, some commentators argued that the Soviets cut the emigration rate in the 1980s because many Jews started using Israeli exit visas to leave Russia but then "dropped out" and went elsewhere. Presumably, that practice undermined the pretext that Jews were permitted to leave for purposes of family reunification. The Soviets allegedly feared that non-Jews might get the idea that emigration for reasons other than family unification was possible. They therefore virtually stopped the outflow of Jews. See, for example, Zvi Alexander, "Jewish emigration from the USSR in 1980", *Soviet Jewish Affairs,* vol. 11, no. 2, 1981, 3-21; Zvi Nezer, "Jewish emigration from the USSR in 1981-82", *Soviet Jewish Affairs,* vol. 12, no. 3, 1982, 3-17. The trouble with this argument is that it fits the facts poorly. Thus the Soviets refused to allow direct Moscow-Tel Aviv flights, an action inconsistent with their alleged desire to stop the westward flow of Jewish emigrants. Between 1979 and 1981 the rate of emigration rose most in precisely those Soviet cities with the highest proportion of emigrants headed to countries other than Israel. And in general there was a statistically significant *positive* correlation between the emigration rate and the proportion of emigrants headed to countries other than Israel throughout the period 1971-87. See Brym, "The changing rate . . . "; "Soviet-Jewish emigration . . . ".

12   Arkady N. Shevchenko, *Breaking with Moscow* (New York: Alfred A. Knopf, 1985), 261.

13   Murray Feshbach, "The Soviet Union: Population trends and dilemmas", *Population Bulletin,* vol. 37, no. 3, 1982, 1-45; Alexander J. Motyl, *Will the Non-Russians Rebel? State, Ethnicity, and Stability in the USSR* (Ithaca and London: Cornell University Press, 1987), 158-9.

14   Peter Reddaway, "Policy towards dissent since Khrushchev" in T. H. Rigby, Archie Brown and Peter Reddaway (eds.), *Authority, Power and Policy in the USSR: Essays Dedicated to Leonard Shapiro* (London: Macmillan, 1980), 186.

15   "Miscellaneous reports", *Chronicle of Current Events,* no. 52, 1980 [1979]), 129.

16   Theodore Friedgut, "Soviet anti-Zionism and antisemitism—Another cycle", *Soviet Jewish Affairs,* vol. 14, no. 1, 1984, 6.

17   "Soviet anti-semitism said to be ceasing", *Canadian Jewish News,* 20 August 1987.

18   Vladimir G. Kostakov, "Employment: Deficit or surplus?", *Kommunist,* no. 2, 1987, 78-89; "Cutback", *Pravda,* 4 March 1988. Fear of a brain drain is still expressed in some circles today. See, for example, Irena Orlova, "A sketch of the migration and refugee situation in Russia", *Refuge,* vol. 13, no. 2, 1993, 19-22.

19   Robert J. Brym, "The emigration potential of Czechoslovakia, Hungary, Lithuania, Poland and Russia: Recent survey results", *International Sociology,* vol. 7, no. 4, 1992, 387-95. The Western desire to promote Soviet emigration also weakened when potential migrants from Central and South America, southeast Asia and elsewhere began making loud and legitimate claims on the Western immigration system.

20   Gregg A. Beyer, "The evolving United States response to Soviet-Jewish emigration" in Tanya Basok and Robert J. Brym (eds.), *Soviet-Jewish Emi-*

         gration and Resettlement in the 1990s, 105-39.

21   Roberta Cohen, "Israel's problematic absorption of Soviet Jews" in Tanya Basok and Robert J. Brym (eds.), *Soviet-Jewish Emigration and Resettlement in the 1990s*, 67-89.

22   Sidney Heitman, "Jewish emigration . . . ".

23   Michal Bodemann, "A renaissance of Germany Jewry?", paper presented at a conference on "The Reemergence of Jewish Culture in Germany", University of Toronto, 6-7 May 1993.

24   Recall that I weighted my sample so that, effectively, it consists of 54.5 per cent Muscovites, 33.2 per cent Kievans and only 12.3 per cent Minskers.

25   In the October 1992 survey I conducted with Andrei Degtyarev in Moscow there were only 23 Jewish respondents, of whom 5 (22 per cent) expressed the desire to emigrate. This is a small sub-sample and one should not read too much into the results. Nonetheless, the fact that 22 per cent of the 535 Moscow Jews in the survey conducted with Ryvkina (weighted n) also expressed the desire to emigrate should increase one's confidence in my findings. Compare Table 5.6, panel 1, with Robert J. Brym and Andrei Degtyarev, "Who wants to leave Moscow for the West? Results of an October 1992 survey", *Refuge,* vol. 13, no. 2, 1993, 24, Table 2. As this book went to press I learned that a survey recently conducted in Russia by Vladimir Shapiro, President of the Jewish Scientific Centre in Moscow, found that a third of Russian Jews wish to emigrate. This is consistent with my findings. The poll surveyed 1,300 Jews in Moscow, St Petersburg and Yekaterinburg. See Natasha Singer, "Poll: Jews staying in Russia", *Forward*, 13 August 1993.

26   Rozalina Ryvkina, "Value conflicts of Russian Jews and their social types", unpublished paper, Moscow, 1992.

27   A large random sample for a 1990 survey in ten republics of the USSR happened to include thirty-four Jews, a fifth of them from Georgia and none from Moscow or Leningrad. When the respondents were asked whether they would like to emigrate permanently, 71 per cent of the Jews said "yes". Note, however, that the sample of Jews is tiny and skewed towards regions with high rates of emigration. The survey was, moreover, conducted during the period of panic emigration. See Lev Gudkov and Alex Levinson, *Attitudes Toward Jews in the Soviet Union: Public Opinion in Ten Republics* (New York: The American Jewish Committee, 1992), 26-7.

28   For example, the USA is apparently planning to implement a new policy allowing people from the former Soviet republics with refugee status only one year to emigrate. This may speed up the pace of departure for some people with refugee status but it may force others to choose to go to Israel and still others not to leave at all. See "One-year limit on US refugee status for ex-USSR", *Monitor: Digest of News and Analysis from Soviet Successor States,* vol. 4, no. 25, 30 July/ 6 August 1993), 1.

29   Natan Sharansky, "The greatest exodus", *The New York Times Magazine*, 2 February 1992.

30   I note that the 1993 Israel budget proposal, tabled in 1992, predicted 154,000 CIS immigrants in 1993. A 1993 Israeli Treasury economic assessment paper lowered the figure to 80,000, but predicted 120,000 CIS immigrants per

year starting in 1994. Based on actual figures for the first ten months of 1993, I project 70,000 CIS immigrants for 1993. See Government of Israel, "The State Budget for 1993: Submitted to the Thirteenth Knesset" (Jerusalem: Government Printer, 1992) (in Hebrew), 114; "Surplus loan guarantees", *Canadian Jewish News*, 17 June 1993, 46.

31   I coded an eighth option ("I do not wish to leave Russia [Ukraine, Belarus]") as missing because in retrospect it seemed simply a restatement of the question. It received only thirty-two responses.

32   Eighteen respondents who said they planned to emigrate but were unsure which country they would go to were coded as missing. It did not make sense to standardize and add the two items because there were 1,000 valid responses for question 74 and only 288 valid responses for question 82. Instead I conducted a regression analysis on each item separately and determined that virtually the same predictors operated on each one and did so in the same direction and with similar magnitudes. This justifies combining the two items.

6 Between East and West

PATTERNS OF ACCOMMODATION

In the year 2000 fewer than half a million Jews will remain in the territory of the former USSR. What was the largest Jewish community in the world in 1900 will constitute less than 4 per cent of world Jewry at the end of the century. The Jews who remain will for the most part be old, highly assimilated and dwindling quickly in number. Already in 1988-9 about 37 per cent of the Jews in the USSR were 60 years of age or older. The total fertility rate was 1.6 children per Jewish woman—24 per cent below the rate needed to replace the population even in the absence of any net out-migration. Half of all marriages were to non-Jews and that rate was increasing over time. Given that the younger and more Jewish Jews are the most likely to emigrate, and that they are continuing to do so in large numbers, one cannot possibly be optimistic about the prospects for the Jewish community in the CIS in the next century.[1]

Meanwhile, the Jews who still find themselves in the CIS seek to adapt as best they can, to work out various patterns of accommodation to the circumstances of their existence. The former USSR comprises fifteen more or less loosely connected states of high anxiety. For each geographical, class and ethnic group in the region, these times of trouble are expressed in a particular form which depends on the group's history and social structure. For the Jews, the general anxiety is most conspicuously expressed as a series of tensions between the Slavic world, the West and Israel. These tensions have been evident throughout my examination of Jewish patterns of identification, perceptions of antisemitism and migration plans. The strains are also apparent in my respondents' general values and political preferences.

Consider in that connection Table 6.1. Respondents were asked whether they regard a whole range of values as very important, important or not important—being successful in business, having a professional career, being part of a good family, enjoying good health, commanding the respect of others, being a leader, participating in making important

Table 6.1
Migration Plans by General Values and Political Preferences (in per cent)

	average	non-emigrants (n=572)	ambi-valents (n=141)	West-bound (n=191)	Israel-bound (n=78)
			migration plans		
value ("very important" minus "not important")					
q152-health	85	86	76	86	87
q151-family	73	74	75	75	67
*q153-respect	49	[51]	{ 38}	50	47
*q154-independence	44	44	38	[51]	{ 29}
*q150-profession	- 8	{-15}	[12]	- 1	- 9
*q157-help Russia, etc.	-17	[- 8]	-29	-32	{-34}
*q149-business	-38	{-50}	[-15]	-20	-32
*q156-imp. decisions	-40	{-44}	-37	[-33]	{-44}
*q155-be leader	-68	{-72}	-64	[-58]	-69
*q158-be in Israel	-75	{-92}	-72	-83	[36]
q159-era preference					
*Yeltsin	33	34	[45]	{ 23}	43
<1917	29	25	35	39	28
Brezhnev	20	21	13	18	21
Khrushchev	7	8	3	5	3
Gorbachev	6	6	3	11	2
Lenin	3	5	0	1	1
Stalin	2	2	1	2	2
total		101	100	99	100
q160-government preference					
*business	51	{ 47}	[63]	55	52
*same as current	24	[28]	{ 15}	18	27
*directors	13	[14]	[14]	13	{ 4}
Communist	4	4	3	5	0
*religious	3	{ 2}	3	4	[10]
military	3	3	0	3	2
national-patriotic	3	2	2	2	5
total		100	100	100	100

*q161-Western influence ("not enough" minus "too much")
14   {- 5} [44] 23   41

Table 6.1 (cont'd)
Migration Plans by General Values and Political Preferences (in per cent)

Note: Items preceded by an asterisk indicate statistically significant differences between maximum and minimum row values at the .05 probability level. For those items, highest row values are enclosed in brackets ([]) and lowest row values are enclosed in braces ({}). The maximum number of valid responses is shown above (n=x) but the exact number varies slightly from question to question. Percentages do not necessarily add up to 100 due to rounding.

decisions, enjoying personal independence, helping Russia (or Ukraine or Belarus) and being in Israel. They were also asked in which era they would prefer to live in if they could choose—that of Yeltsin, Gorbachev, Brezhnev, Khrushchev, Stalin, Lenin or the period before 1917. They were asked what sort of government they would prefer to see in power in Russia (or Ukraine or Belarus)—the same as now or a government led by entrepreneurs, directors of large (mainly state-owned) enterprises, Communists, religious figures, military personnel or so-called national-patriotic forces. Finally, they were asked whether there was too much, enough or not enough Western influence on Russian (or Ukrainian or Belarusian) culture and traditions. Table 6.1 cross-classifies their responses to these questions with their migration plans.

From the first column of Table 6.1 we immediately learn that, overall, the Jews of Moscow, Kiev and Minsk form a pro-Western group who prefer the Yeltsin era over all other periods of Soviet and pre-Soviet history but who would like to see their government led by entrepreneurs more than by any other category of the population. Clearly, the respondents are champions of liberal-democratic and capitalist reform. Like most people in most times and places, they value good health and family above all else. But the fact that they value respect and personal independence so much more than being a leader or being responsible for making important decisions may be regarded as a response to recent Soviet and post-Soviet history. Having suffered countless indignities and dependencies in the Soviet era, they now cherish respect and personal independence. But having survived for so long by laying low and quietly fitting in, they are still cautious about standing out as important decision-makers and especially as leaders.

This general characterization masks interesting dissimilarities between people with different emigration plans. These dissimilarities are brought into relief by comparing columns two to five in Table 6.1. Differences between some maximum and minimum row values are large enough that we can be 95 per cent sure they are not due to chance. Those items are preceded by an asterisk. Their high values are enclosed in square brackets ([ ]) and their low values in braces ({ }).

Compared to those who plan to emigrate, respondents who intend to stay in Russia, Ukraine or Belarus may be characterized as pro-Slavic conformists.[2] Why pro-Slavic? Because they comprise the only group in my sample who tend to believe that there is too much Western influence on Russian (or Ukrainian or Belarusian) culture and traditions. They are, moreover, the most inclined to believe in the importance of helping Russia (or Ukraine or Belarus) and the least inclined to think that it is important to be in Israel. Why conformist? Because they are anything but innovators. Of all four groups, they tend least to value professional and business life and are least inclined to be leaders. They (along with respondents who plan to move to Israel) are also least interested in being involved in making important decisions. True to form, they tend more than members of any other group to support the political status quo. Yet they demonstrate a certain insecurity in so far as they need respect from others more than the members of any other group. In short, they are survivors, and in the socio-historical context in which they find themselves that means being accommodationists *par excellence*.

The respondents who plan on moving to the Jewish state may be characterized as pro-Israel conformists. They are least likely to want to help Russia (or Ukraine or Belarus) and, of course, most likely to want to be in Israel. They tend least to value personal independence and they are tied with pro-Slavic conformists in their lack of desire to become involved in making important decisions. It seems that a small minority of them have an extraordinarily strong attachment to Israel and/ or an exceedingly bitter attitude towards Russia (or Ukraine or Belarus). Thus 15 per cent of them —far more than in any other group—would like to see a government led by religious or national-patriotic forces in Russia (or Ukraine or Belarus). Presumably, like Bakunin, they believe that the worse the better; such governments would in all likelihood force all Jews out and, given the limit on immigration to the USA, that means a huge boon to Israel.

Respondents who are unsure about whether they will emigrate and those who plan to emigrate to countries other than Israel resemble one another in terms of the attitudes measured here. However, they both contrast sharply with the two conformist groups. They thus display an intermediate level of Jewishness compared to the other groups and they are significantly more likely than the others to be innovators in their day-to-day lives.[3]

Respondents who plan to emigrate to countries other than Israel value being leaders, making important decisions and enjoying personal independence more than the members of any other group. Interestingly, however, they also display a high level of nostalgia. They are the least inclined to be happy about living in the Yeltsin era and the most inclined to wish they could have lived in the period before 1917.

The responses of the ambivalents—those who are unsure about their migration plans—suggest that they value autonomy and industry more highly than do other respondents. They thus care least about other people's opinions in the sense that they value the respect of others least. They are the most likely to want more Western influence on Russian (or Ukrainian or Belarusian) traditions and culture. They value their professional and business lives more than any other group of respondents. They are the staunchest supporters of the Yeltsin era but they are also the most eager for political change. Specifically, they are most inclined to support a government led by entrepreneurs.

Figure 6.1
Four Adaptation/Rejection Strategies

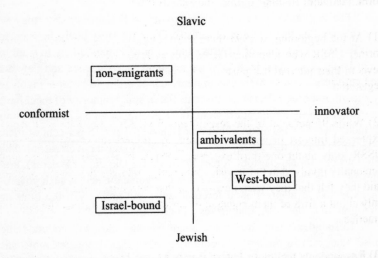

The four patterns of responses that I have just outlined are summarized graphically in Figure 6.1. The Figure suggests that each group is characterized by what might be called a different adaptation-rejection syndrome, a different mechanism for resolving the tensions that characterize

Jewish life in the CIS today. This is most obvious in terms of their different migration plans but it is also clear from the distribution of their attitudes towards issues that have little direct bearing on those plans. The pro-Slavic conformists tend to adapt by assimilating and blending quietly into their societies, rejecting many types of activities and patterns of association that would single them out for notice. The pro-Israel conformists are also keen not to stand out but they reject their country and, in some cases, hope that their country will reject all the Jews. Both the ambivalents and the respondents who are bound for the West adapt by innovation, not conformity. They emphasize eagerness to take initiative and to excel in business and professional life while rejecting the status quo, yearning either for a political regime that will be led by entrepreneurs or, less realistically, for a romantic era long past.

SUMMARY OF MAIN FINDINGS

My analysis has netted some results that are obvious, some that are not self-evident and some that are surprising and may provoke controversy. In point form, the major findings of this study are as follows:

(1) At the beginning of 1993 there were roughly 1,144,000 people in the former USSR who identified themselves as Jews, who were registered as Jews in their internal passports or who had at least one parent who was so registered.

(2) While 95 per cent of the respondents from Moscow, Kiev and Minsk expressed interest in witnessing a Jewish cultural revival in the former USSR, only about one-third expressed interest in remaining or becoming personally involved in the Jewish community, only about a quarter of them said they felt that they were now part of that community and an average of only about a fifth of them engaged in various Jewish religious and cultural practices.

(3) Respondents feel more Jewish if they have a strong Jewish upbringing, if they plan on emigrating, if their mother, spouse or father was or is registered as a Jew in his or her internal passport, if they have experienced antisemitism and fear it, and if they live in smaller peripheral centres (Minsk) as opposed to larger central cities (Moscow).

(4) In Moscow, a relatively liberal city by CIS standards, negative attitudes towards Jews are widespread by North American standards. For example, 18 per cent of Muscovites agree or are inclined to agree that there exists a global "Zionist" conspiracy against Russia and another 24 per cent are undecided. This does not, however, suggest that Jews are in imminent physical danger.

(5) In Moscow negative attitudes towards Jews are more widespread among older people, low-income earners and non-Russians.

(6) Compared to other republics of the former USSR, negative attitudes towards Jews are low in Russia and Ukraine but high in Belarus.[4]

(7) Nearly four-tenths of Jews in Moscow, Kiev and Minsk regard popular hostility as the main source of antisemitism today. A quarter of the respondents mention nationalist organizations, another quarter regard state policy and a tenth view anti-Jewish articles in the press as the taproot of anti-Jewish feeling.

(8) These perceptions vary from city to city. Muscovites regard organized group antisemitism as more of a problem than do Jews in the other two cities. Kievans are most inclined to think that popular hostility against Jews is highly problematic. Minskers are most likely to view the state apparatus as the main source of antisemitism in their country.

(9) While over 90 per cent of respondents in Moscow, Kiev and Minsk believe that antisemitism exists in their respective countries, 15 per cent more Muscovites than Kievans and Minskers believe that pogroms are likely or certain to break out. Ten per cent more Minskers than Kievans and Muscovites have personally experienced antisemitism. And Jews in Moscow perceive by far the largest decline in antisemitism since the rise of Gorbachev.

(10) Nearly a third of Jews in Moscow, Kiev and Minsk express a great deal of apprehension about antisemitism. Heightened fear is most strongly associated with witnessing antisemitism in the mass media, being a woman, having a strong Jewish identity, lacking confidence in one's future and being in one's thirties, forties or fifties.

(11) Extremely rough projections suggest that over 480,000 Jews will emigrate from the USSR between 1994 and 1999. Between 204,000 and 275,000 of them will go to Israel. Between 276,000 and 368,000 of them will go elsewhere.

(12) Nearly six-tenths of respondents with emigration plans said that they planned to emigrate mainly for economic reasons, a third for reasons having to do with political instability and ethnic conflict, and fewer than a tenth for purposes of family reunification.

(13) In contrast, nearly half the respondents said that cultural affinity roots them in their country, over a quarter said they were tied to their country by family and friendship connections and over 10 per cent mentioned economic activities as the most important ties to their country.

(14) About 30 per cent of respondents planning to emigrate to countries other than Israel said that they did not want to go to Israel because it was culturally alien to them. Another 30 per cent said that poor job prospects dissuaded them from choosing Israel as a destination. Twenty per cent of the potential emigrants said they did not wish to go to Israel because they had few friends and/ or relatives there and 14 per cent said they did not want to go because of the Arab-Israeli conflict and the threat of war. About 30 per cent of respondents planning to go the West said that they would go to Israel if they could secure a job comparable to the one they currently hold.

A FINAL WORD ON METHOD

In October 1944 Churchill met with representatives of the Polish government-in-exile in an attempt to convince them to cede Poland's eastern territories to Russia, as Stalin demanded. When Stanislaw Mikolajczyk, the Prime Minister of the "London Poles", said that Polish public opinion would not accept the loss, Churchill shot back "What is public opinion? The right to be crushed!"[5]

In one sense, public opinion matters little, as Churchill clearly understood. It is often shaped by large impersonal forces and at least some of it is an ephemera of everyday life—the raw material for the proverbial newspaper that shouts today's headlines but that tomorrow will be used as wrapping-up paper. From that point of view, a survey is outdated, if not irrelevant, the moment it is conducted. When, in addition, it represents the opinions of only part of the population of interest one is obliged to ask whether its value is out of all proportion to the effort expended in executing it.

I readily admit to the shortcomings implied by Churchill's jab, although not to the conclusions one may hastily draw from it. Yeltsin, Kravchuk, Shushkevich and their regimes now appear to be muddling through—barely. They could, however, be overthrown, much to the serious detriment of Jewish cultural and political freedom in the region.[6] Similarly, a change in American immigration regulations or a further deterioration of the Israeli economy would have serious and direct consequences for the Jewish community of the former Soviet Union. Emigration plans, cultural practice and much else would be bound to alter under such pressure.

Eventually, public opinion would follow suit, at least to a degree. In the long run most people adapt to changed circumstances and rationalize their adaptations by altering their views, even their self-conceptions. One must be careful, however, not to exaggerate the plasticity of public opinion. Some views change from day to day, like the popularity of prime ministers and presidents. Other attitudes are more profound and resist change. Stalin did not, after all, crush the Polish desire for independence.

I believe that many of the attitudes tapped by my survey are deeply held and that the results therefore tell us something enduringly important about the Jews of Moscow, Kiev and Minsk. True, in a couple of places I made some shaky assumptions in order to force my data to say something about the size of the entire Jewish population of the former USSR and their emigration plans. But taken together, doubts about the relevance of public opinion in the face of overpowering circumstances, about the obduracy of some attitudes in the face of changed conditions and about the representativeness of my sample for purposes of making some generalizations suggest to me the need for more surveys, not fewer. Broader-based surveys will yield sounder inferences. Polls taken under a variety of social, economic and political circumstances will give a better sense of how Jews in the former USSR may be expected to act under a multiplicity of conditions, including, if the worse comes to the worst, the exercise of brute force.

In the field of what used to be called Sovietology, and more narrowly among students of Jews in the former USSR, there are few sociologists and many historians who are sceptical of the utility of surveys. The historians inventively stitch together documentary evidence, speculate imaginatively and employ a deep appreciation of Russian, Jewish and other cultures to arrive at explanations and understandings of their subject matter. I do not wish to denigrate the importance of their research. On the contrary, I admire it greatly and have in places relied on it heavily. Based partly on the record of some Sovietologists and students of Jews in the former USSR, however, I strongly believe that documentary investigation, ingenious speculation and deep cultural understanding are often fallible and need to be supplemented by systematically observing, counting and generalizing from the patterns of belief and action tracked by survey and other quantitative data. From my point of view, some scholars in the area build their arguments on meagre evidentiary foundations. When challenged, they sometimes sound like the frustrated *chasid* who, when asked to prove that God actually caused the Red Sea to part, could only extend his arms and indignantly blurt the virtually untranslatable *"Nu du zayst doch!"* (roughly: "Well, you can see!"). Here I have offered another basis for understanding, a basis with its own strengths and its own shortcomings. Documentary investigation, clever speculation and the understanding of deep cultural meaning are important. So are numeracy and the sociological method.

NOTES

1 Mordechai Altshuler, "Socio-demographic profile of Moscow Jews", *Jews and Jewish Topics in the Soviet Union and Eastern Europe*, 3 (16), 1991, 28-9; Mark Tolts, "Jewish marriages in the USSR: A demographic analysis", *East European Jewish Affairs*, vol. 22, no. 2, 1993, 8-9, 17.

2 Note the basis of comparison. The rubric would hardly make sense if the respondents were being compared to a sample of Slavs. An analogous argument holds for the names I use to characterize the other groups. Note also that I initially divided the respondents who did not plan to emigrate into those who ranked in the top and bottom half of my scale of Jewishness. I found no significant differences between the two subgroups in the values examined here. I repeated this procedure after dividing non-emigrants into those who ranked in the bottom two-thirds and the top third of the scale of Jewishness but still found no significant differences. I therefore decided to lump all non-emigrants together.

3 Table 6.1 shows that there is a statistically insignificant difference between the two groups in terms of how much value they place on helping Russia (or Ukraine or Belarus). However, the ambivalents value being in Israel significantly more than do those bound for destinations other than Israel despite their being less Jewish than the latter respondents (as we learned from Table 5.6). This suggests just how ambivalent they are.

4 This generalization is based on an inspection and partial re-analysis of Gudkov's and Levinson's 1992 data.

5 Quoted in Martin Gilbert, *Churchill: A Life* (London: Minerva, 1991), 798.

6 I. V. Chernenko and M. M. Zakhvatkin, "The fascism-socialism dichotomy from the point of view of catastrophe theory", *Rossiysky monitor: Arkhiv sovremennoy politiki*, no. 1, 1992, 92-3; Galina Starovoitova, "Weimar Russia?", *Journal of Democracy*, vol. 4, no. 3, 1993, 106-9.

Appendix A
Methodological Notes

Table A.1 lists the surnames used to select the sample (see Chapter 1 for details).

Table A.2 gives frequency distributions for the basic socio-demographic characteristics of the people in the sample. Comparative data on the Moscow Jewish population according to the 1989 census are given where available.

Table A.3 gives frequency distributions for the sex, age and educational level of nonrespondents, i.e., people who were contacted but who declined to take part in the survey. Data were obtained from other household members. The distributions are very similar to those for respondents. This strongly suggests that nonresponse bias is not a problem in this survey.

As a check on the validity of responses, interviewers were asked after each interview to rank the respondents on a scale of 1 to 5, where 1 indicates that the respondent appeared "very open" in answering questions and 5 indicates that he or she seemed "very closed". The average score was 1.9, which suggests that in general respondents felt comfortable during the interview and gave frank and honest answers.

Interviewers were also asked to indicate which questions, if any, the respondents found difficult to answer. By far the most difficult set of questions concerned the issue of who benefited from the notion that antisemitism existed in their country (q141-q148). An average of 4.7 per cent of respondents found these eight questions difficult to answer. That figure is too low to be of concern.

Table A.1
The Most Common Jewish Surnames in Russia, Ukraine and Belarus (n=405)

Abramov	Bronshteyn	Fish	Igolnik
Abramovich	Bunimovich	Fisher	Ilinets
Abramson		Fishman	Ioffe
Agranovich	Dagman	Fogel	Itenberg
Akselrod	Dashevsky	Fradkin	Itskovich
Altman	Davidovich	Frayberg	Izakson
Altshuler	Davidson	Frayerman	Izrael
Aptekman	Deller	Frid	Izraelson
Arev	Deych	Fridlin	Izrailson
Aranovich	Diligensky	Fridlyand	Izrailev
Aronov	Dimerman	Fridman	
Aronson	Diner	Frishman	Kagan
Arshavsky	Dintan	Fuks	Kagansky
Asbel	Dipman	Funtik	Kalmanovich
Ashkinazi	Domansky	Furman	Kantor
Averbakh	Domnich	Futerman	Kantorovich
Averbukh	Dorfman		Kaplan
Ayzekovich	Dunaevsky	Garfunkel	Kaplun
Ayzenberg	Dverin	Gelman	Kaplunovich
Ayzenshtat	Dvorkin	Gelner	Karpachevsky
	Dvoskin	Gerd	Karpelson
Basin	Dymersky	Gerdt	Karsik
Batkin	Dymshits	Gershenson	Kats
Belenky		Gershikovich	Katsen
Benevich	Fakhzon	Gershuni	Katsman
Beninson	Faktor	Gerts	Katsnelson
Berelson	Faktorovich	Gilevich	Katsner
Berg	Fayn	Gilinsky	Kazakevich
Berger	Faynberg	Gitelman	Kaziner
Bergman	Faynleyb	Glozman	Khashis
Berkovich	Fayntikh	Gofman	Khaymovich
Berlyand	Fegin	Goltsman	Khenkin
Berngart	Feldbeyn	Golod	Kheyfits
Bernshteyn	Feldman	Gorfinkel	Kheynman
Beylin	Feltsman	Gorodetsky	Khidekel
Blyum	Felsot	Gozman	Khmelnitsky
Blyumin	Fiks	Gurevich	Khotinsky
Blyumkin	Finkel	Gurvich	Khurgin
Braude	Finkelshteyn		Kleyman

Table A.1 (cont'd)
The Most Common Jewish Surnames in Russia, Ukraine and Belarus (n=405)

Kleyner	Lurie	Nosonovsky	Ravich
Kofman	Lyublinsky	Noyberg	Ravichbakh
Kogan		Noyman	Ravikovich
Kon	Magaliv	Nudelman	Rekhman
Korman	Maltser	Nudman	Revzin
Krasik	Malkin		Rivers
Kreymer	Malkind	Paperny	Roginsky
Kugel	Margulis	Pekarsky	Rossin
Kugelman	Markel	Pekelis	Rotenfeld
Kunin	Markovich	Pelman	Rotman
Kuperman	Matizen	Perchik	Rovinsky
Kupershteyn	Mayer	Perelman	Roytman
Kushner	Maykin	Peres	Royzman
Kushnerovich	Mayminas	Pevzner	Rozenbaum
	Mayzel	Peysakhovich	Rozenkrants
Lebenzon	Mazo	Pinkhusov	Rozin
Lebin	Meerovich	Pinsker	Rozman
Lebind	Melman	Pinus	Rozovsky
Lefner	Meltser	Plavnik	Rubin
Lerner	Men	Pliner	Rubinchik
Levin	Meyer	Plotkin	Rubinshteyn
Levinson	Meyerkhold	Polyansky	Rukhman
Levintov	Meyerson	Ponizovsky	Rumanovsky
Levit	Milner	Portnov	Ruvinsky
Levitin	Minkin	Portnoy	Ryvkin
Levitsky	Mirkin	Prezent	Ryvlin
Leybkind	Mordkovich	Prigozhin	
Leybov	Mordukhovich	Prilutsky	Sabler
Leybzon		Pritsker	Sakhnovich
Leyfman	Nakhamkin	Pulkin	Saminsky
Leykin	Natan	Pyatigorsky	Sandler
Libin	Natanovich		Seminsky
Lifshits	Natanson	Rabikovich	Shapiro
Likhtenshteyn	Nayshul	Rabin	Shatskin
Lipkin	Nedlin	Rabinovich	Shatsman
Lokshin	Neginsky	Rakovshchik	Shekhtman
Loshinker	Nekhamkin	Ram	Sher
Lukatsky	Neyman	Rappoport	Shereshevsky
Lukhman	Neymark	Rashragovich	Sherman

Table A.1 (cont'd)
The Most Common Jewish Surnames in Russia, Ukraine and Belarus (n=405)

Sheylin	Strokovsky	Volfson
Sheynis	Svecharnik	Volodarsky
Shifman	Sverdlik	Volynsky
Shifrin	Sverdlov	Vorovich
Shifris	Sviridov	Vorovsky
Shikhman		Vortman
Shilman	Tabger	
Shkolnik	Tomarkin	Zak
Shmulevich	Traber	Zakher
Shmurak	Trakhtenberg	Zakhoder
Shnirman	Trakhtenbrod	Zakhtser
Shor	Tubman	Zaks
Shpirman	Tsadik	Zaltsman
Shpulman	Tsetlin	Zalmanov
Shteynberg	Tseydlin	Zaskovich
Shulman	Tsimbal	Zaslavsky
Shusterman	Tsimbalist	Zeldin
Shustik	Tsimernan	Zelkin
Sigal	Tsodik	Zelman
Simanovich	Tsyperovich	Zelmanovsky
Simkin		Zeltser
Sliozberg	Valdman	Zeltsin
Slobodinsky	Varshavsky	Zeltesan
Slobodkin	Vasserman	Zelnik
Slonim	Vatermakhen	Zenkevich
Smidovich	Vatsman	Ziglin
Smigal	Vayl	Zikherman
Smolkin	Vaynshteyn	Zilberg
Smorgonsky	Vayserman	Zilberovich
Smorodinsky	Vaysman	Zilbershteyn
Solomonik	Veber	Ziselts
Solomonov	Vesler	Ziskind
Sorin	Veykher	Zolotar
Sternin	Veysman	Zorin
Stiskin	Vilner	Zul
Stokovsky	Volf	Zusman

Table A.2
Frequency Distributions of Basic Sociodemographic Variables
(in per cent; n in parentheses)

q7-sex			Moscow education (aged 15+)	
male	50		preprimary	1
female	<u>50</u>		primary	2
total	100	(1,001)	incom. secondary	6
male/female sex ratio= 1.00			secondary gen.	12
Moscow m/f sex ratio = 1.14			secondary voc.	14
			incom. higher	4
			higher	<u>60</u>
q8-age			total	99
18-29	18			
30-39	15			
40-49	22		q10-marital status	
50-59	28		married	69
60-90	<u>17</u>		never mar	15
total	100	(1,001)	sep div	10
average=46.5	s.d.=15.8		widow	<u>7</u>
			total	101 (1,000)
Moscow age				
0- 9	5			
10-19	6		q11-family size	
20-29	8		1	9
30-39	11		2	26
40-49	14		3	31
50-59	18		4	22
60+	<u>40</u>		5	10
total	102		6	2
			7	<u>1</u>
			total	101 (1,000)
q9-education			average=3.1	s.d.=1.3
7-8	1			
9-11	13		q12-number of children	
tech/prof	4		0	23
tekhnikum	14		1	43
some univ	62		2	31
phd	5		3	<u>3</u>
dr sci	<u>1</u>		total	100 (993)
total	100	(1,001)	average=1.1	s.d.=.8

Table A.2 (cont'd)
Frequency Distributions of Basic Sociodemographic Variables
(in per cent; n in parentheses)

q14-work status			Moscow occupation		
employed	67		white collar	85	
unemployed	3		blue collar	<u>15</u>	
homemaker	4		total	100	
retired	20				
student	6				
other	<u>1</u>		q29-total monthly income		
total	10	(1,000)	(in roubles)		
			0-5000	28	
q15-sector if employed			5001-10000	20	
state	70		10001-15000	16	
private	19		15001-20000	12	
both	<u>11</u>		20001-40000	16	
total	100	(663)	40000-1 mil	<u>8</u>	
			total	100	(1,001)
q17-occupation			average=23,425	s.d.=57,137	
scientist	8		median=13,800		
engineer	32				
teacher	8				
physician	5		q35-dwelling type		
lawyer	1		state flat	56	
manual	9		priv flat	39	
free profess	6		commun flat	2	
govt service	7		parents' flat	1	
govt admin	6		other	<u>1</u>	
entrepreneur	5		total	99	(997)
private manag	<u>15</u>				
total	102	(656)			

Source for Moscow data: Mordechai Altshuler, "Socio-demographic profile of Moscow Jews", *Jews and Jewish Topics in the Soviet Union and Eastern Europe*, 3 (16), 1991, 24-40.

Note: Due to weighting and missing cases, frequencies do not necessarily add up to 1,000 and percentages do not necessarily add up to 100.0.

Table A.3
Characteristics of Nonrespondents (in per cent; n in parentheses)

sex			education		
male	58		<7	0	
female	<u>42</u>		7-8	2	
total	100	(218)	9-11	12	
			tech/prof	5	
age			tekhnikum	9	
18-29	15		some univ	69	
30-39	10		phd	2	
40-49	23		dr sci	1	
50-59	28		total	100	(214)
60-90	<u>23</u>				
total	99	(213)			
average=48.9	s.d.=15.7				

Note: Due to weighting, the frequencies reported here differ slightly from the unweighted non-response frequency reported in Chapter 1 and percentages do not necessarily add up to 100.0.

Appendix B
The Questionnaire

1. Questionnaire ID number _____

PART A [INTERVIEW IDENTIFICATION INFORMATION. TO BE COMPLETED BY INTERVIEWER IMMEDIATELY BEFORE INTERVIEW IS CONDUCTED.]

2. Month_____ *[Specify 1-12]*

3. Day of Month_____ *[Specify 1-31]*

4. Time of Day_____ *[Specify 1-24]*

5. City_____ *[Specify 1-3, where 1=Moscow, 2=Kiev, 3=Minsk]*

PART B [SCREENING QUESTION. TO BE READ TO EACH RESPONDENT.]

Good evening. I am helping a group of sociologists in Moscow and Toronto conduct a public opinion poll on Jewish emigration from Russia. We would be very grateful if you (or an adult member of your family) would answer our questionnaire.

I want to emphasize that your household was selected at random. All responses will be kept completely anonymous: we do not wish to ask you your name and there is no way to connect your name with your responses. It will take about an hour to answer our questions. You may refuse to answer any questions that you do not wish to answer for whatever reason.

I would like to interview a person in your household eighteen years or older. If you are not alone at home I'd like to interview the adult who had the most recent birthday.

6. May I interview that person or you?

yes   no
1   2

[If "no" go to question 179.]

112

PART C [SOCIO-DEMOGRAPHIC QUESTIONS.]

7. *[Interviewer: indicate by observation whether respondent is a man or woman.]*

male   female
1   2

8. First, would you please tell me how old you are?
[Interviewer: specify figure.]

_____ years   99 don't know or refused

[If "under 18" say:] I am afraid that you are too young to participate in our survey.
Thank you anyway for your willingness to help us, and good evening.

[Ask question 9 only for those who 18 or older.]

9. What level of schooling did you complete?

less than elementary school	elementary school (grades 7-8)	middle school (grades 9-11)	technical-professional school	teknikum
1	2	3	4	5

at least some university	Ph.D.	Doctor of Science (Full Professor)	don't know or refused
6	7	8	99

10. Are you married, never-married, separated or divorced, or widowed?

married	never married	separated or divorced	widowed	don't know or refused
1	2	3	4	99

11. How many people are in your family?
[Interviewer: Specify figure.]

_____ people   99 don't know or refused

12. How many children do you have?
[Interviewer: Specify figure.]

_____ children   99 don't know or refused

[Interviewer: Ask question 13 only for those who have children.]

13. How many of your children live abroad now?
[Interviewer: Specify figure.]

_____ children living abroad   99 don't know or refused

PART D [QUESTIONS ON SOCIO-ECONOMIC POSITION.]

14. Which of the following best describes your present situation— employed, unemployed, homemaker, retired, student, or other?

employed	unemployed	homemaker	retired	student
1	2	3	4	5

other	don't know or refused
6	99

[Interviewer: Ask questions 15-27 only for "employed".]

15. In which sector do you work—the state sector, the private sector, or in both sectors?

state sector	private sector	in both sectors	don't know or refused
1	2	3	99

[Interviewer: Ask question 16 only for employed in both sectors.]

16. What about your main occupation—is it in the state sector, the private sector or equally in both sectors?

state sector	private sector	both sectors	don't know or refused
1	2	3	99

17. And what is your occupation?

scientist	engineer	teacher	physician	lawyer
1	2	3	4	5

manual worker	independendent worker (freelance writer, artist, etc.)			government administrator
6	7			8

employee in state organization	entrepreneur	employee in private organization	other	don't know or refused
9	10	11	12	99

18. What administrative (managerial) post do you hold?

director or deputy director of organization	head of department	professional
1	2	3

other post	none of the above	don't know or refused
4	5	99

19. Do you feel that you are satisfied or not satisfied with your work?

satisfied	not satisfied	don't know or refused
1	2	99

What features of your work do you like or not like?

[Interviewer: Specify 1=like, 2=don't like, 99=don't know or refused.]

20. wages (salary) _____

21. conditions of work _____

22. your relations with managers above _____

23. your relations with your colleagues _____

24. your post _____

25. opportunities for advancement _____

What if anything do you wish to change in your work?
[Interviewer: Specify: 1=wish to change, 2=don't wish to change, 99=don't know or refused.]

26. the organization you work for _____

27. your profession _____

28. How well off is your family in material terms? Please indicate your family's position on a five-point scale where "1" is very rich, "2" is rich, "3" is middle income, "4" is poor, "5" is very poor.

very rich	rich income	middle-	poor	very poor
1	2	3	4	5

don't know or refused
99

29. What is your total monthly income from all sources?
[Interviewer: Specify figure in roubles.]

_____ roubles　　　　　　　　99 don't know or refused

Please indicate how many roubles of your total monthly income comes from each of the following sources:
[Interviewer: specify number of roubles from each source. If respondent does not have income from a source, specify "0".]

30. wages _____　　　　　99 don't know or refused

31. business profits _____　99 don't know or refused

32. unemployment insurance _____　　　　　99 don't know or refused

33. pensions and stipends _____　　　　　99 don't know or refused

34. other _____　　　　99 don't know or refused

35. What type of residence does your family occupy?

single state flat	single privately-owned flat		rooms in communal flat	place in hostel
1	2		3	4

parent's flat	rent a residence	other	don't know or refused	
5	6	7	99	

36. Please tell me which of the following items you own:
[Interviewer: Read options and ask respondent to indicate the items s/he owns.]

dacha	plot of land	car	video tape recorder	don't know or refused
1	2	3	4	99

37. Did you travel abroad in 1991-92?

yes	no	don't know or refused
1	2	99

38. In general, how do you feel about your standard of living--are you satisfied or dissatisfied?

satisfied	dissatisfied	don't know or refused
1	2	99

39. What do you think your standard of living is likely to be in the next 1-2 years--better, the same or worse?

better	the same	worse	don't know or refused
1	2	3	99

40. How do you feel about your current occupational position? Are you satisfied with it, or would you like to occupy a lower or higher position?

satisfied with current position	would like higher position	would like lower position	don't know or refused
1	2	3	99

41. Are conditions favourable to your obtaining a higher occupational position in your country?

yes	no	don't know or refused
1	2	99

PART E [QUESTIONS ABOUT THE ETHNIC COMPOSITION OF THE RE-SPONDENT'S FAMILY.]

I now want to ask you a few questions about your nationality and the nationality of your parents and spouse.

42. What is (or was) your father's nationality according to his passport?

Russian	Ukrainian	Belarusian	Jewish	other
1	2	3	4	5

don't know or refused
99

43. What is (or was) your mother's nationality according to her passport?

Russian	Ukrainian	Belarusian	Jewish	other
1	2	3	4	5

don't know or refused
99

44. What is (or was) your spouse's nationality according to his/ her passport?

Russian	Ukrainian	Belarusian	Jewish	other
1	2	3	4	5

have no spouse   don't know or refused
6   99

45. What is your nationality according to your passport?

Russian	Ukrainian	Belarusian	Jewish	other
1	2	3	4	5

don't know or refused
99

46. Did you ever change the nationality registration in your passport?

yes	no	don't know or refused
1	2	99

47. Some people identify with the nationality listed in their passport while others do not. With which nationality do you most closely identify?

Russian	Ukrainian	Belarusian	Jewish	other
1	2	3	4	6

Jewish and other simultaneously	other	don't know or refused
5	6	99

[Interviewer: Ask questions 48-158 only for those who answered "Jewish" on questions 42, 43, 45 or 47, or "Jewish and other simultaneously" on question 47.]

PART F [JEWISH CULTURAL PRACTICE.]

48. I want to ask you a few questions about your Jewish cultural roots. First, thinking about your upbringing in your parents' home, would you say that your involvement in Jewish culture—that is, languages, religious customs and history—was great, moderate, weak or negligible?

great	moderate	weak	negligible	don't know or refused
1	2	3	4	99

49. Do you speak Hebrew? If so, how well do you speak it—well, moderately well or poorly?

well	moderately	poorly	not at all	don't know or refused
1	2	3	4	99

50. Do you speak Yiddish? If so, how well do you speak it--well, moderately well or poorly?

well	moderately	poorly	not at all	don't know or refused
1	2	3	4	99

[Interviewer: Ask questions 51-55 only for those who responded "well", "moderately" or "poorly" on questions 49 and 50.]

How do you use Hebrew or Yiddish in your everyday life? Do you often, occasionally or never read literature or the press, communicate in family, communicate with friends, communicate with Israelis, communicate in synagogue?

51. read literature or the press

often	occasionally	never	don't know or refused
1	2	3	99

52. communicate in family

often	occasionally	never	don't know or refused
1	2	3	99

53. communicate with friends

often	occasionally	never	don't know or refused
1	2	3	99

54. communicate with Israelis

often	occasionally	never	don't know or refused
1	2	3	99

55. communicate in synagogue

often	occasionally	never	don't know or refused
1	2	3	99

[Interviewer: Ask question 56 only for those who answered "don't know" on questions 49 and 50.]

56. Do you plan to learn Hebrew or Yiddish?

yes	no	don't know or refused
1	2	99

Please indicate whether you usually celebrate the following Jewish holidays:

57. Sabbath

yes	no	don't know or refused
1	2	99

58. Jewish New Year

yes	no	don't know or refused
1	2	99

59. Day of Atonement

yes	no	don't know or refused
1	2	99

60. Passover

yes	no	don't know or refused
1	2	99

61. How often do you visit synagogue--often, occasionally or never?

often	occasionally	never	don't know or refused
1	2	3	99

62. Do you think it is necessary to develop the Jewish religion in your country?

yes	no	don't know or refused
1	2	99

63. Do you participate in the work of any Jewish organizations?

yes	no	don't know or refused
1	2	99

64. Are you a member of any Jewish organizations—cultural, religious, political or social?

yes	no	don't know or refused
1	2	99

65. How often do you read the Jewish press—often, occasionally or never?

often	occasionally	never	don't know or refused
1	2	3	99

66. Do you think that a Jewish community exists in your country?

yes   no   don't know or refused
1   2   99

[Interviewer: Ask question 67 only for those who answered "yes" on question 66.]

67. Do you feel that you belong to the Jewish community?

yes   no   don't know or refused
1   2   99

68. How do you feel about your dealings with Jews--are they enough, too little or too much?

enough   too little   too much   don't know or refused
1   2   3   4

69. How do you feel about your inclusion in Jewish culture? Do you feel a lack of contact with Jewish culture (for example, with well-known Jewish politicians, artists, etc., absence of concerts, exhibitions, Jewish libraries), do you feel you have enough contact, or do you feel you have too much contact?

enough   too little   too much   don't know or refused
1   2   3   99

70. In your opinion, how important is it that Jewish culture be revived in your country today—not important or important?

not important   important   don't know or refused
1   2   99

71. Do the conditions exist for the real development of Jewish culture in your country?

yes   no   don't know or refused
1   2   99

72. Do you feel that it is better if Jews marry Jews, non-Jews or do you feel it's all the same?

Jews   non-Jews   it's all the same   don't know or refused
1   2   3   99

73. Do you bring your children up with Jewish traditions?

yes   no   have no children   don't know or refused
1   2   3   99

PART G [ATTITUDES TO EMIGRATION.]

74. Do you intend to emigrate from the country?

yes	no	don't know or refused
1	2	99

[Interviewer: Ask questions 75-82 only for those who answered "yes" on question 74.]

Why do you want to emigrate? I will read you a list of possible reasons that might be important for you. Please indicate the three most important reasons for you.

[Interviewer: specify "1" for every important reason and "99" for every reasons not chosen.]

_____ **75. to increase standard of living**

_____ **76. due to fear of political instability**

_____ **77. for the sake of children's future**

_____ **78. due to fear of antisemitism, pogroms**

_____ **79. due to fear of violence**

_____ **80. due to lack of belief in any improvement of the situation in the CIS**

_____ **81. in order to keep the family together**

82. To which country are you planning to emigrate?

Israel	USA	Canada	Australia	Germany
1	2	3	4	5

other	don't know or refused
6	99

[Interviewer: Ask questions 83-91 only for those who plan to emigrate to countries other than Israel.]

Why do you not want to emigrate to Israel? I will read you a list of possible reasons that might be important for you. Please indicate the three most important reasons for you.

[Interviewer: Specify "1" for every important reason and "99" for every reason not chosen.]

_____ **83. not enough good jobs there**

_____ **84. fear of losing recent business**

_____ **85. difficulties of living in a Jewish culture**

_____ **86. fear of Arab-Israel conflict and the possibility of war**

_____ **87. too few close friends and/or relatives there**

_____ **88. the Hebrew language is too difficult to learn**

_____ **89. I do not wish to leave Russia (Ukraine, Belarus)**

_____ **90. old age, weak health**

91. If you were assured of getting a job in Israel comparable to your current job, would you emigrate to Israel?

yes	no	don't know or refused
1	2	99

92. Do members of your immediate family or more distant relatives live in Israel?

yes	no	don't know or refused
1	2	99

93. Do members of your immediate family or more distant relatives live in the USA?

yes	no	don't know or refused
1	2	99

94. Do members of your immediate family or more distant relatives live in other Western countries?

yes	no	don't know or refused
1	2	99

95. And do you have friends living in Israel?

yes	no	don't know or refused
1	2	99

96. How about friends living in the USA?

yes	no	don't know or refused
1	2	99

97. Do you have friends living in other Western contries?

yes	no	don't know or refused
1	2	99

98. In your opinion, how many more Jews in your country will eventually emigrate--nearly all, a majority, about half, a minority, hardly any?

nearly all	a majority	about half	a minority	hardly any
1	2	3	4	5

don't know or refused
99

What connects you with the country you live in now? I'll read you a list of connections that might be important for you. Please indicate the three most important connections for you.

[Interviewer: Specify "1" for every connection and "99" for every connection not chosen.]

_____ **99. I have a good job.**

_____ **100. I am accustomed to living in the country.**

_____ **101. I hope to establish a business here.**

_____ **102. I hope to increase my standard of living here.**

_____ **103. I am unwilling to separate from my relatives.**

_____ **104. I am unwilling to separate from my friends.**

_____ **105. I hope for political stability in this country.**

_____ **106. I am closely connected to this culture.**

_____ **107. old age, weak health.**

108. How do you feel about Israel?

[Interviewer: Read the options and ask the respondent to choose one.]

as if it is any other developed country	as if it is an eminent state	as if it is my historical motherland
1	2	3

I have no particular attitude towards Israel	other	don't know or refused
4	5	99

PART H [ANTISEMITISM.]

In your opinion, what does "antisemitism" mean?

[Interviewer: Do not read the options. Specify "1" for the first feature of anti-semitism mentioned, "2" for the second, etc. Enter "99" for each option not selected.]

_____ **109. state policy of restrictions on Jews in some spheres of society and some places of work**

_____ **110. hostility towards Jews from ordinary people**

_____ **111. threats against Jews from nationalist organizations**

_____ **112. anti-Jewish articles in press**

_____ **113. envy of the Jews**

_____ **114. antisemitism doesn't exist, it is a fantasy of Jews themselves**

_____ **115. other**

116. Do you think that antisemitism exists in your country?

yes	no	don't know or refused
1	2	99

[Interviewer: Ask questions 117-124 for those who answered "yes" on question 116.]

What are the main manifestations of antisemitism in your country today?

[Interviewer: Do not read the list of options. Specify "1" for the first manifestation mentioned, "2" for the second, and so forth. Enter "99" for each option not selected.]

_____ 117. state policy of restrictions on Jews in some spheres of society   and some places of work

_____ 118. hostility towards Jews from ordinary people

_____ 119. threats against Jews from nationalist organizations

_____ 120. anti-Jewish articles in press

_____ 121. envy of the Jews

_____ 122. other

123. Have you personally suffered from manifestations of antisemitism?

yes	no	don't know or refused
1	2	99

[Interviewer: Ask questions 124-129 to respondents who answered "yes" to question 123.]

What were the main manifestations of antisemitism you suffered?

[Interviewer: Do not read the list of options. Specify "1" for the first manifestation mentioned, "2" for the next manifestation, and so forth. Enter "99" for each option not selected.]

_____ 124. state policy of restrictions on Jews in some spheres of society and some places of work

_____ 125. hostility towards Jews from ordinary people

_____ 126. threats against Jews from nationalist organizations

_____ 127. anti-Jewish articles in press

_____ 128. envy of the Jews

_____ 129. other

130. Do you fear the manifestations of antisemitism?

very much	not very much	not at all	don't know or refused
1	2	3	99

[Interviewer: Ask question 131 for those who answered "very much" or "not very much" on question 130.]

131. Is your fear of antisemitism now stronger, weaker or the same as compared to 6-7 years ago?

stronger	weaker	the same	don't know or refused
1	2	3	99

132. How likely do you think it is that pogroms will break out in your country in the near future--for sure, possible or impossible?

for sure	possible	impossible	don't know or refused
1	2	3	99

133. Thinking now about the situation over the past year, have you witnessed no antisemitism, a little antisemitism, or quite a lot of antisemitism at your place of work?

none	a little	quite a lot	don't know or refused	not applicable
1 2	3	99	9	

134. How about your neighbourhood?

none	a little	quite a lot	don't know or refused
1	2	3	99

135. How about in the mass media (press, radio and TV)?

none	a little	quite a lot	don't know or refused
1	2	3	99

136. And in state policy?

none	a little	quite a lot	don't know or refused
1	2	3	99

137. Thinking now about the next 1-2 years, do you expect you will witness less antisemitism, about the same, or more antisemitism at your place of work?

less	about the same	more	don't know or refused	not applicable
1	2	3	99	9

138. How about your neighbourhood?

less	about the same	more	don't know or refused	not applicable
1	2	3	99	9

139. How about in the mass media (press, radio and TV)?

less	about the same	more	don't know or refused	not applicable
1	2	3	99	9

140. And in state policy?

less	about the same	more	don't know or refused	not applicable
1	2	3	99	9

The view is becoming widespread that antisemitism exists in your country. In your opinion, who has an interest in spreading this view?

[Interviewer: Do not read the list of options. Specify "1" for the first option mentioned, "2" for the second option, and so forth. Enter "99" for each option not selected.]

_____ **141. political opposition in your country**

_____ **142. certain government officials in your country**

_____ **143. Jews inside your country**

_____ **144. Jewish organizations from former USSR**

_____ **145. Jewish organizations abroad**

_____ **146. Israel, USA and other Western contries**

_____ **147. nationalist parties and groups in your country**

_____ **148. other**

PART I [VALUES OF THE RESPONDENT.]

People have different values. For some people some things are important and for other people other things are important. What things are very important, or important, or not important for you?

[Interviewer: Indicate the degree of importance for each item below. Specify 1=very important, 2=important, 3=not important.]

_____ **149. success in business**

_____ **150. professional career**

_____ **151. good family**

_____ **152. good health**

_____ **153. respect from the people around me**

_____ **154. personal independence**

_____ **155. to be a leader**

_____ **156. to participate in making important decisions**

_____ **157. to help Russia (Ukraine, Belarus)**

_____ **158. to be in Israel**

159. If you could choose, in what era would you prefer to live--before 1917, during Lenin's rule, during Stalin's rule, during Khrushchev's rule, during Brezhnev's rule, during Gorbachev's rule, or during Yeltsin's rule?

before 1917	Lenin's rule	Stalin's rule	Khrushchev's	Brezhnev's
		rule	rule	
1	2	3	4	5

Gorbachev's rule	Yeltsin's rule	don't know or refused
6	7	99

160. If the current government had to resign, what sort of government would you prefer to rule the country next?

a government like the current one	a government headed by the military	a government headed by directors of large state plants
1	2	3

a government headed by entrepreneurs	Communist government
4	5

a religious government	a national-patriotic government	don't know or refused
6	7	99

161. Some people say that the country has reached its current crisis because Russian (Ukrainian, Belarusian) traditions and culture have been weakened by Western influence. Other people say that the country needs even more Western influence in order to solve its problems. Do you think that Western influence in your country now is too much, enough or not enough?

too much	enough	not enough	don't know or refused
1	2	3	99

162. What do you think the political system of your country is likely to be in 1-2 years—freer, less free or the same?

freer	less free	the same	don't know or refused
1	2	3	99

163. Do you have confidence in your own future?

yes	no	don't know or refused
1	2	99

PART J [REMARKS ABOUT INTERVIEW. TO BE COMPLETED BY THE INTERVIEWER AFTER THE INTERVIEW HAS BEEN COMPLETED AND OUTSIDE OF THE RESPONDENT'S HOUSEHOLD.]

164. How many minutes did the interview take?_____

165. Indicate on a scale of 1 to 5 how open or closed the respondent seemed to feel in answering the questions.

very open				very closed	don'tknow or refused
1	2	3	4	5	99

In your opinion, which question(s), if any, were dificult for the respondent to understand? You may indicate up to twelve questions below. Please insert "99" in any positions left blank.

166._____   167._____   168._____   169._____   170._____

171._____   172._____   173._____   174._____   175._____

176._____   177._____

178. In how many households did you try to secure a respondent before succeeding in securing this one? _____

Answer the following questions only if you could not interview the randomly selected respondent from this household. Obtain the information from another household member.

179. What was the sex of the respondent whom you could not interview?

male	female	don't know or refused
1	2	99

180. What was the age of the respondent whom you could not interview?

_____ years   99 don't know or refused

181. What level of schooling did the respondent whom you could not interview complete?

less than elementary school	elementary school (grades 7-8)	middle school (grades 9-11)	technical-professional school	teknikum
1	2	3	4	5

at least some university	Ph.D.	Doctor of Science (Full Professor)		don't know or refused
6	7	8		99

Sources Cited

Alexander, Zvi, "Jewish emigration from the USSR in 1980", *Soviet Jewish Affairs*, vol. 11, no. 2, 1981, 3-21

Altshuler, Mordechai, "The Jewish Community in the Soviet Union: A Sociodemographic Analysis" (Jerusalem: Magnes Press, Hebrew University of Jerusalem, 1979) (in Hebrew)

_____ "Jews and Russians-1991", "The Jews in the Soviet Union" (in Hebrew), vol. 15, 1992, 31-43

_____ "Socio-demographic profile of Moscow Jews", *Jews and Jewish Topics in the Soviet Union and Eastern Europe,* 3 (16), 1991, 24-40

_____ *Soviet Jewry since the Second World War: Population and Social Structure* (New York: Greenwood, 1987)

Antisemitism World Report 1992 (London: Institute of Jewish Affairs, 1992)

Antisemitism World Report 1993 (London: Institute of Jewish Affairs, 1993)

Basok, Tanya and Robert J. Brym, "Soviet-Jewish emigration and resettlement in the 1990s: An overview" in Tanya Basok and Robert J. Brym (eds.), *Soviet-Jewish Emigration and Resettlement in the 1990s* (Toronto: York Lanes Press, York University, 1991), xi-xxii

Benifand, Alexander, "Jewish emigration from the USSR in the 1990s" in Tanya Basok and Robert J. Brym (eds.), *Soviet-Jewish Emigration and Resettlement in the 1990s* (Toronto: York Lanes Press, York University, 1991), 39-50

Bertsch, Gary, "US-Soviet trade: The question of leverage", *Survey,* vol. 25, no. 2, 1980, 66-80

Bestuzhev-Lada, Igor, "Social problems of the Soviet way of llfe", *Novy mir,* no. 7, 1976, 208-21

Beyer, Gregg A., "The evolving United States response to Soviet-Jewish emigration" in Tanya Basok and Robert J. Brym (eds.), *Soviet-Jewish Emigration and Resettlement in the 1990s* (Toronto: York Lanes Press, York University, 1991), 105-39

Bodemann, Michal, "A renaissance of Germany Jewry?", paper presented at a conference on The Reemergence of Jewish Culture in Germany (University of Toronto, 6-7 May 1993)

Bogoraz, Larisa, "Do I feel I belong to the Jewish people?" in Aleksandr Voronel, Viktor Yakhot and Moshe Decter (eds.), *I am a Jew: Essays on Jewish Identity in the Soviet Union* (New York: Academic Committee on Soviet Jewry and Anti-Defamation League of B'nai B'rith, 1973), 60-4

Brodbar-Nemzer, Jay *et al.,* "An overview of the Canadian Jewish community" in Robert J. Brym, William Shaffir and Morton Weinfeld (eds.), *The Jews in Canada* (Toronto: Oxford University Press, 1993), 39-71

Bromley, J. *et al.*, *Present-Day Ethnic Processes in the USSR* (Moscow: Progress Publishers 1982 [1977])

Brym, Robert J., "The changing rate of Jewish emigration from the USSR: Some lessons from the 1970s", *Soviet Jewish Affairs*, vol. 15, no. 2, 1985, 23-35

_____ "From 'The Soviet people' to the refugee crisis in Russia" in Rozalina Ryvkina and Rostislav Turovskiy, *The Refugee Crisis in Russia*, R. Brym, ed., P. Patchet-Golubev, trans. (Toronto: York Lanes Press, 1993), 1-7

_____ "The emigration potential of Czechoslovakia, Hungary, Lithuania, Poland and Russia: Recent survey results", *International Sociology,* vol. 7, no. 4, 1992, 387-95

_____ "*Perestroyka*, public opinion, and *Pamyat*", *Soviet Jewish Affairs,* vol. 19, no. 3, 1989, 23-32

_____ "Sociology, *perestroika*, and Soviet society", *Canadian Journal of Sociology*, vol. 15, no. 2, 1990, 207-15

_____ "Soviet-Jewish emigration: A statistical test of two theories", *Soviet Jewish Affairs,* vol. 18, no. 3, 1988, 15-23

_____ and Andrei Degtyarev, "Anti-Semitism in Moscow: Results of an October 1992 survey", *Slavic Review*, vol. 52, no. 1, 1993, 1-12

_____ and Andrei Degtyarev, "Who wants to leave Moscow for the West? Results of an October 1992 survey," *Refuge,* vol. 13, no. 2, 1993, 24-5

_____ and Rhonda L. Lenton, "The distribution of antisemitism in Canada in 1984", *Canadian Journal of Sociology*, vol. 16, no. 4, 1991, 411-18.

Bútorová, Zora and Martin Bútora, "Wariness towards Jews as an expression of post-Communist panic: The case of Slovakia", *Czechoslovak Sociological Review*, Special Issue, no. 28, 1992, 92-106

Chernenko, I. V. and M. M. Zakhvatkin, "The fascism-socialism dichotomy from the point of view of catastrophe theory", *Rossiysky monitor: Arkhiv sovremennoy politiki*, no. 1, 1992, 92-3

Cohen, Roberta, "Israel's problematic absorption of Soviet Jews" in Tanya Basok and Robert J. Brym (eds.), *Soviet-Jewish Emigration and Resettlement in the 1990s* (Toronto: York Lanes Press, York University, 1991), 67-89

Cohen, Steven M., *American Modernity and Jewish Identity* (New York and London: Tavistock, 1983)

Cole, John P. and Igor V. Filatotchev, "Some observations on migration within and from the former USSR in the 1990s", *Post-Soviet Geography*, vol. 33, no. 7, 1992, 432-53

"Cutback", *Pravda*, 4 March 1988

DellaPergolla, Sergio, "The demographic context of the Soviet aliya", *Jews and Jewish Topics in the Soviet Union and Eastern Europe*, (16, 3), 1991, 41-56

Dunn, John F., "Hard times in Russia foster conspiracy theories", Radio Free Europe/ Radio Liberty Special Report, 23 September 1992

Erlanger, Steven, "As Ukraine loses Jews, the Jews lose a tradition", *The New York Times*, 27 August 1992

Feshbach, Murray, "The Soviet Union: Population trends and dilemmas", *Population Bulletin*, vol. 37, no. 3, 1982, 1-45

"5 million Jews in CIS", *Canadian Jewish News*, 29 April 1993

Frankel, Jonathan, "The Soviet regime and anti-Zionism: An analysis" in Yaacov Ro'i and Avi Beker, (eds.), *Jewish Culture and Identity in the Soviet Union* (New York and London: New York University Press, 1991), 310-54

Freedman, Robert O., "Soviet Jewry as a factor in Soviet-Israeli relations" in Robert O. Freedman (ed.), *Soviet Jewry in the 1980s: The Politics of Anti-Semitism and Emigration and the Dynamics of Resettlement* (Durham NC: Duke University Press, 1989), 61-96

_____ "Soviet Jewry and Soviet-American relations" in Robert O. Freedman (ed.), *Soviet Jewry in the Decisive Decade, 1971-80* (Durham, NC: Duke University Press, 1984), 38-67

Friedgut, Theodore, "Soviet Jewry: The silent majority", *Soviet Jewish Affairs*, vol. 10, no. 2, 1980, 3-19

_____ "Soviet anti-Zionism and antisemitism--Another cycle", *Soviet Jewish Affairs*, vol. 14, no. 1, 1984, 3-22

Gibson, James L. and Raymond M. Duch, "Anti-semitic attitudes of the mass public: Estimates and explanations based on a survey of the Moscow oblast", *Public Opinion Quarterly,* no. 56, 1992, 1-28

Gilbert, Martin *Churchill: A Life* (London: Minerva, 1991)

Gilboa, Yehoshua A., *The Black Years of Soviet Jewry, 1939-1953*, Yosef Shachter and Dov Ben-Abba, trans. (Boston: Little, Brown, 1971)

Gitelman, Zvi, "The evolution of Jewish culture and identity in the Soviet Union" in Yaacov Ro'i and Avi Beker (eds.), *Jewish Culture and Identity in the Soviet Union* (New York and London: New York University Press, 1991), 3-24

_____ "Glasnost, perestroika and antisemitism", *Foreign Affairs*, vol. 70, no. 2, 1991, 141-59

_____ *Jewish Nationality and Soviet Politics: The Jewish Sections of the CPSU, 1917-1930* (Princeton NJ: Princeton University Press, 1972)

_____ "Recent demographic and migratory trends among Soviet Jews: Implications for policy", *Post-Soviet Geography*, vol. 33, no. 3, 1992, 139-45

_____ "Soviet Jewish emigrants: Why are they choosing America?", *Soviet Jewish Affairs*, vol. 7, no. 1, 1977, 31-46

Goldman, Marshall I., "Soviet-American trade and Soviet Jewish emigration: Should a policy change be made by the American Jewish community?" in Robert O. Freedman (ed.), *Soviet Jewry in the 1980s: The Politics of Anti-Semitism and Emigration and the Dynamics of Resettlement* (Durham NC: Duke University Press, 1989), 141-59

Government of Israel, "The State Budget for 1993: Submitted to the Thirteenth Knesset" (Jerusalem: Government Printer, 1992) (in Hebrew)

Gudkov, Lev D. and Alex G. Levinson, *Attitudes Toward Jews in the Soviet Union: Public Opinion in Ten Republics* (New York: The American Jewish Committee, 1992)

_____ "Attitudes towards Jews", *Sotsiologicheskiye issledovaniya,* no. 12, 1992, 108-11

Havel, Václav, "The post-Communist nightmare", *The New York Review of Books*, 27 May 1993

Hechter, Michael, "Group formation and the cultural division of labor", *American Journal of Sociology,* no. 84, 1978, 293-318

Heitman, Sidney, "Jewish emigration from the former USSR in 1992", unpublished paper (Fort Collins CO: 1993)

_____ "Jews in the 1989 USSR census", *Soviet Jewish Affairs*, vol. 20, no. 1, 1990, 23-30

Hertzberg, Arthur, "Is anti-Semitism dying out?", *The New York Review of Books*, 24 June 1993

"Iadov, V. *et al.*, "The sociopolitical situation in Russia in mid-February 1992", *Sociological Research,* vol. 32, no. 2, 1993, 6-32

Immigration data-1991" in "The Jews in the Soviet Union", vol. 15, 1992, 188-91

Karklins, Rasma, *Ethnic Relations in the USSR: The Perspective from Below* (London: Unwin Hyman, 1986)

_____ "Nationality policy and ethnic relations in the USSR" in James R. Millar (ed.), *Politics, Work, and Daily Life in the USSR: A Survey of Former Soviet Citizens* (Cambridge UK: Cambridge University Press, 1987), 305-31

Koltsov, V. B. and V. A. Mansurov, "Political ideologies during the period of *perestroyka*", *Sotsiologicheskiye issledovaniya*, no. 10, 1991, 22-35

Komozin, A., (ed.), *Monitoring: The 1993 Russian Citizens' Opinion Poll Results* (Moscow: Institute of Sociology, Russian Academy of Sciences, 1993)

Kostakov, Vladimir G., "Employment: deficit or surplus?", *Kommunist,* no. 2, 1987, 78-89

"Kosygin on reunion of families and national equality (1966)" in Benjamin Pinkus (ed.), *The Soviet Government and the Jews 1948-1967* (Cambridge UK: Cambridge University Press, 1984), 77-8

Lambert, Ronald D. and James E. Curtis "*Québécois* and English Canadian opposition to racial and religious intermarriage, 1968-1983", *Canadian Ethnic Studies*, vol. 16, no. 2, 1984, 30-46

Lenton, Rhonda L., "Home versus career: Attitudes towards women's work among Russian women and men, 1992", *Canadian Journal of Sociology*, vol. 18, no. 3, 1993, 325-31

Lieberson, Stanley and Mary Waters, "Ethnic groups in flux: The changing ethnic responses of American whites", *Annals of the American Academy of Social and Political Science*, no. 487, 1986, 79-91

Lowenthal, Richard, "East-West *détente* and the future of Soviet Jewry", *Soviet Jewish Affairs*, vol. 3, no. 1, 1973, 20-5

Margolina, Sonja, *Das Ende der Lügen: Rußland und die Juden im 20. Jahrhundert* (Berlin: Siedler Verlag, 1992)

Marnie, Sheila, "How prepared is Russia for mass unemployment?", Radio Free Europe/Radio Liberty Special Report, 11 November 1992

"Meetings between representatives of the French Socialist Party and Soviet leaders (1956)" in Benjamin Pinkus (ed.), *The Soviet Government and the Jews 1948-1967* (Cambridge UK: Cambridge University Press, 1984), 55-8

"Miscellaneous reports", *Chronicle of Current Events*, no. 52, 1980 [1979], 123-33

Morozova, G. F., "Refugees and emigrants", *Sociological Research*, vol. 32, no. 2, 1993, 86-96

Moscow Helsinki Monitoring Group, *Discrimination Against Jews Enrolling at Moscow State University, 1979*, Document 112 (n.p.: 5 November 1979, mimeograph)

Motyl, Alexander J., *Will the Non-Russians Rebel? State, Ethnicity, and Stability in the USSR* (Ithaca and London: Cornell University Press, 1987)

Nationalities Papers, Special Issue on *Pamyat*, vol. 19, no. 2, 1991

Nezer, Zvi, "Jewish emigration from the USSR in 1981-82", *Soviet Jewish Affairs*, vol. 12, no. 3, 1982, 3-17

"One-year limit on US refugee status for ex-USSR", *Monitor: Digest of News and Analysis from Soviet Successor States,* vol. 4, no. 25, 30 July/6 August 1993

Orlova, Irena, "A sketch of the migration and refugee situation in Russia", *Refuge,* vol. 13, no. 2, 1993, 19-22

Pipes, Richard, "The Soviet Union adrift", *Foreign Affairs*, vol. 70, no. 1, 1991, 70-87

_____ "Soviet relations with the USA", Lukasz Hirszowicz (ed.), *Proceedings of the Experts' Conference on Soviet Jewry Today: London, 4-6 January 1983* (London: Institute of Jewish Affairs, 1985), 107-12

Popov, Nikolai, "Political views of the Russian public", *The International Journal of Public Opinion Research*, vol. 4, no. 4, 1992, 321-34

_____ Roussina Volkova and Vadim Sazonov, "Unemployment in Science: Executive Summary" (Moscow: VTsIOM, 1991)

Reddaway, Peter, "Policy towards dissent since Khrushchev" in T. H. Rigby, Archie Brown and Peter Reddaway (eds.), *Authority, Power and Policy in the USSR: Essays Dedicated to Leonard Shapiro* (London: Macmillan: 1980), 158-92

Ribakovsky, L. L. and N. V. Tarasova, "Migration processes in the USSR: New phenomena", *Sotsiologicheskiye issledovaniya*, no. 7, 1990, 32-41

Rosenfield, Geraldine, "The polls: Attitudes toward American Jews", *Public Opinion Quarterly*, no. 46, 1982, 431-43

Rukavishnikov, V. O. *et al.*, "Social tension: Diagnosis and prognosis", *Sociological Research*, vol. 32, no. 2, 1993, 33-65

Ryansky, Felix, "Jews and Cossacks in the Jewish Autonomous Region", *Refuge*, vol. 12, no. 4, 1992, 19-21

Ryvkina, Rozalina, "Value conflicts of Russian Jews and their social types", unpublished paper (Moscow 1992)

_____ "From civic courage to scientific demonstration", *Soviet Sociology*, vol. 28, no. 5, 1989, 7-23

Salitan, Laurie P., *Politics and Nationality in Contemporary Soviet-Jewish Emigration, 1968-89* (New York: St. Martin's, 1992)

Sartre, Jean-Paul *Anti-Semite and Jew*, trans. George J. Becker (New York: Schocken, 1965 [1948])

Schwarz, Solomon M., *The Jews in the Soviet Union* (Syracuse NY: Syracuse University Press, 1951)

Sedov, L. A., "Yeltsin's rating", *Ekonomicheskiye i sotsialnye peremeny: Monitoring obshchestvennogo mneniya*, Informatsionny byulleten, Intertsentr VTsIOM (Moscow: Aspekt Press, 1993), 14-15

Sharansky, Natan, "The greatest exodus", *The New York Times Magazine*, 2 February 1992

Shevchenko, Arkady N., *Breaking with Moscow* (New York: Alfred A. Knopf, 1985)

"The socioeconomic situation of the Russian Federation, January-March 1993", *Ekonomichesky obzor*, no. 4, Goskomstat Rossii (Moscow: Respublikansky informatsionno-izdatelsky tsentr, 1993)

"Soviet anti-Semitism said to be ceasing", *Canadian Jewish News*, 20 August 1987

Starovoitova, Galina, "Weimar Russia?", *Journal of Democracy*, vol. 4, no. 3, 1993, 106-9

"Surplus loan guarantees", *Canadian Jewish News*, 17 June 1993

Swafford, Michael, "Sociological aspects of survey research in the Commonwealth of Independent States", *International Journal of Public Opinion Research*, vol. 4, no. 4, 1992, 346-57

Tolts, Mark, "Jewish marriages in the USSR: A demographic analysis", *East European Jewish Affairs*, vol. 22, no. 2, 1993, 3-19

Tsigelman, Ludmilla, "The impact of ideological changes in the USSR on different generations of the Soviet Jewish intelligentsia" in Yaacov Ro'i and Avi Beker (eds.), *Jewish Culture and Identity in the Soviet Union* (New York and London: New York University Press, 1991), 42-72

Zaslavskaya, Tatyana, "*Perestroyka* and sociology", *Pravda*, 6 February 1987

Zaslavsky, Victor and Robert J. Brym, *Soviet-Jewish Emigration and Soviet Nationality Policy* (London: Macmillan, 1983)

Zotov, Vladimir, "The Chechen problem as seen by Muscovites", *Moskovsky komsomolets*, 12 January 1993

Name Index

Subject Index